Teaching Economic Inequality and Capitalism in Contemporary America

Kristin Haltinner · Leontina Hormel
Editors

Teaching Economic Inequality and Capitalism in Contemporary America

Springer

Editors
Kristin Haltinner
Department of Sociology
University of Idaho
Moscow, ID
USA

Leontina Hormel
Department of Sociology
University of Idaho
Moscow, ID
USA

ISBN 978-3-319-71140-9 ISBN 978-3-319-71141-6 (eBook)
https://doi.org/10.1007/978-3-319-71141-6

Library of Congress Control Number: 2017958631

Printed on acid-free paper

This Springer imprint is published by Springer Nature
The registered company is Springer International Publishing AG
The registered company address is: Gewerbestrasse 11, 6330 Cham, Switzerland

Contents

Introduction 1
Walda Katz-Fishman

Part I Making the Personal Political: The Stories of Capitalism

'Teaching Naked' in Late Capitalism: Instructors' Personal Narratives and Classroom Self-disclosure as Pedagogical Tools 13
Danielle Docka-Filipek

Untold Stories: Bringing Class into the Classroom 27
Adj Marshall and Betsy Leondar-Wright

'Self-made' Success on the Private Dole: An Illustration of the Reproduction of Capitals 41
Roxanne Gerbrandt and Ann Strahm

Financial Stumbles, Consumer Bankruptcy, and the Sociological Imagination 55
Deborah Thorne

Part II Making Marxist Theory Real

Capitalism 101: Teaching First-Year Students How to View the Social World Through the Lens of Marxist Theory 69
Laura Earles

Teaching Global Inequality Through the World of Commodities 81
Eric M. Edwards

Radical Pedagogical Homesteading: Returning the 'Species' to Our 'Being' 91
Phoebe Godfrey

Socialist Grading 103
David I. Backer

Part III Applied Pedagogical Strategies for Course Development

Overcoming Students' Fear: Scaffolding to Teach *Money and Society* 113
Stephanie L. Bradley

Capitalism in the Classroom: Confronting the Invisibility of Class Inequality 125
Charlotte A. Kunkel

Experiencing the Outcomes of Economic Inequality in the Day-to-Day Workings of the Classroom 131
Susan Machum

Teaching Economic Inequality and Capitalism in Contemporary America Using Resources from the Federal Government 145
Andrew E. Kersten

Teaching Social Inequality Through Analysis of Hidden Assumptions in Non-Academic Publications 157
Pidi Zhang

Participatory Action Research as Problem-Based Learning: A Course Study of Rural Poverty, Low-Income Housing, and Environmental Justice 169
Leontina Hormel, Cynthia Ballesteros and Haylee Brister

Inequality and Violence 183
Barbara H. Chasin

Part IV Intersections: Global and Local

Intersectional Marginalities in Rural Teacher Preparation: Teaching Beyond "What I Am Able to See Visibly" 199
Vanessa Anthony-Stevens

Economic Inequality and Race: No, It Can't Be that Bad… 213
Paul R. Croll

Irreversible Punishment: Teaching About Inequalities in Capital Punishment 221
Kristine Levan

Making Room for a Postcolonial Critique in the Introductory STS Curriculum 233
Dilshani Sarathchandra

Utilizing Social Science Theories, Findings, and Comparative Analyses to Create a Framework for Understanding Economic Inequality" 243
Derek J. Robey and Jason P. Robey

Part V Capitalism and Higher Education: Constraints and Opportunities

Capitalism and the Cost of Textbooks: The Possibilities of Open Source Materials 257
Annie Gaines

Writing Against Ideology: Exploring Strategies that Resist Assessment Orthodoxy in the Classroom 267
Joshua Olsberg and Raphi Rechitsky

Lessons on Inequality and Capitalism: Perspectives from a Community College 283
Peter J. Wruck

Capitalism, Racism, and the Neoliberal University: The Case of the University of Missouri (Mizzou) 291
Rose M. Brewer

Against the "Institutional Real": The Structural and Cultural Foundations of Corporate Higher Education and the Challenge to Developing Politically Engaged Students 301
Corey Dolgon

Conclusion: Final Words on Social Class and the Invisible Power Elite 321

Appendix A: Classroom Activities and Assignments 327

Appendix B: Examples of Syllabi 351

Introduction

Walda Katz-Fishman

This political moment cries out for a volume like *Teaching Economic Inequality and Capitalism in Contemporary America* that Kristin Haltinner and Leontina Hormel have so skillfully crafted. The first few months of the Trump presidency are a wakeup call that we are living in profoundly dangerous and volatile times. Resistance and street action are rising up. Analyses of economic inequality and capitalism are critical at this historical conjuncture to teach, and to vision, strategize, and inform today's social struggles. Moving beyond capitalism—and the alienation, exploitation, racial and gender oppression, and dispossession that it produces and reproduces—is vital for the survival of humanity and the planet.

Understanding and teaching about economic inequality within capitalism, the focus of this powerful collection, is one of the burning pedagogical imperatives of this age. How did we get here? How will the ongoing extreme polarization of wealth and poverty shape our experiences and subjectivities, our needs, demands, and movements for transformation? It is increasingly clear that economic inequality and class are central to our lives, and that inequality and class are highly racialized and gendered—both objectively and subjectively. Class and class struggle in twenty-first century America do not look the way they are often portrayed—as the struggle of white, mostly male, industrial workers—and never did. The racial, multinational, and gendered reality of the working class in the United States and globally has always been a historical truth within the capitalist epoch—though observers and scholars often turned a blind eye, and misrepresented these complex realities.

Hormel and Haltinner are part of a new generation of engaged scholars who embrace and embody a liberatory pedagogy and transformative sociology. They have brought together in a single volume a rich diversity of pedagogies, methodologies, and lenses focusing on economic inequality and capitalism in contemporary America that is so urgently needed to reground our sociological imagination,

W. Katz-Fishman (✉)
Howard University, Washington, DC, USA
e-mail: wkatzfishman@igc.org

K. Haltinner and L. Hormel (eds.), *Teaching Economic Inequality and Capitalism in Contemporary America*, https://doi.org/10.1007/978-3-319-71141-6_1

theory, and practice. Their work offers an essential corrective to mainstream sociology that took root in the United States in the twentieth century and continues a century later.

The discipline and the academy tended to put forward mystified analyses of the dynamics of class, economic inequality, and capitalism, and the dialectics of their interrelations with white supremacy, patriarchy, and colonialism. In the post-World War II period, American sociology celebrated the age of American empire, exceptionalism, and hegemonic ideology and power. The dominant and powerful intellectual actors and currents within social science on these questions adapted to the cultural and political context of the day—McCarthyism, anti-communism, Jim Crow racial exclusion, nativism, and gender oppression. They drew on the foundational theoretical and practical orientations of Durkheim and Weber, centering their analysis around cultural determinism and functionalism, subjectivism, status indicators, and authority, with some institutional analysis as the driving forces of social life.

This rendered the diverse working class in America largely invisible conceptually, empirically, and politically. Sociologists replaced the working class with the mythical middle class—so much in vogue in today's political rhetoric. Missing from the analysis was the dialectics of exploitation and oppression within the capitalist epoch. Class, race, nationality, gender, and sexuality were essentialized and located in opposition rather than interrelationship with each other and within the system.

Poverty became an inferior culture and color—most often black—rather than an expression of economic inequality and the economic system. Sociology, for the most part, abandoned anti-systemic scholarship and practice; and capitalism was largely missing from the formulation of social science theory and research. American sociology's distorted conceptualization of economic inequality, stratification, class relations, and power stripped sociologists as scholars and teachers, as historical subjects and change agents of the necessary theoretical tools for analysis and political tools for system change.

To be sure, this was not because sociologists and social scientists did not have a systemic analysis, an understanding of the dialectic between exploitation and racial and gendered oppression, and of the nexus between theory and practice. The works and lives of Karl Marx, W. E. B. DuBois, Jane Adams, Ida Wells Barnett, and many more embodied these dynamics; and their praxis was part of the social struggles of their day. These powerful models of a public and transformative sociology were driven from the center of the discipline and the academy to the far margins. They did not bow to the symbiotic relationship between the university and sociological scholarship that must mask the systemic foundations of class exploitation and racial and gender oppression. They refused to conform to the demands of a university and profession dedicated to producing and reproducing the capitalist, white supremacist, and patriarchal status quo. These scholars, teachers, and political actors enriched our understanding of economic inequality and capitalist exploitation and oppression contextualized within the dialectic of social motion, intellectual production, and education in many settings.

The upsurge and movements of the 1960s interrupted the hegemonic voices and forces in sociology and in the academy. The powerful struggles of the black freedom and civil rights movement, of the indigenous movement, of the women's movement, of the LGBTQ movement, of the anti-imperialist and anti-Vietnam War movements, of the environmental and environmental justice movements, and more cracked the walls of the ivory tower. Expressions of these social forces pushed their way in and informed pedagogy and scholarship in sociology and the university. Marxist sociology, feminist theory, critical theories of race and racism, intersectionality, postcolonial theory, queer theory, etc. and their many applications to history, society, ecology, and change became part of the intellectual and political landscape.

But, even within these more radical frameworks, a clear and holistic focus on economic inequality across race, nationality, gender, sexuality, and region did not fully materialize. These qualities of our lives were too often placed in isolation and/or opposition to each other rather than being relational and rooted within capitalist social relations. What it means to be working class in America within capitalism, and to be part of a multiracial, multinational, and multigendered class that itself was in transition as machine-based production was increasingly replaced by automation was not central to the sociological narrative in the last decades of the twentieth century. In addition, dominant forces within society and the university pushed back. Movement voices were mainstreamed and tamed; their radical, anti-capitalist, and social change edge was dulled, often to the point of non-recognition.

Then came capitalist globalization intertwined with neoliberalism, massive privatization and deregulation, the electronic and robot revolution, social media, and an intensifying and irreversible capitalist crisis in the early twenty-first century. These forces also drove the hyper-corporatization of the university and of society as a whole. The material conditions of global society and ecology—extreme economic inequality and dispossession, climate change, and the commodification of nature—made it necessary to reengage with a deeper systemic analysis of global capitalism and with anti-systemic visions of the future. A more transformative teaching, scholarship, and social motion was on the horizon.

The renewed interest in Marxism in the twenty-first century was one indication that the economic crisis was engulfing the globe in qualitatively new ways. The developing social movements and their many forms—the World Social Forum, including the US Social Forum, the Arab Spring, Occupy Wall Street which gave us the 99% versus the 1%, the fight for $15, Black Lives Matter, immigrant resistance, workers' struggles, global LGBTQ struggles, indigenous and people of color led struggles for the environment, climate, and the earth—and so much more—was another marker. Movement forces put forward demands for human rights for all, including for the necessities of life—food, water, housing, health care, and education—for the commons and enlarging the public sphere, and for cooperative economics, protection of the planet, democratic participation, and the end to state violence and war globally.

The question of how to move politically from the global economic and ecological crisis of capitalism to realizing these demands remained murky at best. Who and what would be the historical subjects for this epochal change? How would movement actors break out of their issue-based silos? The times required a deeper understanding of how the economically unequal and dispossessed might move in alignment with each other, and how a new unity could be forged, nationally and globally.

Guy Standing (2014 [2011]) wrote about the "precariat, the new dangerous class." This was the global precarious working class in low-wage, part-time, informal, and contingent work, if they worked at all. The concept gained traction among some scholars and in movement spaces. The whole question of economic inequality and capitalism re-entered academic and public consciousness with Thomas Piketty's tome, *Capital in the Twenty-First Century* (2014). Media coverage and scholarly examination pushed forward a much needed examination and conversation. Though, most people in Appalachia, the Rust Belt, the South, the Southwest, the Northwest, on Native reservations, and in cities and towns across America from coast to coast, and in most of the world, were already living the daily reality of soaring economic inequality, growing poverty, crisis, and destruction. Scholars and scientists from many disciplines also studied the rapid development and application of automation, robots, and artificial intelligence to work; and mainstream and popular media have been covering this dramatic process. However, again, there is no convergent analysis of the profound impact of today's technological revolution on wage labor, the working class, and the system of capitalism and private property itself (Brynjolfsson and McAfee 2014; Caffentzis 2013; Ford 2015; Frey and Osborne 2013).

As happens throughout history, as happened in the 1960s, and as is happening in the new millennium, the objective conditions of the world propel those most adversely affected to resist; and these conditions and the social response make their mark on the intellectual articulation and media analysis of society. And yet, the systemic root cause of economic inequality and the dynamics of capitalism have not been fully unmasked. The underlying cause of the current capitalist crisis and antagonisms grounded in the economic base of society and the technological revolution remains elusive and unarticulated. Automation, robotics, and artificial intelligence are qualitatively new. They are labor replacing, not labor enhancing, as were machines previously. These new technologies increasingly rupture the fundamental social relations of capital and labor, i.e., capital accumulation rooted in the exploitation of labor power. This upends the dynamics of the labor theory of value at the nexus of commodity production and circulation, capital accumulation, the sale of labor power as a commodity, and work. The systems of global capitalism, markets, and wage labor are being qualitatively disrupted. In conjunction with globalization, the replacement of workers with robots drives economic inequality. Yet, the technological revolution foundational to economic inequality, elimination of jobs and work, and capitalism as a system is rarely, if ever, revealed and analyzed.

Economic inequality and capitalism in contemporary America are also often delinked from analyses of the surge in white supremacy, heteropatriarchy, state violence and the disproportionate incarceration and killing of multigendered black and brown bodies, state repression and disenfranchisement, and ecological destruction. These distortions and omissions in scholarship and teaching leave us without an analytical and practical roadmap to guide political education, strategy, and tactics within the theory–praxis nexus of a critical and liberatory sociology. This societal and sociological context calls for naming and reclaiming a systemic and transformative scholarship, pedagogy, and practice in this political moment. Haltinner and Hormel have stepped up to this task. Haltinner brings a passion for pedagogy, social justice, and social change. *Teaching Economic Inequality and Capitalism in Contemporary America* is one of several collections she has edited or coedited for teaching critical issues of our time—including gender and sex, and race and anti-racism. Hormel shares a passion for scholar activism and teaching, and brings fresh energy and perspective to Marxist sociology, including the ASA Section on Marxist Sociology, and its application to twenty-first-century realities. Her work on rural life takes on new meaning today, as does her commitment to analyzing revolution and political practice.

Hormel's and Haltinner's work challenges dominant ideologies and practices, and engages hot political and social questions for teaching and acting toward a collective future for all humanity. Their collaboration in *Teaching Economic Inequality and Capitalism in Contemporary America* reimagines, for a new century, the deep and often hidden processes of economic inequality and social relations of production and consumption that are essential for human survival within capitalism and the market economy driven by maximum profit. They and the contributors to this volume shine a light on capitalist exploitation and oppression in many and diverse locations. They offer teaching tools and methodologies to move us and our students intellectually, personally, and politically toward greater clarity, a vision for a new society, and critical praxis to get there.

When Haltinner and Hormel began this project, we did not know the specifics of what 2017 would bring. America and global society were already in a qualitatively new period in relation to the economy, the state and politics, society, ecology, and our lives. The whole world was in transition and embodied an ongoing capitalist crisis, and increasing state violence, white supremacy, xenophobia, patriarchy, ecocide, political polarity, and struggle from below.

What undergirded these multiple expressions of the deepening crisis of humanity and the planet was the absolute polarization of wealth and poverty. The global capitalist class, through profit, privatization, and continual commodification of nature, was accumulating greater wealth than ever before. At the same time, the multinational, multiracial, and multigendered working class world over was becoming more impoverished, oppressed, and dispossessed.

Hormel and Haltinner were prescient in their refocus on economic inequality and capitalism. In January 2017, the global corporate and political class met, as they have since 1987, at the World Economic Forum in Davos, Switzerland to strategize about the global economy and controlling the global working class to benefit capital and wealth accumulation. Oxfam International, in preparation for the yearly gathering, released its annual report on global inequality. According to Oxfam, the eight richest billionaires in the world, six of whom are from the United States, had more wealth than the poorest half of humanity, or 3.6 billion people. This represented a dramatic concentration of global wealth from 62 billionaires the previous year down to eight to equal the wealth of the bottom 50% of the world's people. As Oxfam noted, this is "beyond grotesque" (Oxfam International 2017).

Forbes' 2017 annual listing of the world's billionaires offered further evidence of soaring economic inequality. 2016 was a banner year with an increase of 13% in the number of global billionaires between 2015 and 2016. Their numbers rose from 1810 to 2043 (Dolan 2017).

In America, the January 2017 presidential inauguration of Donald Trump ushered in intensifying polarization of wealth and poverty, democracy for billionaire capitalists, and developing fascism for the masses. The Trump Cabinet, the richest in history, boasts total wealth of over $5 billion, by conservative calculations. Its members include two billionaires—Wilbur Ross as Commerce Secretary and Betsy DeVos as Education Secretary—and twelve multimillionaires. Their combined worth is 80% more than that of the previous Obama Cabinet (Harrington 2017).

The 2016 election cycle also surfaced the complexities and lived experience of economic inequality in capitalist America with the eruption into political discourse and public consciousness of the "hidden injuries of class," much of which has been submerged for over a century. The victory of Donald Trump and the Trump administration brought to power a corporate military state grounded in rightwing populism in ideology and rhetoric, and in policy and practice. It mobilizes its social base through appealing to and acting on historic divisions, fears, oppression, and material privilege rooted in the long duree of white supremacy, nationality, gender and sexuality, and religion. It often expresses little regard for science, reality, and facts.

Many white workers, increasingly stripped of their "wages of whiteness"—the marked economic advantage, social privilege, and power in relation to women workers and workers oppressed racially and nationally—responded to this siren call. The 2016 election stirred up the toxic brew of white supremacy, nationalism, patriarchy, and militarism. Even though the effects of the economic crisis on white workers and their declining privilege seemed to be a surprise to the political class and corporate media, they have existed in dynamic relation to white supremacy, patriarchy, and xenophobia for centuries. As economic inequality, unemployment, and poverty rise, all forms of oppression rooted in the capitalist system also intensify.

In this moment, we are reminded by politics more, perhaps, than by the academy that the American working class is multiracial, multinational, and multigendered. As teachers, scholars, and social actors, we forget this at our peril. Within capitalism, workers of all races, nations, religions, and genders must sell their labor and earn a wage—whether at the point of production, in the vast service sector, or in the professional strata. Workers cannot live outside of capitalist labor market dynamics and the markets for housing, health care, and education. Huge swathes of white workers along with workers of all races, now increasingly replaced by robotics and automation, are more and more deemed superfluous by the system and are cast adrift without work and adequate wages to sustain themselves and their families.

The system discards what is to them "surplus" humanity through mass incarceration, police killings, detention, deportation, and war, through environmental toxins, drug addiction, abandonment, and more.

These capitalist processes impinge on the twenty-first century social forces and institutions, including the corporate university. Neoliberalism moves toward fascism—deadly state violence and militarism at home and abroad. These deeply dangerous and unsettling realities are also giving rise to renewed forces of protest, resistance, and revolution. Public schools and universities, and students, teachers, and researchers are once again intertwined with these larger societal motions.

Teaching and learning, and political education inside and outside of the classroom are more critical than ever. Our individual and collective consciousness, worldview, and praxis are, in large measure, informed by the content of formal education at all levels. Within capitalism, educational institutions are purposed by ruling class forces with reproducing hegemonic ideologies and dominant narratives, including social science explanations of society and social change. Yet, we and our students are caught up in today's processes of destruction and reconstruction. In times such as these classrooms can become sites of oppositional and anti-systemic pedagogy and practice. Together we can interrupt, resist, and move toward transformational visions and strategies.

It is in relation to this arc of social history, political economy, ideology and education, and of theory and practice that Haltinner and Hormel give us *Teaching Economic Inequality and Capitalism in Contemporary America*. They have created a broad integrative platform for rethinking and rearticulating economic inequality in contemporary capitalist America within the dialectics of the social relations of class, race, nationality, gender, sexuality, and region. They and the contributors have captured the dynamics and diversity of the lives and experiences of the American people as whole human beings—both their very real differences and their common economic inequality. They have skillfully connected these complicated realities to the educational context of schools and universities and shared transformative pedagogies and tools for teaching.

They have boldly situated economic inequality within capitalist exploitation and super-exploitation at the nexus of the economy and state power, lifting up education and the university as sites of social reproduction as well as contested terrain. This volume challenges the dominant political rhetoric of difference and diversity around race, nationality, gender, and sexuality among workers and the poor as a force of division and opposition. Rather, the deeper analysis embraces the ways in which oppressions of race, nationality, gender, and sexuality are interpenetrated with class relations across time and place. This systemic analysis of root causes opens up the possibility of a unifying process of analysis and social struggle among the exploited, the economically unequal, and the oppressed across their differences.

Hormel and Haltinner's edited volume, *Teaching Economic Inequality and Capitalism in Contemporary America*, embodies the rich tapestry of what economic inequality and capitalism look like and how they are experienced within the racialized and gendered working class in contemporary America. They and their contributors present a critical focus on education as a space for teaching and learning the nuances and realities of inequality and capitalism through lived experience and pedagogical tools. This collection offers a much needed corrective to decades of U.S. sociological scholarship and education that fails to interrogate American exceptionalism and empire, that mystifies the systemic basis of wealth and poverty, and that contributes to the confusion among generations of workers of all races, nationalities, and genders about the source of their exploitation and oppression. Haltinner and Hormel and the chapter authors make an important contribution to reimagining and re-theorizing economic inequality and class exploitation in relation to ideological structures and state violence directed toward today's multiracial, multigendered global working class. Their collection is especially valuable for its critical pedagogies and tools for teaching and transforming our lives and society.

Teaching Economic Inequality and Capitalism in Contemporary America opens with three chapters on "Making the Personal Political: The Stories of Capitalism" [Docka-Filipeck and Gerbrandt and Strahm also in this section] Docka-Filipeck describes results from her classes where the instructor's narratives of "self-disclosure" are used as a tool for learning about class inequalities and intersectionality. Marshall and Leondar-Wright use stories to bring the analysis of class back into the classroom and students' lives. Gerbrandt and Strahm's Harold and Bob exercise helps students see—through detailed, comparative accounts—how financial, cultural, and social capitals shape life chances.

"Innovative Pedagogical Strategies for Course Development" includes four chapters. Bradley uses money and society to teach about economic inequality and recent U.S. financial crises. In the following chapter, Godfrey identifies the problem of students' experiences with "estranged learning" that happens in the classroom and in coursework, and illustrates how may help students return their "species" to their "being." Chasin analyzes spaces of systemic violence by the U.S. military and police forces to quell revolutionary forces globally and domestic protest. Backer analyzes grading as an expression of commodification and power within capitalist education, economy, and society.

In the following section, six chapters on "Helping Students Think Beyond the American Dream" debunk and demystify the myth of the American Dream. Through pedagogies of truth-telling Earles, Thorne, Kunkel, Kersten, Machum, and Zhang challenge students in their worldview and their daily experience to question the middle class, private property, the free market, and the invisibility of class, economic mobility, education as a great equalizer, and the alienation within education and classroom dynamics in capitalist America. For example, Earles shares teaching tools rooted in Marxist theory and the concepts of alienation and reproduction, while Thorne challenges "bootstrap" theory by focusing on students' family financial crises and bankruptcies.

In "Incorporating Intersectionalities" Hormel, Ballesteros, and Brister; Anthony-Stevens; Croll; and Levan build alternative critical analyses based in intersectionality and current and historical realities of capitalism in America. Hormel writes with her undergraduate students Cynthia Ballesteros and Haylee Brister to share their community action research project examining poverty in rural

America in relation to housing and environmental justice. Anthony-Stevens offers pedagogies for addressing educational challenges of students at the intersection of race and poverty in rural America. Croll speaks to the challenges of teaching about the intersectional dynamics of economic inequality and race. Levan ties this discussion to her class discussions and exercises on capital punishment in the United States.

"Tools to Expose Capitalism and Economic Inequalities: International and Postcolonial Experience" includes three chapters that identify systemic structures and relations in different spaces adversely impacted by economic inequality and capitalism. Sarathchandra explores the negative impact on science and technology education in postcolonial spaces. Robey and Robey demonstrate how empirical social science analyses and transnational comparisons can strengthen students' abilities to see how capitalism structures inequalities. Edwards offers pedagogies using commodity production to teach about global inequality.

The volume ends with a reality check for teachers and professors in "Capitalism and Higher Education: Contraints and Opportunities" and regrounds the analysis of capitalism and the transformative potential of teaching in the realities of college students—their educational experiences, critical pedagogies, and tools for grasping the nature of capitalism. Gaines argues for open-source educational materials. Rechitsky and Olsberg go deep into critical pedagogy to link economic inequality and the skills to think and write well. As someone with experience teaching in community college and 4-year college institutions, Wruck describes how the different functions of these institutions affect how one teaches inequality and capitalism to students. Dolgon speaks to the challenge of the corporate university, deeply rooted in structure and culture, to students' political engagement and our teaching to nurture their praxis. Brewer analyzes the 2015 Black student protest at the University of Missouri as a powerful expression of the interrelation of capitalism, racism, and the corporate university, and the need for faculty to connect these forms of analysis and struggle in their critical sociological classrooms.

The depth and breadth of *Teaching Economic Inequality and Capitalism in Contemporary America* reveals the power of analysis and knowledge. Hormel and Haltinner and the chapter authors live within the contradictions of teaching and learning in contemporary capitalism and the corporate university, and of openings for transformative theory and practice. They are part of a generation of scholar and student activists, radical teachers, and historic actors who are building unity between the academy and the street. Critical educators and students, embracing the dialectic of theory, pedagogy, and practice, are informed by today's social movements. Oppositional social science and anti-capitalist analysis are in dynamic relation to the social motion and political struggle in the current moment.

As we embrace today's growing resistance, we are compelled to prepare for the strategic struggle for our collective future. This is an organizing moment. It is also a political education moment. If we do not understand the systemic crisis of our world—in the economy, politics, and ecology—we cannot defeat it. Resistance struggles must be organized into an independent political force, in our schools, universities, and the broader struggle.

Liberatory pedagogy is essential. Despite the hyper-corporatized and neoliberal universities and schools we all work and study in, our classrooms and movement spaces have to be sites of truth-telling and oppositional analysis. Haltinner, Hormel, and the powerful voices in *Teaching Economic Inequality and Capitalism in Contemporary America* are a step forward in this process. A new revolutionary consciousness, vision, and strategic practice is imperative to create a transformed, cooperative, equal, and just society and world. Unity must be forged, inclusive of our racialized and gendered diversities and histories, toward the survival of humanity and the planet.

References

Brynjolfsson, E., & McAfee, A. (2014). *The second machine age: Work, progress and prosperity in a time of brilliant technologies*. New York: Norton & Company.

Caffentzis, G. (2013). *In letters of blood and fire: Work, machines, and the crisis of capitalism*. Oakland, CA: PM Press.

Dolan, K. A. (2017). *Forbes 2017 billionaires list: Meet the richest people on the planet*. https://www.forbes.com/sites/kerryadolan/2017/03/20/forbes-2017-billionaires-list-meet-the-richest-people-on-the-planet/#38b4158362ff. Accessed April 19, 2017.

Ford, M. (2015). *Rise of the robots: Technology and the threat of a jobless future*. New York: Basic Books.

Frey, C. B., & Osborne, M. A. (2013). The future of employment: How susceptible are jobs to computerization? *Oxford Martin School Machines and Employment Workshop, 17 September*. http://www.oxfordmartin.ox.ac.uk/downloads/academic/The_Future_of_Employment.pdf. Accessed December 29, 2015.

Harrington, B. (2017). *Yes, Trump's cabinet is super rich. That's not why we should be worried*. https://www.washingtonpost.com/posteverything/wp/2017/01/19/trump-richcabinet/?utm_term=.fd51d1716eee. Accessed April 9, 2017.

Oxfam International. (2017). *Just 8 men own same wealth as half the world*. Washington, DC: Oxfam International. https://www.oxfam.org/en/pressroom/pressreleases/2017-01-16/just-8-men-own-same-wealth-half-world. Accessed April 19, 2017.

Piketty, T. (2014). *Capital in the twenty-first century*. Cambridge, MA: Belknap Press of Harvard University Press.

Standing, G. (2014 [2011]). *The precariat: The new dangerous class*. New York: Bloomsbury Academic.

Part I
Making the Personal Political: The Stories of Capitalism

'Teaching Naked' in Late Capitalism: Instructors' Personal Narratives and Classroom Self-disclosure as Pedagogical Tools

Danielle Docka-Filipek

> *If we ask academics to hold students in a space of vulnerability and uncertainty in which they can embrace their own beings, it is necessary that we create the kind of environment where academics can explore their own vulnerability and uncertainty.*
> —Blackie et al. (2010: 643)

Author's Reflexive Statement

I am a first-generation college graduate from a very impoverished background. I spent all of my school-age years eating 'free lunch.' Both of my parents and all of my siblings are permanently disabled from either physical or psychiatric illnesses, or some combination of both. Access to housing, healthcare, nutrition, safety, and bodily autonomy have often been precarious or elusive for my loved ones and myself. Additionally, I am a product of the Midwestern rust-belt (my hometown is Kenosha, Wisconsin—a small city known for its infamous Chrysler factory closure), and during my teenage years, punitive "welfare-to-work" reform policies were first pioneered in my home state before introduction on a national scale. While my Ph.D. has afforded me a measure of upward social mobility, I nevertheless occupy a class-liminal position, as most of my biological and chosen family members remain underneath the poverty line. The debts I accumulated to finance my degree will follow me throughout my career, and swimming 'against the tide' has impacted my health in a number of negative ways (as it has for many others with similar life histories—see Miller et al. 2015).

I read as "white," which affords me a good amount of privilege in a variety of circumstances, not least of which is the classroom. In particular, I am granted analytic and other liberties by my students while teaching them about race and

D. Docka-Filipek (✉)
Christopher Newport University, Newport News, USA
e-mail: danielle.dockafilipek@cnu.edu

K. Haltinner and L. Hormel (eds.), *Teaching Economic Inequality and Capitalism in Contemporary America*, https://doi.org/10.1007/978-3-319-71141-6_2

whiteness, yet that's always crosscut by my relatively young age (mid-30s); the visual, embodied markers of my class origins; and my feminine body. I am not able-bodied, I am not Christian, I identify as queer, and I am openly committed to radical, socialist, and feminist ideals. Marxism and historical materialism occupy an important space in my analytic toolkit, and my belief in the moral imperative of fully redistributive justice informs my research, activism, and teaching in a number of ways.

I am especially committed to sharing my own personal narratives and life experiences with students where appropriate, because I feel it is especially important for historically underrepresented scholars to demonstrate to students who themselves occupy marginalized social locations that a successful, professional, intellectual career is not out of their grasp if they do not fit the normative ideal for professor or researcher. For privileged students, I think it is important for them to experience authority from a member of a marginalized group. Further, many of my own undergraduate mentors were members of historically marginalized groups. My mentors were vocal and open about their experiences, with the objective of modeling for me what it might look like to pursue a career in higher education. Because I experience teaching and learning as liberating, revolutionary, and joyful acts that sometimes forge deep intellectual and emotional connections between students and teachers, I maintain my most memorable mentors' commitments to transparency and vulnerability in the classroom.

On the Use of Instructor's Personal Narratives in the Classroom

A growing literature on the use of narrative in the classroom suggests a number of pedagogical benefits: among them, aiding students in building empathy for the 'other' (Bal and Veltkamp 2013); rethinking social myths and stereotypes (Van Rooj 2012); processing the ways in which marginalization is both an interactional and embodied experience (Sy 2013); challenging the ideological hegemony of neoliberal logics (Jones and Calafell 2012); and making visible the "matrix of domination" (Collins 1990; Hooks 1994, 2003). Nowakowski and Sumerau (2015) find that "personalizing the sociology curriculum" via the specific inclusion of emotional/life experiences of the instructor may increase critical sociological awareness, knowledge of patterned disparities, and student engagement. Additionally, both authors reflect that such practices are consistently met with gratitude from students, firm instructor-student rapport, and efficacy in achieving learning outcomes. In the chapter that follows, I argue that my own use of personal narratives, emotional history, and corresponding life experiences via self-disclosure in the classroom together constitute an especially effective pedagogical strategy for teaching students about social class inequality—as well as intersecting oppressions—as they operate under late capitalism. I review student survey data to demonstrate the potential costs and benefits of such an approach.

This project began as an outgrowth of an exchange on the "Teaching with a Sociological Lens" Facebook group, where sociology instructors with a variety of backgrounds exchange resources, ideas, and consider pedagogical questions. At one point, a group member posed the question of exactly how much information other instructors shared about their personal lives in the classroom, and whether or not this was an appropriate or useful practice. I am an instructor trained in feminist pedagogy and, given my committed belief that the "personal is political" (as well as attached to the structural), I came down hard on the side of extolling the benefits of sharing with students, though in limited doses, only when relevant and appropriate, and for very limited amounts of overall classroom time. I argued that such practices are useful in achieving stated learning objectives (especially those related to teaching inequalities), aiding in concept comprehension and application, and building classroom rapport (both between students and the instructor, as well as among students who typically choose to model their instructor and share their own experiences). However, many of the other participating members in the forum were vehemently opposed to the practice as they felt it broke norms of professionalism, compromised classroom authority, revealed instructor bias, and introduced a problematic lack of instructor objectivity. Despite these objections, and perhaps because of my belief in the impossibility of an 'impartial' or 'unbiased' social science, I held firm to my commitments that personal narratives and the life experiences of a sociology instructor can occupy a useful and productive space in the classroom. I came away from this online debate with a resolve to answer the questions posed in the group by gathering and analyzing empirical data on the topic. Subsequently, I set out to test my assumptions at the end of the Spring 2016 semester.

The most recent work on the topic of instructor use of personal narratives in the classroom is likely Nowakowski and Sumerau's "Should We Talk about the Pain? Personalizing Sociology in the Medical Sociology Classroom" (2015). Specifically, the authors consider "biographic incorporation techniques," such as telling the stories of their own experiences with chronic illness/diagnosis/coping strategies, recalling stigmatizing encounters with medical institutions and professionals, sharing the emotional effects these experiences generated, and inviting students to do the same—while always providing the option to opt-out, in order to maintain student consent and trust.

Nowakowski and Sumerau (2015) also provide a thorough overview of existing literature on the topic of the costs and benefits of instructor self-disclosure. Potential benefits of instructors' personal sharing include greater student engagement, the development and honing of students' political/sociological consciousness, facilitating deeper understanding of course content, validation of students' own similar life experiences, and the forging of analytic connections that point to the larger structural causes of disparity and inequality (Adams 2010; Freire 1968; Greenfield

2006; Hooks 1994; Lucal 2015). Despite these benefits, however, a number of graduate programs, pedagogical conference workshops, and existing teacher-training curricula across the discipline of sociology (and in higher education in general) continue to encourage 'distance' from students in teaching—and, from subjects in research—in order to encourage greater 'objectivity' via analytic and emotional remove (Blouin and Moss 2015). However, some scholars argue that the cultivation of such 'distance' can be alienating for students, and indeed that alienation may be amplified for minority students in particular, especially in predominantly white institutions (Gusa 2010).

Research Questions

Data collection was guided by one main research question: Do students perceive instructor self-disclosure (defined as the sharing of narratives rooted in personal experience) as helpful or problematic in fostering their comprehension of concepts, the building of classroom rapport, and learning how to practice radical empathy? Other associated questions I attempted to address via data collection from students included: Which of my personal stories did students recall as especially memorable, and why? Are there additional, unanticipated pedagogical benefits that follow from the practice of instructor self-disclosure? If so, what are they? Are there additional, unanticipated detriments or drawbacks that follow from the practice of instructor self-disclosure? If so, what are they? Do the perceived benefits and detriments of instructor self-disclosure bear any relationship to one another? For example, did students believe that any of the benefits they listed came at the explicitly associated cost of specific detriments? Does deeper learning, validation, rapport, or empathetic capacities for some students (and their identities) come at the expense of detriments for other students, and vice versa?

Telling Personal Stories

Ultimately, I argue the use of instructors' personal narratives, and relating corresponding life experiences via self-disclosure in the classroom, are especially effective pedagogical strategies for teaching students about social class inequality, as well as intersecting oppressions, as they operate under late capitalism. Instructional strategies that include recounting the instructor's significant life experiences may, for example, focus on perspective shifts (such as from colorblindness to racial literacy), the onset of sociological consciousness, or especially telling encounters between the body and oppressive structures.

Speaking specifically about my own practices, there are a wide range of stories I tell my students, when my life experiences speak directly to themes in the course content or the larger structural, institutional, or statistical trends we're examining in class. On a 'normal' day, I generally approach the classroom with plans for a limited lecture (generally, no more than 15–20 min worth), and then as a group we transition into either direct engagement with the text, analysis of a related current event or especially telling media/pop culture artifact, or guided discussion of student-submitted critical discussion questions on the day's material. In general, the classes I teach are small (ranging from 8 to 35 students, with around 20 being most common, though I have deployed similar strategies in classes as large as 80), and the feel of the environment leans towards the informal and conversational. At the time of data collection, generally my classes were roughly 30% students of color (about double the population in the university at large), approximately 1/3 working class or first-generation, 60–70% female, and included a small handful of openly queer students.

When teaching specifically about socioeconomic inequality in the US, the stories I use most frequently in the classroom involve my experiences growing up "dependent" on public aid for my childhood survival after medical crises and disability forced both of my parents out of regular labor market participation. Such stories of navigating social welfare bureaucracies and the stigma that accompanied receipt of public aid are especially relevant as I'm teaching about the welfare state, when debates about 'deservingness' and the merits of cash and food assistance arise. I have explicit recollection of the physical, embodied experience of food insecurity and a deep feeling of shamefulness regarding my family's poverty that dates back as far as elementary school, and I speak of these experiences openly when the discussion turns in that direction.

When addressing the topic of poverty in general, I'll relate to students what it was like to spend a decade in graduate school at a Big 10, research-one university—an environment that often demanded that I learn to study and speak about poverty in "objective," abstract, dispassionately removed, and theoretical terms. This created a jarring disconnect with my personal life, as I continued to live below the poverty line, and members of my immediate family transitioned in and out of homelessness.

When addressing questions about class stratification, class mobility, and cultural capital in the classroom, I'll recount for students what it was like as a first generation student from a highly marginalized socioeconomic background, attending a private liberal arts undergrad institution alongside wealthy and/or economically secure classmates. I'll recall the radical 'code-switching' that was required of me, and the biting humiliation that resulted when I struggled with 'imposter syndrome,' due to the lack of cultural knowledge that would have otherwise allowed me to fully integrate into my new environment.

Additional related subjects I sometimes teach include the social construction of illness, mental health and medicalizing processes, and the institutional intersections of class inequality and disability. When doing so, I'll sometimes tell stories about my experiences growing up with two schizophrenic parents, and what it was like helping them navigate the broken US mental healthcare system in an era of increasing privatization. The ground constantly shifted under our feet due to the neoliberal agenda to dissolve universal state entitlements, and I use my history to help students place an emotional reality to policies, figures, and disembodied claims.

When teaching students about the intersections between class and contemporary racial inequality, I'll relate the difficulties I personally faced in shifting from a color-blind perspective to one of racial literacy, and how that was complicated, and at times, stalled by my experiences of class marginality (as it was sometimes difficult for me to grasp that I was indeed "privileged"). Such conversations are often especially productive for other students who read as white, yet might not yet have 'outed' themselves as class marginal (and often do so eventually, either in class or in private conversation with me), and are struggling to understand the benefits and moral responsibilities of whiteness in the context of their otherwise difficult lives.

Additionally, I'll often push my students to examine the ways in which gender informs race and class, and will then relate to students a variety of instances in my own life and the lives of my friends when biological explanations for gender difference fell short or proved contradictory. It also bears mention that while not all of the items I've chosen to cite are directly or initially 'about' income inequality under late capitalism, they do illuminate the import of considering the ways in which understandings of and experiences with socioeconomic inequality are always cross-cut with gender, race, sexuality, and experiences with living in a differently-abled body.

Altogether, my experiences in the classroom have led me to believe that the limited, yet strategic use of brief personal narratives can serve as powerful antidotes to students' subscription to toxic meritocratic ideologies, tendencies to criminalize the poor, and the mystification of the causes of contemporary inequality. However, I'll also emphasize that the recounting of instructors' personal experience in the sociological classroom must *always* be contextualized with data on larger institutional patterns, else one risks substituting the anecdotal for the empirical (and perhaps fostering an environment where students feel entitled to do so, as well—a situation which proves antithetical to sociological learning). Including instructors' personal experiences in the sociological classroom always risks "the danger of a single story" that threatens to flatten complex lives into stereotype (Adichie 2009). Additionally, I argue that existing scholarship points to the possibility of unique benefits for instructor self-disclosure from teachers with marginalized backgrounds due to the sharpness of their vision "from below" (Sandoval 2000). It warrants emphasis that the personal must *always* be contextualized within the structural, and I'll revisit this matter in the discussion of results and conclusion to the chapter.

Data and Discussion

My data (see Table 1) was gathered in the Spring semester of 2016, when I was teaching at a small, primarily undergraduate-serving, blended liberal arts/professional studies institution (enrolling slightly under 3000 students) just outside of Columbus, Ohio. Students were surveyed across one mid-level seminar on gender titled *Sociology of Gender*, one mid-level seminar on social problems and policy solutions titled *Social Problems* (both courses were cross-listed as electives within the Gender, Women's, and Sexuality Studies major program), as well as an upper-level practicum on sociological praxis and intersectionality titled *Human and Community Services: Organizing Across Race, Class, Gender, and Age* (which met general education requirements for interdisciplinary learning when taken by students alongside a course in organizational leadership). All three classes were open to majors and non-majors and had no curricular prerequisites. Roughly 75% of the students surveyed were sociology majors, and the remainder were non-majors, only some of whom minored in sociology. Surveyed students were spread across class rank, with slightly lower amounts of first-years (roughly, 15% of respondents) than sophomores, juniors, and seniors. Fifty-three (53) total students participated, giving me a response rate of 91% (some of my enrolled students were absent on survey day, though all who were present participated voluntarily). When administering the survey for each course, I always exited the room while students took the survey to minimize discomfort or self-censorship. Surveys were distributed in all courses on the second to last day of class for the semester (Table 1).

Overall, the quantitative data is quite compelling, and builds a strong case for the myriad benefits of instructors' sharing their personal experiences in the classroom. Questions two through eight document the students' feelings about the value of such an approach. The average across the seven measures for student *agreement* with the merits of this very personal pedagogical approach is 91%, while an average of 2.3% of students voiced *disagreement* with the merits of such an approach.

Questions nine through 11 document student concerns about three potential *detriments* of such an approach. Overall, an average of 83% of students *disagreed* that such detrimental circumstances were reproduced in our learning community, while 5.7% of students *agreed* that such detrimental classroom outcomes were possible. Significantly, an average of 22% of students elected that they had "no opinion" on the statements representing the detriments of instructors' inclusion of personal narratives in the classroom, whereas only 6.7% of students felt they had "no opinion" on the merits of such sharing on the part of their instructor.

The remaining three questions in the survey were open-ended. Briefly, I'll recap the main themes that emerged. The student-named benefits of instructor self-disclosure and personal narrative fell largely into five clusters. Students cited:

(1) valuing the validation of their own similar experiences via comparison;
(2) feeling invited to share their own life experience through a sociological lens (which some said enhanced a sense of the classroom as a "democratic" space);
(3) enhancing their capacity to make analytic moves from the abstract to the concrete (which some claimed aided in their theory/concept comprehension and application);
(4) understanding and empathizing with the human and embodied consequences of inequality; and
(5) building greater trust and rapport with their instructor.

Here's a few of the students' direct responses about the benefits of personal narratives from their instructor:

Table 1 Data from student surveys on instructors' use of personal narratives (N = 53)

1. I can recall specific times in the classroom when my instructor shared narratives/stories from her life and personal experience		
YES: 98% (N = 2)	**NO: 2% (N = 1)**	
2. When my instructor shares narratives/stories from her life and personal experience, it helps me better understand concepts and theories from the course material		
STRONGLY AGREE/AGREE: 96%	**NO OPINION: 4%**	**DISAGREE/ STRONGLY DISAGREE: 0%**
3. When my instructor shares narratives/stories from her life and personal experience, it helps me better understand the human and embodied consequences of inequality		
STRONGLY AGREE/AGREE: 91%	**NO OPINION: 8%**	**DISAGREE/ STRONGLY DISAGREE: 2%**
4. When my instructor shares narratives/stories from her life and personal experience, it helps me establish rapport and a relationship of trust with her as a person		
STRONGLY AGREE/AGREE: 94%	**NO OPINION: 4%**	**DISAGREE/ STRONGLY DISAGREE: 2%**
5. When my instructor shares narratives/stories from her life and personal experience, it helps me build empathy for 'others' who are somehow different from me		
STRONGLY AGREE/AGREE: 92%	**NO OPINION: 6%**	**DISAGREE/ STRONGLY DISAGREE: 2%**
6. When my instructor shares narratives/stories from her life and personal experience, it helps me to rethink stereotypes and other social myths		
STRONGLY AGREE/AGREE: 96%	**NO OPINION: 4%**	**DISAGREE/ STRONGLY DISAGREE: 0%**
7. When my instructor shares narratives/stories from her life and personal experience, it helps me to see my own similar experiences as validated, "real," or legitimate by comparison		
STRONGLY AGREE/AGREE: 91%	**NO OPINION: 8%**	**DISAGREE/ STRONGLY DISAGREE: 2%**
8. When my instructor shares narratives/stories from her life and personal experience, I feel invited to share my own life experiences in the classroom		
STRONGLY AGREE/AGREE: 80%	**NO OPINION: 13%**	**DISAGREE/ STRONGLY DISAGREE: 8%**
9. When my instructor shares narratives/stories from her life and personal experience, I am sometimes concerned that the course content is "biased" in a problematic way		
STRONGLY AGREE/AGREE: 11%	**NO OPINION: 11%**	**DISAGREE/ STRONGLY DISAGREE: 77%**
10. When my instructor shares narratives/stories from her life and personal experience, I feel my own experiences are silenced or undervalued		
STRONGLY AGREE/AGREE: 0%	**NO OPINION: 4%**	**DISAGREE/ STRONGLY DISAGREE: 97%**
11. When my instructor shares narratives/stories from her life and personal experience, I feel it encourages a "PC culture" in the classroom that silences unpopular yet necessary opinions		
STRONGLY AGREE/AGREE: 6%	**NO OPINION: 21%**	**DISAGREE/ STRONGLY DISAGREE: 74%**

(continued)

Table 1 (continued)

12. Please recount below any significant examples you can recall from your classroom experiences this semester that involve your instructor sharing stories from her life and personal experience. What sticks out in your mind and why? If you cannot recall examples, please leave this question blank
13. Can you think of any additional assets or benefits to your learning/classroom/overall college experience that are created by having an instructor who openly shares narratives/stories from her life and personal experience? If so, please describe them below. If not, please leave this question blank
14. Can you think of any additional problems, detriments, or hindrances to your learning/classroom/overall college experience that are created by having an instructor who openly shares narratives/stories from her life and personal experience? Please describe them below. If not, please leave this question blank

- "It reaffirms that what we may be experiencing is not something unique to us. It helps for us to participate in the classroom and to know that such sharing is mutual".
- "Because of my experience in this class, and the narratives shared, I have come to realize that empathy is radical AND political. Knowing about how inequality manifests in a person's life—and a person whom I dearly respect—made learning about that pain a lot more accessible for me".
- "There are many benefits to professors sharing stories. I think it creates a better relationship with that professor. These are hard topics, so feeling comfortable about sharing them is critical. It also allows us to feel like Dr. F is more of a knowledgeable peer than a superior. I feel like I'm talking to someone who values my opinion and experiences".
- "You don't have to be a sociology major to be a caring, empathetic person… Stories make sociology a human experience, which is what it needs to be".
- "Before this course I had very little knowledge on oppression and the move towards social justice, nor did I feel invested in any issue. Hearing the stories and personal experiences made this more *real* to me and has ultimately made me more aware. This transformative experience may not have occurred had I simply read the stories of strangers out of a textbook".
- "…I think it is beneficial to hear personal stories because it can help the students have realizations about the way their own social location affects their views…"

And here are a few of their responses on the detriments associated with the approach (again, please recall, these commenters were outliers, though nevertheless important):

- "When your views on certain subjects are SO passionate, I think that people are afraid to share any differing opinions because of the fear of you disagreeing so strongly".
- "Some students may take the instructor's word as law and not formulate personal opinions".
- "May make the classroom feel too biased to one political side or the other".

- "The only problem is being too open which can cause some in the class to be uncomfortable".

Overall, I argue, the benefits listed by students were myriad and represented significant, fairly widespread agreement. Therefore, the data clearly tilts in the direction of students reading such practices as a positive part of their learning experiences. Such data should be further interpreted in the context of relevant institutional circumstances. For example: in addition to enjoying small class sizes, many of my courses were populated by students I'd grown to know over the past three years I'd been teaching at the institution, as I began my full-time tenure track career there after finishing graduate school in 2013. For many students, I'd known them since their first or second year, and I had taught the majority of the courses they had taken in their major and/or minor due to the small size of the department and students' tendency to gravitate towards taking multiple courses with me throughout their education. Despite these circumstances (which would be expected to produce favorable results), the amount of non-majors and students who had not yet taken a course with me were not altogether insignificant, representing at least one-third of survey respondents, if not more.

Furthermore, the amount of students who either felt unsure about the detriments or benefits of their instructor's sharing personal experiences, or came down as clearly reporting *disagreement* with the proposed benefits, or even more problematically, *agreement* with the proposed detriments, must be considered when weighing the extent to which sharing life experiences constitutes sound or beneficial pedagogical practice.

First, regarding agreement with reported detriments: If students experience what they perceive to be a "silencing" of sociologically unpopular views—for example, colorblindness, unwavering belief that we are a society governed by meritocracy, individualism without moral responsibility, etc.—I'm not so sure I consider that a problem. Such opinions are not mere ideas, as they actively contribute to the oppression of marginalized communities, and may be experienced as insulting, triggering, or antagonistic by marginalized students in the classroom. Therefore, creating an environment where such voices and opinions proliferate without sanction may not only fail to further student learning, it may create a hostile environment for targeted students.

Furthermore, my recollection of the semester was such that it was clear in all three classes that these opinions were not entirely silenced as they were consistently debated (sometimes, to the frustration of majors, seniors, and those who occupied targeted identities). Far from being an infrequent subject of conversation, a small but vocal minority of students (some of whom openly identified as "conservative") regularly felt emboldened to make claims and pose questions about, for example, the inherently violent nature of minority communities and individuals, the types of 'pathological' and/or lazy behaviors encouraged in the poor by 'generous' public assistance programs, and even the religiously ordained 'nature' of masculinity and femininity. As the United States is governed by a bipartisan system, the suggestion that such questions and debates were either implicitly or explicitly problematic or counter-productive to learning the sociological perspective are nearly always read as either "Democrat" or "liberal." Though they may be both, or neither, students are nevertheless encouraged by popular culture and dominant ideology to define the world in oversimplified terms of left and right, when often social issues are complex and not reducible to such easy, binary distinctions (Schwalbe 2008). Additionally, despite my best efforts to get students to understand all knowledge, question-asking, and pursuit of scientific or empirical claims are inherently 'biased' (and to encourage them to instead reflect on the benefits of approaching contentious topics and social inquiry with a modicum of reflexivity), many students were either actively resistant to such critiques (which I made space for, respected, and acknowledged), or not present on the days such topics were dissected and discussed in class.

Furthermore, even if students reported sometimes feeling uncomfortable raising 'conservative,' colorblind, neoliberal, or negative views regarding the impoverished in the context of classroom discussion, this certainly did not prevent them from sharing such views in small group work, written work for the course, or in one-on-one office hours exchanges with me (or, for that matter, in end-of-semester teaching evaluations—though these were infrequent). It's also worth mention, though, that many such openly critical students did *not* develop an antagonistic relationship to the course material, or to me as their instructor. For example, in the days immediately following election night for the 2016 presidential election, I had a number of Trump-supporting students approach me during my office hours for emotional support. One white student even came to me with tears of frustration over being called a "racist" after gloating to her coworkers of color that "my guy won last night, so you need to get over it!" My point is that far from feeling alienated, such students felt quite comfortable seeking me out for emotional labor, and while the experience proved quite difficult for me, I would argue that part of the reason they felt comfortable in seeking me out (and providing me with the opportunity to offer my sociological insights) could be directly attributable to the rapport I'd built with them in the classroom via my own willingness to be open and vulnerable. Though not all instructors may see this as a desirable outcome given the weight of the students' requests, again, I'll emphasize that it presented both myself and my students a unique opportunity for teaching and learning that might not have materialized without actively cultivated emotional intimacy.

Perhaps most importantly, upon reflection, I've found that so much of teaching about inequality involves a tightrope walk between (1) creating the type of environment where marginalized students do not feel they're being attacked by their peers' reproduction of marginalizing discourses, and (2) providing a space where privileged students can work through their moral commitments to the logics that secure their continued privilege. Sometimes—though certainly not always—these two imperatives are mutually exclusive. In those instances, I favor the learning and encouragement of my marginalized students, as I see them in need of greater support due to the emotional labor required of them in such exchanges, as well as the circumstances they face in the world outside of my classroom. Ultimately, I would argue, if I'm not having moments in the classroom where this fundamental tension comes to a head, I'm dodging my moral commitments as an educator committed to transformation and liberation.

Discretion in Disclosure?

In closing, I want to acknowledge that the practice of sharing personal narratives with students is not without risk given the potential demands of associated emotional labor, the opportunity for *major* compromise of classroom authority, and the impact of the well-documented possibility of race and gender bias in student evaluations of teaching (Boring et al. 2016). In deciding how much to disclose to students, individual instructors must also consider the political and institutional environments in which they teach.

When engaging in the aforementioned calculus, relevant questions to ask oneself include: Does the campus and/or the department have a more "progressive," "liberal," "radical," "conservative," or "status quo" reputation? Will the Chair and other colleagues 'go to bat' for you if a student or colleague questions your "scientific" or "professional" credentials? What is the student body like in terms of demographics and political leanings, and how do these realities impact the student/teacher relationship, as well as the feeling of classroom environments? How large are classes, how large is the department, how do other faculty in the department teach, and how do all of these factors together influence the norms of the classroom environment one walks into on the first day of each semester? To what extent do you have experiences in your personal history that are directly relevant to the course material? Do you have the protection of tenure or the tenure track, does your tenure status bring additional scrutiny, and are more experimental forms of pedagogy generally rewarded on your campus? Will you be penalized in your professional review for trying new ideas and approaches, or is some level of 'trial and error' expected from faculty in your institution as they learn and grow? Ultimately, how much professional 'risk' can one take, given social location, identity, and the campus environment? Ultimately, though I hope the cost/benefit analysis I've delineated above is helpful for other instructors in deciding the level of self-disclosure they intend to engage, all instructors inhabit different institutional realities, and must therefore decide for themselves what is most prudent, comfortable, and productive for themselves and their students.

References

Adams, T. (2010). Paradoxes of sexuality, gay identity and the closet. *Symbolic Interaction, 33*(2), 234–256.

Adichie, C. N. (2009, July). The danger of a single story. [Video file]. Retrieved from https://www.ted.com/talks/chimamanda_adichie_the_danger_of_a_single_story?language=en.

Bal, P. M., & Veltkamp, M. (2013). How does fiction reading influence empathy? An experimental investigation on the role of emotional transportation. *PLoS ONE, 8*(1), e55341.
Blackie, M., Case, J., & Jawitz, J. (2010). Student-centeredness: The link between transforming students and transforming ourselves. *Teaching in Higher Education, 15*(6), 637–646.
Blouin, D., & Moss, A. (2015). Graduate student teacher training: Still relevant (and missing?) 20 years later. *Teaching Sociology, 42*(1), 5–16.
Boring, A. et al. (2016, January 07). Student evaluations of teaching (mostly) do not measure teaching effectiveness. *ScienceOpen Research*—Section: SOR-EDU. Retrieved from https://www.scienceopen.com/document/vid/818d8ec0-5908-47d8-86b4-5dc38f04b23e.
Collins, P. H. (1990). *Black feminist thought: Knowledge, consciousness, and the politics of empowerment*. New York: Routledge.
Freire, P. (1968). *Pedagogy of the oppressed*. New York: Bloomsbury Publishing.
Greenfield, D. (2006). Understanding social structure through personal experience: The creative use of status and role as explanatory factors. *Teaching Sociology, 34*(4), 404–411.
Gusa, D. (2010). White institutional presence: The impact of whiteness on campus climate. *Harvard Educational Review, 80*(4), 464–490.
Hooks, B. (1994). *Teaching to transgress: Education as the practice of freedom*. New York: Routledge.
Hooks, B. (2003). *Teaching community: A pedagogy of hope*. New York: Routledge.
Jones, R., & Calafell, B. (2012). Contesting neoliberalism through critical pedagogy, intersectional reflexivity, and personal narrative: Queer tales of academia. *Journal of Homosexuality, 59*(7), 957–981.
Lucal, B. (2015). 2014 Hans O. Mauksch address: Neoliberalism and higher education: How a misguided philosophy undermines teaching sociology. *Teaching Sociology, 43*(1), 3–14.
Miller, G., Yu, T., Chen, E., & Brody, G. (2015). Self-control forecasts better psychosocial outcomes but faster epigenetic aging in low-SES youth. *Proceedings of the National Academy of Sciences of the United States of America, 112*(33). Retrieved March 28, 2017, from http://www.pnas.org/content/112/33/10325.abstract.
Nowakowski, A., & Sumerau, J. (2015). Should we talk about the pain? Personalizing sociology in the medical sociology classroom. *Teaching Sociology, 43*(4), 290–300.
Sandoval, C. (2000). *Methodology of the oppressed*. Minneapolis: University of Minnesota Press.
Schwalbe, M. (2008). *Rigging the game: How inequality is reproduced in everyday life*. New York: Oxford University Press.
Sy, F. W. (2013). The artist, the activist, the academic: Building a critical pedagogy of embodied knowledge. *Reflections: Narratives of Professional Helping, 19*(3), 7–20.
Van Rooj, S. W. (2012). Research-based personas: Teaching empathy in professional education. *The Journal of Effective Teaching, 12*(3), 77–86.

Untold Stories: Bringing Class into the Classroom

Adj Marshall and Betsy Leondar-Wright

Authors' Reflexive Statements

Adj Marshall: I first encountered discussions of social class in the classroom while attending a small upper middle class liberal arts college in my hometown city. These discussions, however, rarely moved beyond surface level reflections, despite professors' attempts to have students dig deeper. Very few of my classmates had prior experience with the low-income and working class communities we were learning to organize. As one of only a handful of low-income students at the college, I chose to bring my personal life history of poverty and homelessness into classroom discussions. This allowed me to present a more nuanced understanding of community struggles and raise my peers' and professors' awareness of the social class issues at hand. As an artist, facilitator and educator today, I continue to incorporate my experiences of the social class system into my work in meaningful ways and encourage others to do the same.

Betsy Leondar-Wright: The first time I heard class discussed in a classroom was in a political theory course at Princeton. The topic was abstract Marxist theory, with no connection to my life experience—and of course I had no idea what the professor's class background was. Becoming a community organizer immersed me in the real world of class differences, as my own privileged background made me dissimilar from the grassroots people I organized. I had the good fortune to be trained as an activist by working-class movement leaders, who introduced me to the concepts of classism, class cultures and cross-class alliance-building—the themes I have been writing about, training and teaching about, and attempting to put into

A. Marshall (✉)
Independent scholar, Newton, USA
e-mail: writetoadj@gmail.com

B. Leondar-Wright
Department of Sociology, Lasell College, Newton, MA, USA
e-mail: bleondar-wright@lasell.edu

K. Haltinner and L. Hormel (eds.), *Teaching Economic Inequality and Capitalism in Contemporary America*, https://doi.org/10.1007/978-3-319-71141-6_3

practice for more than 20 years. This article reflects the methods that the foremost non-profit in this field, Class Action, developed to bring our whole selves into our discussions of class. Adj Marshall and I have been Class Action workshop facilitators for many years, doing classism workshops for schools, non-profits and foundations, as well as teaching class topics in college courses.

Introduction

Students often respond with confusion to questions about social class—not surprising given the common assumption that the United States is a "classless society." The fog surrounding class stratification makes it difficult to teach about economic inequality. Why is social class so challenging to teach about? Compared with race or gender, class is less obviously inscribed on the body and more poorly understood, with more gray areas and fewer shared terms for social categories, making identity development a slower and more fraught process. Class background profoundly affects an individual's social standpoint (Collins 2000), but most students have only a latent class identity that they have rarely discussed with anyone.

In our decades of work, both as classroom teachers and as facilitators of Freirean popular education workshops (Freire 1970) for community groups through the nonprofit organization Class Action, we have found it constructive to ground conversations in the lived experience of class—not just workplace experience, but students' and their parents' educations, parents' occupations, type of neighborhood and housing, and so on. Before asking students to disclose their class backgrounds, teachers and facilitators can create a welcoming atmosphere by sharing their own class stories from a subject position (Green 2003). In our experience this mutual disclosure creates an electric learning environment (Adams and Bell 2007).

However, there are pitfalls in educators self-revealing their class backgrounds, as we have each found in our educational practice. We are a mixed-class pair of co-authors, one from a poverty background and one from an upper-middle-class background. In this article, we first describe why class disclosure is worth attempting, then we unpack its risks and difficulties and make recommendations. We offer strategies and insights for readers to adapt these methods into their own personal pedagogical practice, while acknowledging the limited nature of any single teacher's class background (refer to Table 1 for an example of ground rules).

In *Teaching to Transgress* (1994), bell hooks suggests that education is a "location of possibility," noting that "we have the opportunity to labor for freedom, to demand of ourselves and our comrades an openness of mind and heart that allows us to face reality even as we collectively imagine ways to move beyond boundaries to transgress" (207). This liberatory spirit underlies the pedagogical approach in this article. By fostering cross-class dialogue among students from varied class backgrounds, educators can spark a lively interest in economic inequality, and students and educators can together identify and demystify class privilege and oppression. Acknowledging class diversity invites students of varying backgrounds to feel they have a place in the conversation and a responsibility to be engaged and take action for change.

Table 1 Sample ground rules for class story sharing

Ground rules
Listen actively and attentively to each other with respect. Share airspace with everyone. Step up if you tend to be quiet, or step back if you tend to speak a lot.
Speak from your own experience by using "I" statements.
It is okay to disagree with each other respectfully. Commit to learning and dialoguing and not debating. Build on one another's comments to work towards a shared understanding.
Ask for clarification if something is not clear to you. All questions are okay.
Set your own limits on how much risk to take with your self-disclosure. You have the right to pass
Passing on information, ideas and learning after the session is encouraged, but keep everyone's personal statements or experiences confidential.

Why It's Important for Educators to Share Their Class Stories

By sharing their personal experiences with the class system, educators can encourage students to see classist behavior and inequitable class systems as directly linked to themselves and those they interact with. If student disclosure follows educator disclosure, then the pedagogical tool of story sharing creates space for student introspection that moves beyond the textbook, making visible the often imperceptible realities of classist systems. As students combine discovery of empirical knowledge of the wider world with dialogue and self-discovery, they come to more fully understand the U.S. class system.

When the educational goals include generating commitment to work for social justice, the immediacy and humanity of discussing first-person lived experience is essential to raising empathetic awareness of *any* system of oppression. But, this is especially true for social class inequality. In teaching gender, we've found it easy to draw out students' experiences with gender-binary socialization. In teaching race, it may be a touchy subject, but once reluctance is overcome, students do in fact have racial identities and experiences to share of racism and cross-race interactions. But with class, most undergraduates and adult learners have not been categorizing their life experiences and relationships in class terms, and are not conscious of having a manifest class identity. As a result, when educators attempt to ask evocative questions to generate class-related memories, learners frequently report confusion. Many conflate race and class, for example using the terms "black and white" to refer to the class makeup of their hometown, which renders invisible both professionals of color and white working-class and poor people.

Talking about class is often fraught with deep emotions. Shame, guilt, and fear of being judged often inhibit learners from revealing their class stories and fully understanding the experiences of others, particularly for residential college students, who may be experiencing a mixed-class social situation for the first time. In addition, because class identities shift over time as workplace, financial and family situations change, it can be difficult for students to fully identify with one particular class.

Because of these difficulties in teaching about social class, it's important to teach it in a personal way, based on lived experience. The multidimensional and intersectional approach taken by the Working Class Studies Association (Zandy 2001; Russo and Linkon 2005) and Class Action encompasses class dynamics in workplaces, schools, families, neighborhoods, unions, activism, culture, psychology, literature, and among other areas of life. However, this approach is rare within the field of sociology. Most "race, class, and gender" textbooks include only economic topics in the class section, or in some cases have no class section at all, making the word "class" serve the grammatical function of a conjunction connecting race and gender. Critiques of neoliberal capitalism are not the only valuable class analysis. To broaden learners' class awareness beyond economic inequality to the other dimensions of class and classism requires educator creativity in seeking readings, videos, and exercises that bring the topic alive for learners. Because class indicators besides money are unfamiliar to most learners, the educator's prepared personal stories can inject the needed human element into discussions of class, classism, and economic inequality.

We see three main purposes served by educators sharing class life experiences with learners: deepening bonds across roles, illustrating main points, and modeling disclosure to invite student sharing. The first is recommended in most learning situations; the second can be used, as needed; and the third presented only under certain limited circumstances. Each is described below with examples of personal stories one of the authors has shared in an educational setting.

First, educators can break down barriers between themselves and learners by humanizing themselves and by revealing their social standpoint to be similar to or different from each learner's life experience. Students are already making assumptions about who their educators are—sometimes true, sometimes false—and relating to them as similar or different from themselves. Many of us were taught by distant teachers, presumed to be professional-middle-class, and as a result we have an unconscious expectation that classroom relations will be cool and impersonal. Educators' social class story-sharing can create a warmer classroom atmosphere that invites open discussion, which can result from educators' class story-sharing. Since personal storytelling is a more prominent mode of expression in many working-class cultures, this warming effect can be especially meaningful to first-generation college students and others from working-class and poverty backgrounds (Leondar-Wright 2014). Frankly sharing one's class indicators, as well as putting other identities into words, engenders deeper dialogue and often increases mutual respect between educators and learners. Depending on what the educator's class background is, for each student this disclosure invites either a feeling of solidarity about similarities or a bridge across differences that have lost their taboo by being spoken.

Example 1: How and Why Adj Talks About Welfare Office Lines

When I worked as a college success counselor, many of my students were documented and undocumented immigrants, refugees, and recipients of social support programs. They hailed from the Dominican Republic, Cambodia, Puerto Rico, Haiti, Cote D'Ivoire, Guatemala, Cape Verde and other places. Since I am a white woman with the professional status of educator, my students often assumed that we were from completely different worlds, and in some very important ways we were. My family has been in the United States for a few generations now, and I do not face the racism that many of my students deal with on a daily basis.

Where my childhood experience mirrored my students was in the grueling struggle that is life in poverty and the experience of pursuing college as a first-generation college student. Angelika, a young Latina student of mine pursuing her studies in community college while pregnant, was sheepishly providing what she felt I would view as an unacceptable excuse for why her coursework had been suffering that term. She noted that lines at the welfare office and other social service offices were interfering with her ability to complete her homework. In that moment a compassionate smile appeared on my face, one she would later tell me was a surprising response.

I shared with her my experience of standing in the welfare line each month with my own teen mother, waiting some days for hours on end. I described my intuitive childhood knowledge that we were somehow involved in an unfair trade. That of food stamp booklets for bank account statements, dating history and more intimate life details than we would have liked to share. While Angelika and I had established a good working relationship, it was completely altered that day. Our shared social class background became a cementing force in our relationship over the next two years. My sharing earned me Angelika's respect and buoyed us through our frustrations with one another, reminding us of the humanity in each other. Angelika's knowledge of my upbringing allowed her to see me as an elder, someone she could share her struggles with and seek advice from. My deeper understanding for her experience allowed me to see her more fully as a whole person.

Second, educator class stories can be used to illustrate the content being taught. Few examples are as compelling as a crafted narrative told in the first person, especially by someone usually in an authority role. Crafting a story to make a point takes time and effort. Through years of trial and error and seeking out feedback, the two of us have each unearthed and polished many snippets of our past experiences that have served as powerful catalysts in specific educational situations, as the two examples below show.

Example 2: How and Why Betsy Shares Her Childhood Crush Story

In courses about inequality in the US education system, the idea that high-cultural-capital class cultures are not actually superior can be a tough sell to undergraduates imbued with the educational meritocracy myth (McNamee and Miller 2004). Even after I have them read excerpts from counter-hegemonic class-culture texts that are affirming of the strengths of working-class cultures, such as Lareau's *Unequal Childhoods*, (2003), Heath's *Ways with Words* (1983), and Delpit's *The Skin That We Speak* (2003), many students persist in assuming middle-class superiority, for example referring to "bad English," "bad parents," and "bad neighborhoods." Here's a story I have told several times to contradict that classist assumption that working-class cultures only have downsides.

If I had to sum up my upbringing in one word, it would be "sheltered." I was a nice middle-class, Protestant, white girl with no exposure to hardship and who feelings were easily hurt.

In 6th grade I had an intense crush on a Catholic boy named Marc who lived with his mother in an apartment over a store. Marc had a toughness and verbal agility that filled me with longing. When I was picked on, I just stood there silent. I could write with perfect grammar, but I couldn't come up with a witty comeback to save my life. Marc met every put-down with a worse put-down, and went up into a bully's face.

By the rules of our town I was the fortunate kid, and he was the disadvantaged kid. And in material ways there was truth to that. I went to college, Marc didn't. The odds are good that my net worth is now higher than his, and that I get more respect for my work than he does.

But in human terms, Marc and I both had something to give each other. He could have used some of my knowledge about how to get into college. But I needed his thick skin, his assertiveness, and his ability to trash-talk—and I still need it today.

The truth is that my over-privileged class and ethnic upbringing gave me severe limitations that no-one named.

Students tend to enjoy this story because it's about a youthful crush, and afterwards some of them seem to remember the concepts of asset-based and deficit-based depictions of working-class cultures.

Example 3: Why and How Adj Shares Her Checkout Line Memories

When teaching about the effects of poverty, I struggle to find texts for my students that speak beyond the structural elements of oppression: lack of opportunity for educational attainment, vocational possibility, income earning potential, or access to health care. Rarely are there materials from which my students can learn about or understand the deeply personal and psychological effects of poverty, particularly told from a first person perspective.

To bring this element alive for my students I share a story from my adult life exploring how my upbringing in poverty has inscribed itself on my worldview and still permeates my unconscious.

My partner and I were on our weekly pilgrimage to the supermarket, something I could have only dreamed of as a child where shopping occurred once monthly in parallel with the arrival of food stamps and a well-timed bus.

We navigate to the checkout counter where we begin to place the fruits, vegetables, and dairy products, on the belt. My partner places the Tom's Toothpaste on the belt amongst the other food items. I immediately move the toothpaste to the back of the belt. This happens repeatedly with the deodorant, laundry detergent and toilet paper while emptying our shopping cart.

While we wait for the cashier to finish ringing us up, my partner asks, "Why did you keep moving the household items to the back?" He sounds a bit annoyed as if my moving them is a form of judgment on his choice of placement.

I respond quickly with "I don't know exactly. I like similar things to be grouped together"—but before the sentence fully escapes my mouth it occurs to me that I was sorting our groceries in accordance with government benefits requirements.

By the age of seven or eight I knew how to identify items that could and could not be bought with food stamps. It was essential to separate items or run the risk of being chastised by the cashier who might announce loudly that "you can't purchase toothpaste with food stamps".

While I know that being poor did not make me less of a person as a child or today, somewhere deep down I still hold the fear of embarrassment that comes with being called out as poor.

When telling this story I hand out copies of food stamps from the era of my childhood. I talk about how visible people on food stamps were with their colorful booklets and the regulations that required one to rip coupons from the book in front of the cashier. For many of my students, who have only known EBT (Electronic Benefit Transfer) cards, this is illuminating, and can lead to discussions about other ways the poor are put on display as the result of policies.

Third, educator stories can encourage learner self-disclosures of class background experiences, which is eye-opening for story-teller and listener alike. Student sharing of personal class stories is a potent but high-risk activity for certain settings only. If the teacher or facilitator goes first, he or she can model deeper ways to share experiences that learners may then replicate, for example by revealing emotions, avoiding stereotypes, adding race or gender intersections, and drawing lessons and conclusions from stories. By introducing nuance, these moments of personal sharing serve as a guide for students on how to share reflections on class that are grounded in lived personal experience.

In higher education settings, the default assumption is that everyone is or soon will be a college educated professional. The discovery that some students and/or the professor come from a working-class or poverty background shakes up those assumptions, disrupts the middle-class norm and the othering of class-disadvantaged people. Sharing their personal stories, educators can reassure students that their experiences are valid forms of expressions within the classroom. On the other hand, it can also raise discomfort in others whose class story is different, leading to the difficulties discussed in the next section.

Example 4: Why and How Betsy Describes Her Teenage Affluence

Sometimes the most valuable thing I do at classism workshops or during classroom social class units is to describe my teen years factually and in a relaxed tone. When I say calmly, "When I was 15, my dad hit the jackpot in the bond market, so my parents moved to a 15-room house, took us to Europe, and sent me to prep school and an Ivy League college," it gives the message that 'we can be real about class differences here'.

I make it very clear that that my family's upward mobility didn't make us better people than others—and it didn't make us worse people either. It's just where my story happens to fit into a terribly unjust system that I'm not to blame for, but that I can work to change, as everyone can.

Sharing that part of my story creates a space that's welcoming for other very privileged people in particular. I watch their shoulders lower and their faces brighten up, and they become more open to honest disclosure and cross-class dialogue.

The Perils and Pitfalls of Sharing Educators' Class Stories

In a culture where speaking about social class is taboo, teaching students to look at the world through an anti-classist approach can be a difficult and emotionally fraught process, one full of pain, fear, and embarrassment. Despite what's difficult about social class story sharing, we believe that the extra effort needed to bring educators' personal experiences with the class system into the classroom is worth the benefits.

Through our many years of sharing personal class stories, we have discovered some potential pitfalls. Here we identify the pitfalls and provide advice on avoiding and counteracting these potential hazards. These include being clear about your purpose; taking steps to mine and assemble a story; anticipating difficult learner reactions; scaffolding and timing stories well; and, lastly, taking care in preparing to invite self-disclosure.

Knowing Your Purpose, Being Explicit, and Strengthening the Container

Being explicit about the goals of story sharing is one of the simplest ways to avoid pitfalls in the practice of story sharing. Educators should be explicit about the end goal for class story sharing with themselves and their students when choosing to employ this learning tool. We have both had classes and workshops veer far from the intended path because we were not clear about the reasons for sharing our personal stories.

When the two of us share a personal class story to make a point about a reading, we often preface it with our intention: "The author speaks about X in her text; one example from my personal life that illustrates X is ".

If your purpose is to invite students to engage in self-disclosure, it is important you are clear this is what you are asking of students. We have both started classes by stating "In sharing my story here, I have modeled how I hope you will share your own stories, if you choose to." Because class stories are quite personal and students may be wary of sharing them, it is important to set up a strong container of safety and confidentiality (Lakey 2010). For example, state explicitly that students are not required to share and that students may specify if their stories may be repeated outside the classroom.

Preparing Your Stories

While educators can never be fully prepared for the myriad potential student responses, there are things you can do to prepare yourself. Failure to prepare sufficiently for telling a personal story can result in fizzling, backfiring, or veering off track from the intended aim of the course. We have found that sharing and responding to students in a powerful yet inclusive manner requires a well-crafted story that has been vetted by others.

One's own emotions about childhood memories can be triggered by sharing them raw and unprocessed. It's important to do your own work first before bringing class stories into the classroom. Start by writing down your own social class memories. Participation in a cross-class dialogue group (Koch-Gonzalez et al. 2009) is an ideal way to work through your own memories and emotions and find the nuggets of your history that could serve educational purposes. Then we suggest sharing your story with fellow educators, ideally two or more from distinctly different class backgrounds, to solicit feedback before bringing it to the classroom.

Seek out feedback and comments from colleagues about how students from different class backgrounds at your institution might respond. When you build up your network of collaborators, they may be willing share their own class stories in your classroom, providing students with a broader view of the class system than can be provided through your story alone.

Anticipating Difficult Reactions

When sharing our stories, we have encountered widely different reactions from our students and participants, including some difficult or negative reactions. Students may shut down, get confused, be triggered, or become too defensive for dialogue or learning. We have observed that educators may be viewed as antagonists by students from differing class backgrounds than that revealed by the educator. Educators of all backgrounds may lose some credibility after sharing their stories; and those from working-class or poverty backgrounds may encounter a classist lowering of status in the eyes of some students.

While educators' stories about a childhood of poverty are often deeply meaningful to students from similar backgrounds, and eye-opening to students from more privileged backgrounds, such stories have also been met with incredulous responses by students.

For example, Adj has heard, "See, the system works, *you* were upwardly mobile" from low income students. First-generation college students in particular can see themselves as at the beginning stages of upward mobility, and as a result may be especially attached to the American Dream ideology of rising social mobility through education. Deconstructing this ideal can be a hard sell, threatening to students' personal hopes. Adj also notes,

> As someone who has 'made it out' I have to be wary of becoming the unscathed poster child for escaping poverty. When starry-eyed middle- and upper-class students ask 'how did you do it?' I speak frankly about the painful reality of transcending my class background and what I lost in the assimilation process of becoming upwardly mobile. I point out to students that everything is not perfect now that I am part of the professional middle class. In fact, in some senses it is so much more complicated to straddle two class realities (Lubrano 2004).

Betsy finds that the middle-class part of her life story, through age 15, is often met with boredom. She notes, "Few people are interested in hearing how I grew up in a nice little 6-room house and attended a decent suburban public school." In response she has learned to politicize her middle-class story by speaking about the unfair advantages of her middle class upbringing, in comparison to her working-class peers. For other middle class educators, as well, there may be no dramatic secrets to reveal, and the educator's basic story can come across as uninteresting.

Stories of wealth and luxury tend to hold learners' attention and can counteract the presumption that there is no space for socioeconomically privileged student voices in discussions of class. By introducing three-dimensional stories with human flaws, such as Betsy's stories boxed above, the myth that the upper-middle-class culture is the ideal for all to aspire to can be shattered. And on the other hand, the archetype of the greedy, evil rich can also be shaken up by an actual privileged person's story.

Disclosing a privileged background, however, can sometimes alienate working-class and poverty-background students, and may discredit the educator with students as not having a valid standing to teach about class oppression. After describing her affluent late teenage years in a calm, factual tone (as in the boxed examples above), Betsy has occasionally heard students infer meanings that are clearly projections of their own emotions: "Why do you feel so guilty?"; "I don't think you should put down rich people!"; and even "Nice for you, but not everyone got to travel, you know!" Owning-class and top-one-percent educators may get even stronger reactions.

Whereas an educator from a working-class or poverty-class background challenges classist stereotypes simply by their presence in the classroom, a privileged-class educator's presence may reinforce stereotypes about who can become a professional—an assumption that needs to be problematized.

Productive discussions can grow out of initial negative student responses. The further toward either end of the class spectrum an educator's background falls, the more time will be needed for discussion and debriefing. We acknowledge the limited effectiveness of any single educator's class background story and suggest a teaching methodology that allows for a more diverse educator team. Personal class stories work best for student learning when there are two educators with backgrounds at different ends of the class spectrum, with contrasting amounts of privilege or hardship in childhood and adolescence. A racially mixed team is ideal as well.

Hearing a story more similar to their own greatly increases learners' sense of safety to take risks and the likelihood of 'aha' moments. Those from backgrounds of poverty or wealth especially, but others as well, tend to share more deeply after listening to an educator from their own part of the class spectrum. When co-educators model an attitude of warm, respectful listening towards each other it can open a crack in unproductive responses based on stereotypes and unprocessed emotions, such as pity, guilt, envy, and resentment. To see a co-educator from a very different background give rapt attention to the other's story helps establish learning from diverse class stories as a legitimate use of group time and focus.

In typical classroom settings with one professor, this ideal of co-educators may seem difficult to achieve. A colleague from a different class background can be invited into co-teach a session or module. To know whom to invite means opening up sometimes fraught conversations with colleagues about class life stories, which can deepen relationships and create a more class-aware working environment.

Scaffolding and Timing Stories

If educators' personal stories lie far outside the lived experience of their students, it is important to consider *when* to share. If such a story is introduced too early it can cause the students to clam up or not speak openly about their views for fear of offending. It is essential that students are practiced with the tools of responding in a productive manner before introducing them to stories from the extremes of the class spectrum. The same is true of introducing personal stories that convey complex social class concepts.

Because students have a particularly limited experience engaging with their class identity and the class identity of others, educators should consider how they scaffold stories and activities, ensuring to the best of their abilities that students have the background knowledge and social emotional readiness to engage with the content presented.

Example 5: Why and When Adj Reveals Her Family's Homelessness Experiences

When teaching courses on homelessness I often choose not to reveal the fact that I was part of a homeless family until well into the semester, or even well into the chosen text. I often assign Donna Haig-Friedman's *Parenting in Public: Family Shelter and Public Assistance* (2000) sometime in the second half of the course. I explicitly choose to do this because I want students to speak openly in an unfiltered way, constructing and sharing their views, and not hiding their biases towards parents living in homeless shelters.

It can be a learning moment for students when I share my story of homelessness, bringing the 'other' that we have spent the semester talking 'about' into the classroom as an individual that students are speaking to. Students can react to the practice of holding back information strongly. Some are upset, others feel embarrassed or self-conscious about things they said, wondering how I might interpret their views. Sometimes students respond with shock having believed this is an issue that affects only 'other people'. Still others express appreciation for the added element of personal insight brought to the class. By choosing to share this story later in the course, I am able to diversify student responses and allow students the context and time needed to process and respond to such information, recognizing that it can sometimes be difficult for students to hear.

As classism educators, we find that simple digestible stories to which most students can relate can be a good place to begin. As we move throughout the semester, we share more complex and nuanced content, as in the example below.

Example 6: How and When Betsy Shares Her Politeness Socialization

Class culture differences are hard to teach in the abstract without stereotyping (Bourdieu 1984). In Streib's book about mixed-class marriages, *The Power of the Past* (2015), she found that the middle-class spouses tended to plan and manage family life, while the working-class spouses tended to value spontaneity. To introduce this class cultural pattern, near the beginning of the module, I say something about myself that will get less resistance than a generalization, such as: "Growing up middle class, I was taught to quash my emotions and be polite at all times, so it's still hard for me today to be spontaneously expressive."

But because class cultures are such an unfamiliar concept, I always wait to offer that self-disclosure until students have already engaged in some basic reading on the topic.

Inviting Self-disclosure

Successful scaffolding involves gradually increasing the risk level of the classroom activities. Inviting self-disclosure of class background from students falls high on the risk spectrum by opening a well of class-based emotional trauma that educators may not be prepared to respond to. In the worst case scenario, judgmental or mocking student responses to someone's story may devastate the student. Sometimes not encouraging self-disclosure is the best option. For some groups, preparing a class to discuss class identities may take almost an entire semester, while others may spontaneously dive in early. Ensuring your students are prepared and feel safe disclosing is the most essential part of the process.

We have found that questions about other families, not students' own childhood settings, are low-risk enough to ask at the beginning of a course module or workshop. One starter question we have found works well is "What's your first memory of a family that had more or less class privilege than your family?" While most students may have only a latent class identity, they can often pinpoint moments when they have noticed having more or less class advantage than others. Thus, asking students this simple question can be a relatively nonthreatening introduction to sharing surface-level, social class experiences with peers. We advise *not* to expect or actively invite personal self-disclosure in any situation where participants could face consequences for not participating. Having adequate time to debrief what students share is essential, so we also do not advise self-disclosure in brief sessions when there's little time to discuss emotional reactions.

The best possible situation is one in which power dynamics have been mitigated as much as possible and confidentiality ground rules have been set for both inside and outside the classroom. Ideally, students will have been prepared with adequate materials and activities necessary to allow for constructive ways to disclose and respond. In these situations, inviting class background self-disclosure can broaden student perspectives on social class, allow for personal introspection about class advantage and disadvantage in relation to intersecting identities, and turn economic inequality from a dry topic into a subject for heartfelt engagement.

Conclusion

In this chapter we have advocated a high-risk addition to the pedagogy of social class, but one with high potential for student transformation. Even the students who seem to have the least class consciousness do in fact have class-related memories, and they are in fact aware of class stratification. The challenge, which Paulo Freire (1970) took on with Brazilian peasants, is to uncover and politicize that awareness and channel it towards liberatory action. The popular education tradition has provided us with a model in which students and educators share life experiences and unpack them for the purpose of understanding the stratified social world and ideally working to change it. By deeply exploring your own social class stories, crafting them into purposeful vignettes, being vulnerable with your students and inviting them to do the same, you can open a door to powerful cross-class dialogue.

References

Adams, M., & Bell, L. (2007). *Teaching for diversity and social justice*. New York: Routledge.

Bourdieu, P. (1984). *Distinction: A social critique of the judgement of taste*. Cambridge: Harvard University Press.

Collins, P. H. (2000). *Black feminist thought: Knowledge, consciousness, and the politics of empowerment*. New York: Routledge.

Delpit, L. (2003). *The skin we speak: Thoughts on language and culture in the classroom*. New York: The New Press.

Freire, P. (1970). *Pedagogy of the oppressed*. New York: Continuum Publishing Company.

Green, A. E. (2003). Difficult stories: Service-learning, race, class, and whiteness. *College composition and communication*, 55(2), 276–301.

Haig-Friedman, D. (2000). *Parenting in public: Family shelter and public assistance*. New York: Columbia University Press.

Heath, S. B. (1983). *Ways with words: Language, life, and work in communities and classrooms*. Cambridge: Cambridge University Press.

Hooks, b. (1994). *Teaching to transgress*. New York: Routledge.

Koch-Gonzalez, J., Ladd, J., & Yeskel, F. (2009). *Talking across the class divide: A manual for cross-class dialogue and learning*. Boston: Class Action.

Lakey, G. (2010). *Facilitating group learning*. San Francisco: Jossey-Bass.

Lareau, A. (2003). *Unequal childhoods: Class, race, and family life*. Berkeley: University of California Press.

Leondar-Wright, B. (2014). *Missing class: Strengthening social movement groups by seeing class cultures*. Ithaca: Cornell University Press.

Lubrano, A. (2004). *Limbo: Blue-collar roots, white-collar dreams*. Hoboken: Wiley.

McNamee, S. J., & Miller, R. K. (2004). *The meritocracy myth*. New York: Rowman and Littlefield.

Russo, J., & Linkon, S. L. (Eds.). (2005). *New working-class studies*. Ithaca: Cornell University Press.

Streib, J. (2015). *The power of the past: Understanding cross-class marriages*. New York: Oxford University Press.

Zandy, J. (2001). *What we hold in common: Exploring women's lives & working class studies*. New York: The Feminist Press at CUNY.

‘Self-made’ Success on the Private Dole: An Illustration of the Reproduction of Capitals

Roxanne Gerbrandt and Ann Strahm

Authors’ Reflexive Statements

Audre Lorde wrote, “…it is not difference which immobilizes us, but silence. And there are so many silences to be broken” (1984, p. 44). Both authors personally and professionally understand the injuries of class stratification. Our firmly grounded poverty and working class habitus will undoubtedly come across in these pages as we transgress the boundaries of silence.

Roxanne: I would rather not provide a complete biography of my first 25 years of food insecurity (eating air biscuits), precarious housing (homelessness), and the litany of indignities that I have endured by my poverty class position within our class stratification system. But, I want to tell you about a recent experience between a group of students and me, as a faculty participant. We were “practicing” for The Hunger Banquet (a program designed to teach the participants of the dynamics and reality of world hunger and inequality of food distribution). We read from cards describing the biographies and conditions of desperate poverty and hunger.

While it has been many years since I experienced regular bouts of real hunger, I thought I would be immune. I was wrong. My muscle memory returned in full force. My new middle class dialogue to myself was saying, “*Oh, this is all right; students need to know about poverty and hunger. Put up a stiff upper lip and go along with ‘playing’ hunger.*” My poverty class inner dialogue was much different however. She was screaming, “*WTF!—should we also act out rapes in order to teach about sexual assault? Maybe we could have students writhe in pain from smallpox in a First Nations germ warfare-reenactment?*” But, we know that would

R. Gerbrandt (✉)
Austin Peay State University, Clarksville, TN, USA
e-mail: gerbrandtr@apsu.edu

A. Strahm
CSU-Stanislaus, Turlock, CA, USA

K. Haltinner and L. Hormel (eds.), *Teaching Economic Inequality and Capitalism in Contemporary America*, https://doi.org/10.1007/978-3-319-71141-6_4

be highly insensitive to survivors of both deliberate acts. No such sensitivity is extended for survivors of hunger, however, because as a culture we seem to be desensitized to the fact that poverty is deliberative. In fact, poverty and hunger are prescribed outcomes under the logic of capitalism.

Ann: I grew up in a strange social class binary. I am the child of a single mother who worked two jobs and struggled desperately to make ends meet. At the same time, my mother's parents (whom she worked for at one of her jobs) were solidly middle-class, owning three insurance agencies. So I grew up with limited resources and often heard my mother sobbing in despair after she thought I'd fallen asleep, while at the same time having grandparents who would purchase my school clothes and "lend" her money when appliances broke—of course, always reminding us they were doing us a "favor".

My biggest regret is being angry at my mother on Saturday mornings. While my friends were shopping, hanging out at the arcade, or watching cartoons, I was spending my Saturdays cleaning business offices with her (her second job was that of a janitor), and when I turned 14 I went and got a work permit and immediately began a long series of part-time restaurant, fast-food, and retail jobs (always, though, working alongside her and helping on Saturday mornings). As a child I didn't understand why my mother couldn't be like my grandparents or my friends' parents—I was angry that we were so poor and I didn't have the things other kids did—and I told her so. I was never able to tell her how sorry I was for my childhood behavior and how grateful I am now to have had those experiences, because each of them has led to this: the ability to teach students about social class in a truly authentic way.

Authenticity in Teaching

Authenticity in teaching is central to Carreiro and Kapitulik's (2010) extensive review of teaching exercises to aid in the teaching of stratification. In their review of articles from 1987 to 2007 in the journal *Teaching Sociology* the authors found that a significant number of teaching exercises encouraged experiential learning where students would simulate economic disadvantage. They suggest that these "playing the poor and working class" exercises may be ineffective and likely damaging to the students whose experiences are real. We agree with this assertion and would add that while these exercises increase sympathy from the more privileged classmates they fail to provide any look at class privilege, nor do they problematize the threads of classism embedded in the fabric of American society.

As teachers we recognize active learning exercises about poverty are problematic because they force students to "participate in group activities where their classmates pretend to be like them and even more awkwardly, they (poverty and working class students) must "pretend" to be like themselves" (Carreiro and Kapitulik 2010, p. 25), yet we understand that active learning is a High Impact Practice (HIP). This knowledge leads us to a delicate balance of teaching something many of our students understand through lived experiences (knowing) but must learn about theoretically through their formal education (knowledge). One of most interesting aspects of working/lower class students is many of them believe they *are* middle class (Aries and Seider 2007). So, how does an instructor go about explaining social class to a classroom of working/lower class students who identify as "middle class" without doing harm? Our answer to that question is to create a comparative learning exercise that provides a complex, realistic scenario using imagery and data relevant to student's lives, providing students the opportunity to reflect on how their own lives and experiences are similar to or different from the phenomena presented in the classroom. The exercise we have developed is "The Bob and Harold Presentation".

This interactive presentation allows students to actively engage the issue of class stratification concretely in a classroom environment, reflect, then apply previous knowledge onto this new case, and do so collectively, as a community of scholars. It does so without stigma, pretention, or potentially traumatic triggering mechanisms of a Hunger Banquet, or many other well-meaning class exercises. In fact, this is why Bob and Harold works so well. It allows students to relate the objective experience of the presentation to their own lives through a lens of social structure and class reproduction, and the interplay of race and gender within that reproduction. The various capitals that intertwine to produce the disparate outcomes of Bob and Harold are made manifest without directly forcing students to confront their own class status. As the reader will see below we encourage our students to reflect on, discuss, then write in a way that takes this new information and contextualizes it to their own experiences, as well as within the broader historical, globalized sociopolitical economy and culture.

Reflection is an integral part of metacognition and, according to Silver (2013), is the "conscious exploration of one's own experiences" (p. 107). It is constructive because it enhances student learning and critical thinking, and it is a way of working through things that are challenging so that we—literally—change our brains. Reflection is the process of our brains searching for a way to connect new information to what we already know (Zull 2002, p. 164). In this way the Bob and Harold Presentation is an "epistemology of practice" (knowledge informing actions) in which we have constructed a problematic situation that allows students to integrate their knowing and knowledge with Marxist and Bourdieusian theoretical paradigms, thus allowing them to name and frame social class concretely.

Bob and Harold Presentation

The following narrative is a summary of the Bob and Harold Presentation. In the interest of brevity, we use the following "P" for Professor (Roxanne or Ann) voices and "Class" for class responses, whether it is one of Roxanne's Introduction to Sociology classes, or Ann's upper division Social Inequalities class.

The interactive presentation begins by introducing, then comparing, the lives of two fictitious people: Bob and Harold. We begin the presentation with information about both as young boys. Bob is a child from the white working class in the United States and Harold is a child from the white, solidly upper-middle class in the United States. We ask students to describe the houses that each boy most likely dwells in, as well as their habitus—a way of being that develops as individuals interact with the world. Habitus is our acquired dispositions—our tastes, preferences in preferences in food, music, sports, entertainment, and cultural events. It is the lens through which we understand the world—based upon our experiences, all of which seem natural and normal—as though those thoughts, beliefs, dispositions, tastes were ours from the beginning.

We then discuss the kind of neighborhoods the boys would have experienced in their youth and how that might further affect their class status into adulthood. Afterward, we ask students to hold up their hands to answer the following question: "How much influence do you think a person's ascribed social class status has on their future financial success? (a) no influence, (b) a little influence, (c) a moderate amount, or (d) a great deal." It is interesting to note that the thirty times Roxanne has conducted this exercise; answer "b," a little influence, was by far the number one answer for every class of Introduction to Sociology course. As several studies show, this makes perfect sense given the individualistic way of understanding the world that is endemic to most Americans and most American college students (Shaw and Shapiro 2002; Giroux 2010; Lee 2016). We ask students to explain their answers. Most of the responses, even in the upper division sociology classes Ann teaches, tend to explain financial success in terms of individual hard work and sacrifice; it doesn't matter where one comes from, anyone can achieve their dreams if they put in the effort (the boot-strap mythology). Neither of us corrects our students' assumptions at this time, but as the reader will see further in this chapter, after the full presentation and after having the opportunity for reflection and writing about this, virtually every student came away from the experience with a better understanding of the structural constraints of social class in capitalist American society.

We then fast-forward Bob and Harold's lives to the age of 16 years old. We ask students what US teenagers desire at that age and they shout out simultaneously "a car"!

Professors: "Well, how does Harold get that car?"

Class: "His parents give him a car" with close to 100% of the students answering.

P: "Harold gets a nice, used car—worth about $9000—from his parents." However, when we ask how Bob gets a car, the class typically responds,

Class: "He gets a job."

P: "How does he get to his job?"

Class: no immediate response then some students propose, "He takes the bus".

We then engage the class in some discussion of public transportation; availability, access, and relation to class status.

P: "How many of you here (in the class) depend on public transportation?"

Class: two to three students in a class of 45 will generally raise their hands, or nod.

We invite the class to describe public transportation, which typically leads to remarks, like:

Class: "Melt in the heat." "No sidewalks." "Stand by the side of the road—no shelters." "Limited service areas, and generally not on time".

After some conversation, we discuss how public transportation in the US is a class issue. We are a car-dependent nation, and many towns don't have adequate or reliable public transportation systems. This is one of the reasons for the growth of "Buy here/pay here" lots, and is exactly what Bob ends up doing. We explain predatory lending and its system of payments, interest rates, etc. Then, we move to the timeframe after both young men finish high school:

P: "Both Bob and Harold decide that college is very important and they both are very smart and work very hard".

The dominant ideology in the United States argues the cause of poverty isn't the structural barriers in capitalist society, but is a form of liberalism that is too permissive and has nurtured a population of lazy, morally bankrupt, short-sighted "moochers" (or, to put it in the Representative Paul Ryan vernacular, "Takers"). From this perspective, the poor don't succeed in life because their cultural milieu isn't conducive to personal achievement—something subconsciously reproduced by the students at the beginning of the presentation, when asked if there's a connection between social class and opportunities for personal success (Magnet 1993; Schwartz 2000; Murray 1984, 2005; Gilder 1981). As with most individualistic solutions to social problems, people who pull themselves up by their proverbial bootstraps will succeed through their own hard work, sacrifice, delayed gratification, and moxie. The value of educational attainment falls in line with that dominant ideology. Education as the answer to individualistic ideas of poverty isn't wrong—data show earning potential is generally higher for college graduates, while unemployment is typically lower. The notion "education as panacea," though, is problematic, because this perspective ignores the structural barriers to achieving college/university matriculation (much less graduation) for most of the population—particularly for historically marginalized groups and those from the working/poverty class (King et al. 2011; Abrajano and Hajnal 2017; Kucsera and Flaxman 2012; Ochoa 2013; Ward et al. 2012; Guinier 2015).

We continue with Bob and Harold's narrative, explaining that they both attend a state school, and immediately after graduating, go into an MBA program.

P: "How does Harold pay for college?"

Class: "His parents pay for college."

P: "And how does Bob pay for college?"

Class: "He works and takes out loans like we do."

At this point, we spell out how these circumstances shake out for Bob and Harold after college. Bob's undergraduate loans are $24,000, and his MBA loans are $60,000. Bob's total student loan debt is about $84,000 (plus his car loan). Meanwhile, Harold has the same college costs, but his parents and family pay for his college—both undergraduate and graduate degrees. He graduates with no student loan debt.

P: Now—both Bob and Harold go onto the job market and they both land great jobs in Denver, Colorado. Both earn $75,000 per year gross pay. After getting great jobs, they both decide it is time to buy a house. Bob knows he will not receive any financial assistance from his family. Therefore, he must scrimp and save for the down payment on his house. Meanwhile, Harold's family promises him financial assistance for his down payment and, thus, he can use his expendable income on getting a head start on his social capital by attending after work dinner and drink "meetings". It takes Bob about two years to save because the costs for a median priced Junior Executive homes are around $460,000, while costs for an average median priced home are around $270,000.
The story continues,

P: Harold finds a nice house—it's not quite Junior Executive level, but located in a nice neighborhood. His house costs $380,000. His parents give him enough money for 20% down ($76,000), so Harold gets a good interest rate of 4.5% for the $304,000 he finances. Harold's monthly house payment is $1880. Bob needs to be careful (he already has $1165 per month in student loan and car payments) so he finds a house further away from his job for $240,000. Bob has a limited down payment of $7200 (3%), so his loan rate is 6.75%, making his mortgage $2020 (including mortgage insurance because he didn't put 20% down).

We discuss and compare Bob and Harold's homes and neighborhoods, and ask,

P: "What kind of social capital will they acquire?" In other words, what is the social class that Bob's family connected with? How much power do those individuals have to influence institutional decisions?

At this point, we introduce a life event into the classroom narrative. Both Bob and Harold's grandmas die! Harold gets $100,000 in life insurance—tax free! We ask the class what Harold should do with the money.

Class: "Save it!" (Not one time has a student, without prodding, thought of investing in their social capital like Harold does).

We describe to the class that Harold takes the insurance money and buys a nicer, newer house near his boss. The combination of the equity in his old house (20% down!) plus his insurance money means that he can move into the more upscale Junior Executive house for the same house payment he previously had—$1880 per month. Bob's grandma, however, doesn't have anything to leave him. In fact, Bob helps his family to pay for funeral expenses for his grandma, depleting his savings for the down payment on his next car. Therefore, Bob stays in his same neighborhood and does not improve his geographical social connections to people with more power to influence institutional decisions.

The next life event we shift into is that both Bob and Harold finally find the love of their lives and get married. We discuss heterosexual endogamous marriages and reasons why people tend to marry within or close to their same social class and educational level (Ferraro and Andreatta 2012). This also means that Bob and (Cathy) start off their marital bliss with her substantial educational debt as well.

We discuss the symbolic capital of an upscale wedding and the guest list of business connections. It is an opportunity to build strong social capital bonds. Each couple's wedding will cost the average of $33,000. Bob and Cathy borrow $33,000 for their wedding. Harold and Tabitha pay $0, because Tabitha's parents pay for the wedding, as is customary for families who can afford it.

We introduce to students (who are now catching on to the importance of social capital) the best wedding present Tabitha and Harold's parents could give them: Country Club memberships! We also discuss the exclusionary nature of country clubs. As Domhoff explains, this is a key factor in obtaining social capital (2014). Prior to this discussion, students are unaware that social capital's flip side is the power of social exclusion. We further discuss the restrictive history of exclusive clubs as they relate to race, gender, and social class. More examples are presented to demonstrate how divergence continues between Bob and Harold's lives. Bob lives in a smaller house in a lower income neighborhood. He drives to work in an older car. He doesn't replace his wardrobe regularly, so he wears older suits to work and just doesn't look as "put together" as his coworkers. In contrast, Harold lives in an upscale house, near his boss, where he can entertain friends, coworkers, and even clients. He drives a nice car and wears newer suits. Thanks to his parents, he sees his boss and other executives at the Country Club on a regular basis.

P: "At the corporations where they work, who do you think is most likely to get promoted?"

Class: "Harold will!"

We discuss the answers from students and their reasoning. Additional answers to this question are expanded upon in their written reflection papers (optional), some of which we illustrate here.

Student "A" wrote that when she begins her career she will simply "have to work harder to gain more social capital" than her colleagues (3). Student "G" agreed, writing, "I may not have strong social capital … I just have to do a little extra work to get where I want to be" (3). Student "F," disagreed with this conclusion, writing that "the outcome of a situation can depend on the privilege and opportunity one can receive. It does not necessarily apply to hard work and sacrifice" (5). Like Student "F," Student "K" recognized the effect of social class when it comes to promotion. She wrote, "It isn't because we are incompetent, or didn't try hard enough, or didn't want it bad enough" (6). While these students come from very similar backgrounds (working class women of color), they do not share a belief in similar outcomes with regards to opportunities for career-related promotions.

Finally, we ask the "million dollar question":

P: "Did Bob just not work hard enough?"

This inevitably leads to a spirited class discussion, where we as instructors allow the class to work out their anger, and why they are 'suddenly' on the side of the working class.

The presentation and resulting discussions can typically be done in about 80–90 min. However, some classes run 65 min long and three times a week, or are allotted even shorter class periods. In these situations, the presentation can be completed within two class sessions. Each slide from the presentation is able to stand alone for each class session, should someone wish to present the discussion over time. However, presenting incrementally over the term will reduce the effect; the presentation is most effective when presented and completed within the same week to ensure students don't lose the building of knowledge and context, guiding them to a demand that they evaluate everything they've just learned through the question, "*Did Bob just not work hard enough?*"

In addition to class discussions, Ann has her students reflect through writing full essays on the presentation. According to the CSU Enrollment Reporting System (ERSS 2016), select demographics for sociology majors at Ann's university are as follows: 63% are Latina, 87% are first generation college students, and 72% are Pell Grant recipients. The purpose of the demographic data is to show the reader that many of our students come from backgrounds that do not provide familiarity with the rigors of university life and academic pursuit. Additionally, because our students are not "typical" college-going students they require different teaching, learning, and mentoring approaches.

Ann received IRB permission to research students' written responses to the Bob and Harold Presentation in her Social Inequalities class (CSU Stanislaus Institutional Review Board (IRB) 2016). Ann's Social Inequalities course is a senior-level core course required of all sociology majors at her university. The course is centered on communication—written (formal and informal) and oral (presentations, in-class discussion and group activities), along with trust—trust that all voices and experiences are respected in the classroom. The gender and racial makeup of the students who participated in this study are as follows: 12 Latinx, two Indian Americans, two African Americans, one Palestinian American (15 women and two men). After the Bob and Harold Presentation, students were given a paper prompt for a 5-page paper due six days later (see an example of the instructions below).

Paper Prompt for "Bob and Harold Go to College: Class Matters"
You've participated in a lecture/discussion on social capital and its impact on social class. Your papers are to be a minimum of 1200 words and are to be typed and double-spaced. Make sure to use the grammar, language, sentence and paragraph structures appropriate for a formal college paper. Please respond to both the following prompts:

1. Analyze and discuss the information from the presentation. Make sure to include concrete examples in your discussion.
2. Now discuss the presentation within the context of your own life. In what ways does your own social capital help (accumulation of advantage) or hinder (accumulation of disadvantage) your life course. Provide concrete examples to buttress your analysis.

She received permission from all 17 students in attendance for the presentation to use their papers for research. Ann performed a content analysis of the student papers, looking at five specific areas: did students *reference* the presentation in their papers? Did students concretely analyze the presentation and *apply* the analysis to their own lives? Did students correctly *explain* the concept of Social Class in their papers? Did students *relate* to Harold or Bob? Finally, did they *compare* their lived experiences to someone else in their lives (i.e., friend) in the same way we compared Bob and Harold's lived experiences?

The data are as follows:
All 17 students referenced the Bob and Harold presentation in their papers. While the paper prompt referenced the presentation in the title of the assignment, it did not ask/require students to reference the title or the names of the characters, yet the details of the Bob and Harold story took up approximately one-third to one-half of the students' papers. Fifteen of 17 (88%) students applied their analysis of the Bob and Harold presentation to their own lives. Clearly, for these students, Bob and Harold had become embodied symbols of a stratified society.

For example, student "A" provided a comparison of resources available to the two characters, then added herself into the mix, saying on page one of her paper,

> Although they [Bob and Harold] have made similar life decisions, they differ in the resources that are available to them. Their cultural and social capital are substantially different and that will explain why their life course differs from one another.

This same student, later on page three of her paper wrote,

> Similar to Bob, I too come from a working class family, but I also have the double jeopardy of a female and a Latina.

Student "K," an exceptionally talented student who walks this earth bounded to a marginal status by gender, racial, religious, cultural identities wrote this on the first page of her paper:

> Our society loves a good story about someone who grew up in poverty and with hard work and determination, they overcame their adversities and became successful. These stories are used as examples that no matter where you come from, you can do anything if you just work hard enough. While there are certainly people out there who have lucked out in these types of situations, that narrative is not applicable to the majority of us.

Twelve of 17 (70.5%) students correctly explained the concept of Social Class in their papers. The other five simply did not address it. On page one of her paper, student "B" wrote,

> … the only major difference between Bob and Harold is that they belong to different social classes. At every maneuver they make, they both encounter very similar issues and yet these issues impact them differently due to their social classes and family background.

Student "H" wrote (on page three),

> This is really interesting to me because I have always grown up hearing that if you work hard you will make it to the top, but in some cases being a hard worker is not all you need to become successful, you need connections.

Using a narrative format to explain social class, student "K" wrote,

> I can have a higher GPA than a sociology student from UC Davis, for example, but because they come from a higher ranking university, their resume for a job position will likely be put on top of mine (page four).

Fifteen of the 17 students also discussed themselves in relation to Bob and Harold. Specifically, all 15 related themselves to Bob. Student "B" discussed her identification with the Bob character, writing on page two,

> I identify with Bob in many ways. My lack of social capital has affected me throughout my life, and especially throughout my college career. My entire childhood was scarred by financial instability.

Student "L" provided an interesting commentary in her narrative. She wrote,

> I am happy I can relate to Bob and not to Harold. People like Harold sometimes turn out to be ungrateful … (page three).

The final student analysis Ann looked for was a contextual application of the presentation. Would students compare their lived experiences to someone else in their lives (i.e., friend) in the same way we compared Bob and Harold's lived experiences? The answer is a few—18% of the students did compare/contrast their experiences with someone in their life. One of the more heartrending moments for Ann was the narrative of student "F," which included a discussion of the differences between her upper-middle class friend, whose father is a MD, and her own class (her father is blue collar). Both her and her friend want to attend medical school, but she poignantly writes why her friend stands a greater chance to actually get into medical school. After detailing the differences between where she and her friend's parents work and their incomes, houses, neighborhoods, and who's paying for each of their education, student "F" writes,

> Also, [friend's] father is a doctor, her father has access to clinics for her … he also knows what it takes to get into medical school, how the applications work, what they expect and what she [friend] can do. Not only that…she has a better chance of getting in because her father is an alumni. I, on the other hand, have to apply to a clinic in hopes they let me shadow [a doctor], no one in my family has any college background, [and] my parents do not have the income to support me in medical school. This will lead me to also have to apply for student loans just like Bob, and have to search extra hard to find an internship. This portrays the aspect of networking… when it comes to getting into medical school, though I may have worked ten times harder than [friend] and lost more sleep than her, it all comes down to who she knows and how good that looks compared to who I do not know" (page five).

As you can see, the students begin to realize that one's social class trajectory does not begin at a micro level or at a meso level. This is why we end our interactive presentation by drawing a line on the board. It represents the proverbial "race to get ahead." The left side is the starting line and the right side is the finish line. We ask: "Where was Harold born without any effort on his own?" The students place him approximately three-fourths of the way to the finish line. "What was the competition like in this structural place?" We draw dots to mark others in this position. "Where was Bob born?" we query. The students usually place Bob about a third of a length from the starting line and the dots representing competition are filled in. Finally, we add a member of the 'one percent', for example, an heir to the Walton fortune and ask, "Where were they born on this race to get ahead?" The class usually yells out, "They won!" "Against whom did they compete?" we rhetorically ask.

Conclusion

Our presentation of "Bob and Harold" allowed our students to learn about the reproduction of class in ways that respected their social class positions and did not force students to "play poverty" in order to learn. We enabled our students to learn how ascribed class is often reproduced independent of individual effort, and we provided them with concrete tools to challenge the hegemonic ideology of meritocracy. We identified key elements in the presentation that enabled our students to relate their own lives to the lives of Bob and Harold, to see the reproduction of capitals, and to grasp the concept of social class in a concrete and meaningful way. Both authors subscribe to the idea that "[a]ll of us in the academy and in the culture as a whole are called to renew our minds if we are to transform educational institutions—and society—so that the way we live, teach, and work can reflect our joy in cultural diversity, our passion for justice, and our love of freedom" (Hooks 1994, p. 34), a glorious pronouncement to which we would also add the recognition of class and its impact on all of those things.

References

Abrajano, M., & Hajnal, Z. L. (2017). *White backlash: Immigration, race, and American politics*. Princeton, NJ: Princeton University Press.

Aries, E., & Seider, M. (2007). The role of social class in the formation of identity: A study of public and elite private college students. *The Journal of Social Psychology, 147*(2), 137–157.

Carreiro, J. L., & Kapitulik, B. P. (2010). Budgets, board games, and make believe: The challenge of teaching social class inequality with non-traditional students. *The American Sociologist, 41*(3), 232–248.

CSU Enrollment Reporting System (ERSS). (2016). Headcount enrollment by CSU degree program, demographic characteristics, and degree level (fall trends): Sociology. https://www.csustan.edu/sites/default/files/IR/documents/c2t5.headcount.profile.hegis_Sociology_22081.pdf. Accessed April 9, 2017.

CSU Stanislaus Institutional Review Board (IRB). (2016). Protocol #1516-079. "Bob & Harold Go To College: Class Matters".

Domhoff, G. W. (2014). *Who rules America? The triumph of the corporate rich* (7th ed.). New York, NY: McGraw-Hill Education.

Ferraro, G., & Andreatta, S. (2012). *Cultural anthropology: An applied perspective* (9th ed.). Belmont, CA: Wadsworth, Cengage Learning.

Gilder, G. (1981). *Wealth and poverty*. New York, NY: Basic Books.

Giroux, H. (2010). *Youth in a suspect society: Democracy or disposability?*. New York, NY: Palgrave Macmillan.

Guinier, L. (2015). *The tyranny of the meritocracy: Democratizing higher education in America*. Boston, MA: Beacon Press.

Hooks, B. (1994). *Teaching to transgress: Education as the practice of freedom*. New York, NY: Routledge.

King, K. R., McEvoy, S., & Teixeira, S. (2011). 'Remediation' as a civil rights issue in the California State University system. In G. Orfield (Ed.), *The CSU crisis and California's future* (pp. 5–41). Los Angeles, CA: The Civil Rights Project/Proyecto Derechos Civiles at UCLA.

Kucsera, J., & Flaxman, G. (2012). *The western states: Profound diversity but severe segregation for Latino students*. Los Angeles, CA: The Civil Rights Project/Proyecto Derechos Civiles at UCLA.

Lee, E. M. (2016). *Class and campus life: Managing and experiencing inequality at an elite college*. New York, NY: Cornell University Press.

Lorde, A. (1984). *Sister outsider: Essays and speeches*. Freedom, CA: Crossing Publishers.

Magnet, M. (1993). *The dream and the nightmare: The sixties' legacy to the underclass*. New York, NY: William Morrow.

Murray, C. (1984). *Losing ground: American social policy, 1950–1980*. New York: Basic Books.

Murray, C. (2005). The hallmark of the underclass. *Wall Street Journal*. http://libproxy.csustan.edu/login?url=http://search.proquest.com/docview/399001813?accountid=10364. Accessed April 9, 2017.

Ochoa, G. L. (2013). *Academic profiling: Latinos, Asian Americans, and the achievement gap*. Minneapolis, MN: University of Minnesota Press.

Schwartz, J. (2000). *Fighting poverty with virtue: Moral reform and America's urban poor, 1825–2000*. Bloomington, IN: Indiana University Press.

Shaw, G. M., & Shapiro, R. Y. (2002). The polls-trends: Poverty and public assistance. *Public Opinion Quarterly, 66*(1), 121–122.

Silver, N. (2013). Reflective pedagogies and the metacognitive turn in college teaching. In M. Kaplan, N. Silver, D. Lavaque-Mant, & D. Meizlish (Eds.), *Using reflection and metacognition to improve student learning: Across the disciplines, across the academy* (pp. 1–17). Sterling, VA: Stylus Publishing.
Ward, L., Siegel, M. J., & Davenport, Z. (2012). *First-generation college students: Understanding and improving the experience from recruitment to commencement*. San Francisco, CA: Jossey-Bass.
Zull, J. E. (2002). *The art of changing the brain: Enriching the practice of teaching by exploring the biology of learning*. Sterling, VA: Stylus Publishing.

Financial Stumbles, Consumer Bankruptcy, and the Sociological Imagination

Deborah Thorne

Author's Reflexive Statement

I've been studying the social tragedy of consumer bankruptcy since the mid-1990s—and to this day, I still think the topic is pretty darned "sexy." And, as we all know, it is ideal when instructors can share their research with their students. But, despite my best efforts, I struggled to get my students to see the obvious sexiness of bankruptcy. And that's understandable—it's really a pretty complicated event and process. After a couple failed attempts at an exciting course on consumer bankruptcy, I finally realized that, just like my data show, there are typically several financial crises before a bankruptcy is finally filed. It's like climbing down a ladder—there are several rungs before you finally jump off into the water, waves, and boulders below. And, I concluded many of those smaller crises would be familiar to my students. They were the hooks I needed to get them engaged in the broad issue of financial struggle, which would ease them into the exciting world of consumer bankruptcy. What follows are some of the hooks that I've successfully used as enticement.

As an aside, I want to warn instructors to be prepared for the personal stories and emotions that your students will likely share. Financial crises are so common in our country that many of your students will have experienced them. Once they realize that they are not the only ones, the conversations will launch and, of the many subjects I teach, this is hands-down the single most popular and consequential. Students contact me years after our class and thank me for teaching them this material. They have learned to be very cautious with debt—I would expect that their FICO scores are strong, too. They learn how so many financial struggles occur because of institutional changes that are beyond them.

D. Thorne (✉)
University of Idaho, Moscow, USA
e-mail: dthorne@uidaho.edu

K. Haltinner and L. Hormel (eds.), *Teaching Economic Inequality and Capitalism in Contemporary America*, https://doi.org/10.1007/978-3-319-71141-6_5

Introduction

For the past two decades, I have studied consumer bankruptcy. Over that time, I've learned that consumer bankruptcy is, almost without exception, just the final straw in a long line of financial stumbles. I've also learned that causes of consumer bankruptcy are so much more about structural issues rather than individual decisions and choices. For example, a few of the common causes of consumer bankruptcy are job loss (Sullivan et al. 2000; Warren and Tyagi 2003), medical debts (Himmelstein et al. 2009), aging (Porter and Thorne 2008; Thorne et al. 2009), predatory lending, and even student loans (Warren and Thorne 2012). While many of us accuse bankrupt Americans of fiscal irresponsibility or a lack of integrity and ethics, reality is quite different.

When teaching these topics, we need to remain cognizant of the fact that most Americans are reluctant to discuss money matters—financial success is assumed to be a reflection of individual effort, and failures are something of which many are ashamed. As a result of the "bootstrap" assumption, students seriously struggle to accept that financial failures could possibly be outside of their control. Consequently, it can be very challenging for students to incorporate the Sociological Imagination as they move through this unit.

I've long believed that teaching my students about consumer bankruptcy is an excellent way to promote the use of their Sociological Imagination—that they too could understand how household financial collapse in the United States has much more to do with our social institutions rather than an individual's poor money management. However, the reality is that the topic of consumer bankruptcy is often a bit beyond the life experience and educational level of my students.

While my ultimate goal is to familiarize students with consumer bankruptcy, and help them see how structural factors often lead to economic collapse, launching into a lesson on consumer bankruptcy, without first situating it and making it relevant, can be terribly overwhelming and even boring to all but the most curious students. Bankruptcy *is* extremely complicated—law students learn about the topic in their second and third years of law school. And students tend to think of bankruptcy as something that only old people do. Our students are, for the most part, in their early 20s, and relatively few of them have experienced financial struggle—of course, to a large degree, this depends on their social class and the larger economic shifts occurring at the time. More importantly, they tend to think of bankruptcy as something they can choose to avoid regardless of their socioeconomic background—that if they are just smart enough with their money or willing to work harder, they will somehow be immune.

I have found it most effective to initially introduce students to some of the (relatively) smaller financial stumbles that tend to be precursors to consumer bankruptcy. Unlike bankruptcy, these stumbles often resonate with them because they are struggles that can and do happen to people their age. To accomplish this, I rely on two aids. First, I use video clips from John Oliver's, *Last Week Tonight with John Oliver*, to introduce some of the everyday financial stumbles. Students are quite familiar with John Oliver, and he incorporates a beautifully snarky sense of humor into otherwise very depressing topics. Second, I rely on students' shared stories of financial struggles. As they come to recognize how common financial struggles are, they inevitably open up about their own experiences. Essentially, the stories serve to normalize financial struggles and reduce the associated stigma.

Financial Stumbles

Financial Stumble #1: Student Loan Debt

It makes perfect sense to begin with this stumble since the majority of students will eventually have student loan debt. In 2016, the average amount owed at the time of graduation was just over $37,100 (Student Loan Hero 2017). To begin the conversation on the subject of student loans, I recommend the video: "Student Debt: Last Week Tonight with John Oliver" (Oliver 2017d). Oliver briefly describes the history and ubiquity of student loan debt. He also discusses how unique student loan debt is—namely, once you owe it, getting rid of it is next to impossible. Finally, Oliver spends a considerable amount of time exposing the trickery used by many for-profit colleges and universities to increase their profits—at the expense of the students. For several reasons, it is critical that our students think about for-profit institutions, even if they are not attending one. First, for-profits are a powerful driver behind the massive student loan debt crisis—which is well over a trillion dollars. Second, students who attend for-profits are significantly more likely to default on their loans than students at public institutions. Third, these for-profit issues have reached the highest level of our government: President Trump's unlicensed for-profit Trump University was sued for "fraudulent, illegal and deceptive conduct" (Halperin 2013). And finally, President Trump's Secretary of Education, Betsy DeVos, recently hired Robert S. Eitel, who is a for-profit college official and opponent of regulations for for-profit colleges (Cohen 2017). After students watch this video, you might want to consider the following:

(a) I stress the fact that student loan debt has skyrocketed over the past two decades. This gives me an opportunity to talk about how some specific social institutions—politics and education, for example—are directly responsible for these changes. To illustrate the massive shift of financial responsibility from tax dollars to individual students, I tell them that when my husband attended University of Oregon in 1976, tuition was approximately $250 per quarter. (Any example from a generation or so ago will be similarly effective.) Inevitably, they will be quite frustrated and demand to know what's changed. Here is your opportunity to once again stress the power of institutions.
(b) Another effective activity is to ask your students to do a little research on their own university or college to determine how much tuition has increased over the past decade or two. Talk about whether they could realistically work a full-time

summer job and expect to cover the cost of the upcoming year's tuition—like students were able to do about one generation ago.

(c) I also introduce students to a student loan repayment calculator (my favorite is at Bankrate.com). This lets them explore the actual costs of borrowing for college. For example, if they graduate owing the national average of $37,100, with an interest rate of 6%, and they want to repay it over five years, they must pay approximately $720 a month. When we couple this loan amount with their (realistic) monthly income and their other bills, many will be shell-shocked.

(d) We also discuss how lenders can garnish their wages, intercept their tax returns, empty their bank accounts, and sue them in court if they get behind on their student loan payments.

(e) And finally, we discuss the fact that student loan debt *cannot be discharged in bankruptcy*. I stress to them that regardless of what happens in their lives—job loss, medical expenses, injuries, unplanned children, children who are born with expensive medical problems, an increasing mortgage—there is virtually nothing they can do to escape their student loan debts.

Be prepared for students to become quite anxious when you discuss the topic of student loan debt—especially those students who have well above the average total loan amount and who have few prospects. Unfortunately, it is not uncommon to hear from students who will owe $50,000, $60,000, or $70,000 when they graduate with a four-year degree. A few years ago, one of my sociology students told the class that she was graduating with $110,000 in loan debt. You could have heard a pin drop. This subject hits incredibly close to home for them. Many express real anger toward a "system" that encourages if not demands this level of debt among young people who rarely have the financial skills to genuinely understand the implications. Many, justifiably, feel very set up. And many will also realize that their dream of further education, either graduate or professional school, is financially unwise.

Financial Stumble #2: Predatory Auto Lending

I enjoy teaching students about the financial stumble of subprime auto lending as well, again, because it is relevant for so many of them. If you teach in an economically privileged community there may be fewer students who have had to deal with predatory auto lenders. Regardless, this topic will give them insight into the lives of those less fortunate and into the world of predatory lending. For those who are economically disadvantaged and often must rely on the "buy here, pay here—no credit check required" types of lenders, they will likely see themselves in these stories and will be familiar with the ways in which these lenders prey on their financial instability. For this section, I like to have students watch "Auto Lending: Last Week Tonight with John Oliver" (Oliver 2017a). Oliver explains what vehicle subprime lending is, and he walks viewers through the connection between Wall

Street profits and vehicle subprime lending–Oliver makes it quite explicit how the wealthy are profiting off lower-income consumers who need a set of wheels to get to their jobs and schools. This otherwise complex concept is made quite accessible with this video. Finally, the video begins to make that important connection between predatory car loans and consumer bankruptcy. During the conversation following this video, you may want to consider the following:

(a) I emphasize to my students that the vast majority of Americans must have a vehicle to get to and from work. To illustrate this, I ask them to raise their hands if their parents drive to work—and here in relatively rural Idaho, virtually everyone's parents drive to work. In 2015, 86% of all Americans who commuted for work drove rather than took public transit—this is about 123 million people driving back and forth to work every day. No surprise, the people who tend to drive the longest distances to work are in manufacturing and construction—people who typically cannot afford to live closer to their jobs (Lake, 2015). Only those folks who live in fairly progressive cities have access to reliable and affordable public transit. Everyone else, particularly those living in rural spaces, absolutely must have a car.
(b) Another social fact is that the high cost of suburban and urban housing often forces lower-income families to live a considerable distance from their places of employment, in communities where they can afford a roof over their heads. This leaves them even more dependent on their cars. They spend more time on the road, putting many miles on typically low-end cars, and the extra miles often translate into unaffordable repairs—which if they cannot make, may result in job loss.
(c) We also discuss the connection between car loans and consumer bankruptcy. I teach students that when people default on their car loans (stop making their payments), the car will be repossessed, and the buyer *remains responsible for the balance of the loan*. So, for example, if the consumer purchased a car for $10,000, but paid only $2000 on the loan before they could no longer afford it, or it broke down, it will be repossessed and the lender will hold the buyer responsible for the $8000 balance still owing on the car, as well as late fees, interest, and charges that the lender's attorney may have added. I really stress this to my students—the person no longer has the car, but they still owe the debt! As a result of this, many people will file bankruptcy to erase the outstanding balance owed on a car they no longer have.

Financial Stumble #3: When Your Debts Are Bundled and Sold

I like to show "Debt Buyers: Last Week Tonight with John Oliver" (Oliver 2017c) because the bundling and selling of debt is something with which so few Americans, and in particular young people, are familiar. Essentially, "debt bundling" is when the original lender sells a person's delinquent debts to a second party debt buyer, who is also a debt collector. Similar types of debts, for example those that are 90 or more days delinquent, will be bundled into a large financial product and sold to buyers and debt collectors for pennies on the dollar owed. Then these collectors use very aggressive tactics to try to collect from the original debtors. Debt bundling and the corresponding collections are often financially catastrophic for people who get caught in this cycle—and Oliver's video beautifully illustrates how and why this happens.

It is imperative that students are familiar with debt bundling because this is what can happen if they neglect their debts. I've talked with numerous students who, while still in college, have become overwhelmed with their debts, particularly their credit card debts, and they simply stopped paying on them. They may have initially worked quite diligently to remain current on their payments, but found they were not making much if any progress on the balance, so they threw up their arms and simply stopped opening the bills. I use this video to encourage them to think about the long-term consequences of ignoring their debts. I stress to them that even if the original lender writes off their debt and stops trying to collect from them, their financial obligation does not disappear. Instead, the initial lender will sell the debt, and the subsequent owner of the debt will come after them—and often in ways that are quite unsavory. For example, there will be repeated and aggressive collection calls, their bank accounts may be emptied, their wages may be garnished, their tax returns may be taken, they may be sued, and their credit report will likely be severely damaged. In some cases, they will be threatened with jail time, which, while illegal, is still terrifying.

Given their young ages, it is unlikely that many traditional students have ever experienced the consequences of debt bundling and selling. They are still quite new to the game of debt collections. But, this video gives me the opportunity to introduce them to a financial world that is, in so many ways, unforgiving and very aggressive. What follows are some of the topics I cover after we watch the Oliver video.

(a) I talk with students about how fees and interest from an otherwise relatively small debt can grow exponentially if they fall behind on their payments. When a bill is ignored, interest will soon be charged on interest, and there will be late fees and even attorney's fees tacked on to the original balance. It is likely that by the time the debt is sold, it will be many times larger than it was originally. And while students may think that unfair, it is perfectly legal. Again, here is a great opportunity to discuss the intersection of their finances and the law.

(b) Just like when we discuss student loan debt, I again use this opportunity to have students play with a debt repayment calculator. With the calculators, they enter the amount they owe on any loan, in particular credit cards, and then enter the interest rate. Of course, few have any idea what their interest rates are, so this is a great time for them to learn. They then enter what they think they can afford to repay each month. Click enter, and the sad truth of how long it will take them to repay, and the amount they will pay in interest, will appear. This is far and away one of the best activities I do with my students.

Financial Stumble #4: The Credit Report

Like it or not, the three digit number that is otherwise known as our FICO score, or credit score, directly affects numerous things in our lives—which is why I look forward to students watching "Credit Reports: Last Week Tonight with John Oliver" (Oliver 2017b). This video provides a great overview of how the credit reporting industry, the credit bureaus, the credit report, and the FICO score can truly alter their life course—for better and for worse. A low score can make it more difficult to get a job, rent an apartment, and get affordable credit with low interest rates. From this video, we discuss the following:

(a) We talk about how the first three stumbles, student loan debt, auto debt, and delinquent bills, can negatively affect their FICO score.
(b) We discuss the specific ways in which a low FICO score can negatively affect them—when they apply for a mortgage, when they try to rent housing, when they want to purchase a car, when they apply for a credit card, when they apply for a job, when they want to co-sign their children's student loans, and so on (Thorne 2007). When the FICO score is low, things are much more difficult and costly.
(c) I also take this opportunity to have my students get their credit score at CreditKarma.com. At this site, access to their score is free, and they can review their credit report to check for mistakes—which, the sooner caught, the better. And as the video discusses, there is a considerable likelihood that their credit report will include mistakes—some fairly benign, others are seriously problematic.
(d) Studying the credit score also helps students understand the incredible power of this one financial instrument. Expect that they will be shocked and even angry about how much the credit report and FICO score can affect their lives. But, as I tell them, better to appreciate their power now, rather than later.

After your students have learned about the four financial stumbles, I recommend showing the movie, *Maxed Out*, by James Scurlock. While this film is a bit dated (2006), and although it was completed prior to the 2008 financial crisis, it is still one of the best out there. This film synthesizes some of the things that students have learned to this point, and it introduces them to a few other issues such as predatory mortgage lending and the emotional toll, including suicide, that may result from overwhelming debt and aggressive collection tactics.

Bankruptcy

If you don't feel confident teaching students about consumer bankruptcy, you could choose to instead focus on the previous topics and forego the subject altogether. However, even if consumer bankruptcy is completely unfamiliar to you, with just a little background reading, you can be adequately up-to-speed. Of course, you can always spend some time online researching consumer bankruptcy—one good place to start is the "Bankruptcy Basics" section at the website of the U.S. Courts (2017) (http://www.uscourts.gov/services-forms/bankruptcy/bankruptcy-basics). More options for an excellent discussion of the differences between the different types (chapters) of bankruptcy are the books by Sullivan, Warren and Westbrook (2000, 1989), and Porter's more recent work, *Broke: How Debt Bankrupts the Middle Class* (2012). In addition, below is a very simplified description of the two types of consumer bankruptcy—Chaps. 8 and 14.

A (Very) Brief Primer on Consumer Bankruptcy

The two types of bankruptcy that are used almost exclusively by consumer households, rather than businesses or corporations, are Chaps. 8 and 14. In Chap. 8, which is often called a "straight bankruptcy," the debtors typically must sell (liquidate) all of their assets (if they have any equity in them), such as cars and homes, and divide the money up among creditors. (However, most people who file Chap. 8 don't have assets that are worth much—if they have a car or a house, they often still owe so much on them that they don't have any equity.) In exchange for selling any assets, most of the debts are erased, and the debtor returns to the economic system with a clean slate. Typically, the types of debts that are discharged in Chap. 8 are medical bills, credit card debt, and even balances on cars that have been repossessed. This chapter of bankruptcy takes a couple months to complete, and attorney's fees will be approximately $1230 (Foohey et al. 2017).

Chapter 14 is a repayment plan. The debtor gets to keep their assets (often they are filing Chap. 14 to save a car or a house in which they have considerable equity), but they have to continue making their monthly payments on these assets *and* they have to repay a portion of the debts that are in arrears (that they are behind on). So if, for example, they have fallen behind on their house payments, owe some medical bills, some credit card debt, and a veterinary bill, they must continue to make the monthly payments on their existing bills *and* they must repay the amounts they are behind on. This repayment-plan style of bankruptcy often extends for up to five years. Since it requires more work on the part of the bankruptcy attorney, it is also more expensive than Chap. 8, averaging $3217 (Foohey et al. 2017).

When I teach my students about bankruptcy, I remind them that almost without exception, their student loans *cannot* be discharged in bankruptcy. Congress decided that student loans are special and these debts must be repaid. This provides instructors an excellent opportunity to talk with students about how the institution of law can seriously impact their financial lives.

I encourage you to teach your students about consumer bankruptcy—I think it is the proverbial canary in the coal mine for the financial health of many American families, and as such, it should be shared with our students. Consumer bankruptcies are a relatively common phenomenon: since the turn of the century, the annual number of households filing for consumer bankruptcy in the United States has averaged well over a million (http://www.creditslips.org/). And given that most households contain several members, the total number of Americans going through bankruptcy every year is significant. Filing bankruptcy can leave familial relationships in absolute tatters (Thorne 2010). Bankruptcy can negatively affect people's financial lives for years—effectively gutting their FICO score for up to a decade. And most relevant to this audience, few phenomena better illustrate a large social trend that results from structural rather than individual facts (think Sociological Imagination) than consumer bankruptcy.

Their Stories

There is no better feeling than when you are teaching a topic and a student volunteers a personal story that perfectly illustrates your point. It is then that you know they get it—they have made the connection, they have made the information their own. (The best book I have ever read describing this genuine learning is James Zull's, *The Art of Changing the Brain* (2002). If you've not yet read this, put it at the top of your "must read" list.) And other students benefit from the stories—it reinforces the subject matter and often normalizes it. Beginning with the very first financial stumble, I start asking for examples from students. For example, when we are covering student loans, they may talk about how their parents are still struggling to repay their own loans. They may have examples from older siblings who are struggling to repay loans and live on their own. Students have also described how they use their student loans to help their parents with rent, mortgage, utilities, car repairs, or food. And since I also have student loans (they will be repaid when I am approximately 62), I can share my experience, my frustrations, and the choices I've had to make between paying the monthly student loan bill or making additional contributions to my retirement account.

Students will also have stories about car repossessions—the student may have already experienced this or it may have happened to a sibling or a parent. And if they are lower-income and live off campus, the difficulties of a long commute, and an unreliable but affordable car, may be quite real for them.

Most students will still be naïve to struggles with debt collection and poor credit scores, but they are curious about and grateful for the information. This is one of those lessons where you can be confident that the take-home messages will make a big difference in the lives of your students.

And if you do teach the section on bankruptcy, be prepared for how much experience students do in fact have with it. I'm always shocked at the number of students who raise their hands when I ask if their parents have ever filed for bankruptcy—parents who are working-class, middle-class, and professionals. Once we spend time talking about the details of bankruptcy, and exposing the many structural reasons for it, it becomes more normalized. In general, bankruptcy remains quite stigmatized (Thorne and Anderson 2006), but I think the shame and isolation felt by many students from bankrupt households fall away as I, and they, talk about it. Many are willing, and even eager, to share their stories—it seems as though the more they talk about their experience, the less shame they feel. And herein lies the power of the Sociological Imagination. As students share their experiences and I describe the more macro forces behind financial collapse, they are likely to let go of the shame and blame, recognizing that bankruptcy is often well outside of their control.

Finally, it's important to point out to your students the interconnectedness of the many types of financial struggles, and how these combinations, rather than a single isolated incident, more accurately explain how and why bankruptcy happens. For example, a parent gets ill, then loses their job and health insurance, so they cannot make monthly bills, and the car is repossessed, the house foreclosed, and college funds and retirement accounts are drained to put food on the table. Ultimately, in an effort to stay the collection calls and threats, and to enable the family to move forward, a bankruptcy was filed. And so it goes.

A while back, in my Introduction to Sociology course, I was teaching about bankruptcy and the range of reasons for filing. I had nurtured an open and safe discussion environment, so when I asked if any of the students' parents had been through bankruptcy and if they could describe what happened, I was not surprised when several hands were raised. Here is a lengthy (but oh-so-relevant) story from a student:

> Both of the student's parents were college graduates, in fact, his mom had a graduate degree. His parents waited until they had good jobs and good salaries before they had children: his mom was successful in the corporate world and his dad was self-employed in the fine arts. However, "during the recession in 2008, my father's business began to suffer. Since fine art is a luxury and an expensive one at that, revenue to the family sharply declined. My parents made the decision to focus on my mother's career." After 15 years with one telecommunications company, she was hired by a competitor. The student said that "she had been working there for 15 years at this point and had risen in the ranks and our family was fortunate enough to thrive off of her success. Now comes the turning point in which my parents' empire begins to crumble much like ancient Rome (a joke)." Apparently, there was an internal struggle for position and power between the student's mother and another employee. His mom's career was destroyed as a result. She was given the option of either a severance package or partial retirement. His parents elected to take the severance package. They were conservative with their finances and had significant savings and no debt. Unfortunately, "what they did not see coming was both of them suffering from various medical issues—mainly my mother—she lost all sight in her right eye and most in her left. The treatments… were expensive. Then my mother was diagnosed with cancer, which is a hugely expensive medical problem to treat. Then my father had a very major operation himself…. These unexpected medical expenses came when my parents were of age to retire anyways, but the cost of the treatments changed everything. Cars got traded in for cheaper ones, the house got smaller and fell into disrepair, and the college funds ran dry".

This series of assignments, and hopefully the corresponding conversations and stories, will teach your students how so many of our smaller financial struggles, and ultimately bankruptcy, result from social factors that operate well beyond individual effort and determination. Students are often eager to use their Sociological Imagination to make sense of many things, but they tend to struggle to get beyond individualism when it comes to money and finances. Through these examples of everyday financial struggles, most students indeed do develop the awareness of the influence of powerful social structures. And once they develop this perspective to explain the smaller struggles, it is not difficult for them to explain consumer bankruptcy with their Sociological Imagination. When they accomplish this, they have mastered something that most Americans never will—moving past individual blame and shame to fully understand why hundreds of thousands of households file bankruptcy every year. Students can grasp the financial risks in the United States at this point in history—risks that are generated from forces much greater than themselves.

References

Cohen, P. (2017). Betsy DeVos's hiring of for-profit college official raises impartiality issues. https://www.nytimes.com/2017/03/17/business/education-for-profit-robert-eitel.html?_r=0. Accessed March 24, 2017.

Foohey, P., Lawless, R. M., Porter, K., & Thorne, D. (2017). 'No money down' bankruptcy. *Southern California Law Review, 90*, 1055–1110.

Halperin, D. (2013). A nation of Trump universities: The abuses of for-profit colleges. http://www.huffingtonpost.com/davidhalperin/a-nation-of-trump-univers_b_3830007.html. Accessed March 24, 2017.

Himmelstein, D. U., Thorne, D., Warren, E., & Woolhandler, S. (2009). Medical bankruptcy in the United States, 2007: Results of a national study. *The American Journal of Medicine, 122*(8), 741–746.

Lake, R. (2015). 23 commute statistics to know before you go to work. https://www.creditdonkey.com/commute-statistics.html. Accessed March 22, 2017.

Oliver, J. (2017a). Auto lending: Last week tonight with John Oliver. https://www.youtube.com/watch?v=4U2eDJnwz_s. Accessed February 12, 2017.

Oliver, J. (2017b). Credit reports: Last week tonight with John Oliver. https://www.youtube.com/watch?v=aRrDsbUdY_k. Accessed February 12, 2017.

Oliver, J. (2017c). Debt buyers: Last week tonight with John Oliver. https://www.youtube.com/watch?v=hxUAntt1z2c. Accessed February 12, 2017.

Oliver, J. (2017d). Student debt: Last week tonight with John Oliver. https://www.youtube.com/watch?v=P8pjd1QEA0c. Accessed February 12, 2017.

Porter, K. (2012). *Broke: How debt bankrupts the middle class*. Stanford, CA: Stanford University Press.

Porter, K., & Thorne, D. (2008). Better off after bankruptcy. *Norton Bankruptcy Law Adviser, 12*, 1–6.

Porter, K., & Thorne, D. (2006). The failure of bankruptcy's fresh start. *Cornell Law Review, 92*, 67–127.

Student Loan Hero. (2017). A look at the shocking student loan debt statistics for 2017. https://studentloanhero.com/student-loan-debt-statistics/. Accessed February 12, 2017.

Sullivan, T. A., Warren, E., & Westbrook, J. L. (1989). *As we forgive our debtors: Bankruptcy and consumer credit in America*. New York: Oxford University Press.

Sullivan, T. A., Warren, E., & Westbrook, J. L. (2000). *The fragile middle class: Americans in debt*. New Haven, CT: Yale University Press.

Thorne, D. (2007). Personal bankruptcy and the credit report: Conflicting mechanisms of social mobility. *Journal of Poverty: Innovations on Social, Political, & Economic Inequalities, 11*(4), 23–43.

Thorne, D. (2010). Extreme financial strain: Emergent chores, gender inequality, and emotional distress. *Journal of Family and Economic Issues, 31*, 185–197.

Thorne, D., & Anderson, L. (2006). Managing the stigma of personal bankruptcy. *Sociological Focus, 39*(2), 77–97.

Thorne, D., Warren, E., & Sullivan, T. A. (2009). The increasing vulnerability of older Americans: Evidence from the bankruptcy court. *Harvard Law & Policy Review, 3*(1), 87–101.

United States Courts. (2017). Bankruptcy basics. http://www.uscourts.gov/services-forms/bankruptcy/bankruptcy-basics. Accessed February 12, 2017.

Warren, E., & Thorne, D. (2012). A vulnerable middle class: Bankruptcy and class status. In K. Porter (Ed.), *Broke: How debt bankrupts the middle class* (pp. 25–39). Stanford CA: Stanford University Press.

Warren, E., & Warren Tyagi, A. (2003). *The two-income trap: Why middle-class mothers and fathers are going broke*. New York: Basic Books.

Zull, J. E. (2002). *The art of changing the brain: Enriching the practice of teaching by exploring the biology of learning*. Sterling, VA: Stylus Publishing.

Part II
Making Marxist Theory Real

Capitalism 101: Teaching First-Year Students How to View the Social World Through the Lens of Marxist Theory

Laura Earles

Author's Reflexive Statement

When I entered graduate school as a middle-class young woman from a small town in a fairly conservative state without much background in sociology (having majored in psychology as an undergraduate) I did not have much prior experience with Marxist theory. I had read a bit of Marx in an upper-level anthropology class, but beyond that, I was ignorant of the significance of his work. That changed fairly quickly during my first year at the University of Oregon, a program that was known (at least at the time) for its strong Marxist underpinnings. In reading Marx during my first term, especially his thoughts on alienation and primitive accumulation, I found myself finally having words to describe some of my long-felt angst about the social world and the environment. That Marx was shunned by most non-academics because of the admittedly radical implications of his work was such a shame to me given how illuminating I found his ideas. Eight years later as I was starting to teach SOC 101: Introduction to Sociology for the first time at my new job at a small public college in Idaho, I wasn't sure how my students were going to react to their new sociology professor from Oregon, a self-proclaimed Marxist ecofeminist. I reminded myself that I had every right and, in fact, *needed* to cover Marx's ideas in my class, because he was one of sociology's founding thinkers. With that type of earnest intention as my reassurance, I introduced students to Marxist theory in the way that I think it is meant to be taught—straightforwardly and with an emphasis on its fundamental insight: material circumstances matter. As I note below in the introduction to this chapter, this approach has worked even better than I could have imagined. Many of my students are from small rural towns in the Inland Northwest with agricultural or other natural resource-based economies, so they intuitively understand that material circumstances matter, even if they have never thought of

L. Earles (✉)
Lewis-Clark State College, Lewiston, ID, USA
e-mail: leearles@lcsc.edu

K. Haltinner and L. Hormel (eds.), *Teaching Economic Inequality and Capitalism in Contemporary America*, https://doi.org/10.1007/978-3-319-71141-6_6

things in exactly that way before. Similar to me when I started graduate school, they simply need to be introduced to the sociological language that describes what they are already thinking, feeling, and observing.

Introduction

Many students and even some instructors are hesitant to directly engage with Marxist theory because of the political implications associated with this school of thought as well as the perceived abstract nature of theory more generally. However, to the contrary, over the course of nearly a decade of teaching introductory-level sociology courses at a public comprehensive college that serves a socioeconomically diverse student body in a politically conservative state, I have found no better way to help students understand their daily struggles and life experiences than to use Marxist theoretical concepts in an explicit and, importantly, comprehensible manner. In fact, the ease with which students can understand their lives and the lives of others in a more critical and accurate way with the aid of Marxist terminology speaks to the analytical power of the concepts themselves. Quite simply, they help students answer the *how* and *why* questions that implicitly underlie their continual, albeit often subconscious, process of trying to understand why their lives and our society, more generally, are proceeding as they are. Making these concepts a focal point in the classroom gives students permission to acknowledge their struggles and experiences and understand them as products of social structure rather than as personal shortcomings of themselves, their families, and others. Of course, the key to successfully integrating these concepts in the introductory classroom is to distill them down to fairly basic forms and, importantly, to engage students in a way that allows them to understand and apply the concepts using concrete examples.

In this chapter, I highlight the usefulness of two key concepts, in particular, and briefly explain how they can be integrated into introductory-level sociology courses, including both the traditional Introduction to Sociology course as well as introductory Social Problems or Social Inequalities courses. Specifically, I discuss the concepts of alienation and reproduction. I rely on Marx's original formulation of the term alienation in *The Economic and Philosophic Manuscripts of 1844* (Tucker 1978), and my use of reproduction is traced to Carolyn Merchant's (1989, 2005) conceptualization in *Ecological Revolutions: Nature, Gender, and Science in New England* and in *Radical Ecology: The Search for a Livable World.* In discussing how I incorporate these concepts, I explain how I frame each concept's significance and also give examples of questions and pedagogical techniques I use to guide students in applying these terms to understand both the course content and their own life experiences.

Before discussing these specific theoretical concepts, it is useful to step back and consider the place of theory in the introductory sociology classroom. Theory with a capital "T" can be intimidating for first-year undergraduates. (For that matter, it can be intimidating for first-year graduate students.) As instructors, too, we may be hesitant to emphasize theory for fear of losing our students' interest or overwhelming them with the nuances of debates within our discipline, which could serve to further their impression that college professors are an unapproachable, cloistered group who don't have much of import to add to their everyday considerations and experiences. When I have these moments of doubt, I find it useful to remind myself of the point of theory, at least from my perspective. What is theory, after all, but an explanation of the fundamental nature of specific processes? In the case of social theory, it is a way of explaining the essence of a particular social process, interaction, etc. It is, quite simply, elaborating how and why things happen as they do. Viewed in this light, theory, as a basic explanation of a process or interrelated set of processes, loses its intimidation factor. It is no longer grand theory with a capital "T," but unassuming, earnest theory with a lower-case "t," accessible for all who might be curious to learn more about how the social world works. Approaching theory in this way—and, importantly, explaining to students that this is really all that theory actually is—brings it down to earth, making it comprehensible in the introductory classroom. Of course, the tradeoff in approaching theory this way is that your students may not actually remember *the theory* you keep emphasizing to them, but they will remember *the fundamental explanation*, and if our true goal is imparting knowledge that is relevant and likely to be applied again, then there is success in that outcome.

Alienation

To start with alienation, in the original sense it is about, in Marx's words, *estrangement* (Tucker 1978, pp. 71–72). More specifically, Marx saw alienated labor as a key feature of capitalism that has arisen because people are estranged, or separated, from their own means of reproduction (the ability to produce for their own basic needs) and instead work under the power of others to earn wages that they can then use to pay for the necessities of life (Tucker 1978, pp. 70–77). When working in a setting and at a pace controlled by someone(s) other than oneself and aimed at the production of goods and services that are typically destined for unknown others, work becomes something that is less an extension of oneself than a chore one must do in order to get on with the business of living one's more authentically felt life, typically the remaining fifteen or so hours out of the day spent feeding, sleeping, and otherwise caring for oneself outside of work. As much as we all enjoy our downtime engaging in such pleasurable activities as eating and resting, Marx pointed out that these are merely our "animal functions" (Tucker 1978, p. 74). To him, this was the great irony of work in capitalist economic systems; our human creativity, which evolved in the context of (re)productive engagement with the natural world, is reduced to an id-like pleasure seeking in the scant few hours of free time we have remaining after suppressing our creativity for eight to ten hours most days while we are engaged in so-called productive activities, i.e., paid work.

Using this basic observation as a starting point for talking about alienation is itself a revelation, one that is necessary to emphasize to students lest they think you are simply pointing out the obvious. The revelatory insight is this: for hundreds of thousands of years of our evolutionary history, humans and our human-like predecessors labored to provide for themselves and other people they knew. Even under pre-capitalist systems of exploitation, people saw that their work was directly benefiting themselves or someone else (either through their or others' direct use or trade), but with the rise of capitalism, work and the overall process of production take on a somewhat mystical quality in that they turn into processes that happen out of sight or, if in sight in the case of our respective workplaces, into an overall process that most people have little control over. They see and know what their specific roles are and of course can see what others are doing in their immediate work environment, but average wage-workers know little of the overall operations of their place of employment, and much less of its place in a larger network of often global production, and are instead myopically focused on the tasks at hand—as well they should be, given that their performance on those tasks is the only metric on which they are evaluated and remunerated. Pointing out that work as we know it is an historical oddity is the first step in having students grasp both the concept of alienation and why it is important for understanding our work lives (as well as the rest of our lives).

After explaining this basic premise of how work is organized (again, that most people in capitalist societies work for others who determine the nature and purpose of that work) I move on to explaining what alienation actually entails by noting and elaborating the four aspects of alienation that Marx discussed: alienation from self, from the labor process, from others, and from the products of one's labor (Tucker 1978, pp. 71–78). I emphasize that, as a sociological concept, alienation is not a psychological state of mind but rather a structural reality. Namely, the way work is organized in advanced capitalist economic systems is the basis for alienation. Following Eitzen and Zinn (2007), I tell students that another word for alienation is *separation* (p. 375). In this way, when we are considering the four aspects of alienation, we are thinking about how workers are quite literally separated from themselves, others, the way their work and the overall production process is carried out, and the things they produce.

I begin with alienation from self by asking students to think about a job, perhaps one they've held in the past, in which one's body is going through the motions while one's mind can easily be doing other things. The worker herself is not engaged in a skillful craft requiring planning, problem solving, and reflection but rather is carrying out fairly rote movements and tasks that have been standardized precisely so that little thought is needed to do them. This separation of one's body from one's mind leads to the feeling that "even a monkey" could do one's job. This is closely related to alienation from the labor process, since the labor process is simply how work is carried out, from the specific physical motions involved to the larger organization of tasks into the overall process of production. When discussing work and the economy in my introductory Social Problems course, I typically assign excerpts from Eric Schlosser's (2002) instant classic *Fast Food Nation: The*

Dark Side of the All-American Meal to illustrate these first two aspects of alienation. Specifically, my students read the sections of chapter three subtitled "Throughput" and "Stroking" (Schlosser 2002, pp. 67–75). In these sections Schlosser discusses the scientific management of fast food workers, which has led to the extreme form of deskilling that can be seen in that industry. In the process, he perfectly illustrates the basis for alienation from self and from the labor process.

Along with this separation from oneself and from the labor process is separation from other workers. Again, because the mental planning and physical execution of many jobs are two separate processes, there is little reason for collaboration with one's coworkers in such work environments. This type of separation, a separation of workers from each other in terms of the creative engagement they might otherwise have with each other in determining how to carry out their jobs, is one aspect of what it means to be alienated from others in one's work. The other, more far-reaching kind of alienation from others that I note is the separation of workers who are involved in different stages of the production process, stages that are often spatially separated from each other. How often, after all, is the garment worker sewing buttons on shirts thinking about, much less coming into contact with, the retail worker folding those shirts for display in the store where they are sold? The answer, of course, is never in the case of the workers' actual contact with one another and probably rarely in the case of the workers thinking about each other. The point here, again, is that alienation from others is very much a structural feature of work in capitalist economic systems (and as some would argue in any generalized commodity production system, but that is another lecture); workers are quite literally separated from each other in the overall process of production of any given commodity.

The final aspect of alienation, alienation from the product of one's labor is a rather obvious but at the same time revealing feature of commodity production. Workers do not proudly take home whatever it is they have helped produce at the end of the workday. Imagine, for example, as I have my students do, that the average worker on an automobile assembly line was allowed to take home a shiny new car every year. Just mentioning this idea always garners a combination of amused smiles and eye-rolling from my students, because it would clearly be absurd. This alienation from the product of one's labor is the easiest aspect of alienation to illustrate and also the one where students are relatively unfazed when you point it out, likely thinking, "Of course you can't take home something that you've made in your workplace—it belongs to your employer!" Yes, indeed it does, and there lies the crux of the issue: nothing in capitalist production systems belongs to workers. This was Marx's elegantly simple yet profoundly significant point—owners own, and workers work. To drive this point home even further, another example I often share with students of alienation from the product of one's labor, which clearly illustrates the contrast between capitalist relations of production and production geared for use by the producer herself, is the difference between the person baking a pie at home for a holiday dinner and the person working in a factory that cranks out frozen pies by the thousands bound for the freezers of grocery stores. One is a product of creatively engaged labor, the other of alienated wage labor. The product of the labor may be roughly the same on the surface (a pie), but the process and ultimate relationship to the final product are vastly different.

When it comes to applying the concept of alienation to their own lives, I ask students to recall jobs they may have had in the past or currently have that seem to be alienated, based on the four aspects of alienation Marx outlined. I often prompt students to particularly think about those jobs where they may have found themselves day dreaming much of the time, a sign that their minds (what they might think of as their true selves) had become separated from their bodies (their working selves)—an illustration of alienation from self—or a job where they may have just stopped caring or witnessed others who didn't seem to care about the quality of their work—an illustration of alienation from the process and from others. These sorts of questions always elicit stories about retail work in department stores or kitchen and/or cashier work in fast-food restaurants. I encourage students to describe the way the work was alienated with specific references to the four aspects Marx identified, but then I also ask them to think about how they or their co-workers, as the creative human beings that they are, may have tried to add humor or enjoyment to those jobs in an effort to counteract their alienating features. I also bring up management strategies that supervisors sometimes employ to give their workers a sense that their work is not actually alienated, emphasizing, of course, that these strategies do not fundamentally alter the social relations of production but rather provide workers with a superficial degree of engagement in their workplaces. Here again, Schlosser (2002) is useful. In the previously referenced section of *Fast Food Nation* subtitled "Stroking," Schlosser discusses strategies managers use to give their mostly young workers a sense of being on a team with their co-workers to counteract the inherently alienating features of such work.

An important point to make in any discussion of alienation is to have students consider the degree to which various jobs and professions seem more or less alienating. To prime students for such consideration, when I begin coverage of the topic of work (within a larger discussion of the economy) in both my Introductory to Sociology and Social Problems courses, I pose the question, "Work: tedious necessity or fulfilling aspect of life?" After they are introduced to the concept of alienation, it becomes clear to students during the course of our classroom discussion that certain jobs are, indeed, more alienating than others. It also becomes clear that even those jobs that appear to be somewhat immune to the totalizing effects of basic wage-labor's alienating characteristics have features of alienation. It is instructive for students to understand that some of the most alienating jobs are (by definition) those held by working-class people as opposed to by members of the professional-managerial class, which raises important and sobering questions about whose jobs and careers in our society are more satisfying and less taxing, more creative and less dulling. In this way, students are again reminded that alienation is not simply a state of mind of a disgruntled worker but rather a systemic aspect of how much of the work in our society is organized, work that is carried out disproportionately by large segments of the population with little control or influence over this reality. As such, alienation as a theoretical concept deepens students' understanding of socioeconomic inequality as a feature of society that extends beyond easily measurable indicators such as income differences into the more complex terrain of lived experience in different occupational settings and social class locations.

Reproduction

Reproduction is a second fundamental concept that, in my opinion, actually eclipses alienation as a master concept from which many other aspects of social life can be understood (including alienation itself). The conceptualization of reproduction I discuss here is that which is elaborated by feminist scholars writing in the Marxist tradition who seek to explain how laborers are continually *reproduced* so that they are able to contribute their labor power to commodity production. This focus on the processes involved in the continual reproduction of wage laborers reorients attention away from the sphere of formal production and into the informal sphere of the household where such reproductive activities take place. In other words, the focus becomes the unpaid work of those laboring in the everyday tasks of domestic production and maintenance, work which is typically carried out by women. In this way, introducing students to the concept of reproduction is a way to link structural features of capitalism to gender inequality, which, in turn, helps students understand that gender inequality has an economic, rather than a purely ideological, basis and, as such, intersects with other materially based inequalities such as those associated with social class and race.

As Carolyn Merchant (1989) succinctly defines it, "[r]eproduction is the biological and social process through which human beings are born, nurtured, socialized, and governed" (p. 14). Reproduction is especially emphasized by socialist ecofeminists who consider it to be "central to the concept of a just, sustainable world," because it encompasses all of the daily work and longer-term regenerative processes that make life possible (Merchant 2005, p. 208). If we again think of social theory as explaining the fundamental processes and relationships at play in social activity and organization, reproduction holds the key to understanding everything from how we as individuals are sustained day to day to how, in turn, the formal economy is maintained via this sustenance of workers to, most broadly, the social processes contributing to the ecological basis for existence. Quite simply, it is a central concept for understanding how we meet our everyday needs and how society, not to mention our species, assures its continuance. As such, when reproduction is threatened, so is the basis for humanity itself.

With this larger significance of the concept of reproduction as a backdrop, in my introductory classes I tend to use the term more narrowly, focusing on how it can help us understand the economic basis for gender inequality and also how gender relations are complicated by social class and race. I use Merchant's succinct definition of reproduction above when introducing the concept to students, letting them know I will be emphasizing daily nurturance and socialization. I begin the discussion noting Merchant's (1989) key insight that in pre- or non-capitalist, "subsistence-oriented economies, production and reproduction are united in the maintenance of the local community" (p. 14). To illustrate this, I draw a large circle on the whiteboard in the classroom and write "pre-capitalist" above it. I then explain (and write within it) that the circle can be thought of as the household, one of many in a community. Within those various households and also in the broader community in pre-capitalist societies, men and women labored together to provide for their basic subsistence needs (as well as trade in some goods), to socialize the young, and to model (and sometimes enforce) larger community norms, among other things. I ask students to give me concrete examples of these types of activities, and they typically come up with such things as food production and preparation, fiber and clothing production, tool making and repair, and caring for young children. I write these things inside the circle as "food," "cooking," "clothing," "tools," "child care." At this point I emphasize that this discussion is not meant to romanticize gender or generational relations in pre-capitalist societies—there were divisions of labor, and in most known societies women and children were certainly not given equal consideration to men—but rather that I am simply pointing out that the work everyone was engaged in was focused on producing those things that would support and maintain, i.e., reproduce, the household and the community, with trade of goods also acknowledged. I also note that the model of the household I am describing is an ideal type, prominent in the West, but that neither it nor the specific kinship relations implied therein were or are universal.

I then draw another large circle to the right of the household circle, and write above it, "capitalist-industrial," and within it, "formal economic sphere." I tell students that a key insight from Merchant (1989) is that "[u]nder capitalism, production and reproduction separate into two different spheres" (p. 14). I ask students what sorts of things began to be produced in factory settings with the rise of industrial capitalism in places such as Great Britain and the northeastern United States in the late 18th and 19th centuries. They typically immediately catch on and say things like "cloth" and "tools." Clearly, these examples are rather simplistic and straightforward, but it works to illustrate the underlying point, which is that with the rise of industrial capitalism, a formal economic sphere of production develops that is separate from the household, and it doesn't simply involve factories but also mines and mills; banking, accounting, and other financial services and institutions; and eventually industrial agriculture. As I explain this, I write some of the sites of these productive activities ("factories," "mines," "banks," etc.) inside the formal economic sphere circle. I then pause and ask students, "Who initially left the household to supervise and manually labor in this emerging formal economic sphere?" When they answer "men," I draw a little arrow pointing out from the upper right side of the formal economic sphere circle so that the circle resembles the astronomical symbol for Mars, or male. And who, I ask, stayed behind to maintain the household and provide daily nurturance to those men as well as to children? "Women," is of course the class answer, to which I respond by drawing a little cross at the bottom of the household circle, transforming it into the symbol for Venus, or female. I then ask the class what people who supervise and otherwise labor in factories, mines, accounting offices, and other workplaces in the formal economic sphere get in exchange for the work they do. When they inevitably say "money" I draw a dollar sign between the two circles with an arrow pointing from the formal economic sphere to the dollar sign. I then ask what one must have in order to procure clothing, tools, and food in such a system of production where these things or their material components are produced outside of the household, and when students again say "money," I circle the dollar sign and draw an arrow pointing from it to the domestic sphere. I then pause again for effect before asking the question, "Who do you think might have more power in this system?" This leads to a discussion of how having possession of and control over money in a system in which money is the means to get the basic necessities of life gives the people with such possession/control a great deal of power over those who lack such means.

In this simple illustration on the board, students can grasp how men's power over women became entrenched into a historically specific form of gender inequality with the rise of industrial capitalism and the accompanying separation of the production of many essential goods from what had been an integrated system of household production and reproduction. The household, formerly a site of production and consumption united in the overall process of reproduction, increasingly became simply a site of consumption and nurturance, one that was dependent on money earned in the formal economic sphere to purchase the necessities of life. At the same time, those reproductive activities that were still carried out in the household, such as the preparation of food and caring for the young, were obviously unpaid, furthering women's dependence on cash-earning men. I elaborate further that, understood in this way, the split between reproduction and production that accompanied the rise of industrial capitalism has contributed to our ideas about the proper roles for men and women. Modern-day associations we have of women as nurturers and men as breadwinners can in large part be traced to this historical shift in how their respective roles were divided up and, importantly, how those roles were subsequently valued (or not). Taking this insight one step further, I ask students to think about the assumptions we often have, when thinking about ourselves even, about women being more emotional and men being more rational; about women being better at taking care of children and men being more business-minded or adept at hard physical labor; and back to the simple astronomical signs on the board, the sense that "men are from Mars" while "women are from Venus." I ask students to consider how some of these traits that many of us assume to be inherent psychological tendencies and respective strengths or weaknesses of women and men are actually historically rooted in material changes in the way reproductive and productive activities were carried out. In this way, students can begin to see gender roles and gender inequality not as outgrowths of what they assume to be a natural division of labor but as historically conditioned phenomena linked to the structure of economic activity.

This rendering of the origins of modern-day gender inequality is, of course, incomplete, and pointing this out and inviting students to critique the basic model on the board provides the perfect segue for further discussion. I ask students, for example, "Who often worked on factory floors as industrial-capitalism progressed?" to which students can immediately respond that young women and children from the lower classes were often employed in such settings in certain industries, which leads to a discussion of how the historical split between production and reproduction was not a uniform process across social classes. We also discuss how the relatively high incomes of the emerging upper middle class afforded women in such households the luxury of employing working-class girls and women to do most of their reproductive/domestic labor, in the process undermining those economically disadvantaged women's ability to keep up with the reproduction of their own households. Furthermore, the capitalist-industrial system in the United States was heavily dependent on raw materials produced by slave labor in the South, complicating the narrative of the significance of the productive-reproductive split for gender relations when considering the experiences of African American women and men. Finally, I ask students to consider what changes the industrial intensification of the 20th century and eventual post-industrial shift have had on the productive-reproductive split illustrated on the board. I inevitably end up drawing additional arrows between the two circles representing women joining the formal economic sphere in greater numbers; reproductive activities like cooking and childrearing becoming partially subsumed by the formal economic sphere as services that can be bought and sold and that are often performed by socioeconomically disadvantaged women of color; and, more recently, some men contributing more than they have in the past to the domestic sphere in terms of the time they spend on reproductive labor in addition to their paid labor outside the home as men and women try to juggle the demands of dual-earner households. This is also the perfect time in the discussion to critique the heteronormative assumptions underlying the model on the board in light of changing norms regarding same-sex relationships in the 20th and 21st centuries (although my students don't typically point this out, so I usually end up adding this observation myself). This final stage of the discussion gives students practice honing their powers of critique and also enables them to link the historical split between reproduction and production to more contemporary tensions between these two realms, tensions with which they are probably all too familiar from observing their own families growing up and will likely continue to struggle with in the future themselves.

Conclusion

It is worth acknowledging that some may read this chapter and think that I have watered down sociological theory so that it fits with a rather simplified reading of the world. This is a valid criticism. I, too, sometimes wonder if more harm than good may come from replacing nuanced, theoretically sophisticated explanations with broad-brushed, intentionally simplified interpretations of an admittedly more complex social reality. However, when these thoughts of self-doubt creep in, I remind myself of my goal in the introductory sociology classroom, a classroom filled at my institution with non-majors who may never again have two and a half hours a week to think about society and their place in it in a critical manner. When I think about the uniqueness of that opportunity—the opportunity to hold the social world at an arm's length rather than being unreflectively immersed in it—I know that I have to make the intellectual exercise (a) interesting and (b) comprehensible. The half dozen students out of a classroom of twenty-five who might actually be able to read *The Economic and Philosophic Manuscripts* would instead of being inspired by sociology be bored to sleep by it. Instead of feeling sociological concepts as lived experience, my students could end up permanently turned off to anything and anyone who demanded nuanced details over lived, felt understanding. In a world increasingly divided along both educational and ideological lines, I would rather give my students a sense that they can see through at least some of the mystification and understand basic material realities about the world we all inhabit.

References

Eitzen, S., & Baca Zinn, M. (2007). *In conflict and order: Understanding society* (11th ed.). Boston: Allyn & Bacon.

Merchant, C. (1989). *Ecological revolutions: Nature, gender, and science in New England*. Chapel Hill: University of North Carolina Press.

Merchant, C. (2005). *Radical ecology: The search for a livable world* (2nd ed.). New York: Routledge.

Schlosser, E. (2002). *Fast food nation: The dark side of the all-American meal*. New York: Harper Perennial.

Tucker, R. C. (Ed.). (1978). *The Marx-Engels reader* (2nd ed.). New York: W.W. Norton & Company Inc.

Teaching Global Inequality Through the World of Commodities

Eric M. Edwards

Author's Reflexive Statement

I am an academic who comes from a working-class background. We were formerly a rare species, but in more recent years we have become both more common and more visible on college campuses. This is, of course, a positive development. Economic hardship affects billions of people worldwide, but "traditional" scholars (who, one presumes, tend to come from middle-class or elite households) may miss the experiences of desperation, alienation, stress, embarrassment, and material want that dire economic conditions engender. Those of us who have experienced life near the bottom of the socioeconomic hierarchy have insights that potentially could lead to a more robust analysis of class inequality and a more comprehensive view of solutions to poverty.

My experiences as a working-class youth have shaped nearly every aspect of my life, including what I spend my time teaching and researching. I am confident that I would not be a sociologist who studies and teaches about class inequality without the experience of material deprivation in my earlier years. Even though some of the events I detail below happened decades ago, they still stand out clearly to me.

I spent the first nine years of my life in a singlewide trailer. We later moved to a doublewide, but that move did not indicate that times were improving for my family. We never had enough. My father was too proud to take any kind of government assistance, but I am sure that we qualified. My mother worked as a housekeeper at local motels and nursing homes. My father sold industrial parts to area food-processing companies. While we were never in danger of being homeless, we had some lean times. My parents never talked about our poverty, but my siblings and I felt its effects acutely.

E. M. Edwards (✉)
University of Wisconsin-Superior, Superior, WI, USA
e-mail: eedward2@uwsuper.edu

K. Haltinner and L. Hormel (eds.), *Teaching Economic Inequality and Capitalism in Contemporary America*, https://doi.org/10.1007/978-3-319-71141-6_7

I wore second-hand clothes, either from cousins, yard sales, or the thrift store. Other children noticed; the crueler varieties of youth at my school would make fun of me for it when something I wore was obviously from a no-longer-cool era. I did not visit a dentist until I was twenty-six years old. When I entered graduate school, I had dental insurance for the first time in my life. Our pets never went to the veterinarian. They either got better on their own, they died, or my dad would end their suffering with his gun.

As I got older, I started to become ashamed of the poverty I lived in. For example, when I was in eighth grade, my younger brother and I asked our mother to drop us off two blocks away from school so that our classmates would not see our family car: an old, ugly green station wagon. My dad must have kept that car functional by swearing at it! The station wagon was just one of a series of car purchases of a similar nature: buy an old used model, drive it for as long as possible, and then get another similar vehicle. My wife and I bought a new car when I was thirty-five. It was the first new vehicle I had ever owned, been a passenger in, or driven.

It did not take long, though, for my embarrassment to turn to anger and resentment directed toward institutions that promoted systemic injustice. Even as a high school student, I understood that the inequality I was witnessing and experiencing was not my family's fault, but a structural result of the pursuit of profit by capitalists. These views fit in very well with radical sociological views of the world. Once I entered college, I found sociology to be a place that nurtured and developed my own critique of the established social order. Also, my personal interactions sharpened this critique: my first college roommate was able to get into the university only because his wealthy grandfather made a substantial donation to the school. My roommate claimed that it was enough to fund a new parking lot.

It also did not take me long to realize that my own experience of childhood poverty pales in comparison to the deprivation that many people around the globe (including in the economic core) experience. Garment factory workers in Bangladesh, banana plantation laborers in Honduras, and electronics assemblers in China have it far worse than I ever did. I have never had to live or work in a building that was unsafe for human habitation, nor have I ever been faced with chronic malnutrition. A singlewide trailer and second-hand clothes are not ideal circumstances, but it certainly beats living in a one-room house and being unable to afford to buy shoes. I was completely ignorant of the causes of these problems until I was well into my undergraduate career. To me, this tale of global inequality is such a central part of our lives and our history that we need to share it as early and as often as we can. I find it unacceptable that people in the economic core know so little about global poverty. As a sociologist, it is my job to understand why these inequalities exist and to come up with the most effective ways to get rid of poverty around the globe. As a teacher, I need to assist students to come to these conclusions on their own. The way I have found that facilitates an in-depth exploration of global inequality is to focus on the world of commodity production.

Using Commodities as a Lens to Study Global Inequality

Global economic inequality can be a difficult topic for students to comprehend. Some of the causes of the problem both past and present are complex and interrelated. The history of imperialism, efforts by former colonies to remove themselves from direct imperial rule, the role of the global lending agencies like the International Monetary Fund in perpetuating the poverty of former colonies, and the dominance of multinational corporations are some of the major concepts one needs to understand in order to come to terms with the continuing exploitation of the economic periphery. In addition to the lack of student knowledge about the above topics, a teacher has to contend with the problem of student disconnection to the lives of people around the globe. It is too easy either to know nothing about working conditions in other countries or to feel that there is nothing one can do about the problem. Also, students have inherited a disposition from the society they inhabit that encourages them to blame individuals for the poverty these individuals experience.

Students have little difficulty seeing the interconnectedness of the world when it comes to technology and communication. When it comes to understanding the meaning behind the country of origin of one's smartphone, or what is involved in obtaining one's daily dose of coffee, the picture becomes a lot murkier.

I have found that the most effective way to overcome these conceptual blockages is to have students discuss, read about, research, and present on commodities. There are many reasons for doing so, but one of the main ones is the immediacy of commodities. We are all surrounded by things to buy every moment of our lives, yet they remain mysterious. The corporations that attempt to dominate our off-the-job behavior (Dawson 2003) bombard us with advertisements for their products. The Internet is as much a shopping destination as it is a source of collective knowledge or an attempt to communicate with others; in fact, social media companies such as Facebook are far more interested in obtaining marketing information from their users than they are in facilitating social connections. In other words, commodities are a familiar, yet strange, part of all our lives.

Marx (1976 [1867]) felt that the commodity was of such importance to understanding the capitalist mode of production that he began the first volume of Capital with a discussion of how to define commodities. For Marx, commodities are the key to understanding labor exploitation. He separated goods into use values (that is, an item's usefulness) and exchange values (the value a seller receives for the good). Within capitalism, according to Marx, exchange value becomes dominant to the extent that the usefulness of commodities does not matter for purposes of determining what capitalists choose to manufacture. Since companies have to maximize profit—if they did not make this effort, no one would invest in them—they have no choice but to emphasize exchange value over use value. Single-cup coffee makers, for example, do not exist because they make our lives better, but because they turn coffee making into a more profitable endeavor for coffee companies. If studying the commodity was good enough for history's greatest analyst and critic of capitalism, I decided that it was good enough for my students.

The central concept of how we analyze commodities in the class is Marx's (1976 [1867]) theory of commodity fetishism. Marx stated that commodities contain much more meaning than their surface characteristics would lead us to believe. Contained within each commodity is a tale of exploitation. Marx claimed that commodity production in a capitalist economy took on its exploitative character because of the dominance of exchange value. In the effort to maximize profit, companies will pay employees the least amount of money possible and demand the greatest possible amount of labor power. The commodities created in this process represent this exploitation and environmental degradation, but market exchange mystifies the origins of commodities.

A particularly vivid example of commodity fetishism I share with my class is the April 24, 2013 Rana Plaza disaster in Bangladesh. On this date, a building housing garment workers collapsed. Over one thousand people died, and many thousands were wounded (Smith 2016). The workers were making clothing for many familiar Western brands, such as Benetton and J.C. Penney (O'Connor 2014). None of these details, from the low pay to the extremely unsafe working conditions, are apparent to people who buy these clothing brands. Consumers may have an idea that sweatshops exist, but the brands themselves certainly are not sharing any of this information. This point—the location of exchange—is where the commodity takes on a mystified character. Marx (1976 [1867]) used the metaphor of a "veil" that obscures all of us from the process involved with the production of commodities. He stated that, in order to bring these working conditions to light, we have to investigate what happens behind the scenes in commodity production. Hudson and Hudson (2003), referencing Marx's metaphor detailed above, referred to this process as "removing the veil" that obscures the production process.

Commodity-specific research projects have a long history in the social sciences. Some recent examples of these studies are the meat industry (Weis 2014), fish (Longo et al. 2015), chocolate (Off 2008), smartphones (Woyke 2014), and water (Barlow 2007; Feldman 2012). Not only do these types of studies contain important information and analysis about these industries, but also they illustrate to students how to carry out a commodity-based research project themselves.

In other words, every commodity contains a story. The production of nearly every commodity involves exploitation of labor and/or some kind of problematic interaction with the environment. The process of exchange covers up these stories by substituting exploitation with an interaction between a neutral commodity and an individual's money. The class I teach (titled Global Social Problems) is a semester-long effort to get beyond this superficial relationship with commodities, uncover these stories, and in the process expose the structural roots of global inequality. This assignment would also be appropriate for any globally-themed class or as a smaller assignment in any class that has an inequality-based theme.

Class and Assignment Details

At the beginning of the semester, I tell the students that the class they are taking is about commodities. We talk about the concepts and the background material they need to understand in order to explore the world of commodity production. This discussion includes a brief history of how we got to the current state of global inequality. Students learn briefly about the five-hundred-year history of imperialism, anti-imperialist movements in the Global South, and the establishment of the International Monetary Fund and the World Bank. As a part of this history, students explore the development of race and racism, the "white man's burden" approach to global relations, and the creation of capitalism as a class-based system of exploitation. They also learn about and discuss theories of capitalist development, such as monopoly-finance capital (Foster and McChesney 2012) and neoliberalism. These two theoretical perspectives provide contrasting views of why the global economy has taken on the character that it has. Further, they have completely different explanations for why poverty persists for citizens of the global South. Although sociologists correctly dismiss the neoliberal view, we treat it seriously in the class by looking at evidence to determine what the experience of countries has been like during the era of global corporate dominance. The evidence, including the persistence of extreme poverty and hunger in the economic periphery, the proliferation of exploitative "sweatshop" labor rather than meaningful work, and the failure of international lending agencies to help former colonies to improve the lives of people living in these countries (Smith 2016; Toussaint and Millet 2010) leads students to conclude that neoliberal views of development have little merit.

The next stage of the class involves an overview and discussion of Marx's concepts of value and commodity fetishism. I use a large number of examples in teaching about use value, exchange value, and commodity fetishism. These examples include in-class props that both the students and I bring. Often I will ask students to provide an example of a commodity they believe has no use value but has an exchange value, and vice versa. Students have provided many compelling examples in the past; it is a great tool for developing an understanding of value. To explain commodity fetishism, I ask students to name a commodity. Together, we walk through a rudimentary process of what it takes to make the commodity. Common examples my classes have used in the past are t-shirts or meat products. I also like to show students a documentary with details on commodity production. An effective example is the film *Black Gold* (Francis and Francis 2006), which is about coffee production and the plight of Ethiopian coffee growers. The film is 75 min long; I have found that, in a 50 min class session, it is best to start it on a Monday, finish it on Wednesday, and spend the rest of Wednesday and Friday discussing it. Of course, the timing would work better with a 75 min class. By the end of this section, students should have a strong grasp of the exploitation involved in commodity production, why it is obscured, and why it is important to "remove the veil" (Hudson and Hudson 2003) between us and the commodities we purchase.

Shortly after our discussion of commodity fetishism, I provide details on the main assignment: a student research project on a commodity of the individual student's choosing. The culmination of the project is an in-class presentation and/or a research paper. I have had more satisfactory outcomes with the former, as students get to learn from each other about details on specific commodity production practices, but a research paper without a presentation also leads to desirable results. When I teach the global inequality class via distance learning, I have students focus on creating a research paper instead of an in-class presentation. An instructor who is more innovative than I am could find a way to have a distance learning class submit a presentation.

I provide students with a list of commodities from which they can choose. Alternatively, students can propose to research a commodity that is not on my list. Some of the commodities are everyday items such as bananas or cane sugar. Others are a little more obscure, like nuclear energy or flower bouquets. Still others are illegal drugs, such as heroin. I try to make sure that all of the commodities contain a global aspect to their production, but if a student suggests doing research on a commodity that is compelling enough, I will approve the project even if there is no obvious connection to exploitative labor conditions in the economic periphery. For example, a student recently completed a research project on pharmaceuticals. The student presented evidence that pharmaceutical companies are conducting unethical clinical drug trials on impoverished people in the global South (Schipper and Weyzig 2008). Other examples of student-selected commodities are infant formula, wine, hair extensions, and the video game industry. The only danger to doing research on some commodities (such as hair extensions) is that there may not be much information available on how they are made.

Since I teach about global inequality in the context of a general education class I have an additional goal of introducing students to literature searches. I find it helpful to work with my university's librarians to develop a class session led by a librarian on how to do a literature search. In addition, I spend time in class working on the process of doing research, sorting out relevant sources from biased (i.e., corporate) sources, and constructing an effective presentation. It is my hope that devoting time to these subjects assists students both in my class and when they do research and presentations in other courses.

The students are required to submit an annotated bibliography of their sources at least a month in advance of the presentation. This requirement assures me that the students are not going to save their research until the last minute. It also gives me a chance to evaluate their sources. I can determine if a source is either sound or biased, then pass along this information to the students before they engage in serious research. In addition, I can make recommendations for additional books or journal articles that will help the student create a richer presentation.

While they are conducting their research, we discuss global environmental problems. As with our discussion of global economic inequality, we examine relevant sociological concepts and apply them to the experiences of people around the world. The concepts I use here are ecological modernization (Mol et al. 2009) and metabolic rift (Foster et al. 2010). We talk about the connection of environmental problems to economic and social problems, particularly the growth/profit imperative of corporations, the debt burdens of former colonies (Toussaint and Millet 2010), the connection of these problems with structural racism within and between countries, and the growing class inequality in both core and periphery nations. In other words, students build upon what they have learned in the earlier part of the semester in order to obtain a fuller understanding of economic and environmental inequality.

When we have concluded the section on environmental problems, we spend two to three weeks learning about a commodity that we have not yet discussed in class. This section is an exercise in getting students prepared to present on their own commodity. Not only do we learn about the new commodity, but also I encourage students to connect the production of this commodity to all of the concepts we studied earlier. I have students read a book about the commodity we are discussing. While I have used several different books, one that I have found effective is Clapp's book *Food* (2012), which is an exploration of the global food economy. Any example will work, as long as there is no overlap between it and commodities that students have chosen.

We dedicate the final three weeks of class to student presentations and to a discussion of possible solutions to global economic inequality. I tell the students that they have to make their presentations at least seven minutes long, but no longer than fifteen minutes. I require students who are not presenting on a particular day to write down at least one observation or question from each presentation they witness. I find that this requirement both encourages attendance at all presentation sessions and facilitates asking questions when the presenter has finished. The time limit mentioned above assures us that there will be time for questions at the end of the presentations for that day.

While students have a great deal of freedom in the details of their commodity they choose to present, I ask students to focus on the following:

- The working conditions that workers face when creating the commodity;
- Environmental problems associated with the production of their commodity;
- How the production of this commodity relates to relevant class concepts;
- What, if anything, people and groups are doing about the problems that their commodity's production causes.

The first and second categories are, of course, essential to "removing the veil" obscuring commodity production from us (Hudson and Hudson 2003). As stated earlier, most commodities have some kind of negative effect on both labor and the environment. It is the task of students to find out what these problems are. I have observed that students do an excellent job on this part of the presentation. They know what to look for by the time we get to the end of the semester, as they have encountered several examples of commodity analysis in the class.

The focus of the presentation, however, is not only to have students describe the working conditions and effects on the environment that their commodity contains, but also to make connections between their commodity and the concepts that we have discussed throughout the semester. Relating the commodity to class concepts is, without a doubt, the most difficult task students have. Some students do not even make the attempt. Others try to make the association, but have an inadequate analysis. Approximately twenty-five percent of students are able to execute this task successfully. I am still searching for a way to increase the number of students who are able to consistently make connections between the course concepts and the examples they are using. I would anticipate that this percentage would increase if the class consisted of sociology majors and minors, but I teach it as a general education course.

It is also important for students to examine potential solutions to problems that production of their commodity creates. I believe that it is vital for students to understand that people are not helpless, and that people are willing and able to organize for social change. For example, a student who presented recently on the global beef industry pointed out that the amount of beef that people consume in the U.S. and Europe is ecologically unsustainable. She identified the growth of vegetarian and vegan diets as a potential site for social movements aimed at decreasing the amount of meat that people in the global North consume. When students share actions like this one, they can get a sense that they are not helpless individuals trapped in a perpetual system of greed and domination. In other words, they may learn that human agency matters.

Once all presentations are complete, we have a class discussion about similarities and differences in the production processes of commodities. Typically, students are able to successfully point out the important connections between commodities. They talk about how, while there are obvious differences between the production processes of specific products, they all involve a devaluation (both quantitative and qualitative) of human labor. We discuss why this devaluation occurs; the students are able to explain it in terms of the pursuit of profit above all other concerns.

We end the class by talking about small- and large-scale solutions to the global economic crisis and by discussing how people in the United States are affected by global commodity production. The discussion of the former involves thinking about alternatives to profit-driven systems at the local, national, and global levels. It is important for students to understand that such efforts are happening currently and that they are happening all over the globe. In our discussion of how the global economy affects students, we talk about the uncertainty in solid job prospects, the departure of industry, the decline in labor union membership over the last several decades (Dunn and Walker 2016), and the increasing wealth of the richest proportion of the population as some of the consequences of monopoly-finance capital (Foster and McChesney 2012). I make an effort to end the class on a positive note, as mentioned earlier in this paragraph, by talking about the immense capacity of human societies for justice-based social change.

Outcomes and Conclusion

Students have told me repeatedly that the project has a profound effect on their understanding of global inequality. The assignment not only gives students a greater chance at retaining concepts related to global inequality and an increased knowledge about their commodity of choice, but also it:

- Develops their ability to make connections between sociological concepts and experiences of countries, regions, and individuals;
- Allows them to see similarities in the production process of different commodities;
- Gives them a chance to practice conveying complex information to an audience;
- Encourages students to view their own lives in the context of a globalized system of production and exchange;
- Helps students to develop empathy for others who are experiencing difficult conditions. When the abstract becomes concrete, it becomes more difficult to avoid or explain away a problem.

As stated above, the main goal of the presentation assignment in particular, and the class in general, is to assist students in the retention of information concerning global inequality. I am interested principally in their ability to retain and apply conceptual information. The specific details could disappear, but as long as students remember the concepts that facilitate analysis of commodity production, they can find the details themselves. Also, the structure of the class itself is important for retention of concepts. I could lecture to students for weeks about the concepts and examples of global inequality, but I believe they would retain almost none of the material after the semester was over. It is my hope that the active nature of this assignment (and the class in general) assist in the "rewiring" of the brain; that is, students become more disposed to think about the world in social-structural terms when they complete assignments that encourage such ways of thinking. I believe that this task is (or should be) the central goal of all sociologists.

Making this teaching strategy work in a larger class or in a distance learning environment is eminently possible. Since I work in a liberal arts environment, my classes are small, so I can lead our exploration of commodities in a discussion-based style. Also, because I never have more than twenty-five to thirty students in a class, presentations take up three weeks or less of class time. If I had to teach a larger global inequality class, I would use more discussion groups rather than entire-class discussions. Depending on the size of the class, it might make more sense to require students to submit the assignment as a research paper rather than as a presentation. The only drawback to this strategy is that students would not get to learn from each other unless the instructor accounted for this need in some other manner, such as via small groups. The same is true for an online version of the course. In the distance learning environment, an instructor could require a research paper (as I have done in the three times I have taught the course online) or could become more creative with the execution of the assignment.

I will end by stating that I do not believe that we can understand capitalism without coming to terms with the labor exploitation and environmental degradation that are necessary for the system to keep functioning. The reason I have found structuring my class around commodities to be so effective is because it is the best way I can think of to encourage students to explore the systematic global inequality necessary to produce the things the students may take for granted. As this structural inequality has intensified over the last few decades, it becomes more important than ever to help students to attain this understanding. Increased knowledge of the situation does not guarantee positive action, of course, but remaining ignorant certainly guarantees inaction.

References

Barlow, M. (2007). *Blue covenant: The global water crisis and the coming battle for the right to water*. New York: New Press.
Clapp, J. (2012). *Food*. London: Polity Press.
Dawson, M. (2003). *The consumer trap: Big business marketing in American life*. Urbana, IL: University of Illinois Press.
Dunn, M. & Walker, J. (2016). Union membership in the United States." *Bureau of Labor Statistics*. https://www.bls.gov/spotlight/2016/union-membership-in-the-united-states/pdf/union-membership-in-the-united-states.pdf. Accessed 27 March 2017.
Feldman, D.L. (2012). *Water*. Cambridge, UK: Polity Press.
Francis, M. & Francis, N. (producers and directors). (2006). *Black gold*. United States: California Newsreel.
Foster, J. B., & McChesney, R. W. (2012). *The endless crisis: How monopoly-finance capital produces stagnation and upheaval from the USA to China*. New York: Monthly Review Press.
Foster, J. B., Clark, B., & York, R. (2010). *The ecological rift: Capitalism's war on the earth*. New York: Monthly Review Press.
Hudson, I., & Hudson, M. (2003). Removing the veil? Commodity fetishism, fair trade, and the environment. *Organization & Environment, 16*(4), 413–430.
Longo, S., Clausen, R., & Clark, B. (2015). *The tragedy of the commodity: Oceans, fisheries, and aquaculture*. New Brunswick, NJ: Rutgers University Press.
Marx, K. (1976 [1867]). *Capital, volume 1*. New York: Penguin Press.
Mol, A. P. J., Sonnenfeld, D. A., & Spaargaren, G. (2009). *The ecological modernisation reader: Environmental reform in theory and practice*. London: Routledge.
O'Connor, C. (2014). These retailers in Bangladesh factory disaster have yet to compensate victims. *Forbes*. http://www.forbes.com/sites/clareoconnor/2014/04/26/these-retailers-involved-in-bangladesh-factory-disaster-have-yet-to-compensate-victims/#4a20ede657c5. Accessed 27 March 2017.
Off, C. (2008). *Bitter chocolate: The dark side of the world's most seductive sweet*. New York: New Press.
Schipper, I. & Weyzig, F. (2008). SOMO briefing paper on ethics in clinical trials#1: Examples of unethical trials. https://www.somo.nl/examples-of-unethical-trials/. Accessed 27 March 2017.
Smith, J. (2016). *Imperialism in the 21st century*. New York: Monthly Review Press.
Toussaint, E., & Millet, D. (2010). *Debt, the IMF, and the World Bank: Sixty questions, sixty answers*. New York: Monthly Review Press.
Weis, T. (2014). *The ecological hoofprint: The global burden of industrial livestock*. London: Zed Books Ltd.
Woyke, E. (2014). *The smartphone: Anatomy of an industry*. New York: New Press.

Radical Pedagogical Homesteading: Returning the 'Species' to Our 'Being'

Phoebe Godfrey

Author's Reflexive Statement

I was born in the United States to white middle-class parents, both of whom were from the U.K. and grew up in London during World War II. My mother was born middle-class and later worked as an occupational therapist and my father was born working-class but earned a Ph.D. in chemistry and worked in a lab and then as a chemical consultant. These mixed identities, my father being working-class and a chemist and my mother being an occupational therapist meant that in our house my parents, and consequently my brother and I, were always making things, fixing things, building things, designing things and being creative, while also having the educational benefits of being middle-class. Additionally, for much of my childhood we lived in the countryside in Europe (Switzerland and Belgium) and so I wasn't exposed to television until I was 14 when we returned to the US. Therefore, my leisure time as a child was spent doing 'homesteading' type activities—gardening, cooking, sewing, knitting, building (such as bookshelves, sculptures, a patio and deck)—as well as doing artistic activities, such as painting, ceramics, drawing, woodwork—all things that I still do today. I draw from these early creative experiences when designing activities for my classes and these experiences have helped me develop what I refer to here as Radical Pedagogical Homesteading (RPH).

As for my personal commitment to social justice, my parents were both socialists and committed to making a more just and equal world, although my mother did so

I was born in 1964 in New Jesrsey, USA to white middle-class parents, both of whom were from the UK and grew up in London during World War II

P. Godfrey (✉)
University of Connecticut, Connecticut, USA
e-mail: phoebe.godfrey@uconn.edu

K. Haltinner and L. Hormel (eds.), *Teaching Economic Inequality and Capitalism in Contemporary America*, https://doi.org/10.1007/978-3-319-71141-6_8

in a hands-on way, and my father did so in a conceptual way (representing a divide that, as I discuss below, needs to be bridged). Finally, I would say the most influential force in my commitment to social justice came from the school I attended for five years in Belgium—The British School of Brussels—that was started in 1970 by Alan Humphries. Humphries had formally been involved with King Alfred School, London—a school my mother had attended in the late 1940s. King Alfred School, founded in 1898 for boys and girls, sought to break away from conventional educational practices and focus on drawing out "the self-activity of the child," with the emphasis being on learning for its own sake. This emphasis embedded within my psyche the importance for me as a teacher to give students (and ideally everyone) the opportunity to engage in what Marx called 'free conscious activity' and that is fundamental to our 'species-being.' It is therefore for me not just a concept from Marx that I teach, nor merely one that I attempt to practice in my classes so that students may also experience its meaning, but more significantly it is a concept that I consequently live as I continue to practice aspects of Radical Homesteading at home and at work.

Introduction

The first narrative in Studs Terkel's infamous journalistic study *Working* (1974) is from Mike Lefevre, a laborer who muses on his life as someone who does "strictly muscle work." At one point, Mike details what he means:

> You can't take pride any more. You remember when a guy could point to a house he built, how many logs he stacked. He built it and he was proud of it. I don't really think I could be proud if a contractor built a home for me. I would be tempted to get in there and kick the carpenter in the ass (laughs), and take the saw away from him. C'ause I would have to be part of it, you know (p. 1).

One person, although not a builder himself, who did *know* about Mike's desire to be "a part of it" in order to feel "pride" was Karl Marx. In fact, Marx recognized this desire as a visceral and universally human one and termed it *Gattungswesen*, translated as "species-being". As with all opaque philosophical concepts, Marx's included, there is much debate as to their exact intended meaning (Czank 2012). That said, my interpretation of species-being, like that of Czank (2012), is it represents an expression of our "universal nature" (p. 318), that which makes us human. However, what I explicitly add, as does Dant (2010), is the recognition that the expression of this universal nature was for Marx denoted by our unique capacity for conscious and self-directed *creative* production. As Marx states:

> It is just in his work upon the objective world that man really proves himself as a *species-being*. This production is his active species life. By means of it nature appears as his work and his reality. The object of labor is, therefore, the *objectification of man's species life*; for he no longer reproduces himself merely intellectually, as in his consciousness, but actively and in a real sense, and sees his own reflection in the world which he has constructed.

> While, therefore, alienated labor takes away the object of production from man, it also takes away his *species life*, his real objectivity as a species-being, and changes his advantage over animals into a disadvantage in so far as his inorganic body, nature, is taken from him (Marx, as cited in Fromm 1974, p. 102–103, *italics* in original).

In other words, the fashioning of nature through creative work into "his reality" is for Marx central to the construction of human society, as in a humanly intelligible world, as well as the collective and conscious expression of human identity.

Dyer-Witheford (2004) offers that, "…species-being is the social elaboration and expansion of…life-needs. This process entails material capacity, self-consciousness, and collective organization, all feeding into each other. Species-being is a constitutive power, a bootstrapped, self-reinforcing loop of social cooperation, technoscientific competencies, and conscious awareness" (p. 476). As Marx argues, under capitalism the laborer is separated, hence estranged, from his creative capacity and from "the object of his production," since he has no agency in his productive activity. Thus, as Dyer-Witheford (2004) further observes, "'alienation' of species-being,… is not estrangement from a normative, natural human condition, but rather of who, or what, controls and limits the processes of ceaseless human self-development" (p. 477).

Given that the unequal and alienating power dynamics of social class under capitalism permeate all aspects of our society, Marx's concept of species-being can be applied to the realm of academia where much of the labor [learning] done by students is 'estranged labor', hence estranged learning, in that their species-being is not given free and conscious opportunities to thrive. Since most of this estrangement on the part of students happens in the classroom and around course work, where their own learning is 'taken away from their species-life,' the goal of this chapter is to offer instructors an *unalienated* way to not only teach these Marxian concepts but to also illustrate how they can be applied across the curriculum. In so doing, this chapter will present Radical Pedagogical Homesteading (RPH), a term inspired by Hayes's *Radical Homemakers* (2010).

The term 'homesteading' is often used interchangeably with 'homemaking' as in Hayes' choice of term, although nowhere in her book does she use 'homesteading' nor does she say why she chose 'homemaking' over 'homesteading'. I am choosing 'homesteading' despite its historical racist legacy for the reason that other than in Hayes' case, most uses of 'homemaking' based on a Google search do not link it to the larger issue of 'self-sufficiency' which is the meaning I seek to emphasize. Hayes likewise is interested in self-sufficiency, and argues for the reuniting of the day job (done under the extractive economic rules of capitalism) with directly meeting our needs in order to collectively create a "life-serving economy" for us and the planet, as opposed to an alienated one that is subsequently destroying both (p. 13). To further illustrate RPH, examples of classroom based activities that can easily be modified will be offered with the aim to turn the classroom from being based on the tenants of capitalism and the estranged labor/learning of students (and consequently yet to a lesser degree of instructors), to being sites where everyone's 'species' can be an emerging expression of their 'being'.

From Radical Homemakers to Radical Pedagogical Homesteading

Mike Lefevre's intuitively Marxian observation that there was a time when "… a guy could point to a house he built, how many logs he stacked. He built it and he was proud of it" (p. 1) is similar to one that Hayes (2010) makes in relation to food production. She shares her discernment that "Eating local, organic, sustainably raised, nutrient-dense food was possible for every American, not just wealthy gourmets or self-reliant organic farmers. But to do it, *we needed to bring back the homemaker*" (p. 12–13, *italics* in original), the one whose job was to produce goods for the household.

This realization shocked Hayes in that, as a self-described feminist, she recognized how much of feminism was about the "right to go to work, to achieve personal fulfillment through professional accomplishment" (p. 7). However, in researching further she found that "the household did not become the 'women's sphere' until the industrial revolution" (p. 14). In fact, based on the work of historian Ruth Schwartz Cowan in feudal Europe 'housewives' and 'husbands' were terms used for "free people who owned their own homes and lived off their own land" (p. 14). In this time the house was a site of collective production that, although divided by sex in terms of tasks, had "… an equal distribution of domestic work" (p. 14).

With the industrial revolution and the need for workers, adult men (and in some areas teenage girls as well) began to leave for wage labor, thereby slowly transforming the home from a site of production into a site of consumption, stripping in different ways the formally 'free' housewife and the husband of their species-being. The remaining 'housewife' was, by the 1960s, ripe for a feminist revolution and yet, as Hayes explores, many women, as well as men, are now seeking to return to the home but not as mere 'housewives,' as the term is currently understood but as 'homemakers', or rather 'radical homemakers.' Adding the term 'radical' for Hayes implies "men and women who have chosen to make family, community, social justice and the health of the planet the governing principles of their lives" (p. 13). Furthermore, she explains (p. 13):

> Radical Homemakers use life skills and relationships as a replacement for gold [money], on the premise that he or she who doesn't need the gold [money] can change the rules. The greater our domestic skills, be they to plant a garden, grow tomatoes on an apartment balcony, mend a shirt, repair an appliance, provide for our children and loved ones, the less dependent we are on the gold [money].

Recognizing that for most workers gold, hence money, is a product of wage labor, radical homesteading increases creative home production and offers pathways out of dependency on capitalism, thereby offering means to reclaim one's species-being.

Transitioning this definition of radical homemaker to include the term pedagogy, as in radical pedagogical homesteading (RPH), correlates with Freire's (2000) recognition that much of education involves a "banking" method whereby information [like gold] is merely deposited by instructors into the passive minds of students [banks] without them being critically, actively, and/or creatively involved. Thus, students, like workers, have their species-being taken from them when their work—their learning—is estranged. For Freire the antidote to this alienated banking method is to engage students in problem-posing that nurtures reflective critical thinking and that invites a conscious awareness directed towards their liberation and the liberation of their communities. Additionally, I would add that Freire's term '*conscientization*' is instrumental to this process in creating opportunities for students to deepen their levels of awareness through *embodied* activities that involve hands-on collaborative and physically manifested creative production.

Berila in *Integrating Mindfulness Into Anti-Oppression Pedagogy* (2015) recognizes the importance of, "[t]he reclamation of embodiment" within "social justice contexts because oppression is held in our bodies, our hearts, our psyches, and our minds…Part of the work toward social justice, then, *requires* [italics in original] a re-connection to ourselves and to others, so that our profound interdependence is both revealed and treasured" (p. 34). For Berila this 'reclamation of embodiment' involves using mindfulness to help students look within themselves to identify what they are feeling and where they are feeling it within their physical selves in order to counter "the disembodiment that pervades Western culture" (p. 38). She argues, "By developing mindful critical first-person inquiry skills, students learn to see and feel how gendered, racial, sexual, economic, and ableist power dynamics shape their bodily experiences. They also learn tools to cultivate oppositional, more empowered bodily experiences" (p. 39). To achieve this Berila adds that "*embodied learning is generative* [italics in original]" (p. 41). By this she means that students themselves create knowledge through conscious engagement with their own bodies. Ways that such 'generative' practice can manifest are through "journaling, performance exercises, dance, and meditation" (p. 41) a point with which I totally agree.

RPH goes further, recognizing that craft, known as vocational skills, can also manifest embodied learning if the learner is allowed to engage in their species-being. If not, as Marx states, people lose their "… advantage over animals…[in]…that [their] inorganic body, nature, is taken from [them]" (Marx, as cited in Fromm 1974, pp. 102–103). By this Marx means that when we are not engaging our species-being we become alienated on multiple levels. We become alienated from our own bodies/selves, then from each other/our species and from nature.

In *Why School? Reclaiming Education for All of Us* (2009), Mike Rose identifies the split between "the academic and the vocational" (pp. 81–2) as one of the more prevailing and damaging divisions within the high school curriculum. Although there have been efforts to bridging this gap the emphasis for Rose has mostly been on making the vocation more academic thereby continuing to reinforce the bias view of knowledge that separates the two. Integrating more embodied physical work or tasks is generally ignored in higher education, unless such tasks fall within the arts, or if they are done in a laboratory where the emphasis tends to be on the intellectual benefits through research rather than the production of useful objects.

The point being, though, that the bias towards a disembodied 'brain' is deeply embedded in academia and both taints and limits opportunities for student engagement and learning, including learning the *value* of learning. I do not know a teacher, myself included, who hasn't at some point uttered the words "students do not value learning." Yet in Rose's observations, when students are doing vocational tasks, such as carpentry and electronics, they develop values (p. 95). This insight can be extended to traditional academic content and courses via exercises in hands-on, experiential learning (Rose 2009; Dewey 1997; Kolb 1984; Truswell 1975) and such learning engagement was even included as part of the Cuban Revolution (Kozol 1980). Nevertheless, as Rose attests, the struggle to actually achieve this integration continues, with the disintegration increasing the higher up the grade one goes all the way into the academy.

As one example, Lowney (1998) shares an activity of doing puzzles that aims to reduce student anxiety when learning social theory. Unbeknownst to the students, Lowney removed all the edge pieces, leaving students to struggle solving the puzzle without them. She then gives them the edge pieces to illustrate that theory acts as a frame, within which the data (the other pieces) can take shape and become more intelligible. This not only allows students to learn what is meant by theoretical frameworks, but I would argue the exercise also connects hand and brain, which enables students to *think* about theory as a frame and to *create* the frame. I believe this activity comprises 'pieces' of RPH. To fully qualify, the puzzle activity would include some larger use or purpose and thereby meet physical, social or emotional needs, while inviting students to make this bodily connection to concepts, material production and larger philosophical questions around social relations, material needs and collective meaning. As Hayes (2010) states, "Radical Homemakers draw on historical traditions to craft a more ecologically viable existence, but their life's work is to create a new pleasurable, sustainable and socially just society…" (p. 17). These goals also apply to RPH, except as a pedagogical practice they manifest in a specific course based context.

Practicing Radical Pedagogical Homesteading

In *Teaching to Transgress: Education as the Practice of Freedom* (1994) bell Hooks remarks that "class is rarely talked about in the United States; nowhere is there more intense silence about the reality of class differences than in educational settings" (p. 177). To counter the silence around this "uncomfortable topic" (Tablante and Fiske 2015, p. 184), Hooks calls upon progressive professors to "challenge class biases" (p. 187) and to recognize its social influence within the classroom. To achieve this she proposes creatively engaging the "democratic ideal of education for everyone" (p. 189). When teaching Marx in a social theory class, Hooks' point is particularly prescient. Teaching Marx's critiques of capitalism and worker alienation without engaged pedagogy is insufficient for confronting issues of class. Hooks understood engaged pedagogy, as teaching "in a manner that respects and cares for the souls of our students" (p. 13) and as an essential component to student comprehension. My experiences using RPH suggest an additional component that attempts to link 'care for the souls of our students' with embodied activities to further illustrate the full meaning of abstract ideas. In this case, how to engage students' bodies and minds to Marx's critique of capitalism in light of his understanding of humans in terms of 'species-being.'

Attempting to get students to critique capitalism and to fully understand Marx's theory of alienation is certainly challenging as anyone teaching theory can attest (Holtzman 2005; Lowney 1998; Scaraboro 2004). Most university students' class privilege typically means they have not engaged in factory and/or manual labor, and those who have are not versed in critiquing capitalism, and tend, like the rest of the population, to regard Marx with suspicion based on ignorance (Fromm 1974). Yet if we translate the terms 'worker' and 'capitalist' to 'student' and 'teacher' Marx's insights can begin to make sense. This translation makes sense when we consider Marx's observation:

> …the work is external to the worker…work is not voluntary but imposed, forced labor. It is not the satisfaction of a need, but only a means of satisfying other needs. Its alien character is clearly shown by the fact that as soon as there is no physical or other compulsion it is avoided like the plague" (Marx, as cited in Fromm 1974, p. 98–99).

Because most students are exposed to a banking method of teaching and are seeking degrees that are numerically evaluated by their GPA that will, in theory, correspondingly lead to an elevated income, this description of work applies unnervingly well to their experiences in school. However, this correlation is not self-evident and to use an alternative pedagogical practice, not just as a single activity, but throughout the course so students may experience what the alternative is like both conceptually (in mind) and in practice (in body) (Godfrey 2015). In so doing students can begin to recognize the differences between the banking method and engaged pedagogy, while through the use of RPH they are also able to explore and reclaim their species-being by experiencing in the class their own on-going "free, conscious activity" (Marx, as cited in Fromm 1974, p. 100).

According to Eric Fromm in *Marx's Concept of Man* (1974) what is most misunderstood about Marx is the notion that his 'materialism' was "anti-spiritual." Fromm disagrees, instead arguing, "Marx's aim was that of the spiritual emancipation of man, of his liberation from the chains of economic determinism, of restituting him in his human wholeness, of enabling him to find unity and harmony with his fellow man and with nature" (p. 3). I argue that Hooks' concept of engaged pedagogy as the practice of freedom, as well as Hayes' definition of Radical Homemakers are notions consistent with Marx's lofty aim. Likewise, the teaching mission of RPH serves this larger purpose.

Simply stated my invention of the term RPH occurred specifically when teaching Marx's theory of alienation, though it can be applied more broadly to other concepts and theoretical frameworks. What it implies, however, is the direct connection between an intellectual, hence conscious, concept and an opportunity to freely connect that concept into "productive life" (Marx, as cited in Fromm 1974, p. 100).

Productive life is "... life creating life..." as in again the "...free, conscious activity" that "is the *species-character* of human beings" people "make [their] life activity itself an object of [their] will and consciousness" (Marx, as cited in Fromm 1974, p. 100, *italics* in original). As such, my entire class seeks to give students multiple and varied opportunities to integrate "...free, conscious activity" into their academic work through open discussions, journaling based on students' reading choices, and student chosen experiential group projects (all of which students self-evaluate using my prescribed rubrics), as well as art, movement projects, theater and outdoor activities, that all take place during class. My goal for all of my class sessions is to engage in '...free, conscious activities' (some last only a few minutes, others are longer and can take up a whole class period) that have students use their bodies to mindfully do such activities as those listed by Berila—meditation, dance, art, poetry. I include craft activities that fulfill a 'life activity' need or even a social need and are consistent with the aims Hayes (2010) describes for Radical Homemakers who creatively "make family, community, social justice and the health of the planet the governing principles of their lives" (p. 13). Finally, to evoke tenets of place-based education, students freely and consciously connect with themselves, with each other, and with nature—all of which begins with their bodies existing in a place (Godfrey and Brown 2017). I frame the classroom as an intimate community (Hooks 2003) and although students are not homesteading by planting gardens, building houses, making clothes, and cooking together, their classroom activities can inspire their desires to do so. As the quote attributed to Antoine de Saint-Exupéry states, "If you want to build a ship, don't drum up the men and women to gather wood, divide the work, and give orders. Instead, teach them to yearn for the vast and endless sea" (Quote Investigator 2015). In this spirit, RPH is about inviting students to 'yearn for the vast and endless sea' of their own creativity and for collaboration.

One activity I have used is inviting students to make greeting cards. I have done this activity numerous times and students have responded favorably via in-class feedback and journal reflections. The activity follows assigned readings from Marx's *Economic and Philosophical Manuscripts* (Marx 1975) that cover his theory of alienation and his concept of species-being. To prepare for the activity students are asked to buy a greeting card for someone they love and to bring it to class. Instructors must bring sufficient materials to class so that all students (my largest class size has been 70) are equipped to make a greeting card and with enough material choices to enable 'free, conscious activity.' For example, I bring generous amounts of paper in a range of colors, different types of scissors, a variety of colored markers and crayons, images from magazines, and glue. Students are invited to make cards in any way they like and to do so for someone specific. In fact, students can be invited to meditate on that person before beginning their card to further emphasize the relationship between the conscious idea and then the created physical reality that conjures a specific emotional connection. Music can be played while students work, as it helps them to relax into the experience. After a given time (again depending on class length, but no less than 15 min) students are invited to share their cards with a peer and to talk about the person they made it for.

They are asked to describe their feelings about that person, what exactly they wanted to convey to the person, as well as why they made specific material choices in making their card. This can last about 10 min. Class discussion can open with students describing all aspects of the activity, from their own experiences in making and writing their card to reiterating peer conversations. As discussion builds, I slowly invite them to weave in Marx's ideas of species-being and alienation. Students should be asked to compare the card that they bought to the one they made. How do they feel about the purchased card when compared to the one they made? How they judge it? How do the experiences of merely buying a card compare to making one? Significantly, I ask students their perceptions of the store bought card's quality. Do they consider a store-bought card the 'hallmark,' the better one, and the homemade one inferior, quaint, and child-like? Grappling with whether this is the case, and why, is fruitful. Students can be invited to read what they have written in their cards and tell the class who they wrote it for. In the process, students can be asked, "How does this experience compare with the act of buying a card written by someone we have never met?" I try to tie this discussion to Marx's idea of "self-alienation," or alienation from others, highlighting the common practice of purchasing cards that tells someone we care about them, yet relying on a stranger to describe this intimate connection for us (Marx, as cited in Fromm 1974, p. 100).

In comparing cards, students can viscerally understand that making their cards freely and consciously is a small example of embodying their labor in the product. Students may have made conscious choices when picking their store-bought card, they are able to see that such a card does not embody their labor even as the 'gold' (the money) they used to purchase it, no doubt, came from their own or a family member's alienated wage labor. As a final point of discussion, students can imagine that instead of being able to make their own cards in the manner they chose and for whomever they desired, they all worked in a card factory where they would be making cards as dictated to them by those with the power. It can then be recognized that those who design the cards and/or write them (the white collar/brain workers) are less alienated than those who make them (the blue collar/hand workers). But, this difference is merely one of degree rather than kind, because all workers are subject to the larger rules of capitalist production that alienates labor. In concluding this task, students can be asked to share one word that best describes their experience. Overwhelmingly, the aggregate of all my students articulate feelings of being "connected", which is the antithesis of alienation and the goal of RPH.

This is just one specific activity, but there are many other creative activities that illustrate Marx's theory of alienation in class, or even at home, such as other homesteading arts, like sewing, carpentry, leatherwork, cooking, and gardening. Other creative possibilities could draw from arts or mechanics. For example, I have had students make collages, plant seeds, create sculptures out of garbage, write poems using words from readings, cook meals to share and other ideas that invite them to engage their species-being. The central tenet is to take what is being learned intellectually and find a parallel way to teach it that requires that students 'make something'—be it a poem, a skit, a flow chart, a sculpture, a drawing, an experiment, a children's book, a recipe, a model—that further illustrates for them in embodied and experiential ways the very same or similar concepts. For some teachers this proposition may, as Hooks observes, evoke a "fear of losing control" (p. 188). If we are committed to engaged pedagogy, however, then we should welcome "the opportunity to alter our classroom practices creatively so that the democratic ideals of education for everyone can be realized" (Hooks, p. 189). I am sure Marx would agree.

Conclusion

Teaching about social theory, capitalism, social class, and the resulting inequalities, requires teachers to recognize difficulties and necessities (Holtzman 2005; Hooks 1994; Lowney 1998; Scaraboro 2004; Tablante and Fiske 2015). Teaching Marx's theories bring further challenges but also significant rewards. These rewards include what Fromm (1974) sees as the central theme of Marx—"the transformation of alienated, meaningless labor into productive, free labor" (p. 43). In the specific case of students this objective becomes the transformation of alienated, meaningless *memorization* (falsely seen as learning) into productive, free—authentic—learning that invites them to realize themselves not only "as individuals, but also as a species-being" (p. 49). In this capacity the hope is for them to realize how indelibly connected they are to their species and to the natural world from whence the totality of material for their life resides. And once a student regains their species-being it can be assumed that, like Mike Lefevre, they will never not want to 'be part of it' again. RPH is a step along this path in that its goal is to unite for students and teachers in direct and more amorphous ways their hands and their brains and to do so in a manner that, as Hayes concludes, enables us to heal ourselves, society and the larger planet by promoting social justice, creative fulfillment and happiness.

References

Berila, B. (2015). *Integrating mindfulness into anti-oppression pedagogy*. New York: Routledge.

Czank, J. M. (2012). On the origin of species-being: Marx redefined. *Rethinking Marxism, 24*(2), 316–323.

Dant, T. (2010). Work of repair: gesture, emotion and sensual knowledge. *Sociological Research Online*, 15(3), 7. http://www.socresonline.org.uk/15/3/7.html. Accessed March 27, 2017.

Dewey, J. (1997). *Experience and education*. New York: Free Press.

Dyer-Witheford, N. (2004). Species-being resurgent. *Constellations, 11*, 476–491.

Freire, P. (2000). *Pedagogy of the oppressed*. New York: Bloomsbury Academic.

Fromm, E. (1974). *Marx's concept of man*. New York: Fredick Ungar Publishing.

Godfrey, P. (2015). Teaching society and climate change: creating an 'earth community' in the college classroom by embodying connectedness through love. *Journal of Sustainability Education*, 9(1), ISSN: 2151–7452.

Godfrey, P. & Brown, J. (forthcoming). Teaching and learning from within: A placed-based pedagogy for heartfelt hope. In D. Shannon & J. Galle (Eds.), *Interdisciplinary approaches to pedagogy and place-based education: from abstract to the quotidian*. New York: Palgrave Macmillan.

Hayes, S. (2010). *Radical homemakers: reclaiming domesticity from a consumer culture*. Richmondville, NY: Left to Write Press.

Herring, C., Rosaldo, M., Seim, J., & Shestakofsky, B. (2016). Living theory: principles and practices for teaching social theory ethnographically. *Teaching Sociology, 44,* 88–199.

Holtzman, M. (2005). Teaching sociological theory through active learning: the irrigation exercise. *Teaching Sociology, 33,* 206–212.

Hooks, B. (1994). *Teaching to transgress: education as the practice of freedom*. New York: Routledge.

Hooks, B. (2003). *Teaching community: a pedagogy of hope*. New York: Routledge.

King Alfred School website. http://www.aim25.com/cats/72/7212.htm. Accessed March 27, 2017.

Kolb, D. (1984). *Experiential learning as the science of learning and development*. Englewood Cliffs, NJ: Prentice Hall.

Kozol, J. (1980). *Children of the revolution: a Yankee teacher in the Cuban schools*. New York: Dell.

Lowney, K. S. (1998). Reducing 'theory anxiety' through puzzles. *Teaching Sociology, 26,* 69–73.

Marx, K. (1975). *Economic and philosophical manuscripts* (*1844*) (K. Marx, *Early writings* (R. Livingstone & G. Benton, Trans.). New York: Penguin Classics.

Quote Investigator. (2015). http://quoteinvestigator.com/2015/08/25/sea/. Accessed March 27, 2017.

Rose, M. (2009). *Why school? Reclaiming education for all of us*. New York: The New Press.

Scaraboro, A. (2004). Bringing theory closer to home through active learning and online discussion. *Teaching Sociology, 32,* 222–231.

Tablante, C. B., & Fiske, S. T. (2015). Teaching social class. *Teaching of Psychology, 42*(2), 184–190.

Terkel, S. (1974). *Working: People talk about what they do all day and how they feel about what they do*. New York: Ballantine Books.

Truswell, H. (1975). *Made in summerhill*. London: Hawthorn Books.

Socialist Grading

David I. Backer

Author's Reflexive Statement

I write this chapter at a familiar moment in institutionalized schooling: the end of the year, when grades are due. This moment brings with it a combination of joy and disgust. Joy in seeing my students' new understanding and the onset of summer; overwhelming disgust at the need to assign number and/or letter grades to student work. No matter how many rubrics I use to give the appearance of objectivity, no matter how many tests or projects with clear directions and expectations I include, and no matter how many times I have been compelled to assign simple quantities to complex educational qualities as the final class culmination, I cannot avoid the revulsion this moment inspires.

As an educator, I feel most complicit with our exploitative economy in the moment when I assign my students a grade. In the educational sector, grades are positioned at the frontlines of commodification. Grades subject student activity—the embodied forms of their educational labor—to a general equivalent, which—once assigned, like a price—places out of sight the most enriching and meaningful aspects of our time together. Then, the grade—a calculable quantity—is looked at by all manner of institutions, subjecting students to miseducative extrinsic motivators, meaningless competition, and an unhealthy individualism. My nauseous sense of complicity, this disgust, which began when I received my first grades as a young child, continued anew when I first assigned grades as a high school teacher. I still feel discomfort as a university instructor. The nausea has compelled me, though, to find ways of complicating the social power of grading in a capitalist economy.

D. I. Backer (✉)
West Chester University, West Chester, USA
e-mail: dbacker@wcupa.edu

K. Haltinner and L. Hormel (eds.), *Teaching Economic Inequality and Capitalism in Contemporary America*, https://doi.org/10.1007/978-3-319-71141-6_9

This chapter tells the story of those techniques. I present two socialist grading practices that attempt, through the form of teaching, to reduce the commodifying qualities of grading and work against the commodification of education. They could be used independently of course content, whether one teaches the natural sciences, social sciences, humanities, or arts.

I was a high school teacher in South America trying to understand capitalism when I experimented with the pedagogical tactics described below. Since honing them, I have used them with students across class and race positions, from privileged white fourth graders to middle class undergraduates to working class graduate students. The first technique is for grading classroom discussion, the second for final grades.

Socialist Discussion Grading

Two key influences led me to experiment with socialist grading techniques for classroom discussion participation: Marxism and Harkness pedagogy. I was teaching wealthy Ecuadorian juniors and seniors at the American School of Quito, Ecuador. When some of my students didn't respond positively to Socratic seminar, a colleague introduced me to student-centered discussion through the Harkness method (see Backer 2015). Harkness pedagogy requires teachers to act like ethnographer-facilitators. They have to relinquish control over the product of discussion and instead focus on listening, tracking, and guiding the process of discussion, speaking infrequently and encouraging students to talk to one another.

After about a year of experiments with Harkness pedagogy I faced a problem unaddressed by the manuals I had read: how does one grade discussion? How could/should I assign a number value to students' participation?

Meanwhile, I was reading Karl Marx's *Capital, Vol. 1* for the first time and the ideas of exchange, inequality, and distribution were on my mind. I was also reading Polanyi's (1957) *Great Transformation*, along with Freire's (1973) *Education as Critical Consciousness* as part of a master's degree in education I was completing. These latter influences got me thinking about classrooms as societies: that my students and I produced something (education), and my teaching practices and policies set up rules that set prices for that production and distributed value accordingly in the form of quantitative evaluation. There was power and prejudice and freedom and equality and many other social values forming in my classroom society, and the way I taught—the relations of educational production emerging from the economic system of my classroom—could create the conditions for liberation or domination.

While education is productive, it is also reproductive, in the sense that the skills and knowledge students develop in classrooms link to the skills and knowledge they pursue and use in family life, the economy and politics. The ideology that relations of educational production promoted in my classroom could either match or resist dominant ideologies in society. Education is relatively autonomous:

teachers can teach in ways that do not correspond to existing ideologies and promote relations of production that resonate with other political economic arrangements. Grading is a key part of educational production and reproduction, and, due to schools' relative autonomy, can either promote capitalist relations of production, or promote other relations, such as socialist relations of production. After reflecting on all of this, I ultimately modified Harkness pedagogy to generate socialist relations of educational production.

Harkness discussions require students to read something, generate their own questions about the material, and then participate in a discussion using those questions. I listened and tracked the discussion by drawing discussion circles, a form of conversation analysis that counts the number and kinds of comments students make. I focused mainly on turns taken, but also kept notes on the discussion's content. After the discussion, I debriefed with students by showing them my analysis of the discussion. We looked at who talked about what and how many times, and used formulae to calculate number grades. These formulae were the economic policy of my classroom economy.

I first came up with a relatively traditional formula, which reflects capitalist values. Whoever does the "best" earns the "best" grade, and the "best" is whoever talks the most number of times. The formula I used was:

$$grade = (85 + / - d)$$

The 'd' here represents distance from the average. I calculated 'd' by finding the median number of comments offered that day. So, if the median number of comments in a discussion was five and a student said ten things, then she was above the mean by five. Thus, she earned a 90 because:

$$(85 + 5) = 90$$

I used 85 because the class had agreed that, in humanities classes at our school, students expected to get an 85/100 for doing the minimum. So, if a student says nothing but listens attentively she earned 85/100.

When I explained this to my classes, one of my students, J.P. Edgerton, argued, "the person that talks the most shouldn't get the most points." I agreed, politically speaking. Certainly, capitalists would believe that if each person pursues their own self-interest, then the social whole benefits. But I wanted to make a formula based on a socialist imperative and not a capitalist one. I didn't want my students to talk too much and I didn't want them to talk too little. I wanted their abilities and needs to be met in an equal way, mediated through a distribution system that takes the social whole into account. I wanted them to benefit equally from the resource of the discussion space they created together. This discussive energy is a precious resource, like air or water, and I did not want it exploited, wasted, or commodified. I wanted them to pay attention to one another, listen carefully, and share their opinions in a balanced way, and for the educational and quantitative gains to reflect this togetherness. I wanted them to collectively own the means of discussive production rather than competing individually.

In the previous formula one could only get 100/100 if she earned 15 points above the average. This encouraged a kind of race to the top where every student was encouraged to beat every other student to talk the most. I wanted a balanced community, though. How could I encourage students to have the well-being of the group as their goal, while still giving them a number grade?

Along with the socialist texts, I was also reading Mitchell's (1988) translation of the *Tao-te-ching*. A poem in that book inspired the solution. The last line of the fifth poem in Mitchell's translation is "hold on to the center." I realized that, in grading, the apposition of certain qualities of an assignment on the bell curve—like discussion with percentages—is somewhat arbitrary. In principle, depending on what I valued, I could make any point along the distribution worth 100%. If I valued people saying the most number of things, I could give them 100%. If I value people saying nothing, I could give the silent students 100%. So I thought like a socialist: the *average* number of turns taken during the discussion should be worth 100%. Instead of encouraging a race to the top, I'd encourage a race to the center, towards the social whole. If a student said the exact number of things that every other student said, if their number of productive comments was identical to the average number of comments, then that student would be the "best" student, though what "best" means in this calculation is quite different than what a capitalist might think. The "best" student in this case is one who acts with the collective, not out of their own self-interest. If a student says the average number of things during discussion, that would mean they didn't talk too much, or too little. Depending on their distance from the average, I would take off points. I thought of a new formula called the Edgerton formula:

$$grade = 100 - d$$

The student that said ten things, where the median number of comments was five, would get 95.

$$100 - (5) = 95$$

Whomever fits with the average is rewarded and whoever strays from that average, either by talking too much, too little, or disrupting is compensated accordingly. This system is still pretty individualistic, in the sense that distinct individuals get a grade for their own participation. In later years, I modified the approach to give the entire group the same grade by associating certain standard deviations with points out of 100. If there was a standard deviation of zero then everyone got 100, for instance. (I presented these ideas to a group of Harkness teachers, and one replied "this is some kind of wonky communism!" I've wondered whether the formula could inspire a democratic socialist tax code.)

Applying this formula can teach distribution, community, and cooperation, but it has its limits. It is coercive, though the coercion is socialist. It imposes a quantity on something qualitative, particularly by prioritizing turn-taking as the measured phenomenon rather than content of comments: what matters is your awareness of yourself in relation to others as much as (or perhaps more than) what you are saying. Therefore, I like to use it as a classroom exercise to present different kinds of economic ideas. Using the competitive "whoever speaks most" formula, and contrasting that with the Edgerton formula, I can show students the difference between competitive-unequal forms of distribution and cooperative-equal forms of distribution, presuming that the discussion space is a resource and education is a kind of production. The Edgerton formula is a socialist relation of educational production where the best possible outcome is that everyone produces and receives the same amount of value, since everyone gets 100 if they take the same number of turns. While the formula doesn't fully capture Marx's imperative "to each according to need, from each according to ability" (as my second example of grade negotiation below does) it incentivizes shared production and distribution of limited resources, thereby communicating pedagogically what it is like to live in a socialist economic system.

Socialist Grade Negotiation

I first thought to ask students to propose and negotiate their own grades recently, in my first full-time faculty position at a College of Education in Cleveland, Ohio. I was tired of commodifying my students' labor, feeding their addictions to quantitative evaluation, which previous waves of adults had inculcated in them. I could not stand the interpellation of quantitative grading as a student, then as a high school teacher, and as I studied economics and political philosophy further this disdain grew more unbearable.

Grades alienate. I frequently ask my students what they remember most vividly about their classes, the knowledge or the grades they received. It is a rhetorical question meant to communicate that number grades, like a wage, separate you from the embodied form of your labor. They put out of sight the complex, particular, and concrete results of an educational activity by translating them into a discourse of equivalence ultimately boxing individual production into easily tradeable labels, which permit the movement of bodies into hierarchies. The exchange-value of grades represses education's use-value. Now with the power of a full-time faculty position, I could do something about this.

In Ranciere's (1991) re-telling of Jacob Jacotot's pedagogy, *The Ignorant Schoolmaster*, Jacotot bids his students to take measure of their own learning. In my first classes in Cleveland, teaching Jacotot, I thought, "Why not try it?" I remembered the way I settled prices while living in Ecuador, specifically by haggling taxi rides: I proposed my fare to the driver who either agreed or disagreed. If grades reflect the scholastic commodity price, then I would tell my students to haggle with me. I would ask them to take the measure of their own learning at midterm and at final through an online survey, which included questions about the strengths of the course, weaknesses of the course, things they learned, their goals for themselves, and then leaves space at the bottom for a quantitative proposal. I would read their responses and proposals and write back, agreeing or disagreeing. The exact protocol for this grading tactic is:

(1) Tell the students at the outset about this grading procedure, making sure they understand it.
(2) Create an online survey. In the survey, ask qualitative questions about the course, students' measurement of their own learning, and a quantitative proposal for a grade. (I like to ask about specific things students remember—one anecdote, activity, or idea—they think about a lot now, or something they understand).
(3) Ask for responses with whatever frequency is appropriate (I do midterm and final since these are the traditional grading times in undergraduate programs, though I have thought to do it more frequently).
(4) Read responses online, then respond with agreement or disagreement giving reasons for either. If you disagree, make a counter-offer and ask the student if they accept this.

I would later realize that, while this is a negotiating tactic, and markets are negotiation structures, this negotiation fulfills Marx's ethical imperative "to each according to need and from each according to ability". In this case, I use negotiations and self-evaluation to determine with students what they need in terms of compensation and what they deserve based on what they are able to contribute. They take the measure of their own learning and determine the quantity they think best represents that learning, and I tell them what I think about their evaluation. This method also takes into account students' particular contexts: what grades they might need to maintain scholarship status; their achievement given certain social, economic, or political circumstances; and any other context for their needs and abilities. Rather than grade commodification, this negotiation method draws from what you might call a labor theory of grading value where the general equivalent of grades as an exchange value is abolished, at least in the classroom context.

Among the interesting outcomes of this technique is the decoupling of assignments' worth from the final grade. Since the students proposed their grades at midterm and final as reflections on their learning through the assignments, I did not have to grade those assignments with any numbers. The assignments were vehicles for an experience that the students themselves evaluated in its entirety, rather than vehicles for me to calculate a number through a one-way fragmented process. Each assignment became just an assignment with its own specific educational integrity rather than worth a certain percentage of the final grade. This particular integrity prioritizes the use-value of education over the exchange-value of education, without getting rid of the latter since I could still enter a grade for student transcripts.

Conclusion

Much of the anti-capitalist literature on education, beginning perhaps with Bowles and Gintis's (2011) *Schooling in Capitalist America*, makes an important inversion in sociological thinking about teaching and learning. Put simply, the idea that better schools will make a better society is a distinctly liberal-capitalist promise. From Horace Mann, to Lyndon B. Johnson's Great Society legislation, to the repetitive calls that a college degree will guarantee young people good jobs, these discourses and programs presume that society will improve as citizens achieve more and better schooling. Anti-capitalist educational thinkers like Bowles and Gintis demonstrate that this presumption is false. Observing the data on inequality and educational attainment in the United States also leads us to broach this question: why has educational attainment increased exponentially, both in secondary and tertiary graduation rates, yet income inequality has also increased exponentially? The amount of money people make has not increased proportionally with educational attainment and unemployment has fluctuated violently. Good schools do not guarantee a good society. Rather, a good society guarantees a good society. Economic crises happen whether or not much of the populace has attended certain schooling institutions. Schools reproduce and alter the character of society in a relatively autonomous way, but they cannot make society more just if structural injustices persist. It is with this in mind that I use the above grading procedures to teach students to think differently about capitalism and then seek to change capitalism. Socialist grading techniques in a capitalist economy, therefore, may inspire big structural changes in small ways.

References

Backer, D. I. (2015). Listening for discussion: the conference method or Harkness pedagogy. *Listening to Teach: Beyond Didactic Pedagogy*, SUNY Press: New York, 97.

Bowles, S., & Gintis, H. (2011). *Schooling in capitalist America: educational reform and the contradictions of economic life*. Haymarket Books.

Freire, P. (1973). *Education for critical consciousness* (Vol. 1). Bloomsbury Publishing.

Mitchell, S. (1988). *Tao te ching (Lao Tzu)*. New York: HarperPerennial.

Polanyi, K. (1957). *The Great transformation: the social and political origins of our time*. Boston: Beacon.

Rancière, J. (1991). *The ignorant schoolmaster: five lessons in intellectual emancipation*. California: Stanford University Press.

Part III
Applied Pedagogical Strategies for Course Development

Overcoming Students' Fear: Scaffolding to Teach *Money and Society*

Stephanie L. Bradley

Author's Reflexive Statement

Before entering graduate school I spent 16 years developing a banking career. My former career consisted of two main phases. Right out of college, from 1994 to 2004, I served as a branch manager and retail lender. I mainly worked in affluent markets and lent money to people buying and leveraging luxury real estate during periods of atypical appreciation. In an interesting juxtaposition, many hardworking members of my teams struggled financially while tending to the banking needs of our affluent clients. My employers required close scrutiny of the working hours of non-salaried employees in efforts to maximize corporate revenues and stockholder dividends. I became keenly aware of the income and wealth gaps among individuals with whom I frequently interacted. The inequality puzzled me.

The second phase of my banking career spanned 2004 to 2010. During this period, I worked as a retail credit trainer and subsequently managed our retail credit training department. Instead of being "bankers who could teach," we were trained as professional instructors. Though I have always had an interest in instruction, during my time as a corporate trainer both my passion for teaching and my interest in understanding the forces that contribute to economic inequality came alive.

As a banker-turned-sociologist, I am passionately curious about topics pertaining to money, such as taxes, credit, economic inequality, and capitalism. In my early years as a graduate student, I would zealously launch into discussions about these interests with anyone who would listen. It only took a few glazed-eye responses to learn that these topics challenged people. Many colleagues and students told me that they struggled to stay engaged because they had a preconceived dislike of these subjects. They commented that they felt intellectually challenged because they feared subjects with which they lacked familiarity. I speculate that the latter often

S. L. Bradley (✉)
Radford University, Radford, USA
e-mail: sbradley20@radford.edu

K. Haltinner and L. Hormel (eds.), *Teaching Economic Inequality and Capitalism in Contemporary America*, https://doi.org/10.1007/978-3-319-71141-6_10

caused the former. That is, a lack of familiarity caused the fear that often led to individuals' disinterest in these topics. Undeterred, my research and teaching interests took root in issues of public policy and economic inequality.

Introduction

Imagine my excitement when offered the chance as a graduate student in sociology to design a new upper-level course based on my interests! I titled the course *Money and Society*. The initial eagerness I felt about creating my own course eventually turned to apprehension. The course I developed requires students to analyze the claim that money and society are inextricable concepts by exploring the history, social construction, and social meaning of money; theories on money; forms and uses of money; and societal and institutional influences on, and effects of, money. I expected most of the topics we analyze—such as markets, economic inequality, taxation, corporate governance, and the U.S. financial crisis—to be particularly nebulous for many students. Admittedly, I also designed a rigorous course. Course objectives include that students should be able to explain the consequences of capitalism and free market systems on economic inequality; think critically about abstract concepts such as money, capitalism, inequality, poverty, greed, and privilege; and define the U.S. financial crisis as an economic, political, social, and cultural event. To meet these objectives, students need to understand gross domestic product, commodification, subprime loan, collateralized debt obligation, and other potentially challenging concepts. While courses frequently expose students to unfamiliar topics, I have the additional challenge of helping them overcome their fears and feel confident that they have the aptitude to understand and learn material they may instinctively resist. Students need to build a shared vocabulary and an individual confidence in order to analyze complex concepts and meet course objectives.

I consider myself a conductor in the classroom—students take an intellectual journey and it is my responsibility to guide their voyage. Aware of these objectives, challenges, and responsibilities, I turned to the technique of scaffolding, a pedagogical concept with roots in cognitive psychology (Vygotsky 1978). The term 'scaffolding' originated with research assessing tutor-child relationships as the child learned how to solve a puzzle (Pea 2004). Extant pedagogical literature now defines scaffolding as a technique that allows students to gain confidence about a specific concept before moving on to a more complex, yet related, concept (Sawyer 2006). This instructional technique calls for the teacher to break a larger topic down into smaller units that students master before bringing the whole together. The content begins simply and becomes more complex as student understanding develops. My ultimate goal in *Money and Society* is for students to develop the language and understanding necessary to analyze the financial crisis that began in 2007. The financial crisis provides an ideal case study with which students can explore the effects of capitalism, power, and institutions across social dimensions such as race and class. Though the financial crisis acts as the pinnacle to which the scaffolding leads, along the journey students learn about topics that are independently important to a survey of *Money and Society*.

Complex social, economic, and political conditions contributed to the financial crisis. Broadly, the crisis is often thought of as the product of a subprime mortgage boom followed by a housing market collapse. These forces led to a high default rate of subprime mortgage loans. A subprime loan is usually defined as financing offered to a borrower who does not meet traditional lending standards, such as someone with poor credit or low income. The borrower pays more for the loan to offset the additional risk. Banks have routinely sold mortgages to investors who assume the loans' risk. However, the risk of these investments became more opaque when collateralized debt obligations (CDO) began to include mortgage-backed securities of varying risk levels. Due to the perceived risk diversity and the blessing of ratings agencies, banks were able to sell off high-risk loans with little regulatory oversight by repackaging them as part of a CDO. The newly expanded market for subprime loans led to predatory lending by creditors incentivized based on their loan production who assumed they would not bear the risk. Black and Latino borrowers came to represent a disproportionate share of outstanding subprime mortgage loans during the boom (Faber 2013). However, market conditions changed and the perceived risk protections dissolved. America's housing market declined and loosely regulated loan structures transformed into burdens too great for lenders to refinance or borrowers to pay.

Subprime mortgage loan defaults led to the financial crisis. However, additional forces beyond mortgagors simply unwilling to pay their debts brought about the near demise of the U.S. banking system. Contributing forces included a profit-driven capitalist system, a regulatory environment seemingly unaware of the potential hazards of new forms of securities, power dynamics that prized lending production over the long-term financial security of borrowers, and predatory lending practices that put unwitting borrowers in precarious financial predicaments. For our semester to culminate in a unit on the financial crisis, students first need to understand topics such as markets and capitalism; stratification, income and wealth gaps, and intersectional economic inequality; and government, banking, and corporate governance. In summary, the recent financial crisis is often characterized as the result of a greedy Wall Street that encouraged the sale of subprime loans to homebuyers and homeowners, the effects of which led to a global economic crisis. Though the effects of the financial crisis were felt around the globe, we focus specifically on the U.S. financial crisis.

Money and Society is structured around six conceptual units—an introduction, money and inequality, the social meaning of money, money and institutions, the U. S. financial crisis, and money's power to inspire (a table illustrating these units is provided in the conclusion). The last unit serves as a less academically rigorous end-of-semester farewell. The second-to-the-last unit, the unit on the financial crisis, is the primary target of our scaffolding. The units act as building blocks, each becoming more complex as they integrate information obtained in prior models while collectively constructing a body of knowledge. To that end, *Money and*

Society incorporates traditional journal and book readings, popular in- and out-of-class activities, and novel uses of available technology. By ascending a scaffold that exposes students to course concepts in a deliberate order, students actively learn—reading, listening, journaling, participating, and watching—throughout their academic journey. Classes often incorporate some amount of instructor-led lecture or discussion and common activities such as write-pair-share. In addition, various assessment techniques are employed throughout the course. Rather than present lecture topics, standard activities and readings, and assessments incorporated throughout the entire course, this chapter focuses on novel content-specific material and activities related to economic inequality and the financial crisis. I hope this chapter serves as a resource educators can utilize as they guide students' intellectual journey through *Money and Society*.

Reading and Listening

In *Money and Society* students read material outside of class in advance of most class meetings. Readings intentionally vary by type and source to maintain student interest and engagement. Reading types include hard-copy monographs, downloadable articles and chapters, and online content. Sources include leading disciplinary journals and non-academic, yet highly related, sources such as the Pew Research Center and NPR's Planet Money. When accessed by computer, each Planet Money podcast comes with a short article and the ability to download a transcript. Additional reading material comes from the Inequality.org website. A project of the Institute for Policy Studies, this mission-based source provides access to a range of data and resources including lists of books, reports, videos, and films addressing wealth and income inequality. Students read sections of one particular Inequality.org resource several times during the units on money and inequality and money and institutions. "Growing Apart: A Political History of American Inequality" by Colin Gordon presents information on the basic dimensions, conventional explanations, and contributing politics and policies of financial inequality in America. This source contains interactive tables and graphs, allowing students to manipulate data to show a range of effects and outcomes as they make sense of complex concepts.

Podcasts produced by This American Life provide another source of pre-class exposure to complex concepts. This American Life's thematic-episodes focus on a host of socially relevant topics. Select podcasts are assigned during the units on money and institutions and the U.S. financial crisis. Like Planet Money, This American Life provides access to full transcripts when using a computer to access the site. Even so, students are directed to access the transcript and still listen to the full podcast. This way they do not miss content as they busily take notes on the hosts' conversation. Instead, students can take notes in the margins as they decipher the discussion. It is important for students to have this type of private 'first pass' at challenging material. The conversant and investigative style of the podcast's hosts allows for learning to occur casually. In addition, out-of-class podcasts allow students to move through the material at their pace, revisiting challenging topics without the scrutiny of their peers. On their learning journeys, students do not simply complete assigned readings or listen to the podcasts. Students interact with assigned readings and podcasts by completing daily semi-structured journal entries.

Journaling

Extant pedagogical literature suggests that the most effective educators approach teaching as an enterprise that moves beyond simply transmitting knowledge. In addition to exposing students to universally or disciplinarily accepted information, the best teachers create an environment in which students can construct their understanding (Bain 2004). Reading is considered one of the more important tools for learning, particularly with difficult material (Svinicki 2011). However, students often encounter unique difficulties when reading challenging text (Bean 2011). Research shows that students benefit from reading guides, but such an exercise may lead students to read to answer rather than read to understand (Svinicki 2011). This semester-long semi-structured exploratory writing assignment encourages students to engage with, reflect on, and express their perceptions related to course material. Pre-class journal entries provide much of the scaffolding that supports course participants' development of both a shared vocabulary and independent understanding.

For each class with assigned pre-work, students prepare by (1) writing one paragraph about each assigned reading or podcast and (2) developing a glossary of assigned words and their definitions. The number of paragraphs written for each journal entry varies based on the number of pre-class materials assigned for the day. However, the organization of each paragraph stays consistent. Students are provided with the structure they should use to prepare their journal entries, but not content-specific questions. In the first sentence, students explain the authors' or speakers' main argument. The next few sentences contain evidence provided in support of the main argument. In the remaining sentences, students document their reactions, thoughts, and questions about what they read or heard. This last section of the journal entry reflects the students' critical thinking and independent understanding. Instead of simply stating that course material surprised them or reinforced their current knowledge, students explain why the material produced their reactions. Why did the student disagree or agree with the content? What questions do they have? What else should have the source considered? In addition to the learning benefits this activity affords the students, the journal entries provide feedback the instructor uses to identify misunderstandings and concepts that require additional attention. The class revisits confusing topics prior to advancing to the next material. The journals require students to interact with material and provide feedback essential to gauging understanding.

In addition to the summary paragraphs, students define select terms relevant to the current topic. For example, in the beginning of the course, students define terms to which we refer throughout the semester, such as economy and capitalism. Towards the end of the course they define terms related specifically to the U.S. financial crisis, such as collateralized debt obligation and predatory lending. The course's online library contains a list of each day's selected glossary terms. Students include the terms and their definitions at the end of their journal entry. While the students may reference a dictionary or other resources with appropriate citation, they are expected to write definitions in their words.

Journal entries are collected in class at random times throughout the semester and graded based on their thoughtfulness, development, and completion. The grading occurs fairly quickly, as it is more cursory than the kind of in-depth grading that takes place on formal papers. Submissions are returned to students with feedback so they can build an annotated bibliography and glossary for use throughout the semester. They can add glossary words and modify their glossary as their understanding of terms develops with future use and exposure. For many students, this resource serves as their main resource for graded work, such as exams and the final paper. Though the student journals serve an important role in building student knowledge, they are a lot of work. Many students express their dislike for the journal assignment in mid-term evaluations. Responding to a question asking what they liked the least about the course, one student commented, "The journals—not because they don't help me. Just because I don't like doing them (I'm sure I will appreciate [them] come test time)." Usually, approximately a third of the class makes similar comments. This feedback allows us to revisit an earlier discussion about the benefits of the journal entries, including that their compiled journal serves as the foundation for their final paper. Though students provide a lot of comments in end-of-semester evaluations, students generally only comment positively about the journals by the end of the course.

Participating and Watching

Teaching by lecture is mostly a one-way exchange that places students in a passive role wherein they receive information (Bean 2011). While some educators debate the importance of this technique, many agree that it provides some utility in transmitting information. However, research shows that lecture alone is less effective than other methods in promoting independent thought and understanding (Bligh 2000). Instead of being passive recipients of information, this course's design incorporates in-class activities that require students' active participation as they learn and make sense of foundational topics. I develop the scaffolding that students use to construct their understanding.

The ethos of American individualism implies that everyone is responsible for their life outcomes. Given this deeply entrenched belief, some scholars suggest that social stratification is one of the more difficult topics to teach in the social sciences

(Coghlan and Huggins 2004). The financial crisis was possible, at least in part, because of the power wielded financial elites with the ability to exacerbate growing economic inequities (Carruthers 2009). Thus, students need to be exposed to causes and consequences related to economic inequality. With this understanding they become prepared to analyze how the financial crisis both impacted and was impacted by individuals differently. Short videos, interactive websites, and games are used to help students better understand social stratification.

We view short video clips in class throughout the semester, but one source is utilized far more than others. The series "We the Economy" (wetheeconomy.com) aims to help viewers better understand the U.S. economy through its 20 short films. Through collaboration between well-regarded filmmakers and economic experts, these five- to eight-minute shorts organize into five topics. Topics include the economy, money, the role of government in the economy, globalization, and causes of inequality and the minimum wage. We watch select short films in class during the introduction unit to explore the economy's origins, define GDP, and assess the meaning of money. In other units we watch films pertaining to inequality and the debt and the deficit. A film related to taxation is assigned for homework with a reflection on our complicated tax system due the next class period. When we start our unit on the financial crisis, we watch a film on how Wall Street influences the economy. Each film's home page includes relevant facts and interactive questions. I ask these questions, plus original questions, in class after each film ends. I want students to answer each question anonymously so I can immediately gauge group understanding. Educators can use "clickers" or any similar student response system to administer the questions. I use Poll Everywhere (polleverywhere.com) to capture answers to these low-stakes questions. As suggested by pedagogical literature, we debrief student responses to questions and incorporate additional questions or lecture as needed (Svinicki 2011). The films' engaging, often cinematic, style resonates with students and contributes to their developing an understanding of many key course concepts.

In addition to short videos with response questions, multiple online interactive websites construct student understanding about social realities to which many students are not exposed. Exposure to such realities primes student attentiveness to the interplay between financial wellbeing and class, race, gender, and other social dimensions. This awareness is important for later analysis of social dynamics related to the financial crisis. The Economic Policy Institute created and hosts the Inequality.is website. Through the website's interactive tools and videos, students can explore income gap data and factors contributing to economic inequality in the U.S. This source further offers a range of ideas regarding ways to address and solve economic inequality. Spent (playspent.org) is another interactive tool. This online simulation offers users the opportunity to try to make their money last over the course of a month while making life decisions commonly faced by lower-income individuals. Marketed by the developer as a "game about surviving poverty," this activity is helpful in getting students to consider choices related to housing, healthcare, employment, and other life events. Educators can use these interactive activities in a variety of ways, including navigating through the sites in class under the direction of the students while guiding discussion. Alternatively, students can access these sites outside of class in conjunction with writing reflections.

Games and group activities are used to advance understanding related to economic inequality and other course concepts. For instance, students play the game commonly known as "Stratified Monopoly." Originally created by Coghlan and Huggins (2004), several modified versions are easily available for educators wishing to stratify the game along different dimensions. My students play the original Stratified Monopoly with some minor revisions. Students are put into groups of six or seven members. Five students play Monopoly using the standard board and accessories, while the remaining students are silent observers. Observers and the instructor meet privately before game play. Observers are instructed to note how players interact with each other and avoid participating in the game. They also receive a note sheet to complete throughout the game along with the game boards they take back and distribute to their groups. The money allocation differs in this game from the standard game. Each of the five players represents an economic quintile. The starting money, starting property, and money received each time they circle the game board are all allocated based upon their assigned income and wealth quintile. Players receive little direction before the game begins other than to receive their randomly selected distribution of cash, property, and game piece. While students are not informed about their economic status or the intent of the game beforehand, they are told how much money each will receive for passing "Go." Advance exposure to the game is not required, as it is a social experiment in itself to allow students the chance to develop game rules. Play usually lasts 30–45 min. Players who run out of money during the game are expected to stay engaged and take notes on what they observe during the remaining play. Immediately after the game concludes, students count their money and property and record their tallies on papers. After their game materials and tallies are collected, players and observers complete a guided, independently written reflection on their experience. Due to time constraints, class concludes after students complete and submit their written reflections. The next class period we debrief the activity by assessing players' wealth attainment, mobility, and reflections. In addition, we examine select observer comments. To conclude the activity, we watch a portion of the TED Talk "Does Money Make You Mean?" I find that many students are uncomfortable with the Monopoly activity. The students placed in the lower economic quintiles express frustration, while some students in the higher economic quintiles act uncomfortable upon reflecting on their behavior, such as greed. This video highlights a social psychologist's research that employed a similarly rigged game of Monopoly with groups of students. An awareness of income and wealth gaps seems to contribute to a range of reactions, including helplessness to dominance. Seeing the reactions displayed in the video helps students move past their individual feelings, allowing them to be more open to learn about power dynamics and long-term implications of economic inequality.

We watch two documentaries towards the end of the course. By this point, students have developed the vocabulary necessary to view full-length documentaries filled with technical jargon and an independent understanding of topics such as money, markets, capitalism, and inequality, among others. Students receive viewing guides to complete as they watch each documentary. The viewing guides contain specific questions listed in the same order as the topics are presented in the films. Guides are collected at the end of each documentary, and later returned to students after the instructor assesses student learning and provides feedback. The first documentary we watch is *Enron: The Smartest Guys in the World* (2005). This video complements our unit on money and institutions, specifically the section on corporate governance. Students, many of whom have had little to no exposure to the roles and responsibilities of corporate executives, learn about the actors and actions that contributed to one of the largest business scandals in U.S. history. This awareness lays the foundation for students to learn about the corporate actors and actions involved in the financial crisis. The second documentary we watch is *Inside Job* (2010), a critical exploration into the regulatory environment, housing market, banking practices, and actors that created the financial crisis. This movie brings together prior course activities and concepts into an exploration of the most devastating recession since the Great Depression.

The unit on the financial crisis spans class periods devoted to an overview of the crisis, the players, and the impact. To prepare for this unit, students listen to and take notes on two This American Life podcasts. The first is "The Giant Pool of Money" and the second is "Return to the Giant Pool of Money." In addition, they read an article reflecting on the impact of rating agencies, financial elites, and the political aftermath (Carruthers 2009). To prepare for the second day of the unit, students read Chap. 4 from *Griftopia* (Taibbi 2011). The book asserts that the very rich, deemed the "grifter class" because they have a grip on the political process, caused the financial crisis. Finally, in advance of the last class, they read a peer-reviewed article connecting residential segregation with foreclosure activity (Rugh and Massey 2010). The authors assess the degree to which racial housing segregation created attractive markets for the subprime lending activity that led to mass foreclosures. They found black residential segregation to be a significant factor in the foreclosure crisis. Throughout the unit we watch *Inside Job*, debriefing it along the way. Students employ the vocabulary and understanding they developed sequentially throughout the semester in their assessment of the financial crisis' causes and consequences.

Conclusion

Money and society are complex, entangled concepts. In Table 1, below, I outline course tools employed to help students intellectually connect with these ideas. During the first half of our course, we investigate the conceptual relationship between money and society by engaging critically with sociological theories, learning how to think about and define money, and becoming acquainted with the history of money (Unit I); understanding the causes and consequences of economic inequality (Unit II); and examining how the meaning of money differs based on its

Table 1 Select tools used to teach money and society

Units and topics	Select teaching tools and sources
Unit I: Introduction to money and society • Overview of the course • Foundations • Theories of money • What is money? • Historical development of money	• Pre-class journals with glossary terms • Planet Money – The invention of 'the economy' • We the Economy – Cave-O-Nomics – GDP smackdown – That film about money
Unit II: Money and inequality • Social stratification and structural inequality • Income gap and the minimum wage • Wealth gap • Poverty	• Pre-class journals with glossary terms • Growing apart: a political history of American inequality • We the Economy – The unbelievably sweet alpacas – Monkey business aka economic inequality – The value of work • Inequality.is • Spent (playspent.org) • Stratified Monopoly
Unit III: The social meaning of money • Introduction • Money in the home • Policing poor people's money	• Pre-class journals with glossary terms
Unit IV: Money and institutions • Government • Taxation • Banking and credit • Corporate governance	• Pre-class journals with glossary terms • This American Life – Take the money and run for office • Growing apart: a political history of American Inequality • We the Economy – Amazing animated film on the debt and the deficit – Taxation nation • *Enron: the smartest guys in the world*
Unit V: The U.S. financial crisis • Overview of the crisis • The players • The impact	• Pre-class journals with glossary terms • This American Life – The giant pool of money – Return to the giant pool of money • We the Economy – The street • *Inside Job*
Unit VI: Money's power to inspire • Alternative forms of currency • The sharing economy	• Pre-class journals with glossary terms

origins, users, and uses, and how these meanings impact social relationships (Unit III). In the second half of the course, we devote attention to the connection between institutions and money—paying specific attention to the government, tax policy, banking and credit, corporate power, and the recent U.S. financial crisis (Units IV and V). The course follows a scaffolding design whereby students construct their understanding of course concepts that grow in complexity as we ascended the scaffold. I instruct select topics and provide semi-structured activities while students develop their understanding with my feedback and redirection as needed.

Anonymous midterm and end-of-semester qualitative feedback suggests that scaffolding works to instill confidence in students and provide a structure within which students can develop their understanding of challenging topics. In an end-of-semester evaluation students are asked what they enjoyed the most about *Money and Society*. One student commented on the activities employed throughout the course:

> I enjoy the clips and videos that you show that go more in depth on some of the concepts. It helps to better understand some of the more difficult material. I also enjoy doing the glossary words before each class, so that I already know what some words mean, because I have no prior experience with some of these terms. I also think the Monopoly game day was a great, fun, interesting way to illustrate money in society.

For me, the most important feedback relates to knowledge attainment and mastery of course objectives. In the final exam students are asked to reflect on the purpose and benefit of the course. The following example is representative of many student responses:

> This is the single most informative class I have taken as an undergraduate. Past generations experienced nothing like the past U.S. financial crisis, and it's hard for most people to understand the way our economy works without formal education about it. Understanding the way money impacts our government and politics can lead to more informed decisions and voting. Facts about welfare and government assistance can relieve stigmas about the poor. Overall, this class looks directly at the "elephant in the room," and that is money and how it affects each and every one of us on a daily basis.

References

Bain, K. (2004). *What the best teachers do*. Cambridge, MA: Harvard University Press.

Bean, J. C. (2011). *Engaging ideas: the professor's guide to integrating writing, critical thinking, and active learning in the classroom* (2nd ed.). San Francisco, CA: Jossey-Bass.

Bligh, D. A. (2000). *What's the use of lectures?*. San Francisco, CA: Jossey-Bass.

Carruthers, B. G. (2009). A sociology of bubbles. *Contexts, 8*(3), 22–26.

Coghlan, C. L., & Huggins, D. W. (2004). That's not fair!: a simulation exercise in social stratification and structural inequality. *Teaching Sociology, 32*(2), 177–187.

Faber, J. W. (2013). Racial dynamics of subprime mortgage lending at the peak. *Housing Policy Debate, 23*(2), 328–349.

Pea, R. D. (2004). The social and technological dimensions of scaffolding and related theoretical concepts for learning, education, and human activity. *The Journal of Learning Sciences, 13*(3), 423–451.

Rugh, J. S., & Massey, D. S. (2010). Racial segregation and the American foreclosure crisis. *American Sociological Review, 75*(5), 629–651.

Svinicki, M., & McKeachie, W. J. (2011). *McKeachie's teaching tips: Strategies, research, and theory for college and university teachers* (13th ed.). Belmont, CA: Wadsworth, Cengage Learning.

Sawyer, R. K. (2006). *The Cambridge handbook of the learning sciences*. New York: Cambridge University Press.

Taibbi, M. (2011). *Griftopia: a story of bankers, politicians, and the most audacious power grab in American history*. New York: Spiegel & Grau, Random House.

Vygotsky, L. S. (1978). *Mind in society: the development of higher psychological processes*. Cambridge, MA: Harvard University Press.

Capitalism in the Classroom: Confronting the Invisibility of Class Inequality

Charlotte A. Kunkel

Author's Reflexive Statement

As the daughter of Midwestern farmers, I grew up knowing we didn't have much money, but never thought we wanted for anything. It was self-evident in high school that homemade clothes were readily identifiable next to name brand fashion. I learned to fit in, if not entirely so. I was a good student and had lots of friends. I didn't think class identity marked me much. One incident made it clear to me, however, that class location was definitely an influential construct in my upbringing. In graduate school at some social gathering with my fellow students, I had the occasion to utter the phrase "borrowed your book." I don't recall the details of who borrowed what, but I distinctly remember being taken to task for using the term "incorrectly." I was told "you loaned" the book, you did not "borrow it." Chastised and flummoxed I had to research the usage of the term so I could avoid further embarrassment with my new crowd. Whether a local colloquial usage or low class vernacular, I rarely use the terms today, still scarred by that reminder that I was not one of them—well schooled and high classed. Though I am clearly part of the upper middle class today, I struggle between a working class desire to "own" land (the mark of wealth and stability I learned growing up) and an intellectual critique of capitalism, and a political belief in socialism.

C. A. Kunkel (✉)
Luther College, Decorah, IA, USA
e-mail: kunkelch@luther.edu

K. Haltinner and L. Hormel (eds.), *Teaching Economic Inequality and Capitalism in Contemporary America*, https://doi.org/10.1007/978-3-319-71141-6_11

Introduction

When teaching about socioeconomic or class inequality and capitalism, I find I first need to raise awareness about social location. Most students I encounter are not class conscious. Then I need to debunk stereotypes about how we find ourselves in these locales and, finally, question the ideologies of inequality (and capitalism) that keep us there. I use a series of strategies to achieve these goals in an Introduction to Sociology course at a private liberal arts college. My students are disproportionately white and wealthy, although we also have a significant population of first generation college students.

Most of my students have never questioned their class identity; they are comfortably "middle class." This subjectivity isn't closely connected to objective measures of income or wealth but rather ideas about social value/s. They hold deeply the embedded ideologies of private property and competition, and extol the virtues of the free market. They report adhering to the values of education and family as strong middle class values. I find we have to unpack these statements to articulate that valuing family means: most traditionally a heterosexual two-parent family even though we know only twenty percent of households are such [married couples with children under 18 make up only 20.2% of households in the US (Newman 2014: 201)]. Valuing education means going to college without thinking about how many young people are unable to achieve that regardless of their values (or income!). Nearly seventy percent of 18–24 yr. olds were attending college in 2015 (Bureau of Labor Statistics 2015). In other words, purporting to hold these values is idealistic and symbolic and not always based in the reality of behavior.

I will share and discuss two classroom activities that I employ with some success. In this essay, I will describe the income quiz and "train game" activities and provide commentary about how they work best to expose class invisibility in the classroom.

The Income Quiz

The income quiz simply asks two questions: what is your socioeconomic class identity/label and what is your parent's annual income. Students submit this anonymously on a piece of torn out notebook paper. They write two responses, class label and income. I create a chart with this data and present it to the class the next day, with data from the Statistical Abstracts of the United States about median family and quintile distributions of annual incomes.

On the following day of class I present the students' responses back to them in an anonymous table with incomes ranging from high to low and their corresponding class labels adjacent to the income (see Appendix A). I ask students to comment. ("Tell me what you see?" "Are we class conscious?" "How do you know?"). We talk about class consciousness, middle class bias, invisibility, and ideology. In my private college classroom the distribution is often skewed toward the upper quintiles, with most students claiming incomes over the median family income—sometimes in the millions. Most students also claim an identity label of "middle class" sometimes qualified by "upper middle" or "lower middle," but nonetheless, "middle class." And these monikers are not consistent with actual incomes—they are applied when making an estimated $20,000, $200,000, and $700,000 annual income. The median annual income of families was $70,697 in 2015 dollars (US Census Bureau 2015). Students are forced to confront concepts like objective and subjective class, middle class bias, class consciousness (and false consciousness), invisibility, and relative deprivation, while looking at their own class labeling and distribution. We debunk stereotypes of the poor and the rich, and introduce the concept of ideology (see examples of assignments in Appendix A).

During discussion, the students are encouraged to problematize these labels and consider the effect of false consciousness and middle class bias on the economic conditions in the United States. I introduce the sociological use of the word ideology as "a set of beliefs that justify social structures" and then we identify class ideologies in the United States that they have learned and explore how they learned them. It is helpful to ask them to think about their families and how and when they talk about money. Students readily answer that they learned they are supposed to work hard to pull themselves up and improve upon their parents' class status. They believe they will, if they work hard.

Class discussion often reveals that students are unaware of their parents' annual incomes. When I ask them why they don't know how much their parents make, they give these answers: my parents don't want me to worry, they say it is none of my business, it is just something we don't talk about. When I ask if they filled out FAFSA forms they, of course, say they do. "Is your parent's income listed?" I ask. "We don't look," they say. Only one of twenty students this fall 2016 said they regularly discuss income—but only with her mother, not her dad.

I ask them about their own jobs and whether or not they have ever been told to "not talk about" their pay. It is common for at least a few students to share stories about being given a starting salary or a raise and having been asked (or told) not to tell their coworkers what they get paid. I ask them why. We may talk about unionization at this point, or do a mini lecture on Marxism, the proletariat, and the bourgeoisie. We may talk about religion as the 'opiate of the masses' and what our ideologies of class are today.

I connect these concepts to the text and they are forced to think about what they know and how they learned about class and ideologies of pulling themselves up by their bootstraps, hard work, meritocracy and equal rewards. At the same time they believe in the notion of meritocracy—that you earn what you deserve— they also know about the gender wage gap, for example, or that people of color are disproportionately poor. We look up the numbers in the text to reinforce the facts of class inequality. I ask them to reconcile these disparate beliefs with the objective data and they come to understand that ideologies of class mask the objective realities of class stratification.

The Train Game

On the next day, we begin class by playing a game,[1] for which I provide complete directions in Appendix A (based on Brinkerhoff et al. 1995). The instructor brings to class envelopes with two colors of cards inside. The classroom must have moveable chairs. Students are broken into groups which line up like a train in a circle—so one student is facing the next student's back—and are given the rules of scoring (I typically write these on the board) and told to pass cards—all without talking. Without explicit instruction they will most likely revert to cultural assumptions about competition and winning to play the game. They are forced to choose between competition and cooperation—and get points based on individual choices. As the game proceeds opportunities for discussion among members and team play develop, but students ultimately have to choose what to follow. After several rounds, and breaks for controlled communication, we tally results and discuss outcomes. I typically have three rounds of seven passes such that the total possible (if all passed white) would be 210 points each. If they play competitively I have had high scores in the 300 s and low scores in the negative numbers. The point spread can be as large as 400 or 500. I have students report their individual scores when finished as well as highlight the spread of points in each group or "train." In addition to discussing their individual choices in how to play, it also becomes clear whether the group played competitively or cooperatively based on the spread of points –do all members of the small group have similar points or is there a great distribution (or inequality) of points? Further, ask them what they discussed when they had the opportunity to talk to each other: What did they say to each other when given a chance to communicate? Did they agree collectively on a strategy? Did they follow it? Why or why not? When? If they changed their practice they can tell you why and try to connect it to business practices in a free market, e.g., loyal customers deserve better deals or one-time transactions are high risk for deception and fraud.

This simulation game allows students to see the cultural assumptions of competitive individualism, capitalism, and its ideologies, and how we reproduce it in everyday practices—such as, childhood games, education, sports, and business transactions. We end the unit by identifying class-based ideologies prominent in our culture. I ask them what games they played as kids, in school, and now. I ask them about childhood games and school yard games—can they think of games that are played cooperatively? The most common examples are clearly competitive, e.g. Monopoly, Sorry! Parcheesi, Aggravation, or card games such as War. Few students can identify games that teach principles of cooperation. Even team sports compete against other teams. I provide them a website i.e. citation "10 cooperative

---

[1]I received permission (and blessings) to reproduce/incorporate and modify Harrod's (1983) activity.

games" and then include the website in works cited Top 10 cooperative games for families. http://www2.peacefirst.org/digitalactivitycenter/files/top_ten_games_for_families_0.pdf that offers some basic cooperative activities. Beyond the parachute activity on the playground, few examples of cooperation are familiar to them.

Next, I provide a handout with a very basic outline to compare and contrast structural characteristics of capitalist and socialist systems. I have to remind the students that we do not live in a purely capitalist system (there are many government interventions, e.g., minimum wage, monopoly laws, permits and licensing). Students struggle with the stereotypes they have learned about communist systems as well but can rarely progress in the conversation beyond simple assertions that communism is "bad". I ask them where they learned this information and how it was conveyed to them. Standard images in their minds are of the bread lines in the former USSR or "repression" in communist Cuba. Further, while they are generally aware of the outcomes regarding productivity (high and low), no student typically identifies the outcome of inequality (high and low). Using Marxist theory we talk about the need for an underclass or unemployment in a capitalist economy to keep wages down. After discussion and exposing the very basic lack of information, students report seeing socioeconomic class in new ways and begin to question notions of culture and capitalism that they have not encountered before.

Summary

After using these two class activities and providing the handout on capitalism and socialism, students are less able to blindly herald capitalism's benefits and forced to confront the pitfalls of a "free market" system. We are able, as a class, to discuss the ideologies of economic class as beliefs that pervade our culture and that justify our social practices, from games to educational pedagogy, to business practice. Most significantly students begin to question their own family norms not just about money but even about how they talk about money. Many students come back to class telling of conversations they had with their parents—for the first time! They also come confused, sometimes angry, and with feelings of guilt for perpetuating inequality. I mention this to prepare instructors to be ready to deal with emotion in the classroom. What I find effective is to work through how we come to class consciousness and the perpetual interactions between individuals and society—using the sociological imagination. It is helpful to remind them social systems are set up to reproduce themselves and now that we are class conscious we can work to change the systems of class inequality. Ultimately, these two activities help me to expose or make visible class stratification in the United States and provide students some information to raise class consciousness, such that students move beyond just words in a text, but rather through simulation must confront both the realities of their own class location and the practices of class ideologies in their own lives.

References

Brinkerhoff, D. B., White, L. K., & Ortega, S. T. (1995). *Instructor's manual to accompany essentials of sociology* (3rd ed., pp 169–171). New York: West.

Bureau of Labor Statistics. (2015). College enrollment and work activity of 2016 high school graduates. *US BLS Economic News Releases*. Retrieved from https://www.bls.gov/news.release/hsgec.nr0.htm.

Harrod, W. (1983). Social dilemma: A teaching game. *Teaching Sociology, 10*(2), 266–274.

Newman, D. M. (2014). *Sociology: Exploring the architecture of everyday life* (10th ed.). New York: Sage.

US Census Bureau. (2015). Historical income tables: Families. Retrieved from https://www.census.gov/data/tables/time-series/demo/income-poverty/historical-income-families.html.

Experiencing the Outcomes of Economic Inequality in the Day-to-Day Workings of the Classroom

Susan Machum

Author's Reflexive Statement and Context for the Described Classroom Activity

In their innovative research on elementary school students' awareness of social class, Baldus and Tribe (1978) illustrated that between grade one and grade three students acquired a keen awareness of their own social class position in relation to others. Despite early knowledge, I find university students in the liberal arts university I teach in—who are much older than third graders—reluctant to acknowledge or discuss social inequality and class differences. In addition, students frequently camouflage their own class origins. Dorling (2014) also reports "young people try to hide their class backgrounds by means of how they dress and behave" (p. 33). Regardless of their family's actual economic wealth, students tend to self-identify as members of the nebulous "middle class".

I don't think this discomfort with social inequality is new. I remember very clearly being an undergraduate student at the same liberal arts university in which I now teach, grappling with social inequality and the practices that produce and reproduce it. I came to university in the early 1980s with a scholarship, a small bursary, and a student loan. My first year marked both the end of the province's student bursary program and early days of government austerity—what would later become structural adjustment and neoliberalism.

As an undergraduate student, I was not keen to share with my classmates the fact that I grew up poor, on a subsistence farm in rural New Brunswick. In retrospect, I am not sure why. Was it from shame or embarrassment of not being as wealthy, as I thought, my classmates were? Then and now, I have no empirical evidence of most fellow students' wealth or social class background. So I was definitely working off

S. Machum (✉)
St. Thomas University, Fredericton, NB, Canada
e-mail: smachum@stu.ca

K. Haltinner and L. Hormel (eds.), *Teaching Economic Inequality and Capitalism in Contemporary America*, https://doi.org/10.1007/978-3-319-71141-6_12

of assumptions. Was it because through my education I was seeking to achieve social class mobility? Was it because I was afraid if people knew I was from a working class background I would not credibly become a member of the consumptive 'middle class' or as it turned out 'the petit-bourgeosie'? I have no clear recollections of my thinking process at the time. But I believe this awareness of my younger self's discomfort is what draws me to role-playing and simulation activities as a means to challenge my students to recognize privilege, advantage, and disadvantage within existing social structures and institutions, without calling on them to disclose the personal details of their own lives.

Simulations in Higher Education

In my office, a significant amount of space is devoted to books that are filled with exercises, role-plays, games, and discussions designed to creatively engage students in critical analysis. This is the legacy of my time with Canada World Youth, an international exchange program, as both a participant and group leader. Falling within the popular education tradition, these activities are intended to provide a shared experience from which debate, dialogue, and discussion can emerge. As the first book I read on the subject explains: "[Popular education] is a collective or group process of education, where the teacher and students learn together, beginning with the concrete experience of the participants, leading to reflection on that experience in order to effect positive change" (Burke and Arnold 1983, p. 7).

Popular education, as defined by Freire (2000), is a form of education that poses problems and asks questions in a setting that calls on participants to be active. Students 'do' something; and then they are called on to describe their experience, to reflect on it, to share how the activity made them feel, and to analyze and question how this event is linked to other social processes. In popular education a distinction is made between the content of the activity (i.e. what the group talks about) and the process (i.e. *how* the group learns about and discusses the subject matter).

Some popular education activities are very simple, others incredibly complex. To get student engagement and buy-in in a university classroom, it is important to introduce simulation and interactive popular education activities at the outset of the term, beginning with simple exercises before moving to more complex undertakings. It is also critical that instructors have a clearly identified learning goal that is well thought through and directly linked to the exercise. Otherwise students will feel like they have wasted their time, and such a feeling can undermine the success of future activities. To ensure maximum learning, time has to be budgeted to 'debrief' students immediately after the event; in other words you should never do an activity in one class, with plans to reflect on and discuss lessons learned the next because the time gap can allow frustrations to fester. If students are too emotionally engaged without an opportunity to vent and reflect, they may even prematurely withdraw from the course. Always plan time for students to provide immediate feedback and, if time is short, layout some of the follow-up discussion points that will be picked up next class. I can assure you, I have learned these lessons the hard way.

The exercise that I lay out here emerged from a conversation with a former colleague about her daughter's homework assignment. Students in a local New Brunswick elementary school had been given one week to make a booklet on birds in the region. As part of the instructions the teacher had forbidden them to draw, sketch or color pictures of these birds to include in their report. Instead they were to find and include photographic illustrations of each species and they would be graded on how 'colorful' and detailed their assignment was. Living in a small, rural town, my colleague said she had spent almost $70 on printer ink to ensure her daughter successfully completed this homework. Over coffee we discussed how teachers routinely ask students to bring in pictures, Bristol board, magazines, color pencils and other material resources to undertake work. More recently students are also being asked to have personal electronic devices and resources for use during school hours. But not everyone has easy access to these resources to use at home or carry to school at a moment's notice.

At the time I was teaching a second year course on social inequality. We were studying intersectionality and I was emphasizing how, through everyday acts, we 'do' racism, gender, ageism, and so on. I realized this elementary school homework assignment represented a real opportunity to illustrate how the education system practices and 'does' social class. Especially as students strongly believe their grades reflect their own intellectual abilities and performance as opposed to other social dynamics. My goal was to create a simulation activity that showed how teachers influence academic outcomes—and reinforce existing social class inequities—through particular assignments. As Atkinson (2015) explains, through such means "class differences get translated into academic differences" (p. 125). The following section provides a detailed explanation of the in-class 'poster' making activity I devised for students to experience how varying class backgrounds can impact student grades and educational outcomes.

The Exercise: Education and Social Class

While in primary and secondary schools students are routinely asked to bring resources to school in order to carry out in-class activities, this scenario is less common in university where students generally carry only pen and paper, relevant books, and perhaps a calculator or appropriate lab supplies for in-class use. Consequently, this exercise requires students to bring items they would not normally transport with them to university classes and to search out and find materials they may not have on hand. As students are packing up and preparing to leave class, I announce that between now and the next class they have a homework assignment. In order to create an in-class poster on gender stereotypes they are to bring the following items to the next class: a piece of Bristol board, colored crayons, markers, scissors, a ruler, glue, tape and magazines that they are willing to cut up. As a memory aid, each student is handed this list on a small strip of white paper as they leave the class but no other reminders or contact is made with students between giving the list and beginning the next class. The piece of paper is intentionally small, to encourage it being lost and forgotten between one class and the next.

The following class is spent doing the exercise and undertaking an initial debriefing. This simulation exercise works best in a class that has a ninety-minute or longer time slot. The first twenty minutes of class are spent setting up the exercise and splitting students into groups. At the beginning of class, students are told that the main agenda for the day will be to create a colorful poster, intended to teach their peers about gender stereotypes. They are reminded that their homework assignment was to bring materials to class for this activity and they now need to pull out their resources and create a pile of all the materials they brought with them. Invariably at this moment some students groan as they forgot to do their homework and have nothing, while a few students have amassed a large pile of materials and might be described as 'over-prepared' for the task at hand. Once their piles are created, students are asked to pick up all of their materials and with 'arms loaded' or 'empty', to create a line up along the perimeter of the classroom according to those with the most to those with the least amount of resources. What quickly emerges is a sense of abundance at one end of the line and a dearth at the other.

At this point, if there is a lot of grumbling, students can be reminded social inequality is present in all classrooms—even if students have an unequal access to resources—they all had an 'equal opportunity' to bring materials to class. They were each given the same instructions at the same time, nobody was discriminated against, and nobody was given an advantage by receiving differential information.

Given they all had the same opportunity to bring resources to class, they need to accept that what is in their hands right now represents their current wealth and access to resources for the duration of the class. They cannot ask for, borrow, or lend materials from one person or from one group to the next because 'homework' assignments are normally done at home and do not, as a rule, enable a redistribution of resources amongst students. Everyday homework assignments are completed according to a students' real access to materials.

Once students are lined up according to their resource wealth—depending upon the size of the class—they are divided into five or ten equal size groups. A class with fewer than 50 students would generally be divided into five equal size groups to represent quintiles; and a class of more than 50 students would be divided into ten equal size groups to capture deciles. The divisions occur according to the quantity of resources on hand. For example, in a class of 30, the six students with the most materials are formed into a group; the next six students form the next group; and so on. The fifth group will have the least amount of resources to work with for completing the exercise. These 'quintiles' are intended to symbolically capture income inequality among a given population. Before moving forward, students can be reminded of what portion of income and wealth are in the hands of the richest versus middle versus poorest quintile within their region and/or the nation.

Once divided into groups, students are given 30 min to work together as a team to create one group poster on gender stereotypes. They are told at the end of the exercise their poster will be assessed according to: how colorful it is; how informative it is; its use of photographs, pictures and illustrations (they are informed mechanical visuals will be given more value than any hand drawings); its overall neatness; and the clarity of its message. In addition all members of the team will be given the same grade—as this is often standard practice for group work within the education system.

What I have observed as students undertake the task of creating their group poster is that the group with the most resources is often the most overwhelmed. They tend to have too many resources to process in the allotted time and their quandary is over what to include and what to exclude in their quest for the 'best' outcome. I have witnessed scissors flying across pages, disagreements over what images to use, and struggles over what message to convey.

On the other end of the spectrum, I have seen the 'poorest' quintile have nothing to work with but a pen and sheets of loose leaf, and sometimes a highlighter. On occasion there has been a student with incredible artistic talent in this most disadvantaged group and they have effectively drawn—albeit on small pieces of paper —an effective message about gender stereotypes (but in the end, they lose marks for not fulfilling the artistic and presentational criteria).

The groups in-between are working with fewer resources than the quintile groups above them and more than those below them, with mixed results. Of course, creativity plays a key role in the actual outcomes of each group; but the exercise, and the evaluation criteria, is deliberately skewed to advantage those with the most economic resources.

Of note, students without resources report thirty minutes feels like a really long time, while those with a plethora of magazines, pictures, markers and pencil crayons report it feels like an insufficient amount of time. Nevertheless, at ten-minute intervals, students are reminded of how much time is remaining. After thirty-minutes of poster making, ten to fifteen minutes is spent collectively evaluating the posters according to the criteria noted above: Is the poster colorful? Is the message clear? Does it use photographs and detailed illustrations? Based on the criteria listed the class is asked what grade the poster would receive. At this moment students can be reminded that classroom assignments and assessment criteria effectively capture what the teacher—and the school system they work in—values; so there is always a subjective component to marking, even when the criteria is seemingly objective.

Debriefing the Exercise

The teaching value of doing simulation activities is that they provide a relevant shared experience for students to reflect on, discuss, and debate. It moves students from hypothetical to lived scenarios. Students can now talk about what they did and how they felt rather than how they might act in a given situation. To be effective and gain maximum learning students need to be guided through a 'debriefing' or evaluation phase of the exercise in order to extrapolate and apply what happened in the simulation to 'real world' events.

I use this activity to teach students several key concepts about social inequality and social justice. On one hand we look at the overt or stated curriculum agenda of the exercise, which was to examine gender stereotypes. On the other I use the exercise to introduce students to Bowles and Ginitis's (1976) concept of the 'hidden curriculum'. In this case, the hidden curriculum is to examine the effects of social class and economic inequality on student grades and outcomes. Working through the dynamics of the hidden curriculum and its invisibility leads to a discussion of the dominant ideology embedded in early 21st Century capitalism, the key concepts it endorses—such as meritocracy and 'equality of opportunity'—and the broader features of the liberal ideological framework.

In a forty-five minute class it is not possible to do the exercise and address all of these issues. But the exercise paves the way for these discussions to emerge throughout subsequent classes. Immediately after collectively 'grading' the posters it is important to capture students' emotional responses to the activity because this is when they will be strongest and it may be necessary to diffuse them, especially if people feel particularly wronged. In fact, every 'debriefing' should encompass two phases—first, time needs to be allotted for capturing and validating participants' initial reactions; and secondly, instructors need to help students extrapolate and link their experiences from this exercise to the theories and concepts they want them to learn.

Phase One: Capturing Emotional Responses

Immediately following an activity, we, as instructors, can feel pressured for time, especially if the end of class is looming. We might be tempted to skip over immediate reactions in favor of theoretical messages. However, for deep engagement students need to express how the exercise made them feel. This step captures the 'process' side of popular education, whereas our theories and concepts fall on the content side. Listening to and gaining an appreciation of students' feelings immediately after the event helps them identify—and later reflect on—points of discomfort. Did they feel angry, empowered, enlightened, hurt, frustrated, scared, annoyed, or indifferent as they carried out the assigned tasks? Why? What exact events or behaviors made them feel this way? Did they feel that the activity was fair? Or did they experience feelings of injustice? What was going on at those points?

If students are reluctant to speak, to tease out the range of reactions I witnessed during the activity, I will identify specific moments of engagement and ask them to elaborate on what was happening and how they felt at that particular moment. It is best to focus on specific incidents as this approach can be used to draw attention to the structural, rather than the personal, dimensions of the exercise.

During phase one of the debriefing, it is critical to not only validate students' feelings but also to remind them that they and others were acting according to the structures and the 'rules of the game' imposed upon them. If they were among the poorer groups they should not see their peers as 'greedily hoarding materials' from them, but instead recognize that their peers were bound by the rules to behave in the ways that they did, even if doing so made them feel uncomfortable.

In acknowledging emotions, I emphasize that the exercise is designed to not simply illustrate how social inequality unfolds in an abstract, theoretical sense but also to provide an awareness of how it can feel to have too much or too little. Depending upon the neighborhood people live in, where they work and go to school, they many never have the sense of having 'too much' in relation to others. However, those living outside their neighborhood are almost always aware of their relative situation and often seek to hide it. In *Poor-bashing*, Swanson (2001) lays out the politics of exclusion and documents how children deny being poor in order to avoid being ridiculed or undermined. Dorling (2014, p. 33) also reports children try to hide their class backgrounds. But here, in a small classroom where everybody has shared the same experience, inequality of wealth and its consequences permeate the space without students needing to reveal their own class position.

Sometimes in the process of talking about their feelings, the 'resource rich' students indicate they wanted to give up some of their materials to others. When this happens, the window is opening to engage in phase two of the debriefing: theoretical reflection. I ask them why they wanted to give their items away. I challenge them on whether they were going to give their best resources or the least useful ones. I ask the 'poor' students how they would have felt to receive the wealthier group's charity. Swanson (2001) is a great resource for exploring how charity helps the rich feel better about their wealth, how it reinforces social inequalities and short-circuits the potential for real social justice. Swanson (2001) reports "charity creates a relationship of power and dependence instead of equality and respect" (p. 135). And while I acknowledge students could have shared resources in this classroom setting, I ask them how they could do so if they were all in their individual households doing their homework? After all, by its very nature, homework means working with the resources you have at home. Should it be surprising, then, that "class and material wealth [are] the best predictors of [academic] outcomes" (Atkinson 2015, p. 126)?

In a 45-min teaching slot, it is usually only possible to barely scrape the surface of potential learning outcomes. The key is to spend the limited time at the end of class listening to, recognizing, and acknowledging students' emotional responses. It is particularly necessary to diffuse strong emotions as this is important for continued student engagement and moving on to the second stage of debriefing.

Phase Two: Engaging with Theoretical Concepts and Debates

As noted above, there are multiple layers of social inequality and its effects that I aim to illustrate through this exercise. I elaborate on each of them here—though I would stress that my discussion is not exhaustive. These theoretical dialogs begin in the subsequent class and can continue throughout the term through referrals back to this exercise. Indeed what can be learned from this simulation is open-ended, as the depth the exercise affords is dependent on what you as an instructor, and your students, bring to the discussion.

The next class begins with all the posters being prominently placed on the classroom wall. Our goal at this moment is to address the explicit or overt curriculum agenda of the poster exercise—to examine gender stereotypes. I query students on what their posters and the images embedded upon them tell us about gender inequality. How do the images they encountered (or conjured) portray women and men? How are class, age, gender, and ethnicity—what McMullin (2010) calls CAGEs—depicted? How homogenous or diverse are the social media images? How reflective of students' life experiences are the messages and images presented in their posters? What stereotypes do their posters and the sources they used reinforce? Is intersectionality present? If so, how? If not, what is missing?

I introduce McMullin's (2010) argument that social injustices are witnessed and experienced inside physical bodies—literally the body is a CAGE—that is classed, aged, gendered, and ethnically diverse. Every individual's CAGE is developed and transformed through the social, economic, political, and cultural encounters they have. As we move through the life course our experiences can reinforce or challenge our class, gender, cultural and ethnic identity. I also challenge McMullin's CAGE and suggest an expanded notion of CA^2G^2ES allows for a more comprehensive discussion whereby we could analyze class, age, ablebodiedness (and disability), gender, geography (urban/rural; North/South), ethnicity, and sexuality.

The key in this process of reflection is to raise questions about who is included (and how) and who is excluded (and why) in the posters they produced in order to tease out how everyday actions subtly 'do' social inequality, even when it is not the intention. Critically questioning and examining the messages and images of gender stereotypes conveyed in social media and reproduced in their posters is the first layer of learning but it is not the reason for doing the exercise. Everybody could have been given a comprehensive and identical package of resources to work with to achieve this outcome. Instead the goal was to illustrate how economic inequality and social class emerges inside the education system.

I want to increase their knowledge of how a lack of resources for school assignments—and subsequent marks—reflects real world social inequalities. Is it fair what happens to students who do not have the resources to meet the evaluation criteria? I reveal that recognizing the effects of class inequality was the real purpose of the exercise. Is it fair that I did not tell them this from the beginning? Some students say yes, others no. My strategy at this point is to introduce Bowles and

Gintis's (1976) notion of a 'hidden curriculum'. Basically Bowles and Gintis (1976) argued the stated school curriculum and outcomes masked the real purpose of school, which was to produce compliant workers. The 'hidden curriculum' was for students to learn to take orders, to follow instructions, to eat and go to the bathroom on a particular schedule, and so on. Students who are the most compliant and excel at obeying the rules, not those with the most academic skills, make the best workers. Of course the actual training that students receive is very much dependent on their existing class position because local schools reflect the working or middle class neighborhoods in which students live. The curriculum, learning environment, and assignment and testing expectations capture existing privilege, or its dearth, and reproduce it.

For example, the absence of homework captures a working class person's reality—they do their job, come home and forget about work. Having homework, on the other hand, parallels the working reality expected of managers and professionals who routinely bring work home to catch up and prepare for the next day. Hence the debate over the value of homework is an ideological debate based on social class locations. The 'hidden curriculum' thesis thus seeks to demonstrate how education systems foster and legitimatize class inequality (Atkinson 2015, p. 128).

I also point out this process continues in post-secondary education: in part through streaming students through different universities ('top' ranked, research institutions versus smaller, liberal arts colleges) and different programs (commerce and computing versus arts and humanities); and through the reproduction of an ideological framework that promotes meritocracy—that is the Davis-Moore thesis that pay (and grade) differentials are and should be based on 'personal merit' (Atkinson 2015).

Given students want to believe the education system is fair and just, and has treated them all according to their individual merit, arguments in favor of 'equality of opportunity' generally emerge in the class discussion. Students maintain it was their own—or their peers'—fault that they did not have the resources needed. They were all asked and expected to bring resources to class. Here I like to talk about the difference between 'blaming the victim' whereby social inequality is attributed to individual flaws and failures as compared to structural/system flaws. My poster exercise is deliberately structured to produce unequal outcomes—even if the poorest quintile has a lot of resources, relative to their peer groups they will have less.

This also permits a discussion of absolute versus relative poverty. In terms of schooling, what if children do not have the resources asked for, and parents do not have the money to buy them, should children be punished for their lack of resources? In the 'real' world, children often are punished for their family's lack of resources, which is something they have no control over.

In studying social inequality in Canada, Duffy and Mandell (1994) reported how many school children are excluded and need to sit on the sidelines during school bike hikes or skating days because they do not own a bike or skates. For these children, parts of the school day and life turns into "a spectator sport". You watch, but you don't participate. I ask if this is what it felt like being in the resource poor groups. How did they feel about wealthier groups throwing away or discarding materials they could use? I recount how, even though I could afford to, I refused to buy skates for my child to wear four times for a gym class module. My son and his friends who did not own skates were effectively punished for not having the resources in that they were expected to walk to the skating rink, and then spend the ensuing hour, while others skated, walking around the skating rink watching those with skates engage in the activity. One week he refused to walk and sat down during the skating session. That day I got a phone call from a school administrator about his non-compliance. But as my son pointed out, the skaters got to take breaks all the time. They could go sit on the benches, but the walkers could not. From his perspective it wasn't fair. I ask students if they can recall such events throughout their school years. Were they the excluded participants observing the privileged or the privileged watching the excluded participants sitting on the sidelines? Can they recall any efforts to redress or shift these experiences in ways that everybody could participate equally, without discrimination?

Even after the poster exercise and elaboration of other real life examples, students still want to believe that their classmates from elementary school and high school who 'dropped out', or didn't do well, or never went on to university ended up where they did because they weren't motivated, or skilled, or able. My students become very uncomfortable when I point out their dialogue mimics the language of exclusion outlined by Swanson (2001) in *Poor-bashing*. Students who do poorly are labeled as "lazy, unmotivated, and undisciplined"; and when they end up poor later in life they will also be called "uneducated". I ask: Why do we believe that students with poor grades and, later, low incomes were unwilling or unable to work hard? What driving force leads to the collective propensity to blame individuals for their 'poor' grades and failure to 'succeed' in what is in fact an educational environment that reinforces existing social inequalities?

It is at this juncture that I introduce the dominant ideology pervasive in capitalist societies. The dominant ideology promotes individualism, liberalism, utilitarianism, and materialism (Allahar and Côté 1998). But before elaborating on these specific features I summarize Allahar and Côté's (1998) review of the five dimensions inherent in any ideology. First, Allahar and Côté (1998) argue the cognitive dimension of an ideology captures the complex, and often messy, mix of knowledge and beliefs its adherents follow. Knowledge statements can be questioned and verified whereas the strength of a belief is so strong that proof is not needed. They note beliefs are often based on myths rather than actual evidence so critical investigation can be hindered by the cognitive dimension of an ideology. Secondly, ideologies embody an emotional dimension in that people are often blindly passionate and emotionally attached to their beliefs. As a result people's actions can appear highly irrational to those who do not share the same ideological position. Thirdly, ideologies have value judgments embedded in them, since any given ideology aims either to endorse or to challenge existing social systems, institutions and social relationships. Fourthly, an ideology embodies a 'call to action' whereby followers recognize what should be done to maintain the *status quo* or to overturn or correct its wrongs, deficiencies and weaknesses. It is the type of action that an ideology calls for that differentiates conservative, radical, and reformist ideologies. Finally, an ideology must have a societal base—a group of people whose perceived interests are served by promoting and endorsing this way of thinking. This last dimension is critical because while an individual can embrace an ideology, they don't just develop it on their own. In summary Allahar and Côté (1998) argue ideologies are frameworks that we use to evaluate both how the world is *and* how it ought to be. Consequently ideologies provide a *description* of unfolding events, as well as a *prescription* for appropriate action.

So how do the features of the dominant ideology within capitalism—individualism, liberalism, utilitarianism, and materialism—promote and validate social inequality and the dynamics we saw playing out in the poster exercise? First and foremost, the cult of the individual presents and insists that personal success and failure (in this instance school grades and later 'career' earnings) is the result of individual efforts, skills, hard work, and motivations (Allahar and Côté 1998). This dimension of the dominant ideology is directly challenged by the poster exercise, in that it is a group project and a group mark. This is a dynamic that students reluctantly accept in the exercise, but generally challenge in course assessment schemes. Students passionately believe a group grade will hinder rather than enhance their final mark. Generally students cling to the premise that as an individual they will achieve the most.

The second feature of the dominant ideology, liberalism, is premised on the separateness of each individual person, and on the notion that the 'invisible hand' of the market metes appropriate and fair rewards to each individual on the basis of their skill and efforts. Within this dimension, society is understood to be a collection of individuals, each free to pursue their own individual goals within the marketplace (Allahar and Côté 1998). In the case of the exercise, individuals were 'free to' bring whatever materials they wanted. It was their freedom to act that saw those with a lot of resources act responsibly, while those without materials clearly acted irresponsibly. The results, therefore, reflect their individual efforts. From a dominant ideology perspective, this is fair.

The utilitarian facet of the dominant ideology promotes the idea that if each individual pursues what is best for them, then it will lead to the greatest good for all (Allahar and Côté 1998). By bringing materials and doing the best possible job on the poster, the individual student will gain the most. In group work, on the other hand, their efforts will lead to others' success, which is the very aspect students tend to dislike the most about group work. Students tend to argue group work always produces some freeloaders—students who get grades they did not earn because they did not do their portion of the work. Challenging this notion and questioning the extent to which this is actually true can lead to interesting debate.

Finally, the notion of materialism validates and encourages the relentless drive of individuals to acquire and own more and more material possessions (Allahar and Côté 1998). The materialist dimension is supported through our tendency to measure personal success and achievement through our possessions (see Schor 1999). This aspect of the dominant ideology is challenged by the exercise requiring students to share the resources they brought to class with the other members of their group. Questions around how comfortable they were with sharing their pictures and resources with fellow group members, their desire to keep the best materials for themselves, and the challenge even of sharing ideas can allow students to probe how wedded they are to their material possessions. Further probing can involve asking students: Who took 'left over' resources home? The person who brought them, or somebody else? After the magazines were used and cut up, did the 'owner' want them back? Why or why not?

While each facet of the dominant ideology is present within, and to some extent challenges, our capacity to work collectively, students still manage to work in their groups and complete the task assigned. A fundamental question is how did they do that? How have they learned to work within competing paradigm structures in order to carry out day-to-day expectations and events? Understanding our malleability, our capacity to at once question social inequalities, while at the same time maintaining them is an important lesson for students. Understanding social inequalities and the spaces and places where they intersect is critical for breaking down social inequalities and changing the behaviors that 'do' social class, gender, ageism, sexism, racism, homophobia, and so on. This exercise provides a shared experience from which students can extrapolate and explore how the social world has come to be what it is and how it might be changed.

Conclusion

Freire (2000) keenly believed that power emerges from critical analysis and awareness of everyday experiences. Our capacity to analyze our behaviors and see the linkages between them and larger social processes is how we will understand our own role in the creation and maintenance of oppressive structures. A simple classroom exercise like the one presented here is structured to illustrate how social class emerges in the day-to-day operations of the classroom. It shows how everyday educational practices serve to reproduce those inequalities by disproportionately rewarding those with resources, while punishing those without. This learning goal is intentionally hidden at the outset, just as the 'hidden curriculum' is hidden from students. The strength of popular education techniques is that they call on participants to question social structures, and to apply their learning to multiple situations. Moving from the concrete to the theoretical enhances overall student learning and shared activities create a deeper level of discussion than external or abstract examples. Your own students will bring their backgrounds and experiences to bear on this exercise leading to varied theoretical threads of discussion than I have presented here. And you will bring yours.

References

Allahar, A.L., & Côté, J.E. (1998). *Richer and poorer: The structure of social inequality in Canada*. Toronto: Lorimer.

Arnold, R., & Burke, B. (1983). *A popular education handbook. An educational experience taken from Central America and adapted to the Canadian context*. Toronto: Ontario Institute for Studies in Education.

Atkinson, W. (2015). *Class*. London: Polity Press.

Baldus, B., & Tribe, V. (1978). The development of perceptions and evaluations of social inequality among public school children. *Canadian Review of Sociology/Revue canadienne de sociologie, 15*(1), 50–60.

Bowles, S., & Gintis, H. (1976). *Schooling in capitalist America*. New York: Basic Books.

Duffy A., & Mandell, N. (1994). The widening gap: social inequality and poverty. In D. Glenday & A. Duffy (Eds.), *Canadian society: Understanding and surviving in the 1990s* (pp. 49–85). Toronto: McClelland and Stewart.

Dorling, D. (2014). *Inequality and the 1%*. London: Verso Books.

Freire, P. (2000). *Pedagogy of the oppressed*. London: Bloomsbury Publishing.

McMullin, J. A. (2010). *Understanding social inequality: Intersections of class, age, gender, ethnicity, and race in Canada* (2nd ed.). London: Oxford University Press.

Schor, J. B. (1999). *The overspent American*. New York: Basic Books.

Swanson, J. (2001). *Poor-bashing: The politics of exclusion*. Toronto: Between the Lines.

Teaching Economic Inequality and Capitalism in Contemporary America Using Resources from the Federal Government

Andrew E. Kersten

Author's Reflexive Statement

I am a historian of the United States with research and teaching interests in politics, economics, and social movements. In 2014, I became the dean of the College of Letters, Arts, and Social Sciences at the University of Idaho. As I assumed this new job, my contact with students lessened. That said, by assisting undergraduate and graduate students with their research, I still engage many on the historical issues relating to working people, particularly in the United States. When I was teaching full time, I focused my courses not only on the stories that workers tell but also on the data that illuminate the structures of their lives. In other words, I helped students gather qualitative and quantitative sources. In some ways, I have been trying to teach students what I do from my own perspective.

As a son of working class parents who went to college and a son of an immigrant, I have always been interested in the stories that people tell and in finding out how unique or common those stories are. This chapter reflects my thinking on how to handle one type of source material: federal publications. These sources contain both qualitative and quantitative information but are especially helpful with the latter. I have used these stories to ask questions like this: my mother was a Cuban immigrant who arrived in 1954. How many Cubans arrived in the United States in the year she came? I know from teaching and from counseling young historical researchers that the answers can be found in federal publications. The problem is finding these sources and then understanding the data sets. This chapter is designed to help based on more than 20 years of teaching and mentoring.

A. E. Kersten (✉)
University of Idaho, Moscow, ID, USA
e-mail: andrewkersten@uidaho.edu

K. Haltinner and L. Hormel (eds.), *Teaching Economic Inequality and Capitalism in Contemporary America*, https://doi.org/10.1007/978-3-319-71141-6_13

Introduction

The U.S. federal government is among the largest publishers in the world. Each year, it releases hundreds of books, reports, and pamphlets. Each one is full of information and data (both quantitative and qualitative) about the conditions of contemporary America. As such, they provide a treasure trove for exploring issues of inequality and capitalism. This has long been the case. These historical sources are rich for analysis. More recently, with the advent of the worldwide web, using these sources have become more challenging. First, there are so many documents and so much more information available that the volume of information itself can be quite overwhelming. Second, getting to the sources and the data is not always straight-forward: some are in print sources; others are on government websites; and still others only can be accessed through social media. For teachers and students who are interested in exploring issues of inequality and capitalism in contemporary America, there are some good guides and shortcuts to gain access to the information. This essay is designed to introduce some common federal resources and provide a method of accessing them. This chapter will highlight the following publications: *Yearbook of Immigration Statistics*; *Income and Poverty in the United States*; and *Digest of Education Statistics*; It will also focus on a few web sites including those of the Bureau of Labor Statistics, the Center for Disease Control and Prevention, and Federal Reserve Board. In the context of this volume, the focus is on inequality and contemporary American capitalism, but the method outlined below should work for any topic about American life and history.

Currently, I am the dean of the College of Letters, Arts, and Social Sciences at the University of Idaho. I am also a U.S. historian. When I regularly taught classes, I frequently had courses about U.S. labor history, U.S. immigration history, and comparative and interdisciplinary courses about work and working people. I often had assignments in which I asked students to use federal resources to investigate conditions for workers in the past, in the present, and around the world. The sources I feature in my discussion below are perfect for any class dealing with inequality and capitalism within the larger contexts of economics, history, sociology, politics, and anthropology.

When teaching with the resources of the federal government, the first step is to provide students with an orientation. I suggest spending no more than one class period on this and, if possible, to have this session in a library that is a federal government document repository. The orientation, ideally conducted by a government documents librarian, would cover three basic aspects of federal resources. First, it would provide an overview of the Government Printing Office (GPO). Created in 1861, the GPO is the official publisher of federal documents and has churned out these resources for more than one hundred and fifty years. There are three nice official histories of the GPO. Each is available online at the GPO's web site (https://www.gpo.gov/about/gpohistory/).[1] Finding specific documents within

[1] Kerr (1881), Harrison (1961), and Boarman (2011).

the corpus of GPO publications can be a challenge, but there are a few helpful guides. The first is the GPO's *Monthly Catalog*, which has been published in various forms since 1895. For the period 1789–1909, there is a checklist of public documents, which the GPO published in 1911. The GPO's online bookstore has now replaced the monthly catalog. One can access it here: https://bookstore.gpo.gov. One particularly useful feature of this site is that one can browse by agency. For example, by clicking on the Department of Labor, one has access to lists of books, pamphlets, and other materials related to the mission of the Department of Labor and its bureaus and offices.

Let's take an example to demonstrate one method to use the GPO online bookstore and connect it to a common question about the economy and American society. Suppose one wonders: how many immigrants obtained green cards in 2015? By typing in "immigration" into the search box or by clicking on the "Department of Homeland Security," one can quickly access publications regarding immigrants. Among the top hits is the 2015 *Yearbook of Immigration Statistics*. Selecting that publication provides the opportunity for purchase. But, knowing that it is published, also gives one the chance to see if a local library has this title or to check out the Department of Homeland Security's web site. The 2015 *Yearbook* is also available as an interactive website with yearbooks going back to 1996 (see: https://www.dhs.gov/immigration-statistics/yearbook/2015). Clicking on Table 1 gives access to the data.[2]

These are large numbers! When a foreign national receives green card, it means that they are lawfully allowed permanent residence in the United States. This would include people who were granted asylum or refugee status or were naturalized. While not everyone inside those large numbers were workers, many were. That means that our economy draws workers from around the world, and consistently so. This is an important point of understanding of modern capitalism in the United States. Despite all the changes in the economy and the society for the last thirty years, the number of green cards issued has been a constant. The contemporary capitalist economy relies heavily on foreign-born workers.

The interplay between GPO publications and web-based resources is an important point to impart to students as they begin to ask more sophisticated questions about economic inequality and contemporary capitalism. In my teaching experience, this is the key to unlocking the treasure trove of federal resources to answer big questions in classroom. One question that is appropriate to a classroom studying this theme is: Has the rate of poverty in the United States been increasing or decreasing since the turn of the millennium? A search of the GPO bookstore web site yields the essential government publication: *Income and Poverty in the United States*. The U.S. Census Bureau publishes it annually. Going to the Census Bureau's web site allows one to access a wealth of statistical tools and reports,

[2]"Table 1. Persons Obtaining Lawful Permanent Resident Status: Fiscal Years 1820–2015," *Yearbook of Immigration Statistics 2015*, accessed March 20, 2017, https://www.dhs.gov/immigration-statistics/yearbook/2015/table1.

Table 1 Immigrants Entering the United States, 1999-2015

Year	Number
2015	1,051,031
2014	1,016,518
2013	990,553
2012	1,031,631
2011	1,062,040
2010	1,042,625
2009	1,130,818
2008	1,107,126
2007	1,052,415
2006	1,266,129
2005	1,122,257
2004	957,883
2003	703,542
2002	1,059,356
2001	1,058,902
2000	841,002
1999	644,787

Source "Table 1. Persons Obtaining Lawful Permanent Resident Status: Fiscal Years 1820–2015." *Yearbook of Immigration Statistics 2015*. Accessed March 20, 2017. https://www.dhs.gov/immigration-statistics/yearbook/2015/table1

including the latest *Income and Poverty in the United States* (2015), which is available for free download as a PDF. The report begins to provide a framework for understanding economic inequality.

Using Government Data to Understand the Social-Historical Dynamics of Economic Inequality

Government data can be used by instructors to help students understand the dynamic nature of economic inequality over time and by social location. For example, *Income and Poverty in the United States* (2015), which is based on U.S. Census data, provides a wealth of information that can be used by students or in classes on topics related to economic inequality. This includes essential and basic demographic information. For example, in 2015, there were 125,819,000 households reported by the U.S. Census Bureau. Of those, 107,081,000 (85%) were native born and 18,738,000 were foreign born (15%). Most of the foreign born households were in metropolitan areas.

This document can also be used to show and analyze economic trends by various factors such as gender and race. For example, looking at this data reveals a few critical aspects of economic inequality: women earn less than men. The median income for men was $51,212 while the median for women was $40,742.[3] As a snapshot in time, this statistic—that women earn 80% of what men earn—does not indicate the trend, which has reflected slow and steady growth in the female-to-male earnings ratio since the mid-1980s, when the percentage was about 60%.[4] However, students can compare Census data over time to analyze social change. In terms of race, if we slice the income data another way to account for race and Hispanic origin, other patterns emerge. The median household income for African Americans in 2015 was $36,898; for Hispanics of any race $45,148; for whites (not Hispanic) $62,950; and for Asians $77,166. Looking at trends from 2010 to 2015, one can see that since the end of the Great Recession incomes have been rising, but much more slowly for African Americans than for other groups.[5]

Census data also can be used to show the contemporary (or historical) nature of capitalism and inequality in the United States. For example, income distribution reveals a structure of social class where the top income earners have a commanding share of the wealth. In 2015, the highest quintile of earners earned 51.1% of the money income. The top 5% earned 22.1%. The lowest three quintiles earned a combined 25.6%. In other words the top 5% earned nearly as much as the lowest 60% of the income earners in the United States.[6]

This income information question provides a foundation for the answer to the question about the trend in poverty and poverty rates in the United States. In 2015, 43.1 million Americans lived in poverty. The official poverty rate was 13.5%, down from 14.8% in 2014. That rate was one percent higher than the 2007 rate. In other words, in 2015, the United States had essentially returned to a pre-Great Recession poverty rate. That said, the poverty rate in the United States is still higher than it was in 1995. In fact, the Great Recession wiped out all the gains of the late 1990s and early 2000s. Furthermore, the United States remains near the high water mark for the number of poor Americans. In 1960, there were almost 40 million Americans in poverty. That number declined to under 25 million in the 1970s, and it has been on the increase since then with periods of decline such as the mid-1980s and the mid-1990s.[7]

As reported in *Income and Poverty in the United States, 2015,* the U.S. Census data tell even more about the poor in 2015. Most were white (66%). African-Americans made up 23%, and Hispanics of any race constituted 28%. Most poor were women, born in the United States, and aged 18–64. There were more than three times as many poor children as there were poor seniors. Most poor live in the South and the West.[8] Teachers can create interesting student assignments, since they may use this data filtered and sorted for state, counties, and localities. For

---

[3]Proctor et al. (2016).

[4]Proctor, Semega, and Kollar, *Income and Poverty in the United States: 2015*, 10.

[5]Proctor, Semega, and Kollar, *Income and Poverty in the United States: 2015*, 5.

[6]Proctor, Semega, and Kollar, *Income and Poverty in the United States: 2015*, 9.

[7]Proctor, Semega, and Kollar, *Income and Poverty in the United States: 2015*, 12.

[8]Proctor, Semega, and Kollar, *Income and Poverty in the United States: 2015*, 13.

example, you might have a group of students working on collecting the national level data on income and poverty. Then other groups in the class could find the state, county, and city data. Working in teams, students could then report out using a collaboration platform such as Google Docs, building toward a reveal in the classroom when the teacher takes the class through all the data, zooming in from the national level to the local level. This assignment could even have a public element by having a local government official in the room as the presentation is made.

Using Government Data to Analyze Areas of Possibility for and Barriers to Change

Once students have an understanding of socio-historical patterns of inequality, they will likely want to understand: (a) how people can improve their class position and (b) why people remain in poverty. Federal documents and statistics can also provide some information about what poor people can do to get ahead now and in the future as well as barriers to these changes.

For example, one method of economic advancement is to secure higher paying jobs. Looking at the Bureau of Labor Statistics web site is essentially the only place to go for information about jobs and income relative to contemporary American capitalism (https://www.bls.gov). Among the myriad of statistics available, four points of data indicate what it is like for average Americans. First, unemployment—a measure of people who are looking for work and who have not found employment—is now nearing levels not seen since the years prior to the Great Recession. In February 2017, the national rate was 4.7%. At the comparable time in 2007, it was 4.5%.[9] One of the stark differences, however, is that the labor participation rate has declined. In January 2007, 66.4% of the civilian labor force over the age of 16 was working or seeking work. In January 2017, that rate was 62.9%.[10] Thus by only looking at the unemployment rate, we might get a false sense of the vibrancy of contemporary American capitalism. It is not yet producing enough jobs to support the growing working population. Unemployment is relatively low, but many have ceased to look for work.

Obtaining a job is only part of a path out of poverty. Many of the kinds and numbers of jobs that are being created are at the lower level of the income scale. The BLS has projected that for the period 2014–2024 the great number of jobs that will be created have relatively low median incomes (Table 2).[11]

---

[9]"Bureau of Labor Statistics Data,." U.S. Bureau of Labor Statistics, accessed March 28, 2017, https://data.bls.gov/timeseries/LNS14000000.

[10]"Bureau of Labor Statistics Data," U.S. Bureau of Labor Statistics, accessed March 28, 2017, https://data.bls.gov/timeseries/LNS11300000.

[11]"Most new jobs: 20 occupations with the highest projected numeric change in employment." U. S. Bureau of Labor Statistics, accessed March 28, 2017, https://www.bls.gov/ooh/most-new-jobs.htm.

The jobs that pay higher rates frequently require degrees beyond high school, which is the next step many have to take to get out of poverty. Although college and university degrees are important achievements unto themselves, the costs of attainment, measured not merely by tuition but also by total cost of attendance year over year, is increasing. Finding that information is also relatively easy using our belt-and-suspenders approach of checking for published resources and web resources. First, checking the GPO online bookstore for current statistics about higher education yields two important sources for purchase or for check out at a library that is a federal repository: (1) *Digest of Education Statistics 2016* and *The Condition of Education 2016*. They are also available online at the U.S. Department of Education's web site. Second, digging into the statistics reveals the stark reality of the challenges of higher education in the United States. As state-sponsored support has dwindled over the last three decades, the cost of attendance has risen. Comparing 1986–2016, in constant, inflation-adjusted dollars, we see that the average cost of attendance (tuition plus room and board) for all institutions (public and private), was $10,969 in 1986 and $22,432, a 104% increase.[12] At the same time, student debt has increased to accommodate the rise in costs of degree attainment. The Board of Governors of the Federal Reserve System maintains data about consumer debt. The latest information is on its website (https://www.federalreserve.gov/). Student loan debt has increased from $1055 billion in 2012 to $1406 billion in 2016.[13] The Federal Reserve has only tracked this information since 2006. The percentage increase has been 192%.[14]

The challenges for most Americans in paying for higher education comes at a time and in a context of other rising costs, particularly for health care. Given the relative costs of health care and of higher education, many Americans choose one or the other. The U.S. Department of Health and Human Services' Center for Disease Control and Prevention (known also as the CDC) issues an annual publication titled *Health, United States*. The 2015 installment provides a wealth of information about disease, wellness, and the health care industry. It's available for purchase; in libraries, and for free download (https://www.cdc.gov/nchs/data/hus/

[12] "Average undergraduate tuition and fees and room and board rates charged for full-time students in degree-granting postsecondary institutions, by level and control of institution: 1963–64 through 2015–16," National Center for Education Statistics, *Digest of Education Statistics* 2016, Accessed March 29, 2017, https://nces.ed.gov/programs/digest/d16/tables/dt16_330.10.asp?current=yes.

[13] "Consumer Credit—G.19, January 2017," Statistical Releases and Historical Data, Board of Governors of the Federal Reserve System, Accessed March 29, 2017, https://www.federalreserve.gov/releases/g19/current/default.htm.

[14] "Consumer Credit—G.19, Historical Data," Statistical Releases and Historical Data, Board of Governors of the Federal Reserve System, Accessed March 29, 2017, "Consumer Credit—G.19, January 2017," Statistical Releases and Historical Data, Board of Governors of the Federal Reserve System, Accessed March 29, 2017, https://www.federalreserve.gov/releases/g19/current/default.htm.

Table 2 20 occupations with the highest projected numeric change in employment

Occupation	Number of new jobs (projected), 2014–2024	2015 Median Pay
Personal care aides	458,100	$21,980 per year
Registered nurses	439,300	$68,450 per year
Home health aides	348,400	$22,600 per year
Combined food preparation and serving workers including fast food	343,500	$19,440 per year
Retail salespersons	314,200	$22,680 per year
Nursing assistants	262,000	$26,590 per year
Customer service representatives	252,900	$32,300 per year
Cooks, restaurant	158,900	$24,140 per year
General and operations managers	151,100	$99,310 per year
Construction laborers	147,400	$33,430 per year
Accountants and auditors	142,400	$68,150 per year
Medical assistants	138,900	$31,540 per year
Janitors and cleaners, except maids and housekeeping cleaner	136,300	$24,190 per year
Software developers, applications	135,300	$100,080 per year
Laborers and freight, stock, and material movers, hand	125,100	$25,980 per year
First-line supervisors of office and administrative support workers	121,200	$54,340 per year
Computer systems analysts	118,600	$87,220 per year
Licensed practical and licensed vocational nurses	117,300	$44,090 per year
Maids and housekeeping cleaners	111,700	$21,820 per year
Medical secretaries	108,200	$33,730 per year

Source "Most new jobs: 20 occupations with the highest projected numeric change in employment." U.S. Bureau of Labor Statistics. Accessed November 4, 2017. https://www.bls.gov/ooh/most-new-jobs.htm

hus15.pdf). The same information, though in a different format, on the CDC's National Center for Health Statistics web site. If you had the question of how many Americans have no health insurance, the answer is easily accessed there (Table 3).[15]

[15]"Uninsured: Table 105. No health insurance coverage among persons under age 65, by selected characteristics: United States, selected years 1984–2014," National Center for Health Statistics, Center for Disease Control and Prevention, accessed March 30, 2017, https://www.cdc.gov/nchs/data/hus/2015/105.pdf.

Table 3 Americans under age 65 without Health Insurance, 1984–2014

	1984	1997	2000	2004	2010	2012	2014
Total in millions	29.8	41.0	41.4	42.1	48.3	45.2	35.7
Total as percentage of population	14.5	17.5	17.0	16.6	18.2	16.9	13.3

Source "Uninsured: Table 105. No health insurance coverage among persons under age 65, by selected characteristics: United States, selected years 1984–2014," National Center for Health Statistics, Center for Disease Control and Prevention, Accessed March 30, 2017, https://www.cdc.gov/nchs/data/hus/2015/105.pdf

Using Government Data to Assess the Impact of Contemporary Inequality

These data provide some indication of what life is like for contemporary Americans. By examining the information about jobs and income, we get a rough portrait of the kinds of inequalities that exist. But, how do they affect people? What can we say about them? Federal sources in print and online provide some answers here as well. In particular, the *Monthly Labor Review*, a publication of the Bureau of Labor Statistics since 1915, provides reports and information on particular topics drawing from many sources of information. First published in 1915, most of the MLR is widely available for purchase and in many libraries. Some of it is also available online. From the period 1981 to 2017, the entire issues are accessible. Prior 1981, it is hit and miss, at least for now.

Examining or searching the MLR provides a place to see how inequality and contemporary American capitalism intersect. Let's take the relationships between income and health care. In a February 2017 *Monthly Labor Review* article titled "Income and Health Outcomes," Serah Hyde summarizes some recent research that indicates that as income disparity has grown since the 1970s mortality rates among the middle aged have risen among those are in the middle to lower income earners. As she explains, "individuals in this [top income] group were more than twice as likely to report being in very good or excellent health than individuals in the bottom [or lower income] group… The number of those who reported very good to excellent health," she continues, "have eroded over time, but for the top income group, that erosion has been negligible." Thus higher incomes point to better health outcomes. Lower income Americans are in a worse situation generally.[16]

Hyde's report points to two caveats of using federal sources to discuss inequality and contemporary American capitalism. The first is that to use sources like the *Month Labor Review* one needs beyond the web site and to go to the library. Similar data sets also exist that require that trip. One of the most useful sources of information about the United States was the *Statistical Abstract of the United States*,

[16]Hyde (2017).

published yearly from 1878 to 2011. The U.S. Census Bureau's web site has some the information, but there is no substitute for the books, which for the most part are unavailable for purchase. The last difficulty with federal sources is that statistics do not tell the story of people. In this context, inequality can boil down to numbers and ratios. But what does it mean for people who have lived in the past and are alive now? Taken together, these comments point to the need to head to the library and dig into some additional sources. Again, the federal sources can help.

There are a few go to places for finding print-only federal sources regarding inequality and contemporary American capitalism. I have already mentioned the *Monthly Labor Review* and the *Statistical Abstract of the United States*, which are in most libraries. In addition, there are some other go-to sources which can help students and researchers alike. Before the worldwide web, the Government Printing Office published a *Monthly Catalog*, which is essentially an index to its publications and a useful way to find materials not included in the GPO online catalog. Finally, there are two other statistical compellations that one needs to know. The U.S. Census Bureau published two versions of *Historical Statistics of the United States*. Utilizing data sets from the U.S. Census, these volumes offer historical tables on population, work and welfare, economic structure and performance, economic sectors, and governance and international relations. The first was released in time for the bicentennial. The second appeared at the start of the new century. The *Historical Statistics of the United States: Millennial Edition* was subsequently sold to Cambridge University Press. The set has a companion web site (http://hsus.cambridge.org/HSUSWeb/HSUSEntryServlet). All the tables are only available for purchase. It is no longer a free federal resource. They are available at many libraries.

Using Government Data to Hear the Stories of Americans

There is a final but important point to make. Federal sources provide an ocean of statistics to wade through. For every question about inequality or the structure of contemporary capitalism, there are many data sets that help provide an answer. And, there is a methodology for gaining access to those sources, which I have outlined above. But, what about the stories of Americans? By focusing on the quantitative, we risk ignoring the quantitative data. There is a large body of published work, perhaps the subject of an additional essay. One place to begin are the reports of federal blue-ribbon committees. There is a long tradition of these, which constitute an incidental canon of federal publications. To take the long arc on conditions of inequality and the structure of American capitalism, I suggest beginning with two sources. One source, *Recent Social Trends in the United States*, was published during Herbert Hoover's presidency and gives a detailed overview of the conditions on the eve of the Great Depression. Another source is the reports of President Franklin D. Roosevelt's National Resource Planning Board, particularly its multi-volume reports issued in 1943 *Security, Work and Relief Policies* and *National Resource Development*, which pointed the way to a postwar world.[17]

A few more are worth mentioning in the context of this topic. The report of President Harry S Truman's Committee on Civil Rights not only summarized briefly the seriousness of inequality in American life but also charted a course for public policy.[18] The difficulties in achieving improvements is at the heart of another federal report. At the end of the 1960s, after several massive riots in American cities, the federal government empaneled a U.S. Riot Commission, under the direction Illinois Governor Otto Kerner. Its report began with a stark and startling assessment: "Our nation is moving toward two societies, one black, one white—separate and unequal".[19] The federal government has fallen out of habit of these ceremonious committees and reports, especially as they relate to inequality and the economy. Every once in a while, they still come out as with the 9/11 Commission's Report. Inequality and the nature of contemporary capitalism, though, are unlikely to receive similar attention. To fill the void, some newspapers have been publishing their own in-depth reports based on their reporting. Some valuable reports from the *New York Times* include *The Downsizing of America: Millions of American are Losing Good Jobs, This is Their Story* (1996) and *Pulling Together, Pulling Apart: How Race is Lived in America* (2001).[20] These sources contain the stories of individuals that provide direct qualitative examples that make the quantitative data come alive.

In teaching about inequality in America and its connection to contemporary capitalism, the quest for resources is as important as the analysis that can be done. There are more resources than one person would have time to investigate. Even at the federal level for a simply stated question such as how many people are currently working, many resources can be brought to bear. Expanding the search into state, county, and local data sets makes the project richer yet more difficult. This makes such an investigation perfect for the classroom. Acquiring the data—both quantitative and qualitative—is not easy but it is engaging.

References

Boarman, W. J. (2011). *Keeping America informed: The U.S. government printing office, 150 Years of Service to the Nation*. Washington, DC: GPO.

Ehrenreich, B. (2001). *Nickel and dimed: On (not) getting by in America*. New York: Metropolitan Books.

---

[17] President's Research Committee on Social Trends (1933), National Resource Planning Board (1943a, b).

[18] U.S. President's Committee on Civil Rights (1947).

[19] U.S. Riot Commission (Kerner Commission) (1968).

[20] New York Times (1996, 2001). Without the aegis of their newspapers, some reports have gone on to publish important works about inequality and the American economy. See Ehrenreich (2001), and Greenhouse (2008).

Greenhouse, Steven. (2008). *The big squeeze: Tough times for the American worker*. New York: Anchor Books.

Harrison, J. L. (1961). *100 GPO Years, 1861–1961: A history of United States public printing*. Washington, DC: GPO.

Hyde, S. (2017, February). Income and health outcomes. *Monthly Labor Review*, Accessed March 30, 2017 https://www.bls.gov/opub/mlr/2017/beyond-bls/income-and-health-outcomes.htm.

Kerr, R. W. (1881). *History of the Government Printing Office with a brief record of the public printing: A Century, 1789–1881*. Lancaster, Pa.: Inquirer Printing and Publishing Company.

National Resource Planning Board. (1943a). *Security, work and relief*. Washington: D.C.

National Resource Planning Board. (1943b). *National Resource Development*. Washington: D.C.

New York Times. (1996). *Special report: The downsizing of America: Millions of Americans are losing good jobs, this is their story*. New York: The New York Times.

New York Times. (2001). *Pulling together, pulling apart: How race is lived in America*. New York: The New York Times.

President's Research Committee on Social Trends. (1933). *Recent trends in the United States*. New York: McGraw-Hill.

Proctor, B. D., Semega, J. L., & Kollar, M. A. (2016). *Income and poverty in the United States: 2015* (p. 6). Washington, D.C.: GPO.

U.S. President's Committee on Civil Rights. (1947). *To secure these rights: The report of the President's committee on civil rights*. Washington, D.C.: GPO.

U.S. Riot Commission (Kerner Commission). (1968). *Report of the national advisory commission on civil disorders* (p, 1). Washington: U.S. Government Printing Office.

Teaching Social Inequality Through Analysis of Hidden Assumptions in Non-Academic Publications

Pidi Zhang

Author's Reflexive Statement

When I first began teaching, I was puzzled by how students would demonstrate mastery of a particular sociological perspective learned in class and then struggle to apply that concept or theory to real-life social issues. Rather, time and time again, I saw students return to individual explanations for social phenomena. One particular event really sticks with me. I had a student, struggling to complete their school work while laboring at two minimum-wage jobs, yet who was adamant that increasing the minimum wage would hurt him and others like him. He believed that such a policy shift would cause inflation, compel employers to hire fewer workers and reduce work hours, and, as a result, hurt the minimum wage earners. Another time, a senior sociology student expressed that an online "article" they read—which purported that there was virtually no poverty in the United States—was "eye-opening". Experiences like this convinced me that something must be changed about how we teach critical thought and data analysis to students.

With rapidly expanding access to information, resultant over over-information, the prevalence of misinformation and overt distortions in the information system are overwhelming to our students. It is no wonder that they are often confused with the world around them. As high school students, their critical thinking skills remain incomplete—they are used to trusting what they read. As a result, upon entering college, students are not prepared to attune to the information they need and screen out harmful misinformation. I have found that, college students need tools to help them process information and news they encounter in their every day lives.

P. Zhang (✉)
Georgia Southern University, Statesboro, GA, USA
e-mail: pzhang@georgiasouthern.edu

K. Haltinner and L. Hormel (eds.), *Teaching Economic Inequality and Capitalism in Contemporary America*, https://doi.org/10.1007/978-3-319-71141-6_14

Introduction

Professors teaching about inequality report various reactions from their students upon first learning about economic inequity, ranging from outright denial to moderated resistance (Davis 1992; Forbes and Kaufman 2008; Hedley and Markowitz 2001; Kleinman and Copp 2009), from feeling overwhelmed to expressing intense rage (Davis 1992). Students enter classes having been socialized with ideologies at odds with the sociological perspective on economic inequity (Forbes and Kaufman 2008). The situation may be worsened by the acceptance of the notion among college students that all views are equal (Benton 2008). To some extent, these attitudes are byproducts of the American democratic process which holds dear the tenet that people should be allowed to think and express themselves freely on any subject, even when speaking against the idea of democratic society (Postman and Weigartner 1969). However, this tenet is not typically paired with its essential twin: the intellectual power and perspective to critically examine the popular texts they encounter.

In practice the power elites use schools to promote their own interests and claim that as a part of the democratic process (Postman and Weigartner 1969). Schools and universities serve as political instruments that legitimize and conserve the existing system that benefit elites by maintaining a commonsensical understanding about a class meaning system. Bourdieu (1977: 169) calls it "a system of euphemisms, of acceptable ways of thinking and speaking" that describes the dominant system as natural, self-evident and undisputed and rejects heretical remarks as blasphemies. This meaning system produces unquestioning agents who in turn help maintain the dominant system (Bourdieu 1977; Chabrak and Craig 2013). Wysong et al. (2014) discuss the opinion-shaping information and entertainment industries funded by the superclass and the involvement of these industries in the reproduction of the dominant system.

Given that students are products of the existing social structure and their cultural upbringing, professors are faced with the difficult task of teaching critical thinking and the sociological imagination. Postman and Weigartner (1969: 3) pointed out nearly half a century ago that,

> Our intellectual history is a chronicle of the anguish and suffering of men who tried to help their contemporaries see that some part of their fondest beliefs were misconceptions, faulty assumptions, superstitions, and even outright lies. ... We have in mind a new education that would set out to cultivate just such people – experts at "crap detecting."

Nardi (2006: 286) translates "crap detecting" into the more familiar "critical thinking," a skill college professors find rare among present day students. In this chapter, I discuss methods for teaching students to distinguish between information and misinformation in non-academic publications and introduce a two-step strategy for instructors to help students develop the critical thinking skills needed to accomplish this task.

Over-Information and Misinformation

Mills (1959) discusses the "Age of Fact," the contemporary reality in which people, though in need of information to understand the rapidly changing world, are overwhelmed and dominated by the information to which they are exposed. The situation has only worsened in recent decades. The amount of information and misinformation from cultural products such as movies, televisions, the Internet, radio, music, DVDs, video game, newspapers, magazines and books that "reflect and influence the content of American culture" has grown at an unprecedented rate (Wysong et al. 2014: 262).

Wysong et al. (2014) demonstrate that corporations, foundations, and the wealthy fund think tanks, which produce messages heavily used by the information industry. The information industry operates via three interrelated control processes: the mainstream ideology process, the opinion-shaping process, and the spin-control process. These processes shape the ethos of the existing economic system as legitimate, upper-class behaviors and lifestyles as desirable, and existing inequality as fair. Chabrak and Craig (2013) illustrate the impact of the ethos on accounting students in a study of their responses to a disastrous business practice that contradicts their own values but is in line with the evolving ethos of capitalism. The authors find that most students compromise their own values and adopt behaviors consistent with the dominant meaning system because of the persuasive power of capitalist ideology (Chabrak and Craig 2013).

It is a challenge for students to detect flawed arguments skillfully crafted to misinform and mislead them. For instance, students in my Inequality class were given an online article to analyze and critique about poverty in the United States. The article (Rector and Sheffield 2011) provides statistics showing that 99% of American households have refrigerators or televisions and other amenities. The statistics are used to support the argument that poverty in the United States is grossly exaggerated by academia, government, and the media. Most students were convinced by the statistics presented in the article of the argument that poverty did not exist. One student who regularly did well in other class activities even exclaimed that the article was "eye-opening," as she "never realized that there was actually so little poverty in America!"

This article is an effective vehicle that shapes opinions about poverty even though access to refrigerators, televisions, and other amenities is not valid evidence of poverty. Similar publications sponsored by powerful interest groups appear online and in print. They add to the growing amount of overinformation and misinformation that often becomes conventional wisdom. Educators cannot afford to ignore the powerful influence of non-academic publications in shaping students' ideologies and perspectives about the world. Attention must be directed toward helping students develop effective working strategies to "debunk the social fiction" in non-academic publications and make "a first step toward freedom" (Berger 2011: 75).

Limitations of Academic Sources

Information from academic sources and knowledge gained in sociology classes constitute a tiny fraction of what students encounter compared with the amounts of information they come across from other sources. Few students acquire information and knowledge about social issues through reading academic publications unless required by professors. Most students do not care to fully understand what they read (Horowitz 1987). Although academic sources provide information that meets rigorous scientific standards, social scientists normally do not highlight sources of biases that would otherwise flaw their research and therefore do not alert readers of various potential methodological defects they guard against. In that regard, academic sources do not constitute an effective counterweight against biases in non-academic sources. Educators must play an active role in helping students develop critical thinking skills (Chabrak and Craig 2013). One specific strategy that can be used by instructors is to provide students with tools they can use to critique information and uncover misinformation.

Analyzing Hidden Assumptions Versus Providing Counterarguments

The strategies I propose in this article seek to pinpoint defects in arguments through identifying and analyzing their hidden assumptions rather than providing counterarguments. For example, the Rector and Sheffield (2011) article, while never operationalizing the concepts of poverty or economic status, successfully persuades many readers into accepting its argument that the United States has very little poverty mainly because readers unknowingly accept its implicit assumption of access to refrigerators, microwaves and other common household amenities as valid indicators for a household's economic condition. Readers without a rigorous training in social science methodology are likely to take the data for granted and get hoodwinked into accepting the intended message.

A common student response to the problematic argument is raising counterarguments. However, juxtaposing arguments against one another without analyzing the validity of their evidence fails to undermine misleading arguments and may leave students even more confused. The strategy discussed in this chapter, instead, helps students recognize and critique the hidden assumptions of problematic arguments. Returning to the example at hand, when asked whether access to household appliances is a valid measure of economic status or poverty, most students are able to recognize the measure's deficiencies and suggest more valid measures. Directing students' attention to the invalidity of the hidden assumption helps them debunk the seemingly plausible but truly misleading argument of the article.

As mentioned, most students have not been trained to question the validity of a measure. Roberts and Roberts (2008: 125) note that, in high school, students are taught "surface learning" rather than "deep learning". Surface learning involves repeating factual information while deep learning prepares students to "make meaning and construct a strong argument." Identifying the hidden assumption about evidence usage entails deconstructing and reconstructing meaning. The key is to help students develop the ability or the habit of searching for hidden assumptions when reading online, news, or academic articles. The following section introduces a two-stage method of analyzing hidden assumptions. The first stage is to use the sociological imagination and identify an article with truly problematic arguments. The second stage is to identify and analyze hidden evidenced-based and reason-based assumptions.

The General Approach

The Sociological Imagination

A few years ago I designed a writing assignment in which students were required to identify and critique a seemingly plausible but misleading argument in a non-academic publication. Over half of the class found articles with largely sound arguments and mistook them as misleading. American society's propensity toward micro level thinking makes it difficult for students to think sociologically and the students' faulty selections were due to this fact that Americans are accustomed to thinking in individualist terms, at odds with the sociological imagination. Thus, armed with an understanding of macro-level perspectives and the sociological imagination, students are less likely to select articles with sound arguments to criticize in this activity. The activity below, titled "Identifying Problematic Arguments", provides a list of questions I ask my students as they examine the arguments in articles to help them employ their sociological imagination and, thereby, a macro-level lens.

Identifying Problematic Arguments

Pedagogical Goal of Activity

Given the increase in access to information with the expansion of the Internet and social media, along with a decrease in lessons about critical thinking in K-12 education, college students are in need of learning to critique the information they read. This activity seeks to help students critically analyze an argumentative article.

Assignment Description and Instructions:

Step 1. Have students bring a news or academic article to class.
Step 2. Verify that the article is argumentative using the following questions. For example, one could have students read two articles, one by James Sherk on minimum wages and the other by Rector and Sheffield, and answer the following for each:

1. Does the article describe or report something without making any specific argument?
2. Does the article make a specific argument?
3. What is the argument? Specify.
4. What does the article use to support the argument? Mainly evidence or reasoning? Specify.

Many non-academic publications are descriptions or reports that do not have a clear argument. Such articles should be excluded in this first step. The questions listed above crosscheck potential selections and verify the selected article has an argument to meet the basic requirement.

Step 3. Step three involves using the sociological imagination and ensures that the argument of the selected article is not sociological. This is verified by whether the selected article takes a structural or individualist approach and whether the article makes an argument that denies a problem. Students should be alerted to think and recognize why denying a problem is tantamount to denying the structural causes of a problem. The tool helps identify two types of arguments that may not be mutually exclusive: evidence-based and reasoning-based. Students would need assistance to make sure they identify an article with problematic arguments. The instructor should keep a list of problematic articles for them to choose from.

Apply the sociological imagination. Ask students the following questions to help them see the role of micro-level and macro-level analytic claims.

1. Does the evidence provided in the article specify or point to individual motives as major support to the argument? Specify if any.
2. Does the evidence provided in the article specify or point to individual behavioral factors as major support to the argument? Specify if any.
3. Does the evidence provided in the article specify or point to something beyond individual thinking, feeling, preference or behavior as major support to the argument? Specify if any.
4. Does the evidence provided in the article specify or point to any social, historical, societal, or cultural factors as major support to the argument? Specify if any.
5. Does the reasoning in the article specify or point to individual motives as major support to the argument? Specify if any.
6. Does the reasoning in the article specify or point to individual behavioral factors as major support to the argument? Specify if any.

7. Does the reasoning in the article specify or point to factors beyond individual thinking, feeling, preference or behavior as major support to the argument? Specify if any.
8. Does the reasoning in the article specify or point to any social, historical, societal, or cultural factors as major support to the argument? Specify if any.

Validity Check for Evidence-Based Arguments

Problematic arguments based on evidence can be scrutinized with a construct validity check (Singleton and Straight 2010). As mentioned, the argument of Rector and Sheffield's (2011) article is that there is virtually no poverty in the United States. The major concept used in the argument is poverty. Measures used as evidence include access to a long list of amenities such as refrigerators, televisions, stoves and ovens, and microwaves, etc. The construct validity check asks the question: "Is the instrument measuring the intended concept (or construct), or can it be interpreted as measuring something else?" (Singleton and Straight 2010: 140). The activity below, titled "Teaching Students about Argument Validity", uses the Rector and Sheffield article as a case study and provides a tool for instructors to use when helping students conduct a "validity check" regarding arguments and their evidence. Identifying the hidden assumption about the validity of the evidence usage entails reconstructing meaning and reveals the defect of an argument's construction. In turn, a students' analytical power and their ability to build strong arguments is strengthened.

Teaching Students About Argument Validity

Pedagogical Goal of Activity

These questions seek to help students examine the validity of arguments made in scholarly and news articles they encounter.

Instructions

Have students select an article related to poverty, economic inequality, or capitalism. Then ask them the following questions about the article.

1. What is the main argument of the article?
2. What is the key concept in the argument? Focus on the argument for a few minutes and you will find out the concept.
3. Specify the evidence or measures the authors use in the article as support for the argument. (Tables and graphs may contain such information as well.)
4. Do the authors discuss how appropriate the measures of the concept reflect the related concept (poverty)?

5. If the authors do not discuss the appropriateness of the measures, do they assume that the measures correctly exemplify the concept?
6. Evaluate whether the measures as evidence sufficiently exemplify the concept. (For example, evaluate access to refrigerators as a measure for poverty status, etc.)
7. According to published information you know of or based on your own knowledge, what may be important measures that appropriately exemplify the concept (in this case, poverty or economic status)? Make a list.
8. Compare your list with the author's measures, discuss their appropriateness (validity) or lack of it.
9. Synthesize the above information and draw a conclusion about the authors' argument.

As an instructor, you will likely need to help them with question number six, as students often fail to see when measures do not 'measure up' to the claims made by authors.

After completing this activity, discuss the articles as a class and uncover all or any bias in the claims made by authors.

Detecting Bias in Reason-Based Arguments

Many articles, columns, or editorials online or in print are discursive and based on reasoning that is intended to persuade the reader into accepting their arguments. A misleading argument based on reasoning may appear appealing to uncritical readers. However, the flawed nature of the claim may be revealed in the argument's connotations, which, upon analysis, may highlight the problematic messages of the argument. In these cases, instructors should direct students to detect bias in the connotations of the arguments rather than flawed use of evidence.

For example, in my "Inequality" course, I ask students to critique the article: "Raising the Minimum Wage Will Not Reduce Poverty" (Sherk 2007). The author uses three reason-based arguments to support his claim. First, he argues, the only workers who benefit from a higher minimum wage are those who earn that higher wage. Others are detrimentally affected as raising the minimum wage reduces many workers' job opportunities and working hours. Second, he claims, few minimum-wage earners actually come from poor households, many are teenagers. Third, Sherk claims, most poor Americans do not work at all, for any wage, so raising the minimum wage does not help them (Sherk 2007). The author also uses existing research findings (Neumark et al. 2004) as supporting evidence for the reasons why minimum wage policies do not reduce poverty. I then employ the following activity, "Examining Reasoning-Based Articles: Detecting Bias in Reason-Based Arguments", to support students in analyzing reason-based arguments.

Examining Reasoning-Based Articles: Detect Biases in Connotations

Pedagogical Goal of Activity

These questions seek to help students examine reason-based arguments in articles to detect biases.

Instructions

Have students read "Raising the Minimum Wages Will Not Reduce Poverty" by James Sherk. Then ask students the following questions:

1. What is the main argument of the article?
2. Describe the motives, reasons or reasoning the author uses in the article as support for the argument.
3. Find out connotations of the argument or reasoning that the author does not explicitly discuss but that may appear at odds with the values of mainstream society. The connotation must be logically related to the reasoning of the argument. Admonishment: The purpose is not to show the argument is invalid (impossible for reason-based arguments), but to reveal less acceptable or unacceptable implications of the argument.
4. Deliberate the (social, political, economic) importance of the connotation and how it comes into conflict with society's values and even with the way the author's argument appears. For example, Sherk (2007) in effect argues against increasing the minimum wage because it does not reduce poverty, and because most people who benefit from it are not poor. One connotation of the argument is that it is reasonable or acceptable for the small proportion of poor people who need an increase in minimum wages not to have it. This connotation may go against some basic human values of modern society and is surprisingly different from the innocent appearance of the argument that minimum wages do not reduce poverty.
5. Compare the unacceptable connotation and the author's seemingly plausible argument. Draw a conclusion based on all the above.

Following this initial discussion, have students attune to the following arguments made by Sherk and pose the following questions to shift their thinking about the veracity of his claims.

Sherk's reason: "First, the only workers who benefit from a higher minimum wage are those who actually earn that higher wage. Raising the minimum wage reduces many workers' job opportunities and working hours."

Suggested Questions:

1. Why does the author seem to suggest that the increased minimum wage for workers who benefit from it indicates something negative?
2. The author discusses that raising the minimum wage reduces workers' job opportunities and working hours but does not discuss whether the same amount

of work would be done with the fewer workers and reduced work hours. What could be the moral or legal implications of that practice?

Sherk's reason: "Second, few minimum-wage earners actually come from poor households."

Suggested Questions:

1. If minimum wages help many people who do not need help, does that mean it is reasonable or acceptable to deny those of the help who do need it?

Sherk's reason: "Third, the majority of poor Americans do not work at all, for any wage, so raising the minimum wage does not help them."

Suggested Questions:

1. If the minimum wage does not reduce poverty, does that indicate the increase is not large enough?
2. Why does the author not point to the need to further increase it?
3. Does the author seem to suggest getting rid of it?
4. Would getting rid of the minimum wage solve or worsen the problem?
5. Based on the sociological perspective bring up a hypothesis about a condition that causes poor Americans not to work.
6. Based on the above analysis, reevaluate your initial conclusions drawn from the article.

Intellectual Challenge About the Real World

The need for "crap detecting" Postman and Weigartner (1969) envisioned nearly half a century ago continues to be relevant today as the information to which students are exposed online consistently reflects capitalist bias and ideology (Wysong et al. 2014; Berners-Lee 2017). James and Brookfield (2010) note that deep learning occurs when people suddenly see unexpected patterns emerging. The strategies discussed in this paper are a useful toolkit that should enable students to "detect crap" that they encounter on a daily basis.

Acknowledgements The author is grateful for the valuable comments and input provided by William L. Smith and Kristin Haltinner.

References

Benton, T. H. (2008). On Stupidity. *The Chronicle of Higher Education, 54*(47), A27–A30.

Berger, P. L. (2011). *Adventures of an accidental sociologist: How to explain the world without becoming a bore*. Amherst, NY: Prometheus Books.

Berners-Lee, T. (2017). I invented the Web. Here are three things we need to change to save it. https://www.theguardian.com/technology/2017/mar/11/tim-berners-lee-web-inventor-save-internet. Retrieved March 15, 2017.

Bourdieu, P. (1977). *Outline of a theory of practice*. Cambridge, UK: Cambridge University Press.
Chabrak, N., & Craig, R. (2013). Student imaginings, cognitive dissonance and critical thinking. *Critical Perspectives on Accounting, 24,* 91–104.
Davis, N. (1992). Teaching about inequality: student resistance, paralysis, and rage. *Teaching Sociology, 20*(3), 177–187.
Forbes, C., & Kaufman, P. (2008). Critical pedagogy in the sociology classroom: Challenges and concerns. *Teaching Sociology, 36*(1), 26–33.
Hedley, M., & Markowitz, L. (2001). Avoiding moral dichotomies: Teaching controversial topics to resistant students. *Teaching Sociology, 29*(2), 195–208.
Horowitz, H. L. (1987). *Campus life: Undergraduate cultures from the eighteenth century to the present*. Chicago, IL: University of Chicago Press.
James, A., & Brookfield, S. D. (2010). *Engaging imagination: Helping students become creative and reflective thinkers*. San Francisco, CA: Jossey-Bass.
Kleinman, S., & Copp, M. (2009). Denying social harm: Students' resistance to lessons about inequality. *Teaching Sociology, 37*(3), 283–293.
Mills, C. W. (1959). *The sociological imagination*. New York: Oxford University Press.
Nardi, P. M. (2006). Sociology at play, or truth in the pleasant disguise of illusion: 2006 Presidential address to the pacific sociological association. *Sociological Perspectives, 49*(3), 285–295.
Neumark, D., Schweitzer, M., & Wascher, W. (2004). Minimum wage effects throughout the wage distribution. *The Journal of Human Resources, 39*(2), 425–450.
Postman, N., & Weigartner, C. (1969). *Teaching as a subversive activity*. New York: Dell Delta.
Rector, R., & Rachel, S. (2011). Air conditioning, cable TV, and an Xbox: What is poverty in the United States today?" http://www.heritage.org/research/reports/2011/07/what-is-poverty. Retrieved January 5, 2015.
Roberts, J. C., & Roberts, K. A. (2008). Deep reading, cost/benefit, and the construction of meaning: Enhancing reading comprehension and deep learning in sociology courses. *Teaching Sociology, 36*(2), 125–140.
Sherk, J. (2007). Raising the minimum wages will not reduce poverty. http://www.heritage.org/research/reports/2007/01/raising-the-minimum-wage-will-not-reduce-poverty. Retrieved January 5, 2015.
Singleton, R. A., Jr., & Straight, B. C. (2010). *Approaches to social research*. New York: Oxford University Press.
Wysong, E., Perrucci, R., & Wright, D. (2014). *The new class society: goodbye american dream?*. Lanham, MD: Rowman & Littlefield.

Participatory Action Research as Problem-Based Learning: A Course Study of Rural Poverty, Low-Income Housing, and Environmental Justice

Leontina Hormel, Cynthia Ballesteros and Haylee Brister

Author's Reflexive Statements

Leontina: Back in 2009, I taught Introduction to Sociology to a class of nearly 200 students. Two of the students, a military veteran and an ROTC trainee, were Syringa Park residents. Syringa is a mobile home park just three miles outside of Moscow, Idaho's, city limits. Along a popular and scenic biking and running route, many people in the area are familiar with the park. Now fairly run-down, the park has been an affordable and idyllic setting for retirees, military veterans, families, and college students to live. Since Moscow has the third most expensive housing and rental market in Idaho, mobile home parks like Syringa play a valuable role in providing affordable housing. In December 2013, I learned through local news media that Syringa residents' water was shut off after water lines froze and fears of sewage contamination ensued. Though I tend to follow such stories closely, the fact that I knew that two of my students were residents in the park connected me more closely to who these residents are and the kinds of dreams and aspirations they have for their future. Unlike many stories of mass tragedy Americans see, Syringa residents were not a faceless group to me.

The local media coverage regularly covered grim news about Syringa: first, residents' struggles with water crisis and then residents' class action suit that started in 2014. What was clear in these stories was that the owner, Magar E. Magar, had not been reinvesting much of his revenues from residents' property lease payments into the maintenance of Syringa Park, which included the maintenance of the owner's private drinking water and sewage systems. What local readers have learned via media since then is that Syringa is a perpetual zone of crisis. But, what locals learned was only part of the story. The class research project we describe in this chapter is an effort to humanize poor people, most especially those who live in

L. Hormel (✉) · C. Ballesteros · H. Brister
University of Idaho, Moscow, USA
e-mail: lhormel@uidaho.edu

K. Haltinner and L. Hormel (eds.), *Teaching Economic Inequality and Capitalism in Contemporary America*, https://doi.org/10.1007/978-3-319-71141-6_15

trailer parks, and to highlight the fact that Syringa residents are proactively trying to save their community.

Cynthia: I came into this class peering through several lenses, which quickly merged in the class project we describe in this chapter. I am a first generation college student, a Chicana; I am from a working class background, a household of eight, and my parents, in addition to their other jobs, are landlords. Entering a class that sought to examine the U.S. class system from a sociological perspective, I didn't know (1) what to expect nor (2) how much I already knew about the topic until we began reading *Evicted: Poverty and Profit in the American City*. At first I was surprised to hear that evictions happen on a massive scale in the United States, but it sounded accurate. I began to take apart the pieces of information we gathered in the class and applying it to the experiences my parents had with tenants and special circumstances. It seemed as though I had never paid enough attention to the realities my parents and their residents faced. Now that I started, I am committed to applying the information we learned in class to improve the lives of Americans in poverty.

Haylee: Prior to attending the University of Idaho and beginning my education at the undergraduate level, I had no real, in depth, understanding of the socio-cultural disparities that my friends, family, or fellow students experience every day. I had been raised in a middle class home where I was never knowingly exposed to any structural narratives that may contribute to social stratification or a person's class position. My formal education, through the activity we describe in this chapter, has given me significant insight.

Introduction

This chapter reflects three individuals' vantage points: Leontina (course instructor), Haylee and Cynthia (students) regarding a classroom activity (that can be extrapolated for use at a variety of institutions) used in a course Leontina created called, "Sociology of Prosperity: Social Class and Economics in the 21st Century," and taught during fall term 2016 (course syllabus provided in the appendices of this book). As you have already observed in the reflexive statements, Haylee and Cynthia brought distinct backgrounds and interests that influence how they experienced the course and the PAR (participatory action research) project. The first section explains problem-based learning (PBL) and participatory action research (PAR) and how they complement one another as opportunities for learners (students and research participants) to be investigators and knowledge producers. The next section describes how Leontina organized the PBL-oriented class research project. Cynthia's and Haylee's insights allow us to understand students' perspectives about their learning, which elements of the course project design helped build their abilities to ask questions and seek answers, which parts did not fulfill this as effectively, and why. The final part of this chapter asks what different ways this type of course project can be improved to meet the combined aims of PBL and PAR.

What Is Problem-Based Learning and Participatory Action Research?

Problem-Based Learning (PBL)

In past courses I have organized group projects that employed problem-based learning (PBL) techniques (Hormel 2009). A key goal for instructors when using PBL is to reduce the instructor's role in the learning environment and create opportunities for students to take responsibility for the direction of their learning. Greenwald (2000: 28) outlines three key components within PBL assignments: they begin with a problem, the problem must be "ill-defined," and instructors guide students in the process of problem solving. Central to PBL instruction is the belief that when problems are ill-defined, students learn and are motivated to raise "questions about what is known, what needs to be known, and how the answer can be found" (ibid.). Reinforced with a teacher's willingness to support (rather than lead) the learning process, PBL enables student-driven discovery in which students are "creators and holders of knowledge" (Ross and McNeil 2004). For sociologists who regularly critique oppressive social structures, this is a valuable model for teaching and learning since students can often perceive critiques of capitalism and its dependence on economic inequalities as political and, therefore, biased. These perceptions short-circuit students' learning abilities, since they often reduce their willingness to accept that they may not know much about different social phenomena. Ross and McNeil (2004: 89) contend PBL enables students to analyze topics more objectively since PBL assignments "remove the focus of controversial topics from the faculty member, specific assigned readings, or particularly vocal students and center the learning experience on the issue at hand." Creating an environment in which students discover issues and formulate solutions on their own can diminish students' resistance to social critiques and can help students see themselves as part of the social world they are studying.

Participatory Action Research (PAR)

Just as PBL tries to create an environment where students are knowledge builders, PAR is motivated by the desire to empower community members. PAR seeks communities' leadership in investigations and through this process seeks to enhance communities' capacity to advocate for themselves using knowledge they need and are able to interpret for their purposes. As participatory action researcher Randy Stoecker (38) describes it:

> The idea of participatory action research is to intervene in the power/knowledge/action cycle. But because it is a cycle, if the community or group itself is not involved in leading the process that produces knowledge, they can't understand the knowledge and its relationship to action and power.

As a researcher who has slowly been figuring out how much PAR resonates with her ethics and epistemological approach and how this kind of research really needs to unfold, I could not help but finally see the parallels between PAR and PBL intentions. Both approaches seek to 'intervene in the power/knowledge/action cycle' so students and community members are makers of their learning and, consequently, their futures.

A Matter of Perfect Timing

An important note for others considering integrating PBL and PAR in their courses is that it may not always be the best time in your own work life to do it. In my own case, I was able to seize this opportunity, since I was faced with a major dilemma trying to juggle time for teaching and researching. I had started doing research with Syringa trailer park residents (from now on I just refer to the park as "Syringa") in spring 2015, but I could not seem to gain consistent momentum to dig deep into the various institutions shaping their lives. After nearly a year-and-a-half of researching and interviewing in fits and starts, I was beginning to lose clarity about the different elements that made Syringa a fascinating and disturbing example of how poverty, housing shortages, and environmental justice intersect in rural Idaho and create vulnerable, unstable living circumstances. At the same time, I have been puzzling over the best way to teach this newly minted course "Sociology of Prosperity." I had envisioned this course being a means to teach political economic theories and the ways different social class arrangements are assumed in these perspectives, but after the first try in 2015, I wasn't satisfied that students got this connection or felt any more in touch with how intricately social class is woven within oppressive systems like racism, sexism, heterosexism, and ableism that have a tendency to mutually reinforce one another.

Including students from Sociology of Prosperity in my research project with Syringa residents seemed an exciting opportunity to combine the forces of PBL and PAR principles and to sensitize my own understanding of the issues affecting Syringa residents by looking at the case through the fresh lenses of the students. As I mentioned above, PBL and PAR are motivated by the principle of empowerment by engaging students and research "subjects" in the cycle of making/interpreting knowledge and acting on what they know. By bringing a local social and environmental justice case to the class and asking them what puzzles about it pop out at them, without too much of my own understanding shared, students generated their own questions and interests to investigate about Syringa. This is the stuff PBL is made of. In this class research project, PAR became more relevant as students—toward the last six weeks of the term—met residents from Syringa and were taken on a (very chilly, windy) resident-guided tour of the park. What mattered to me in this process was that residents were the knowledge producers, presenting their interpretations of their circumstances, and that students generated questions for the residents in the learning process. This was PAR and PBL interaction. More details will be described in the following pages, as I explain specifically how I organized this project in tandem with themes from class readings and how students, represented by Haylee and Cynthia, perceived this project.

The Set-up

The first priority for this project was to make sure every student in the class was listed as research personnel in the IRB Protocol for my ongoing research project on Syringa Mobile Home Park. Before the term started, I emailed all registered students to inform them they needed to take the university's mandatory training (at University of Idaho we use the CITI modules for human subjects research training) by the end of the first week of class. I explained they needed to do this to participate in the main course project and to be able to access research data used for the project. Students responded fairly promptly—by the end of week all three students were listed in my IRB Protocol as research personnel.

What Is Prosperity?

The first week of the course, students were asked to define prosperity. The first day of class discusses the roots to why the course is titled, "Sociology of Prosperity." Though I usually joke that it was an effort to finally make sociology focus on something that sounds positive and hopeful, I also turn to what drives so much of social philosophical debates: social and political economic theorists are all basically arguing about what makes societies *prosper*. In fact, once one opens his or her/their eyes and ears to the word "prosperity," he/she/they realize that it is spoken regularly in media interviews with politicians and talking heads of all stripes.

Core Text

For the specific course we are describing here, we also embarked on a four-week reading of Matthew Desmond's ethnographic book (2016) *Evicted: Poverty and Profit in the American City*. Desmond writes like a novelist, comparing the day-to-day circumstances of poor people living in two distinct Milwaukee neighborhoods, the predominantly black North Side and the predominantly white South Side. This research design allows him to compare racial-class experiences, plus—conveniently for a class preparing to study Syringa trailer park—the South Side research is conducted with residents of a trailer park, called College Mobile Home Park. The book not only introduces students to these different experiences, but Desmond also demonstrates the institutional arrangements that serve to dig poor people deeper and deeper into unstable housing, debt, and criminalization. It served as a perfect introduction for understanding that there are a variety of forces shaping poor people's circumstances that go beyond the stereotype that "poor people make poor decisions." In fact, as Matthew Desmond illustrates, people make a lot of money when poor people are perpetually living in limbo. And, for launching a PBL research project, the book's story gets students thinking about dimensions of poverty and housing that pique their personal interests.

Giving Students Tools for Investigation

Starting the third week of classes, once we had started building rapport with one another, students were introduced to different tools of investigation. One day, we took a tour of the library to learn how to conduct archival research of newspapers using microfiche and of various materials available in special collections. Another day, one of the county commissioners presented in class on the way county and municipal governments are organized, answering: "What is available?" and "Who does what?" Since Syringa is not sited within municipal boundaries, it was important for students to learn what governing capacity counties have in comparison to cities. Students were also able to ask the county commissioner what the county was doing about issues affecting Syringa, most especially their intent for "red-tagging" vacated trailers (Cynthia will talk more about "red tags" later). To introduce students to the District Court system and how to request court documents available to the public, we took a field trip to the County Courthouse where one of the District Court judges sat with us in a trial room and explained how the system works and what things in particular students investigating Syringa trailer park should know about the law. We learned about the state repositories that are now all online for public use, allowing investigators to look at the complete history of court cases involving individuals, individuals like the owner of Syringa park (who has a long rap sheet). Ideally, we would have also met with a representative of the Idaho Department of Environment Quality, but time did not allow. We, instead, listened to the 45-min interview one of my colleagues, Dilshani Sarathchandra, conducted with Idaho DEQ in spring 2015. The goal with these different presentations was to give tools to students and to expose them to the complex, historical institutional arrangements intersecting with Syringa residents' personal and everyday lives. All of this took place before introducing students to residents' lives.

Connecting Theory to Real Life

As students were introduced to the investigation tools described above, we began reading different theories of political economy—Adam Smith, Thomas Malthus, David Ricardo, Karl Marx, Maynard Keynes, and Karl Polanyi. A major shortcoming is obvious here, since I usually include feminist and critical race readings (e.g., Marilyn Waring and Himani Bannerji) in a class without a research project, though I do incorporate these angles of critique in discussions and lectures. I was nervous about how this would shake out in the midst of doing a PBL research project. Would these theories make any sense when students are simply trying to get their heads wrapped around this disturbing, complex case? Below Cynthia and Haylee discuss student learning of these connections, but how I saw this working for instruction was that the assumptions about social class inherent in each of these theorists' works could be shown to operate, some more obviously than others, in the case of Syringa trailer park. What assumptions about poverty, whether people deserve their lot in life or not, seem to operate in the kinds of actions and processes that have taken place to help residents and in ignoring them? Having a real life experience to work with seemed an eye opening way to show how old theories—notably, from white male perspectives—continue to make their mark in policies and social and environmental catastrophes today.

Meet the Syringa Community

Though I puzzle over whether the timing worked okay, I postponed acquainting students with Syringa community members until the last six weeks of the term. Some of this delay simply grew from the complexities of residents' lives, as they often deal with uncertainty and were forced to cancel some of our appointments. I organized this class, though, with the idea that I wanted students to get familiar with the institutional view of rural poverty, housing, and environment—a perspective they are likely to have greatest exposure to in their future careers—before challenging that view with on-the-ground realities residents navigate. One of the first ways I introduced students to residents was sharing an interview with one of the residents, playing the audio while we viewed the transcript. Students were asked what themes struck them in the interview, plus to share any questions they had that they thought needed to be asked in the future. I remember one interesting theme that arose during the interview and class discussion concerned the conditions for the big population of cats at the park. Most, if not all, of the residents have at least one cat and many cats—according to the resident interviewed—are dumped off at a nearby junkyard. We explored the important role cats must play for people facing uncertainty. Another interesting angle Cynthia posed was, "If people can't drink the water because of sewage contamination, wouldn't this also mean the health of the park's cats are also jeopardized?" This was a point of inquiry I hadn't considered and, in a recent meeting with a couple of residents, this concern was raised. Residents do, indeed, feel their pets' health is affected by ongoing water quality problems.

It was important, though, that residents and students interacted face-to-face. Thus, I arranged with two of the key, public figures at Syringa—Dawn Tachell and Shannon Musick—to come to class to conduct a formal presentation introducing their experiences as well as the park's history with the current park owner. Dawn and Shannon described why they moved to Syringa, how the community mattered to them, and the kinds of things they hoped the class would learn and do for them. We also worked out a schedule for students to visit Syringa, during which Shannon (who had been until recently the on-site manager for the park) and Dawn would tour them through the park, showing red-tagged homes, showing places that wore the scars of changes in the park, and also showing the places they wanted to improve to get the community back to its better self. During these tours, residents came out to visit and find out what they were doing. This presented students the opportunity to hear different voices and to hear how important it is to residents that young people hear them and do something about it.

Team-Writing a Research Report

The outcome of this research was a written report, in which each student was responsible for writing out a section describing their specific research area and what they found. The goal was to distribute the report to residents and to county organizations, such as the county commissioners and the county-level Human Rights Task Force. The substance of students' experiences and findings is shared in the next section of this chapter.

Students' Investigations: What They Asked and What They Found

Haylee: The class was structured into three different parts. The first gave us an introduction to life in poverty through reading the book, *Evicted: Poverty and Profit in the American City*, by Matthew Desmond. This book gave me important insights on the everyday struggles faced by low income renters; explaining how difficult it is to maintain a home and a quality life when there is a whole economic niche benefitting from evictions in places like Milwaukee. Prior to enrolling in Sociology of Prosperity, I had some knowledge about who was affected by poverty and why, but I never really understood how the cycle of eviction was perpetuated to ensure that those in poverty had very few chances of getting out. Reading Matthew Desmond's book helped to me to better understand how vital a stable home is for one's mental health, familial success, and economic stability.

The second portion of the class was focused on economic theory, educating students on ideas from theorists like Marx, Polanyi, and Keynes; giving us a brief understanding as to how poverty was explained by different theorists and what solutions they suggested for solving poverty. While I have, in the past, taken some classes on economics, they were focused on macro level effects of economic structures on the national or global stage, instead of the individual and community level. Sociology of Prosperity gave me a better understanding of the direct effects of capitalism on the individual, particularly on those in poverty, and explained, through the lenses of different theorists, how the problem of poverty should or shouldn't be solved.

The final section was the more hands-on section of the class. This portion integrated the experiences of residents of the Syringa Mobile Home Park into the class. It also consisted of conducting research on the crisis facing residents and its ongoing consequences.

One of the most important aspects of the class was being able to see a real life example of how the current capitalistic structure has allowed for inequality within my own community. For me, our lessons had meaning. Instead of rote memorization, I was able to apply information on collective efficacy or economic theory to Syringa, a small community near where I live, with people who I met and interacted. Being able to integrate myself into the community through resident-guided tours and reading court files gave me insight on real life people with families who have been directly affected by and taken advantage of through the capitalistic system. It made what I was learning in class much more poignant. Meeting different people throughout the term, who were key individuals in the Syringa Crisis—including former on-site park manager Shannon Musick, Syringa resident Dawn Tachell, and Latah County Commissioner Tom Lamar—helped me understand the different complexities of the case.

Each student in the class was given a different aspect of the Syringa case to focus on; some of my peers studied red tagging while others focused on the declining market value of the homes before and after the crisis. Each part was important in telling the Syringa story, shedding light on the intricacies of the situation that may have been overlooked by the different actors involved in the crisis. My contribution focused on creating a timeline of events based on information gathered from different district court files I analyzed at the county courthouse. Following these different investigatory paths, and merging knowledge, allowed our class to fully understand why the residents were filing a case against Magar E. Magar and connect it to the bigger picture of the Syringa story.

Cynthia: It was clear since the very beginning that this project was going to be multifaceted in the fact that we all had to work together to piece the puzzle of this huge story. At first I thought of "the boonies" when I pictured rural poverty or food deserts; I didn't know how close to Moscow one of these places would be located. In the winter of 2013–2014, I had heard of a mobile home park running out of water because its water was contaminated. Around the same time, it was discovered that the tap water in our housing complexes on campus had too much chlorine. One could smell it while they showered or when they tasted the water. As a result, we were instructed not to drink water from drinking fountains. Despite this experience, I couldn't fully imagine the financial and emotional hardships low-income families experienced when abruptly losing precious water sources. It didn't seem possible for them to go on unscathed; bottled water adds up, this is usually not only used to drink, but to cook as well. To go 90 days without on-site water, they were stuck buying water in Moscow, which meant their water costs added up quickly, especially in such large increments. Later on, there was news that both government officials and church affiliated entities were taking water out to the park and that was the last I heard of it. It wasn't until I enrolled in this class that I understood that the situation had not gone away, but there was a need to keep fighting.

The class divided up the project and I chose to conduct research on the process of "red tagging" homes. This part of the project was interesting to me because of its complexity and significance: there are a number of factors that shape the county's decision to red tag a home and, more importantly, the red tagging process creates negative and unintended outcomes for Syringa residents.

According to the Latah County Commissioners Office and their executive order for the Syringa Mobile Home Park, "red tags" are placed on mobile homes after a tenant vacates the property. They are issued to restrict further habitation (by owner or renters) of the mobile home. Red tags are placed near the front door after the mobile home is vacated and automatically deemed in noncompliance with Building Code #318. Latah County Building Code Ordinance #318 allows for a person to enter the structure and make repairs to it, but makes it a misdemeanor for anyone to inhabit the structure (Latah County, State of Idaho 2014). This means a homeowner cannot rent the residence, even if it is structurally habitable, and also leaves little incentive for homeowners to invest in any structural improvements. The most difficult part about this scenario is that it is not clear what conditions need to be met to enable red tag removal in the park, and all of the conditions are dependent on the park owner's actions to make infrastructural improvements—improvements that have been deferred for over two decades already. Thus, those who own red tagged homes have no idea if red tags can or will be removed. Moreover, residents like Shannon and Dawn (mentioned earlier) are watching more and more of their neighbors leave and, as red tagged homes multiply, see a dying community with no definite end in sight.

The mobile home park owners do not lose ownership over the property. They still have the option to move it, but it costs anywhere from $5000 to 8000 to move a trailer, which in some cases is more than the home is valued at right now (BSU 2007). County officials hope it will motivate Magar E. Magar to invest in fixing the water and sewage systems. Red tags reduce the number of people paying leases on the land, which is the incentive for Magar to fix things. Another benefit the commissioners see in red tagging is that as more residents leave, fewer are affected by frequent water stoppages and crises.

As a private landowner, Magar E. Magar has a high degree of control over Syringa Mobile Home Park, and therefore, the repairs made to the park's water wells. Since the winter of 2013–2014, Latah County Commissioners have placed red tags on mobile homes at Syringa Park, in an effort to push its owner, Magar E. Magar, to pay for water system repairs. The class met with the previous on-site manager of the park, Shannon Musick, who made efforts to fix the system, but before any progress was made, left the job as a result of being denied back pay and being mistreated during her employment. Shannon worked alongside the park maintenance personnel who noted that the situation with the park's water system was complex; knowledge of water system operations was necessary and water testing was needed often and at various times of the day. Weather was a significant factor in trying to keep the water lines running and, in an effort to keep the water system working, both the park manager and maintenance personnel needed to wake up at ungodly hours of the night to make sure everything was running smoothly. Sometimes, this meant Shannon had to crawl under mobile homes with flashlights in the middle of the night to fix leaking pipes or to add pipe insulation, for less than $1000 in monthly pay.

Red tags have not only led to tenants leaving their trailers unoccupied but the situation has escalated to the point where people come into the park to scavenge building materials and steal belongings from the red tagged trailers. The homes' property values have gone down significantly. Though Commissioners appear to have assumed that mobile homes were mostly owned by Magar, most are actually owned by other individuals. I found that the issue of title ownership is crucial, since it means that, in an effort to squeeze Magar's control of the park, the homeowners have actually been the ones immediately harmed financially. In this sense, the situation is highly challenging and convoluted.

As mentioned, red tagging has significant, unintended consequences for residents. In addition to being accidentally harmed financially, the stigma of being a Syringa Mobile Home Park resident means that they have very few housing alternatives in the nearby city of Moscow. Residents shared with us their frustration that locals nickname their community "Syringe Park," which is one of numerous ways that they experience stigma as a low-income county resident. This stigma spreads to rental companies, many of which will not agree to rent apartments and homes to people whose current address is out at the park.

What Tinkering Can Be Done to Improve This Project? Some Closing Comments from Leontina

Our above discussion outlines the organization of the course and illustrates some of the knowledge and skills gained by students from this class project. It is clear, though, that continuing with this or a similar project presents challenges. PBL is intentionally designed so that students are given a problem from which students develop questions and strategies for solving. This means, as an instructor, that one leaves some ambiguity about how "exactly" to proceed or what to ask. It is possible, though, to be too vague and this is one area that will need improvement in future classes. For example, the students felt they needed to meet the residents and be introduced to the park, itself, much earlier. Haylee explains how more time with residents and earlier discussion of the final product would have helped her and the class:

Haylee: While overall, the project was structured well, there were two things that I would have liked to see integrated into similarly structured classes in the future, (1) better integration of Syringa and its residents into the class from the very beginning and (2) a more concrete end product. Our class did not begin to put major focus on the Syringa project until the second half of the semester. This, I felt, limited how much we were able to accomplish when it came to researching and contributing to the project. While I personally understood what Dr. Hormel wanted to see with the project, the limited guidance in the beginning made it difficult to jumpstart my research and to feel like a productive contributor to the report. I think it would have been very beneficial to my learning experience had we outlined exactly what we wanted our end goal to be and set more finite deadlines so the project would have connected with the class more seamlessly.

Leontina: As the instructor for this course, Haylee's feedback makes sense. Though, in some ways, how we approached this project was very much like the reality of research for sociologists in everyday experience. We often are not handed information or understanding of an end product until we have collected enough puzzle pieces that enable us to start seeing the connections between individuals, organizations, and institutions. The mission, though, is tied to the classroom, which is limited by time in a 15-week semester (or even a 10-week quarter) and institutions are increasingly demanding instruments for demonstrating outcomes assessment. Moreover, as a classroom experience tied to PAR, the importance to residents that students give back to them for the knowledge they have shared as a community cannot be overlooked. In fact, for students this is the most critical part of their learning experience, and of mine. For this reason, I would carefully reorient the timing of students' introduction to the community, envisioning it more as a sandwich in which students go to the community to learn about it and visit residents, then learn about different institutions that factor into residents' lives, and ultimately go back to residents with more informed questions. I will need to think about this a little more, since I delayed introductions with the purpose of protecting residents until students had been introduced to the complex, sociological forces shaping poverty in rural America.

The last part of the section has focused mostly on necessary improvements, though both Haylee and Cynthia have also described the positive experiences they had with this pedagogical approach to learning. Students would have preferred to have had more exposure to Syringa and community residents earlier, though the fact they did end up working with residents the latter part of the term was transformative for them. They described how good it felt to feel involved in making a difference for people who were experiencing such injustices. Theorists posing different definitions of, and paths to, prosperity made more sense to them when given a case study: it was easier to see how the dead white men of the past posed arguments that continue to be inherent to people's explanations of poverty and prosperity right here and right now. Below, Cynthia and Haylee share how they saw theorists arguments relate to our project.

Cynthia: Malthus was among the theorists who connected the most with the problem of red tags in Syringa. Social stigmatization of residents at Syringa tied back to Malthusian thoughts about impoverished populations and the role of welfare. He argued that those who were lower class had tendencies to live off of welfare, and, as a consequence, had large families they couldn't support. For this reason, he argued that welfare perpetuated a cycle of poverty, because being able to receive money they didn't earn led them to make bad choices. Unfortunately, this is not exclusive to the time period in which Thomas Malthus lived, as many today assume residents of Syringa have the power to make better choices, but have not and, thus, remain in the trailer park. Collectively, the information we compiled showed a set of circumstances which were out of park residents' control. As a student, this connection made the experience in this class valuable. Applying theory to everyday life doesn't always have to come in a textbook assigned in a classroom—it can happen while walking through the living spaces of neighbors and understanding how the socio-political and economic status of a person can set trends and stigmas that continue to linger, experiences we may have seen centuries ago. I don't think this connection could have impacted me to the level that it has if it were done in a space that didn't provide this opportunity.

Haylee: Through working with the court documents, I was able to create a timeline which guided us through the story of Syringa, starting with the beginning of the crisis, all the way to when the case action suit was stalled due to Magar E. Magar filing for bankruptcy. Working on this portion of the report highlighted two important concepts for me. The first being the importance of collective efficacy in a society. Collective efficacy allowed for the residents to stand up for themselves and file the suit because they knew that the livelihood of every person in the park relied on giving a voice to the residents. The crisis allowed them to mobilize and the suit provided them with a voice. I also was able to connect the idea of fictitious commodity, which was first coined by Polanyi, to the Syringa story. The idea of a fictitious commodity helps reveal how the market system commodifies things that are essential to society, such as land and labor. Magar, a landlord who has control also over the life-essential good of water, has greatly benefitted from land, and what it brings (like water), being a commodified good. He has been collecting rent since his purchase of the land and the water/sewage systems, yet he has failed to maintain the infrastructure of the park, allowing to generate vast sums of money at the expense of the residents' health and security, who rely on him contractually to meet these conditions. Polanyi's argument became much more obvious when looking at it through the lens of Syringa residents' dependence on Magar for these basic necessities in their lives.

Considering the insights Haylee and Cynthia have shared about their experiences in this chapter, I feel like my first try at combining PAR and PBL was successful, even with the necessary areas of improvement. One thing is certain, there are many community members in Moscow whose class location marginalizes them and, for this reason, I am intent on incorporating this and similar action projects into this course in the future.

References

Boise State University (BSU) Center for Idaho History and Politics and Public Policy Center. (2007). *Mobile home living in Boise: Its uncertain future and alarming decline*. Boise, ID: Boise State University.

Greenwald, N. L. (2000). Learning from problems. *The Science Teacher, 67*(4), 28–32.

Hormel, Leontina. (2009). Practicing social activism through problem-based learning. *Humanity & Society, 33,* 169–184.

Latah County, State of Idaho. (2014). Ordinance #318: Latah County building code ordinance.https://www.latah.id.us/pzc/Ordinances/Building%20Code%20Ordinance.pdf. Accessed December 8, 2016.

Ross, S. M., & McNeil, H. J. (2004). Problem-based learning: An exercise on Vermont's legalization of civil unions. *Teaching Sociology, 32*(1), 79–93.

Inequality and Violence

Barbara H. Chasin

Author's Reflexive Statement and Introduction

With the Vietnam War escalating in 1963, I, like many others, found that my conception of our country did not fit the facts. While a graduate student at the University of Iowa, I joined campus protests and was introduced to Marxism and activism. The connections between capitalism, the war and other aspects of American society became too obvious to be ignored. Marxist concepts helped me understand social reality far better than the traditional sociology I had been learning. Later, I discovered that many of my students found this form of analysis made sense to them, as well.

I was influenced by the radical directions within the profession occurring in the late sixties. The discipline's progressive movement can be traced to Martin Nicolaus's "Fat-Cat" Sociology speech at the American Sociological Association's 1968 meeting (Nicolaus 1968). This was an example of liberation sociology, a movement urging sociologists to ask "which side are you on," to acknowledge that our teaching has consequences, and to help students understand ways the structure of society causes problems in efforts to find solutions. Feagin and Vera (2001, p. 12) explain: "Liberation sociologists" raised concerns "about social inequality and the illegitimacy of the powers that be," an exciting idea for those of us beginning our teaching careers. This was not without risks, as numerous radical academics found themselves fired, or had other difficulties in their workplace.

Influenced by liberation sociology and against the backdrop of the social movements and urban disruptions of the 1960s, I developed a course in 1970 called the "Sociology of Conflict and Violence." When the US military or local police forces were used to deal with revolutionary movements or domestic protests these were seen as legitimate uses of violence, while those protesting social conditions in

B. H. Chasin (✉)
Montclair State University, Montclair, USA
e-mail: chasinb@mail.montclair.edu

K. Haltinner and L. Hormel (eds.), *Teaching Economic Inequality and Capitalism in Contemporary America*, https://doi.org/10.1007/978-3-319-71141-6_16

the Third World or the US were severely criticized and punished for allegedly choosing violence as a course of action.

This chapter describes a key element of the course: understanding the violence endemic in capitalism. It further explains strategies that instructors can use to convey this information and help students critically examine American capitalism.

Context for the Course

At the time I developed Sociology of Conflict and Violence, the systemic violence that occurs as a result of American capitalism was not thought of as violence. Employing concepts of Marxism, I was able to challenge this invisible narrative by emphasizing the role a capitalist ruling class plays in perpetuating the types and incidence of violence we discuss. I taught the course almost yearly until 2006. Since the overall structure of US capitalism is not changing, the general points discussed here remain valid.

When I first began teaching the course, few books were available to demonstrate the violent nature of US capitalism. Most of these have since gone out of print and none of the books took an explicitly sociological approach. Thus, I decided to write my own text identifying three major types of violence within capitalism and showing their links to American social structure (Chasin 2004a). Instructors can organize this course referring to contemporary issues and movements that fit in with the course's themes.

In the course, I supplement/ed my textbook with handouts from newspapers, periodicals, and scholarly journals. Today it is also useful for students to search for relevant websites, bring in their findings, and to discuss their criteria for deciding their sources' validity. This seems especially important given concerns about false news and the frequent dismissal or ignoring of valid scientific findings. Mainstream media can also be problematic, though, so it is important not to add to students' sense that no source can be trusted. Students, thus, appreciate having a handout of sources the instructor finds credible (see Appendix A).

Inequality, Conflict, and Violence: Defining and Measuring Inequality

Inequality

In teaching this course, it is important that students have a shared understanding of language. Thus, early in the semester we clarify what the terms in the course title mean starting with inequality. Partly as a result of social movements, particularly Occupy, more students recognize that there are high degrees of inequality than they did when I first taught this course.

We begin with a review of traditional measurements of inequality, such as the Gini Coefficient. Cross national comparisons indicate the United States has the highest income inequality among comparable nations. Other statistical measures show the growth in inequality since the 1970s. There are enjoyable exercises that can show how much inequality there is in the United States. One (previously published) exercise can be done with chairs so that the most affluent have chairs to spare while the lower income groups do not have enough (c.f., Ender 2004; Giecek 2017).

Discussing inequality means discussing social class, as well as race/ethnicity, and gender, all of which can operate simultaneously—as the concept of intersectionality indicates. Many students assume class is based on life-style choices, like clothing, food, leisure activities, and one's occupation. To counter this dominant narrative, I introduce Marxist categories based on relationships, such as between workers and capitalists, as an alternative way to conceptualize the nature of class inequality specific to the capitalist system.

Conflict

For this course conflict is defined as differences in the goals, strategies, values, and ideas of individuals or groups. We consider the following questions, with the students providing specific examples:

- What is causing the conflicts of capitalism?
- How serious are the conflicts of capitalism?
- Are there mechanisms for resolving the conflict non-violently?

Then we consider more general questions:

- What are the social rules or norms for resolving conflicts?
- What causes these rules/norms to change? This is a place to mention social movements.
- Why does conflict sometimes become violent?

The dispute about the protests against the Dakota Access Pipeline at Standing Rock, North Dakota can provide a good case study to illustrate the intersection of class, ethnicity, and gender, methods of protest, including non-violent ones, and the conflict between armed patrols and water protectors.

Violence

I define violence as acts, intentional or otherwise, that result in physical harm to other persons, or a person. Students are asked to bring in examples of violence before discussing my definition. Most will bring in some example in the media of a shooting, rape, or domestic violence. Sometimes there is an example of violence caused by a corporation and, currently, I would imagine there might be examples of well-publicized police violence.

The course identifies three major types of violence: interpersonal, organizational, and structural. Students' examples usually fit the first two categories, but they are less likely to bring in instances of structural violence. Instructors can introduce sociological analysis of students' examples that use relevant concepts for the course. For instance, organizational violence is illustrated when individuals in decision-making bureaucratic *roles* choose policies that harm others.

When students present different examples of violence, instructors can illustrate why social class matters. Interpersonal violence is what most people think about when asked for examples of violence. Particular individuals directly injure others and are usually aware that they have done so. This form occurs most often among people of the same social class and often between members of the same community or household. Organizational and structural violence, on the other hand, are a direct or indirect result of decisions made at the elite level of society, while the victims are usually from less privileged groups.

One way we know that structural violence is occurring is to draw comparisons between groups living in the same society. If one group is healthier or safer than another we can demonstrate that these disparities are caused by more than just individual life-styles or attitudes.

We can compare infant mortality rates between African-American, Native American, and white infants. In 2013, for every 1000 African-American infants born 11.1 died before reaching their first birthday. For Native Americans it was 7.6 out of 1000 births, while for whites the figure was 5 of every 1000 births (Mathews et al. 2013). These figures are lower than in previous years and there are ways to lower the figures with different social policies, which demonstrates these can make a difference in levels of structural violence.

The forms of violence can interact with one another. Specific organizations make decisions, at given historical moments that maintain, increase, or reduce people's vulnerability to structural violence and/or affect the likelihood of interpersonal violence. I provide Table 1 illustrating differences between the three types of violence.

There are several reasons for broadening our conception of violence beyond interpersonal violence:

1. Structural and organizational violence account for more deaths and injuries each year than interpersonal violence.
2. We need to understand structural violence in order to gain a fuller understanding of the dangers many people in our society face.
3. We need to analyze structural and organizational violence in order to overcome stereotypes about who the violent people in our society are. In a statement that too many would agree with Boston City Councilman, James Kelley noted, in 1994, that "People feel very intimidated by these black males in hooded sweatshirts" (quoted in Herbert 1994).

Table 1 Summary of the characteristics of the three types of violence

Characteristic	Type of violence		
	Interpersonal	Organizational	Structural
Number of victims	Few	Many	Many
Victim(s) can identify perpetrator(s)	Usually	Rarely	No
Perpetrator(s) can identify victim(s)	Usually	Rarely	Very rarely
Characteristics of perpetrator(s) and victim(s)	Similar or identical social class	Different classes	Different classes
Time between decision and violence	Short—often less than one day	Sometimes months but may be years in creating the conditions involved	Months to years
Number of decision makers in incident	One or a very few	Usually a few	Cumulative effect of many decisions
Example	George Zimmerman shoots and kills Travon Martin	NYPD police choke Eric Garner to death	African–American life expectancy of 75.6 years compared to 78.8 years for whites

4. We need to understand the nature and causes of all types of violence in order to learn what we have to do to create a more humane and less violent society.

When we outline the relationship between inequality and violence we show that:

1. Inequality leads to organizational violence and to structural violence when part of the population is denied the needed resources for a healthy life and environment.
2. Organizational violence leads to dangers to workers, consumers, and the public. In the forms of domestic repression and militarism organizational violence is used to maintain and even further inequality.
3. Interpersonal violence is a way in which the less privileged react to their situation, for instance, by engaging in street crime. They may direct their anger at an unjust social order against the weaker and more vulnerable sectors of society—scapegoats.

In the following sections, I describe how I have developed students' understanding of inequality and violence in society, emphasizing the different levels of violence. Violence not only happens at various levels—interpersonal, organizational, and structural—but is always shaped by intersecting institutions of racial, ethnic, gendered, and class oppressions. These complexities should be interwoven throughout the course and each can be examined in the course to help students understand their distinct qualities in relation to the course subject. For purposes of saving space, I am not able to include discussion of intersectionality in this chapter.

The Sociological Imagination and Its Alternatives

Teaching sociology is often challenging since sociologists have to contend with the dominant mind-set of individualism and "powerful vested interests" (Wilkinson and Pickett 2009, p. xi) who find sociological reasoning threatening. I have found that teaching about conflict and violence is a way to introduce students to several sociological perspectives, with my course focusing on conflict theory.

The sociological imagination means seeing how our lives are shaped by living in a particular historical period in a particular social environment (Mills 1959). Asking about students' education choices clarifies this. *Why did you go to college? Why did you choose this one, and did you decide between public or private? How did you choose a major?* The relevance of social class and economic inequality can usually be drawn out of their answers.

As Mills' sociological imagination helps us understand, one's personality alone cannot explain an individual's circumstances. Individuals are embedded in social circumstances, some obvious, others less so. This is in contrast to the dominant US paradigm, which gives primacy to individual choices—as when Trump's HUD Secretary Ben Carson said "Poverty is really more of a choice than anything else" (quoted in Malmgren 2017). The reality is we make choices from a menu but one that is created by larger social forces at several levels as the diagram that I developed indicates (see Fig. 1). Examples abound and can vary according to when and where the course is being taught. A 2017 scalding death of two young homeless sisters in New York City brings together the effects of being born into poverty, the subsequent lack of safe affordable housing, and the effects of class inequality in the city as market based housing prices have been driven upwards by demands from the wealthy (Newman et al. 2016). The example illustrates that homelessness—and the dangers this status brings—was not a lifestyle choice, but shaped by these larger social forces.

In addition to bias toward individual choice arguments, another anti-sociological approach is the human nature argument that ties our biological make-up to the main reasons for violence. This approach only attempts to account for interpersonal violence and cannot explain structural nor organizational violence. It cannot adequately explain non-violent societies such as the Semai (Dentan 1968) nor examples of modern non-violent groups; including the Amish, Jehovah's Witnesses, Mennonites, Hutterites, and non-violent, even when attacked, Civil Rights activists. As we discuss these positions, we also consider how increasing social distance

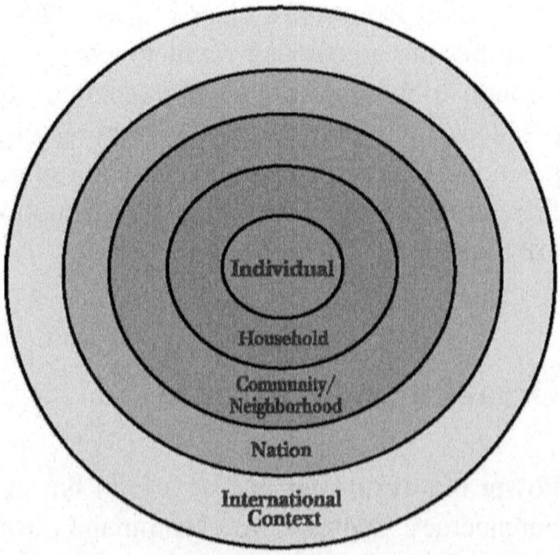

Fig. 1 Levels of Larger Social Forces. *Image source* Chasin (2004a)

facilitates violence by decreasing our ability to empathize. It is easier to stereotype and dehumanize people with whom you are not in routine, egalitarian contact. We consider other ways empathy is lessened, emphasizing the role of bureaucratic structures.

Capitalism as a Violent System

Though my course concentrates on the contemporary United States, capitalism has been violent since its inception. Capitalism's global nature has meant that large numbers of people in many parts of the world have been subjected to its violence including enclosure movements, slavery, the Irish potato famine, and fascist regimes (Guerin 1973). When the material interests of a few with great power take precedence over others and other values violence is a likely outcome.

All types of violence in the United States are caused by high levels of economic inequality. The United States has the highest level of economic inequality among advanced capitalist democracies, the highest levels of interpersonal violence, and higher levels of those kinds of structural violence that we can measure, such as infant mortality. Organizational violence is more difficult to compare in this way, though with less corporate regulation than in comparable countries the drive for profits can be shown to produce physical harm.

Profit maximizing goals resulting in violence include weak regulations, controlling resources here and abroad, lowering the cost of labor, and having lower taxes. Less tax revenues means less money for social services that could reduce all forms of violence. As noted earlier, it is not difficult to show that there is widespread economic inequality, nor that political power and class are deeply intertwined. The nature of the linkage, however, needs to be explained to show how a ruling class actually rules and how this produces violent outcomes.

William Domhoff's classic work *Who Rules America?* is useful here, since it describes the processes by which economic power is translated into political power, through lobbying, campaign financing, corporate executives staffing government positions, and through policy-creating organizations (Domhoff 2005). The composition of Trump's key players in his administration seems particularly blatant, but there are examples from other administrations showing the systemic nature of these linkages.

Organizational Violence

Power is a result not just of wealth but of occupying a role at the top of a major bureaucracy. Mills' phrase "command posts" describes elite positions in the "major hierarchies and organizations of modern society" (1959, p. 4), with the corporation being the most powerful of these bureaucracies. Being wealthy and well-connected may help an individual achieve such a position but it is still the position that is the source of power.

Role theory, which stresses the social context in which a person is acting, is one traditional lens sociologists have used to examine how bureaucratic structures are implicated in violent outcomes. Experiments by social psychologists are useful to illustrate this point, showing how social roles can influence individuals likelihood of engaging in violent acts, or not. For instance, Stanley Milgram's classic work *Obedience to Authority* demonstrates how the immediate presence, or absence, of an authority figure can enhance or diminish one's obedience to commands that may inflict harm on others. Philip Zimbardo's well-known Stanford prison experiment demonstrates that situations provoking inhumane behavior can be orchestrated by those in powerful positions, and that a desire to assert power over others can be a motive for violence (Milgram 1974; Zimbardo 2008).

Different features of bureaucracies can enhance violence-causing decisions (Chasin 2004a, pp. 75–85). Students could be asked to look for examples of these characteristics, listed below, to share with the class.

1. The "chain of command" feature of bureaucracies allows those lower down the hierarchy to claim they were only following orders while those higher up can claim subordinates are responsible for any harmful outcomes. Personal feelings of responsibility can be avoided in this scenario.
2. "Social distance" means members of the ruling class rarely suffer from the results of their decisions, nor do they have to face their victims.
3. "Groupthink" means elites are surrounded by people who share and reinforce their world view.
4. "Language manipulation" allows for the masking of harmful actions. For example, Abu Zubayadah, a CIA torture victim, reported that the agency's waterboarding made him feel as if he were 'dying' and said 'I really felt I was drowning….' The CIA report merely said of its actions 'Water treatment was

applied.' The *New York Times* account of this wording described it as "bloodless bureaucratese" (Fink et al. 2017). Steve Bannon, a Trump advisor, described the administration's deregulation, mentioned below, as "the deconstruction of the administrative state" (Lipton and Appelbaum 2017, p. A1).

5. An "appeal to higher values" can be used to make it seem that a particular decision, actually harmful, serves the public good. For instance, abolishing or not enacting regulations is justified as a job-saving measure. Allegedly protecting national security allows for military violence and repression of citizens and non-citizens.

Comparing interpersonal violence to organizational violence illustrates the dangers arising from corporations. Because of the close ties between economic and political elites, regulations of business are relatively weak. This leaves workers, consumers, and the general public more vulnerable to corporate decisions where profit is the goal and not the general welfare of the public.

Deaths on the job are higher than homicide fatalities. In 2015, there were 15,696 murders reported (FBI 2016). According to the AFL-CIO (2016) "In 2014, 4821 workers were killed on the job in the US, and an estimated 50,000 died from occupational diseases, a loss of 150 workers each day from hazardous working conditions." Since the creation of the Occupational Health and Safety Administration (OSHA), these numbers, are lower than they used to be, illustrating the importance of social policies and government regulation when discussing structural and organizational violence.

Both the Democratic and Republican parties are influenced by corporations but the Republicans are more corporate-friendly (Chasin 2004b; Gilligan 2011). Organizational violence is greater when Republicans are in power, which can be attributed to the fact that Republicans are less likely to promote health and safety regulations. For illustration, former President Clinton enacted strong ergonomic rules in the workplace, with a goal of reducing repetitive stress injuries that affect nearly two million workers. When George W. Bush took office in January 2001, Congressional Republicans and several Democrats, with White House backing, used the Regulatory Review Act—never before invoked to overturn a major regulation—to repeal this move toward worker protection (Dewar and Skryzicki 2001). Another more recent example is evident when one observes the Obama administration's enactment of regulations to protect streams from coal-mining pollutants—a public health measure. Soon after taking office, Donald Trump abolished these (Henry 2017). Additional deregulation has focused on forbidding the use of Social Security data to prevent mentally ill individuals from buying guns. In fact, over 90 regulations have been reversed, suspended, or delayed since Trump's inauguration in January 2017 (Lipton and Applebaum 2017).

Corporations as violent organizations also face fewer penalties when they are caught. The class biases in criminal justice can be illustrated by the difference in punishments meted out to those committing interpersonal violence and those responsible for organizational violence. Regardless of which party is in office, fines for organizational violence are relatively small. The government continues to do business with companies that have violated OSHA laws.

Foreign Policy, Militarism, and Violence

Militarism is a major example of organizational violence promoting ruling class interests. Very few students are aware of the extent of US military interventions since World War II or their consequences. I have a handout to show how many interventions there have been and who have been the primary victims (refer to Appendix A). Students could look at the National Priorities Project website which shows the trillions of dollars that have been spent on militarism and what social needs could be met instead. Meeting these social needs would improve the health and safety of many. Alternatives to military spending can also produce more jobs than weapons manufacturing (National Priorities Project 2016). Among the consequences of military violence are psychological problems for those serving in the military. Some students will have, themselves, served or have experience with those suffering from PTSD. Videos are available that describe how harming others can lead to serious psychological damage to oneself and to others (c.f., Alpert et al. 2010).

Capitalist Influences on Our Thinking About Violence

Corporate-controlled media have an influence on thinking about violence (Glassner 1999; Media Education Foundation 2010). C. Wright Mills' discussion of "the cultural apparatus" illustrates how profit-seeking and ownership patterns shape our media experiences which in turn can influence our thinking and political actions (1963). The journalistic slogan "If it bleeds it leads" sums up the emphasis on interpersonal violence. The dangers from systemic corporate or governmental organizational violence are usually minimized.

The weapons industry and the organization it supports, the NRA, benefit from the manipulation of fear (Harkinson 2016). Conservative political figures, loath to fund needed social services, and depending on the time period, gain votes by claiming to protect the public from terrorists, immigrants, gangs, or communists. Between 2001 and 2014, 3412 Americans were killed by alleged terrorists with most of the assailants citizens or permanent residents. In the same period there were 440,095 firearms fatalities (Bowen 2016).

Controlling information is another way in which organizations protect themselves from criticism and reduce the likelihood of regulation. A well-documented example is the role of tobacco companies in perpetuating the myth that smoking is not a health hazard. The sugar industry is engaging in the same type of obfuscation regarding sweeteners and health while Exxon-Mobil covered up its knowledge of the connection between fossil fuels and global warming. Discouraging whistleblowers, such as Chelsea Manning is a way to prevent information leaks while actively concealing information is another tactic. For example, there is the Trump's administration censoring of data from the EPA and other federal agencies.

This could be a place in the course to discuss some real threats that are not being adequately addressed: harmful products, the easy availability of weapons, and climate change. Looking at the latter there are many victims, especially persons in communities of color, and, those in Third World countries. Richer individuals and countries create the conditions leading to climate-driven disasters that mostly impact on others lower down the income ladder (Bullard 1994; Kristof 2017).

Strategies for Non-violence

While our Constitution says the government is instituted to promote the public's general welfare, it is corporate welfare that is promoted the most. My course concludes by looking at non-violent strategies for addressing this, examining nonviolent strategies' effectiveness, their limitations, reasons for using them, and what non-violent resistance and its consequences can tell us about the nature of power relationships (King 1986).

From a sociological perspective many of the effective strategies of nonviolence involve individuals and/or groups not playing their expected social roles. Actions are taken that require some response from the targeted organizations. Among the tactics are boycotting, going on strike, sit-ins, and mass walk-outs from class. Examples of successes, locally, nationally, or internationally, demonstrate the effectiveness of non-violent resistance. However, non-violence has limitations, too. It is hard to think of many non-violent examples which resulted in major distributions of wealth and power. Even successful movements often have some form of violence associated with their successes. The Civil Rights Movement, with federal troops' involvement, and the ending of South African apartheid come to mind.

The students' cynicism levels are very high usually and, unfortunately, this course can reinforce their pessimism. Examples of successful progressive changes illustrate that organized opposition to inequality has made a difference and can continue to do so. There are local activities that can usually be suggested. Urging people to vote is something I think is important to do as well. Individual actions, like using socially responsible credit card companies and being a socially responsible shopper, at least, gives them a sense that personal activities do have social consequences. I urge them to become better informed about the choices they do have power to make.

Recalling past social movements such as anti-racist movements, the anti-apartheid movement in South Africa, environmental movements, women's movements, transgender and gay rights movements I hope has motivated my past students to think about how we can deal with the consequences of inequality and move to a fairer, more humane, and less violent society.

References

AFL-CIO. (2016). Death on the job report. http://www.aflcio.org/Issues/Job-Safety/Death-on-the-Job-Report. Accessed March 27, 2017.

Alpert, J., Gandolfini, J., Kent, E. G., & O'Neil, M. (Producers). (2010). *Wartorn: 1861*-2010 (DVD).

Bowen, E. (2016). American deaths in terrorism vs. gun violence in one graph. *CNN.com* http://www.cnn.com/2016/10/03/us/terrorism-gun-violence/. Accessed March 27, 2017.

Bullard, Robert D. (Ed.). (1994). *Unequal protection: Environmental justice and communities of color*. San Francisco: Sierra Club Books.

Chasin, B. H. (2004a). *Inequality and violence in the US: Casualties of capitalism* (2nd ed.). Amherst, NY: Humanity Books.

Chasin, B. H. (2004b, April). The Bush administration: hazardous to our health and safety. *ZNet*.

Dentan, R. K. (1968). *The Semai: A nonviolent people of Malaya*. New York: Holt, Rinehart and Winston.

Dewar, H., & Skryzicki, C. (2001, March 8). House scraps ergonomics rule. *Washington Post*. https://www.washingtonpost.com/archive/politics/2001/03/08/house-scraps-ergonomics-regulation/. Accessed March 27, 2017.

Domhoff, W. G. (2005). *Who rules America? Power, politics, & social change*. New York, NY: McGraw-Hill.

Ender, M. (2004). Modified monopoly: Experiencing social class inequality. *Academic Exchange Quarterly, 8,* 1096–1453.

FBI. (2016). 2015 Crime in the US. https://ucr.fbi.gov/crime-in-the-u.s/2015/crime-in-the-US-2015/offenses-known-to-law-enforcement/murder. Accessed March 27, 2017.

Feagin, J. R., & Vera, H. (2001). *Liberation sociology*. Boulder, CO: Westview Press.

Fink, S., Risen, J., & Savage, C. (2017, January 20). New details of CIA torture, and a new clash. *The New York Times* (pp. A1, A6).

Giecek, T. (2017). Teaching economics as if people mattered. *Teachingeconomics.org*. http://www.teachingeconomics.org/content/index.php?topic=tenchairs. Accessed March 27, 2017.

Gilligan, J. (2011). *Why some politicians are more dangerous than others*. Cambridge, England: Polity Press.

Glassner, B. (1999). *The culture of fear: Why Americans are afraid of the wrong things*. New York: Basic Books.

Guerin, D. (1973). *Fascism and big business*. New York: Pathfinder Press.

Harkinson, J. (May+June 2016). Fully loaded: Inside the shadowy world of America's 10 largest gunmakers. *Mother Jones*, 24–31.

Henry, D. (2017). Trump signs bill undoing Obama coal-mining rule. *The Hill online*. http://thehill.com/policy/energy-environment/319938-trump-signs-bill-undoing-obama-coal-mining-rule. Accessed March 27, 2017.

Herbert, B. (1994). The soap-opera machine. *The New York Times online*. http://www.nytimes.com/1994/11/09/opinion/in-america-the-soap-opera-machine.html. Accessed March 27, 2017.

King, M. L. (1986). Letter from Birmingham city jail. In J. M. Washington (Ed.), *A testament of hope: The essential writings and speeches of Martin Luther King, Jr* (pp. 289–302). New York: HarperOne.

Kristof, N. (2017, January 8). As Trump Denies climate change, These Kids Die. *The New York Times, Sunday Review* (pp. 1, 11).

Lipton, E, & Applebaum, B. (2017, March 6). Regulatory leashes coming off Wall St., gun sellers and more. *The New York Times* (pp. A1, A13).

Malmgren, E. (2017). The Cabinet normalized. *The Nation, 304*(5), 10.

Mathews, T. J., Marian, M. F., & Thoma, M. E. (2013). Infant mortality statistics from the 2013 period. *Center for Disease Control, 64*(9). https://www.cdc.gov/nchs/data/nvsr/nvsr64/nvsr64_09.pdf. Accessed March 27, 2017.

Media Education Foundation (Producers). (2010). The mean world syndrome: Media violence & the cultivation of fear. (DVD).
Milgram, S. (1974). *Obedience to authority*. New York: Harper & Row.
Mills, C. W. (1959). *The sociological imagination*. New York: Oxford University Press.
Mills, C. W. (1963). The cultural apparatus. In I. L. Horowitz (Ed.). *Power, politics and people: The collected essays of C. Wright Mills* (pp. 405–422). New York: Ballantine Books.
National Priorities Project. (2016). Retrieved from https://www.nationalpriorities.org/cost-of/war/. Accessed March 27, 2017.
Newman, W., Stewart, N., & Goodman, J. D. (2016, December 9). Sisters' deaths reveal strains in city system. *The New York Times* (pp. A1, A25).
Nicolaus, M. (1968). Fat-cat sociology: Remarks at the American Sociological Association convention. http://www.colorado.edu/Sociology/gimenez/fatcat.html. Accessed March 27, 2017.
Wilkinson, R., & Pickett, K. (2009). *The spirit level: Why greater equality makes societies stronger*. New York: Bloomsbury Press.
Zimbardo, P. (2008). *The Lucifer effect: Understanding how good people turn evil*. New York, NY: Random House.

Part IV
Intersections: Global and Local

Intersectional Marginalities in Rural Teacher Preparation: Teaching Beyond "What I Am Able to See Visibly"

Vanessa Anthony-Stevens

Author's Reflexive Statement and Introduction

In the American imaginary, schools have been seen as democracy's great equalizer. As one of the only institutions in U.S. society where equal access and opportunity is said to be provided to *all* children, public education has been coined as the vehicle through which social mobility becomes possible. Still, gross inequities among the educational experiences of students in poverty and/or of color compared to their White, middle-class counterparts underscores a disconnect between aspirations, actions, and outcomes. In the United States, it is estimated that one in four children live at or below the poverty line (Berliner 2013), and one in two of those children are children of color (Milner and Laughter 2015). The vast majority of poor children do not experience success in schools (Nieto 2013). Statistics indicate that children in poverty have less than 10% chance of obtaining higher education, and minimal chances of making it out of poverty in their lifetime (Berliner 2013). Proportionally, more students of color live in poverty than white students (Milner and Laughter 2015). Race and poverty are salient factors in school achievement across the United States. Research and policy reports indicate that public schools consistently fail to support those living in poverty and/or in a racially minoritized group (Ladson-Billings 2006a, b).

The gulf between what schooling claims to provide, and what it actually provides, is a pressing issue in the preparation of teachers. Preparing teachers for diversity and equity is perhaps the most challenging task facing the field of education (Darling-Hammond 2011; Milner 2010). This urgent need is especially complicated as teacher preparation programs across the nation have become more monolithic, monocultural, monolingual and middle class (Festritzer 2011; Nieto

V. Anthony-Stevens (✉)
University of Idaho, Moscow, ID, USA
e-mail: vstevens@uidaho.edu

K. Haltinner and L. Hormel (eds.), *Teaching Economic Inequality and Capitalism in Contemporary America*, https://doi.org/10.1007/978-3-319-71141-6_17

2000), while, conversely, U.S. schools have become increasingly diverse (Cruz et al. 2014).

In this chapter, I reflect on my own journey preparing pre-service teachers to teach for equity. As faculty at a public university in Idaho, the rural Inland Northwest region of the U.S., the challenges of engaging a mostly white and middle-class student body in the two-fold process of (1) recognizing factors which create educational inequity, and (2) developing pedagogies which offer more equitable learning experiences to underserved children. These are complex tasks. Indeed, the complexity of this work contends with entrenched (and outdated) educational theory, which inundates pre-service teachers with simplistic explanations for student success and failure. Stereotypes which locate school failure as a problem of low self-esteem, a lack of family values, and/or the culture of poverty are common place in teacher preparation (Delpit 2006; Ladson-Billings 2006a, b). My work has grappled with how to push my students and colleagues to engage complexity, and get specific about *what* plagues our schools: racial inequity and economic inequity, and the nexus between the two.

When I arrived at my current institution in 2015, it was made known to me by faculty that our teacher preparation program had a diversity "problem", and it needed "help". Unearthing exactly what kind of diversity "problem" the program felt it had, and gauging the perceived value of preparing teachers to combat inequity generated innumerable conversations with pre-service teachers, practitioners and faculty. In the span of two years, these conversations revealed that diversity was often thought of as "what I am able to visibly see" (e.g. race and ethnicity); however, many believed that our regional schools did not deal with *that* kind of diversity. Instead, socioeconomic difference, particularly rural (White) poverty was highlighted as the significant, and potentially invisible issue of inequity in the region. My teaching and research have led me to examine the disconnect between diversity (e.g. race and ethnicity) and rurality (non-urban settings), and to propose that diversity and rurality are not the binaries our regional discourses predominately portray them to be. A pressing question for me has been, "Can teachers talk about poverty without talking about race?" My response is, "No." That said, the challenge in mapping the apparently invisible lines between intersecting marginalities, such as the links between race-poverty in school failure is significant. This reflective analysis walks through how I have attempted to map these seemingly invisible lines with teachers.

Is This Just an Idaho "Problem"?

To zoom out for a moment, the research on practicing teachers indicates that the diversity "problem" faced by my university is not entirely unique. Teachers across the nation report feeling under-prepared to work with children living in poverty (Milner and Laughter 2015), and experience personal difficulties relating to poor students and their families (Ng and Rury 2006). Teachers feel even more uncomfortable teaching children when they are both living in poverty and also students of color (Milner and Laughter 2015). These realities indicate that race and poverty, and the intersection of the two, are of alarming importance for teachers to understand if they aim to help children thrive in schools. To be fair, we know that societal ills such as poverty and racism are not created or dismantled by teachers alone; however, we also know that teachers do play a significant role in interrupting the damages of racism and poverty in the educational lives of students (Ladson-Billings 2016; Nieto 2013). The robust research on preparing future teachers to equitably serve historically underserved students indicates that pre-service teachers need explicit opportunities to develop knowledge, skills and perspectives which enable them to place equity at the center of public education (Nieto 2000). To do this, teacher preparation needs to change dramatically.

Zooming in on my region, the nation-wide challenges in preparing future teachers to "see" inequity are more acute in rural settings like Idaho. In rural teacher preparation programs there is even less emphasis placed on preparing teachers to understand the complexities of diversity and inequity among their students (Hickey and Lanahan 2012; Storey 2000; Wenger and Dinsmore 2005). Relative geographic isolation, presumptions of cultural homogeneity among university students and faculty (Hickey and Lanahan 2012), and perceptions of rurality as non-diverse (Panelli et al. 2009), contribute to the normative neglect of diversity and equity preparation. Common tropes such as: "rural teachers don't have to deal with *that* kind of diversity" pose considerable obstacles to effectively engaging pre-service teachers in critical examination of how, for example, race matters in the inequities produced (or reproduced) in institutions of schooling.

Teacher preparation programs are not bound to prepare future teachers for service in a single state. But quality teacher preparation draws upon regional issues to provide significant application for the in-depth study of education "on-the-ground" in schools (Darling-Hammond 2016). When looking at the nexus between racial diversity and poverty in Idaho, data from Idaho's Department of Education State Report Card (2017) tells a specific story about the relationship between race-poverty-school achievement. Across the state, school districts with the highest rates of poverty (70% and above) have the highest rates of racial minorities. Within that category, American Indian and Hispanic families experience the state's most statistically significant rates of poverty and school achievement disparities. The districts which serve the state's five Tribal Nations and the agricultural regions which serve high rates of Hispanic children experience both high rates of poverty, and the lowest rates of school achievement on statewide measurements (State Report Card 2017; Dearien 2016a, b). This is not to say that *only* students of color experience poverty and low-rates of school achievement. It does, however, reveal that school failure is more common among students who experience racial minoritization and economic stress, patterns which mirror national trends (Milner and Laughter 2015). This brief glance at the intersections of race-poverty-achievement, makes clear that rural states do deal with complex and overlapping inequities, not just related to race, and not just related to poverty. However, the conversation among educators rarely reflects this reality.

As an entry point to address this complexity, I have begun to conceptualize rurality as diverse, a theoretical framework which allows intersectional marginalities to become visible in our lives and the lives of classrooms. I use the concept of *diverse ruralities* to help teachers explore their beliefs about communities and schooling in rural regions such as the inland Northwest. I use this framework as a foundation to push future teachers to conceptualize their future students, and themselves, beyond normative visions of Whiteness, middle-class neutrality and cultural homogeneity, and toward seeing the intersections. My emergent experiences across two years of teaching a core teacher preparation course titled "Teaching Culturally Diverse Learners," and eighteen months of ethnographic data collection with pre-service teachers, teacher preparation faculty, and regional teacher practitioners inform how I think about diverse rurality. I do this through three interlocking concepts: Rurality, Diversity and Intersectionality. Let me scaffold the explanation of each concept to paint an image of the whole:

Rurality: Rural is often used as "a catchword denoting everything that is not urban or metropolitan," a fixed construct which "overlooks the complexity of rural communities and school districts, as well as the considerable variation within them" (Monk 2007, p. 156). In order to debunk rurality as a fixed construct, the neutrality of the rural as homogeneous needs to be problematized. Dominant histories must be (re)read through lenses which understand power, difference, identity and disadvantage as social constructions in and around the space of schools (Green and Letts 2007). Rural space as White, pastoral and culturally static fails to acknowledge the varied processes of exclusion, racism and abjection at work in homogenizing *whose* experiences are considered legitimate in the social and cultural geography of rural spaces. The dominant narrative of rural space erases narratives of diversity from the discourse of rurality (Panelli et al. 2009, p. 355). For example, the seizure of Indigenous lands, the economic exploitation of poor and non-European labor to build rural infrastructure, the gendered nature of capital ownership, and heteronormative laws are all human experiences in rurality. Yet these histories are all too often glossed in the historic record. Rural spaces are and have always been multicultural spaces (Panelli et al. 2009). Contemporary rurality continues and expands such a trajectory: rurality is dynamic and interconnected to global flows of economic, social and political movements (Appaduri 1996). In the 21st Century, rural schools increasingly serve a broad range of linguistically and culturally diverse students, making their diversities even more present (O'Neal et al. 2008; Wenger et al. 2012).

Diversity: In teacher education, diversity is regularly associated with multiculturalism, e.g. race, ethnicity, and/or culture (Grant and Gibson 2011). I present to students this idea: diversity is not just about race, but race, and the ways that has become associated with culture, is significant. With that, diversity includes multiculturalisms, as well as contemporary visions of diversity which "also encompass age, gender, sexual orientation, (dis)ability, religion, language, and socioeconomic class" (Cruz et al. 2014, p. 13). Diversities make up and influence larger networks of sociocultural and economic movements in society, within which schools form a part. Using the term diversity as a centerpiece of public education requires teachers to conceptualize teaching and learning as building upon the multiplicity and mixture of human experiences across geographies. Acknowledging diversity additionally makes space for understanding that difference, whether race-, gender-, or class-based, have served as a basis for injustice and inequity in U.S. society (Banks 2004). Inequity is not experienced equally in the United States; thus, teacher diversity preparation recognizes that while many diversities make-up the educational spaces, race and culture are important and cross-cutting in the educational opportunities afforded to students. Diversity preparation focuses on content integration, knowledge construction, prejudice reduction, equity pedagogy, and empowering school cultures for historically underserved students (Banks 2004). Colleges of education prepare teachers for state, national and international venues, requiring diversity to be conceptualized through local and global examples.

Intersectionality: Poverty, race, and geographic location are all identity categories on their own. However, when viewed in isolation, they tend to be oversimplified into static categories which overgeneralize students, their families, and ways of learning. Drawing on the work of feminist scholars of color (Crenshaw 1989; Hill Collins 2015), educational scholars advocate for teachers to consider how the intersection of multiple identity categories produce distinct lived experiences with inequity and oppression, both inside and outside of schools (Grant and Sleeter 1986). Intersectionality "holds that the classical models of oppression within society, such as those based on race/ethnicity, gender, religion, nationality, sexual orientation, class, species or disability do not act independently of one another". In schools, the perpetuation of academic failure is better understood if conceptualized through more than just one axis (Grant and Zwier 2011), as stand-alone variables fail to adequately explain educational achievement across groups (Milner 2013). For example, there is evidence that even when we hold a constant for socioeconomic status, Africa-American youth do not achieve at the same rates as their White counterparts (Ladson-Billings and Tate 1995; Owens et al. 2016). Hence, the term intersectionality is used with teachers to underscore how poverty impacts students differently based on its intersections with other factors such as race, gender, language, and geographic location. Teachers must develop and strategically use intersectional knowledge about their students in order to impact positive change with regard to curriculum, instruction, and assessment (Grant and Sleeter 1986). Normative statements about rural culture are more obviously problematized when viewed through the perspective of a middle-class American Indian students, or a female African-American student or a Latina queer student. An intersectional lens to view diverse ruralities brings into relief patterns which disproportionally find students of color living in poverty and at greater risk of academic failure.

The concept of diverse ruralities is complex and its transfer to teacher preparation requires a significant cultural shift. Because of this, I try to bring rurality, diversity and intersectionality into relief through examples from my region. This way pre-service teachers have a greater chance to see themselves, and those around them, through these new lenses. In many cases, my students have attended rural schools prior to university, or participate in field experiences in the region. There are five school districts in the county surrounding the university, a handful of charter schools, and another three to four districts in each of the state counties to the north, south and east. Two of the nearby districts serve sovereign American Indian Nations. The schools in the area surrounding my university can be characterized by the following statements: they are rural; they are impacted by poverty; they are *not* racially and culturally homogeneous.

Mapping Diverse Ruralities—Nexus of Poverty and Race

> …in a society where race matters but people do not want to acknowledge or talk about why and how it matters, many students do not experience poverty at the same rate and they consequently do not experience living in poverty identically (Milner and Laughter 2015, p. 345).

Given the available evidence, education has not made adequate strides to acknowledge that race is a salient factor in poverty. Teacher education's failure to help pre-service teachers map the intersections of diversity and inequity *is* the "problem" to be redressed if teacher preparation programs want to prepare future educators to support all students to find success across diverse classrooms and communities. But this understanding is often isolated from the general discourse on student achievement. Take a common example: a 2013 news headline on Idaho public radio read, "Idaho's Lowest Performing Schools Have Among the Highest Rates of Poverty" (Cotterell 2013). In the printed version of the radio program, an education professor is quoted stating, "We have made some progress as a nation closing racial achievement gaps…but the one that has persisted is the gap between kids who live in poverty and their more affluent peers" (Cotterell 2013). This message is echoed locally. Through my research, I have found that most pre-service teachers in my context conceive of diversity as race: "what am I able to visibly see" but that race was not really what pre-service teachers *see* in our region. A formal interview with a regional practitioner who spent two years as a clinical professor in teacher preparation echoed this sentiment when discussing the perceptions of pre-service teachers and regional educators. Rather, what one *sees* is "the socioeconomic disparity between the haves and the have nots". Addressing issues of poverty and race—e.g., diversity—has historically focused on urban multicultural education (Ball and Tyson 2011), yet clearly rural education is also impacted by racism and inequity. One of the pressing questions posed by my pre-service students who have limited experiences engaging with diversity is, "Why should I care about this?" Reflecting the regional discourse, many pre-service teachers and practitioners alike have little experience considering race and racism in society or education, and/or believe racism is a thing of the past. An anonymous course evaluation from my first year of teaching framed this dilemma well:

Question: Overall, how would you rate the quality of this course?

Student Response: I get that we have to learn how to be multicultural teachers, but a lot of what we discussed felt very one sided. Basically every conversation we had ended up with "white people have more privilege." and this is not true, but I felt I could not state what I was feeling because all things came back around to this idea. I think we did discuss some important issues with racism but I think after the first few weeks it seemed like we were beating a dead horse. Overall I am a little disappointed because as a education course [sic] I feel like we only touched the surface on [sic] how to make lesson plans, curriculum maps, etc.

As an instructor, I was struck by this student's perception that understanding race was not as relevant as technical aspects of teaching such as lesson planning; however, I was even more struck by the strong claim that "basically every conversation we had ended up with 'white people have more privilege' and this is not true." As an education student in a class with predominantly White peers, the clear majority of whom attended rural or suburban schools in Idaho and the Northwest, it is my responsibility to help students like him/her map what he/she was not able to see, and to become self-reflective in the process. I have used these kinds of comments as an opportunity to become more intensional in regards to guiding pre-service teachers through the specifics of the evidence on just how race, poverty, and achievement are central issues all teachers need to understand in order to equitably support *all* students.

Ideas to Engage Intersecting Marginalities

While my experiments with diverse ruralities is emergent, I will offer two brief examples of ways I challenge pre-service teachers to explore the nexus of race-poverty, inside and outside of the classroom.

Use the Numbers

I find it important to show pre-service teachers the information from national and local data banks in order to demonstrate links between poverty and race. Mapping the "unseen" is aided by seeing the numbers. This also helps students consider how trends play-out broadly, as well as locally. National data banks indicate that poverty rates among children in American public schools has been as high as 25% in the past decade; most of these children reside in inner-city neighborhoods and isolated rural regions (Ng and Rury 2006). Rural students make up a quarter of the U.S.

Table 1 Poverty and race in Idaho

Poverty in Idaho	Total population: 1,622,116 Population living in poverty: 245,551 Percentage of people living in poverty 15.1% Percentage of children living in poverty 17.4%				
Idaho by race (census estimates)	2% African American	1.5% Asian American	12% Hispanic	2% Native American	89.1% White
Poverty in Idaho by race and ethnicity	33.4% African American	11.2% Asian American	23.9% Hispanic	26.7% Native American	14.4% White

Statistics from: Center for American Progress (2016), U.S. Census Bureau (2010), Pew Research Center (2014)

primary through secondary (K-12) public school population. Students of color comprise 25% of rural students in the United States color and 41% of rural students are living at or below the poverty line (Strange et al. 2012). In many regions of the inland Northwest, culturally or linguistically minoritized students can comprise the majority of the student body (Wengner and Dinsmore 2005). Table 1 presents basic statistics on poverty in the state of Idaho. Idaho ranks 31st in the Nation on the poverty index, and mirrors national trends which maintain a racialized reflection of poverty. This broad view helps student gain an understanding of intersectionality, and primes them to look more specifically at data from K-12 schools.

Using the numbers, teacher educators can ask pre-service teachers to go deeper by giving them the assignment to create their own data tables of poverty rates, ethnicity categories, and achievement scores comparatively across a region. I have assigned students to work in small groups researching five districts throughout the region (each pre-service teacher group should be assigned different combinations of school districts). Once each group compiles their data table, pre-service teachers can be asked to look for patterns, and tables can be compared with groups who researched districts different from their own. This activity helps students to *see* for themselves how diversity and intersectional inequities at play in schools across geographies.

Provide First Person Experiences

Since beginning to re-shape my course "Teaching Culturally Diverse Learners" I saw a need for pre-service teachers to gain intentional and first-hand experiences with diversity in the region. Over three semesters, I have built in a series of experiences where guest speakers come to my class to speak first-hand about issues of diversity and equity in schools. I use class time to work in a series of guest panels and dialogue sessions where individuals share their experiences with diversity as teachers or students in schools. Invited guests have included, but are not limited to:

guest panel of college students who arrived in the United States as refugees or immigrants during their K-12 years; regional teachers who do innovative work in their approaches to diversity in curriculum and instruction; and family "funds of knowledge" interviews (González et al. 2005) where pre-service students share dialogue with parents from a variety of backgrounds to explore the knowledge of families' everyday practices and connect them to schooling. These experiences have been cited as impactful and eye-opening for my students.

I have also structured a series of "diversity field practicums", where each pre-service teacher is required to attend one diversity field practicum trip outside of class (ranging from 3 to 6 h). Access to neighboring school districts requires instructors to manage transportation logistics and distance connections in rural environments. However, with limited funds and departmental support, I have transported cohorts of students—12 to 15 students, three to four times a semester—to visit select schools/educational centers in the region. These experiences include visiting schools impacted by rural economic depression, schools serving sovereign Tribal Nations, refugee settlement organizations, charter schools addressing diversity through inquiry-based learning, and a selection of professional development activities focusing on cultural and linguistic diversity in teaching. In order to help pre-service teachers process these experiences in terms of diverse ruralities, I have used post-experience assignments such as field notes, compare and contrast diagrams, blog posts, and small group dialogue to push students to analyze how equity and inequity related to diversity in a variety of contexts.

While these are just a few examples of potential activities college instructors can use to help pre-service teachers explore the nexus between race and poverty, each challenges the dominant discourse that rural teachers do not deal with *that* kind of diversity. A broad collection of first-person experiences, whether doing personal research, or interacting with others, have been instrumental for helping my pre-service teachers begin to see the connections been race-poverty-achievement in relief. As teacher educators, we must be willing to recognize that it is hard for pre-service teachers to imagine that which they are unfamiliar. By bringing a variety of voices into pre-service classes, and pushing pre-service teachers to experience the worlds of others, future teachers may begin to see the intersectional nature of inequity in society and schools. Research in diversity preparation in rural settings, although sparse, indicates that rural teachers in my region overwhelmingly feel unprepared to work with culturally and linguistically diverse families (Wenger et al. 2012). When teachers compare the "haves and have nots", they should be able to see not only the impact of poverty on children, but should also understand the factors which create and perpetuate poverty, such as the nexus of race-poverty, and its impacts on school achievement. To isolate race from the conversation of poverty, is misleading for teachers, locally and nationally. Statistics, field experiences and first-person narratives are important to help students conceptualize the diverse ruralities that surround schooling.

(Re)Shaping Knowledge and Opportunity in Teacher Preparation

My journey preparing pre-service teachers to teach for equity can be described as emergent at best. The conceptual framing I have outlined in diverse ruralities is merely a way to open up space for new kinds of dialogues about educational achievement. The work that remains is just as urgent and as complex as the issues stated at the beginning of this chapter. Education needs to work to eradicate poverty for all children, that said, "all teachers can benefit from opportunities to engage race and poverty and the ways in which they overlap and compound" (Milner and Laughter 2015). As I have used the concept of diverse ruralities in an attempt to begin new conversations within my teacher preparation program, challenges to equity work persist on a daily basis. Significantly, acknowledging the nexus between race-poverty-achievement may occur, but subsequent paradoxes have emerged. For example, even when I speak about teaching and learning through a diverse ruralities lens, and those around me conceptually agree, our teacher preparation program practices remain slow to change to reflect an awareness of diverse ruralities. Institutional resources and class time are necessary structural changes which must be prioritized to ensure pre-service teachers gain access first-hand experiences with diversity. Thoughtful faculty and students may agree that teachers must combat one-size-fits-all pedagogies, yet pre-service teacher coursework remains heavily over-simplified and restricted to analyzing learning within the four walls of the classroom. Additionally, practitioners and faculty members may champion that good teaching includes individualized attention, yet individualized attention uncoupled with understanding the larger sociocultural context of learning—structures of inequity within which students and teachers exist—does not produce long-term or systemic change. These challenges are well documented in the literature on equity and social justice in teacher education (Cochran-Smith et al. 2016). They remain, however, little documented in rural setting (Wengner et al. 2012), despite the reality that rural spaces are distinctly characterized by intersectional human identities, and overlapping marginalities.

Clearly, teacher education needs to more systematically prepare future teachers to understand the intersections of diversity and inequity that impact classroom interaction and learning (Nieto 2009; Milner 2010). Students of color and/or living in poverty are grossly underserved by U.S. schools, both urban and rural. Interrupting this phenomenon necessitates new conversations in teacher preparation. Commonly, such conversations are maintained as "urban issues" or addressed in add-on isolation, negating the intersection of poverty and race in the lives of school children. My work tries to advocate for a conceptual shift which preemptively challenges static notions of place and identity, in order to invite future teachers into nuanced study of the salient ways poverty-race-achievement characterize local and global school realities. In rural landscapes dominated by overwhelming Whiteness, getting serious about preparing teachers to effectively educate *all* students requires future teachers understand local complexity, and analyze the multiple acts of inequity which marginalize diverse narratives from rural landscapes. To do so in contexts of rural teacher preparation, I use diverse ruralities as a conduit to prepare future teachers to serve *all* students.

References

Appaduri, A. (1996). Sovereignty without territoriality: Notes for a postnational geography. In P. Yaeger (Ed.), *The geography of identity* (pp. 40–58). Ann Arbor, MI: University of Michigan Press.

Ball, A. F., & Tyson, C. A. (Eds.). (2011). *Studying diversity in teacher education*. Lanham, MD: Rowman & Littlefield Publishers Inc.

Banks, J. A. (2001). Multicultural education: Goals, possibilities, and challenges. In C. F. Diaz (Ed.), *Multicultural education in the 21st century* (pp. 11–22). New York: Addison-Wesley.

Banks, J. A., & McGee Banks, C. A. (Eds.). (2004). *Handbook of research on multicultural education* (2nd ed.). San Francisco, CA: Jossey-Bass: A Wiley Imprint.

Bates, V. (2011). Preparing rural music teachers: Reflecting on "shared visions. *Journal of Music Teacher Education, 20*(2), 89–98.

Berliner, D. (2013). Effects of inequality and poverty vs. teachers and schooling on America's youth. *Teachers College Record, 115*(12), 1–26.

Center for American Progress. (2016). *Talk poverty: Idaho report*. Retrieved from https://talkpoverty.org/state-year-report/idaho-2016-report/.

Cochran-Smith, M., Ell, F., Grudnoff, L., Haigh, M., Hill, M., & Ludlow, L. (2016). Initial teacher education: What does it take to put equity at the center? *Teaching and Teacher Education, 57*, 67–78.

Cotterell, A. (2013, August 5). Idaho's lowest performing schools have among the highest rates of poverty. *Boise State Public Radio*. Retrieved from http://boisestatepublicradio.org/post/idahos-lowest-performing-schools-have-among-highest-rates-poverty#stream/0.

Crenshaw, K. (1989). Demarginalizing the intersection of race and sex: A black feminist critique of antidiscrimination doctrine, feminist theory and antiracist politics. *University of Chicago Legal Forum*, 139.

Cruz, B. C., Ellerbrock, C. R., Vásquez, A., & Howes, E. V. (Eds.). (2014). *Talking diversity with teachers and teacher educators: Exercises and critical conversations across the curriculum*. New York: Teachers College Press.

Darling-Hammond, L. (2011). Forward. In A. F. Ball & C. A. Tyson (Eds.), *Studying diversity in teacher education (ix-x)*. Lanham, MD: Rowman & Littlefield Publishers Inc.

Darling-Hammond, L. (2016). Research on teaching and teacher education and its influence on policy and practice. *Educational Researcher, 45*(2), 83–91.

Dearien, C. (2016a). *Idaho at a Glance: American Indian education, 7*(5). McClure Center for Public Policy Research, University of Idaho.

Dearien, C. (2016b). *Idaho at a Glance: Hispanics: Education, 7*(4). McClure Center for Public Policy Research, University of Idaho.

Delpit, L. (2006). *Other people's children: Cultural conflict in the classroom*. New York, NY: The New Press.

Ellis, C., & Bochner, A. B. (2000). Autoethnography, personal narrative, reflexivity: Researcher as subject. In N. K. Denzin & Y. S. Lincoln (Eds.), *Handbook of qualitative research* (2nd ed., pp. 733–768). Thousand Oaks, CA: Sage.

Festritzer, C. E. (2011). *Profile of teachers in the United States 2011*. Washington, DC: National Center for Education Information. http://www.edweek.org/media/port2011final-blog.pdf.

Gay, G. (2010). *Culturally responsive teaching: Theory, research, and practice*. New York, NY: Teachers College Press.

Gay, G., & Howard, T. C. (2000). Multicultural teacher education for the 21st century. *The Teacher Educator, 36*(1), 1–16.

Gollnick, D. M., & Chinn, P. C. (2013). *Multicultural education in a pluralistic society*. Pearson Higher Ed.

González, N., Moll, L. C., & Amanti, C. (2005). *Funds of knowledge: Theorizing practices in households, communities, and classrooms*. London, UK: Routledge.

Grant, C., & Gibson, M. (2011). Diversity and teacher education. In A. F. Ball & C. A. Tyson (Eds.), *Studying diversity in teacher education* (pp. 19–62). Lanham, MD: Rowman & Littlefield Publishers Inc.

Grant, C. A., & Sleeter, C. E. (1986). Race, class, and gender in education research: An argument for integrative analysis. *Review of Educational Research, 56*(2), 195–211.

Grant, C. A., & Zwier, E. (2011). Intersectionality and student outcomes: Sharpening the struggle against racism, sexism, classism, ableism, heterosexism, nationalism, and linguistic, religious, and geographical discrimination in teaching and learning. *Multicultural perspectives, 13*(4), 181–188.

Green, B., & Letts, W. (2007). Space, equity, and rural education. In K. N. Gulson & C. Symes (Eds.), *Spatial theories of education: Policy and geography matters* (pp. 57–76). London, UK: Routledge.

Hickey, M. G., & Lanahan, B. K. (Ed.) (2012). *Even the janitor is white: Educating for cultural diversity in small colleges and universities. Critical Education and Ethics* (Vol. 4). Peter Lang: New York, NY.

Hill Collins, P. (2015). Intersectionality's definitional dilemmas. *Annual Review of Sociology, 41* (1), 1–20.

Idaho State Department of Education. (2017, March 25). *School report card*. Retrieved from http://apps.sde.idaho.gov/ReportCard.

Ladson-Billings, G. (2006a). From the achievement gap to the education debt: Understanding achievement in US schools. *Educational Researcher, 35*(7), 3–12.

Ladson-Billings, G. (2006b). It's not the culture of poverty, it's the poverty of culture: The problem with teacher education. *Anthropology & Education Quarterly, 37*(2), 104–109.

Ladson-Billings, G. (2016) Toward a theory of culturally relevant pedagogy. *American Educational Research Journal, 32*(3), 465–491.

Ladson-Billings, G., & Tate, W. F. (1995). Toward a critical race theory of education. *Teachers college record, 97*(1), 47.

Locke, S. (2005). Institutional social and cultural influences on the multicultural perspectives of preservice teachers. *Multicultural Perspectives, 7*(2), 20–28.

Mills, C. (2008). Making a difference: Moving beyond the superficial treatment of diversity. *Asia-Pacific Journal of Teacher Education, 36*(4), 261–275.

Milner, H. R. (2010). What does teacher education have to do with teaching? Implications for diversity studies. *Journal of Teacher Education, 61*(1–2), 118–131.

Milner, H. R., IV. (2013). Analyzing poverty, learning, and teaching through a critical race theory lens. *Review of Research in Education, 37*(1), 1–53.

Milner, H. R., & Laughter, J. C. (2015). But good intentions are not enough: Preparing teachers to center race and poverty. *The Urban Review, 47*(2), 341–363.

Monk, D. H. (2007). Recruiting and retaining high-quality teachers in rural areas. *The Future of Children, 17*(1), 155–174.

Ng, J. C., & Rury, J. L. (2006). Poverty and education: A critical analysis of the Ruby Payne phenomenon. *Teachers College Record, 18*.

Nieto, S. (2000). Placing equity front and center some thoughts on transforming teacher education for a new century. *Journal of Teacher Education, 51*(3), 180–187.

Nieto, S. (2009). *Language, culture, and teaching: Critical perspectives*. London, UK: Routledge.

Nieto, S. (2013). *Finding joy in teaching students of diverse backgrounds: Culturally responsive and socially just practices in US classrooms*. Portsmouth: Heineiman.

Nieto, S., & McDonough, K. (2011). "Placing equity front and center" revisited. In A. F. Ball & C. A. Tyson (Eds.), *Studying diversity in teacher education* (pp. 363–384). Lenham, MD: Rowman & Littlefield Publishers Inc.

O'Neal, D. D., Ringler, M., & Rodriguez, D. (2008). Teachers' perceptions of their preparation for teaching linguistically and culturally diverse learners in rural eastern North Carolina. *The Rural Educator, 30*(1).

Owens, A., Reardon, S. F., & Jencks, C. (2016). Income segregation between schools and school districts. *American Educational Research Journal, 53*(4), 1159–1197.

Panelli, R., Hubbard, P., Coombes, B., & Suchet-Pearson, S. (2009). De-centring White ruralities: Ethnic diversity, racialisation and Indigenous countrysides. *Journal of Rural Studies, 25*(4), 355–364.

Pew Research Center. (2014). *Demographic profile of Hispanics in Idaho, 2014*. Retrieved from http://www.pewhispanic.org/states/state/id/.

Sleeter, C. E. (2001). Preparing teachers for culturally diverse schools research and the overwhelming presence of whiteness. *Journal of Teacher Education, 52*(2), 94–106.

Sleeter, C. (2011). An agenda to strengthen culturally responsive pedagogy. *English Teaching, 10* (2), 7.

Sleeter, C. E., & Owuor, J. (2011). Research on the impact of teacher preparation to teach diverse students: The research we have and the research we need. *Action in Teacher Education, 33* (5–6), 524–536.

Strange, M., Johnson, J., Showalter, D., & Klein, R. (2012). Why Rural Matters 2011-12: The Condition of Rural Education in the 50 States. A Report of the Rural School and Community Trust Policy Program. *Rural School and Community Trust*.

Storey, V. J. (2000). The first five years: A follow-up study of a rural teacher cohort. *Journal of Research in Rural Education, 16,* 40–50.

U.S. Census Bureau. (2010). *QuickFacts: Idaho*. Retrieved from https://www.census.gov/quickfacts/table/BZA010214/16.

Villegas, A. M. (2007). Dispositions in teacher education a look at social justice. *Journal of Teacher Education, 58*(5), 370–380.

Wenger, K. J., & Dinsmore, J. (2005). Preparing rural preservice teachers for diversity. *Journal of Research in Rural Education, 20*(10), 1–15.

Wenger, K. J., Dinsmore, J., & Villagómez, A. (2012). Teacher identity in a multicultural rural school: Lessons learned at Vista Charter. *Journal of Research in Rural Education, 27*(5), 1–17.

Zeichner, K. (2011). Embracing complexity and community in research on multicultural teacher education. In A. F. Ball & C. A. Tyson (Eds.), *Studying diversity in teacher education* (pp. 329–337). Lenham, MD: Rowman & Littlefield Publishers Inc.

Economic Inequality and Race: No, It Can't Be that Bad…

Paul R. Croll

Author's Reflexive Statement

"The wealth of white households was 13 times the median wealth of black households in 2013, compared with eight times the wealth in 2010… Likewise, the wealth of white households is now more than 10 times the wealth of Hispanic households, compared with nine times the wealth in 2010." (Kochhar 2014). There is a large racial wealth gap in the United States and it has gotten worse since the Great Recession of 2008.

"No, it can't be that bad…"

This is an actual response I have heard from students when presenting these statistics on racial inequality in the United States today. Presenting this information to our students often challenges their notions and understanding about our society. If one believes we have already reached a level playing field and there is already equal opportunity for all, then the difference in wealth of this magnitude between whites, African Americans, and Latino/as raises some serious questions.

And, it gets worse.

Studies show that African American job applicants are far less likely to receive a callback for a job than their white counterparts (Pager 2003) and resumes with "African American-sounding" names are less likely to get called for an interview (Bertrand and Mullainathan 2004). White Americans not only have more wealth, on average, than people of color, but they also face less discrimination in employment. Resources and opportunities are greatly affected by race in the United States.

In this chapter I present a number of strategies I use in the classroom to empower students to understand how economic inequality is deeply connected to race in the United States and how historical legacies in our country, that seem dusty and distant

---

P. R. Croll (✉)
Augustana College, Rock Island, IL, USA
e-mail: paulcroll@augustana.edu

K. Haltinner and L. Hormel (eds.), *Teaching Economic Inequality and Capitalism in Contemporary America*, https://doi.org/10.1007/978-3-319-71141-6_18

to students, have direct consequences on their lives and their generation in ways they often cannot even imagine. I have two goals when teaching this material to my students. My first goal is to provide my students with the facts and statistics about racial economic inequality in the United States. Whether students know, like, disagree, or even hate it, they need to know the facts. These vast economic inequalities exist and it is our job to educate our students on this topic. My second goal is harder, but even more important. As best I can, I try to help my students to see that these inequalities are not simply the result of individuals' lack of effort, but that structural forces and institutions—both historically and today—have produced and reproduced these racial differences.

It is also important to consider our own personal background and the demographics of our students when teaching about inequality. Social location matters. I am a white male who grew up in the suburbs outside of Detroit. I attended a well-funded, suburban, mostly white high school and was firmly part of the white, suburban middle class. My life experiences impact how I understand racial and economic inequality. Thinking about my students, their life experiences matter as well. Augustana is a private, small liberal arts college in the Midwest. As a result, many Augustana students come from similar backgrounds as my own. However, we are seeing steady increases in the diversity of our student body, both racial and socioeconomic status. Our incoming first year cohorts are now typically about 20–25% non-white and we are seeing more diversity in socioeconomic status within our student body including a greater number of first generation college students. We have a sizable number of white, middle to upper class students, but our demographics are changing. I need to keep all of this in mind when I walk into the classroom.

Teaching students about any form of economic inequality can be challenging. Incorporating racial differences makes this even harder. Discussing the intersection of economic inequality and race in the classroom can be a significant challenge for educators. Our students have grown up in a society that cherishes core American values such as individualism, hard work, and effort. These values are so deeply ingrained in the fabric of our society that it is difficult to get students to see the vast differences that exist today in terms of wealth, education, and opportunity between racial groups in the United States. The stark racial inequalities we present to our students challenge the very notion of our individualistic society—a society that many of our students desperately want to believe allows anyone to make it if they just work hard enough.

We could simply present students with facts regarding racial inequality. However, we then face the challenge of helping students understand this is not simply our opinion or political agenda. Thus, it is important to help our students understand that facts are real and facts do matter: that there are real, stark economic differences by race in the United States that have been created and maintained by racial policies in the United States, both intentional and unintentional. My goal is try to get students to see how the legacy of historical policies and actions in the United States continue to produce and reproduce racial inequalities today.

Introducing Racial and Economic Inequalities in the Classroom

When I teach about economic inequality and race (and other sensitive topics), I often start with a video clip or a documentary. I have found that doing this can diffuse the tension in the room and shift the focus away from a "me against them" dynamic. By bringing other voices into the room, we can discuss and analyze what the scholars and experts in the video argue, rather than creating a situation where a student has to directly argue against the professor, which can set-up an adversarial relationship in the classroom. It is often the case that I agree with the arguments presented in the videos, but it becomes less personal for the students and the teacher when the focus is on the evidence and arguments we watch together. I can argue in favor of the points raised in the video, but when students disagree, they are disagreeing with the video and not directly with me.

Showing a video also provides another important advantage. Students can't easily disrupt the video and the dissemination of the information and ideas we have chosen to show. If this same information was presented in lecture format by a professor, an angry or disruptive student could interrupt, argue, protest, or even challenge the authority of the professor on the topic. It is possible on a topic such as economic inequality and race that student questions and pushback could disrupt the lecture to a point where the main information is not even fully presented within the class period. Showing a documentary or video avoids this potential problem. Like it or not, students in most cases will sit and listen to a video without interruption.

My strategy for teaching about economic inequality and race is to use two class periods to cover this material. On day one, I show a full hour-long documentary in class. For this specific topic I usually start with the documentary *Race: Power of an Illusion*, Episode Three: The House We Live In (2003). This PBS documentary walks students through the construction and reproduction of race, wealth, and economic inequality through the 20th century in the United States. This documentary presents history and racial policies in the United States that are challenging and uncomfortable for many of our students. It explains the creation of the Federal Housing Administration, the use of redlining, the creation of the suburbs (an almost exclusively white racial project in the mid-20th century), and how racial differences in home ownership have led to significant differences in wealth, passed on through inheritances and the intergenerational transfer of wealth over several generations.

This documentary interviews elderly white couples today who in the 1940s were able to purchase homes in Levittown that began a trajectory of wealth accumulation for their families. We also powerfully watch an interview with an African American couple denied this same opportunity after the husband returned from fighting in World War II. This difference between the experiences of white families and black families at the same time in the same place in the United States in the 1940s is powerful and sticks with my students. We also hear from multiple scholars reinforcing these same ideas, explaining that the federal government used explicit policies and unwritten practices to aid white families in the purchase of homes and prevented African American families from the same opportunity. The scholars interviewed in the documentary then explain how home ownership has directly resulted in the accumulation of wealth for white families in the United States. Real examples are provided regarding the differences in the home values between white families and African American families. One African American scholar explains that his father's house in Detroit is probably worth about $20,000 but that the same house in the largely white suburbs outside of Detroit would probably be worth about $320,000. This idea is reinforced by an elderly white man who chose to stay in a racially-integrated neighborhood throughout his life. He explains that his house would probably be worth about $80,000 more if it was located a few towns away from where he lives. These racialized policies and practices have real financial consequences.

Once we have watched the documentary, students need time to let all the information soak in and percolate in their heads. For this reason, I try to show the documentary on day one and continue the topic on day two. During day two, we get into it. We roll up our sleeves and work together to make sense of the topic and the significance of racialized institutions and policies on racial inequality today. I always start this day asking students to share their thoughts, reactions, and feelings about the video we watched in the previous class period. I think this is important for a few reasons. First, the video often generates strong emotions and feelings and I want to make it clear that these are valid and should be shared. Second, if a student has something on their chest and needs to get it off, we get it done at the start of class. Third, if there are students resistant to the ideas presented in the video, I want to know at the start of our discussion. Comments in the first two categories (strong emotions and the need to say something) are often along the lines of shock and surprise that things were as bad as they were. Students tell me they knew there were problems, but they didn't realize the extent, depth, and institutional aspects of racial discrimination and inequality. Comments in the third category (resistance) often take the form of trying to minimize the problem. Students who are resistant to the ideas from the video will often say, "Well, maybe it was bad for the people in the video, but it probably wasn't that bad for everyone," or something along those lines. I encourage all these comments, both positive and negative, but try my best not to weigh in or judge the comments that students make at this point in the process. I am just asking for student reactions to help me get a read on the class, where they are at, and how they feel about the ideas we are about to explore. I find this extremely helpful to know as we proceed with the material.

In terms of readings for the day, I often assign a reading by Melvin Oliver and Thomas Shapiro. Oliver and Shapiro's book *Black Wealth/White Wealth* (Oliver and Shapiro 1995) was one of the first works to critically examine the racial wealth gap, moving beyond income as the main measure of economic standing. As they argue, wealth is a very important factor in socioeconomic standing and upward mobility in the United States. Simply looking at income misses much of the story. I typically assign a short reading from an edited volume based on their work (e.g., Shapiro 2012). Also, Melvin Oliver is one of the scholars featured in the video

Race: The Power of an Illusion, so it pairs nicely to read some of his work to prepare for the following day after watching the documentary.

In class, we talk about how the racial wealth gap got so large and how historical and structural forces are the primary cause. I use Oliver and Shapiro's argument to do this work and walk my students through their main argument, including their very specific, controversial phrase "unearned inherited wealth" (1995). I ask my students what they think of Oliver and Shapiro's work, specifically their choice of the term "unearned" with regard to inheritance and the intergenerational transfer of wealth. Many students push back on this and do not like the idea. I often have students (typically white, but not always) who tell personal stories at this point about how their parents or grandparents started with nothing, worked hard, built careers and businesses, bought houses, and earned their successes. In this personal context, students grapple with the idea that the inheritance their parents or they themselves received is "unearned." I let this conversation occur and acknowledge these stories and personal experiences. I do not argue or push back as students share these stories. This is the process students need to go through to understand what we are trying to teach. We need these examples in the room to work through where we need to go.

Once students share these personal stories, we turn back to the video and the readings. My transition back to the course material is usually something like "Ok, we now have several examples of earlier generations who struggled and succeeded. Why does this matter? Is this something every American in the 1940s or 1950s could do? What did we learn from the video? Are there any groups who could not take advantage of this?" The answer is usually clear and obvious, but I make someone say it. The success stories in the video and in the room are almost exclusively the stories of white, European Americans who were allowed to take advantage of all the benefits given to them at the time. African Americans and other people of color were excluded from this path to success and prosperity. This is what matters. This is the point that hits home. This is a moment that needs to be allowed to linger in the room. If you reach this point, let it sink in. Previous generations of people of color in the United States were systematically denied the same opportunities and level of success as their white counterparts.

The pushback from students about historical economic inequality is often "but my family didn't own slaves." But in the context of the documentary we just watched in this class and the discussion of racialized housing policies in the 20th century, a better question is who could own their houses and who had to rent? Who was allowed to take advantage of systems of wealth generation and who was not? At this point in the class, we have established the financial advantages of home ownership. I then ask "what can you do with head start assets?" Students can then work through this in our class discussion. With wealth and head start assets, you can buy a better home in a better neighborhood. What does that get you? A safer neighborhood, more community resources, and better schools. What do better schools provide for you and your kids? A better education, more opportunities. What can the next generation then do with a better education? Go to a better college. What can they do with a better college education? Get a better job. What happens when you have a better job? You make more money? What can you do with more money? Buy a nicer house, in a nicer neighborhood, with nicer schools, and it goes on and on and on. You are spiraling upward, or not. Is this fair? Is this right? What do you think? This is when I start to see light bulbs going off in the classroom. This path to economic success is clear—but only some were given the chance to get on this path toward wealth and prosperity. This discussion helps students begin to see the structural and institutional causes of persistent inequality in the United States.

I also always make this personal, for both the students and for me. To foster deep learning, it has to be personal and relevant. Again, turning back to Oliver and Shapiro, "Homeownership is by far the single most important way families accumulate wealth." (Shapiro 2012). Why does this matter? What happens if going back several generations some families could own homes and accumulate wealth and others could not? I work hard to make this real for my students. I ask them to talk about their own experiences. Do their parents own their own homes? Did their grandparents own their own homes? Why might this matter? I also share my own story. My own history consists of several generations of white homeowners in largely white suburbs. I explain how I have benefited from this very system we are studying. I had help from relatives for the down payment on my first house and I was able to then buy a car years later by taking out a home equity loan on the house I was able to buy with help from previous generations of wealth accumulation. I also walk my students through a hypothetical example where two people work side by side in an office, same job, same pay, but one person has parents who have benefited from generations of wealth accumulation and homeownership and the other person comes from several generations of renters, excluded from wealth accumulation and home ownership. Let's imagine the person who comes from generations of homeowners receives assistance to buy a house and the other person has to rent. What happens after twenty years of home ownership versus renting? First, there are tax-breaks for the homeowner. Second, homes typically appreciate in value allowing homeowners to tap into their home equity to pay for things they want or need. And, third, home appreciation often leads to significant profits upon the sale of a house. The homeowner could walk away with tens of thousands of dollars in profit when they sell. The person renting gets none of these financial advantages.

These systems of advantage and disadvantage are not the result of individual effort and hard work. Rather, they are the result of generations of racial practices and policies that excluded many people of color but provided relative advantage to many whites in the United States. The cumulative advantage grew and grew for generations, resulting in the racial disparities we see today. The goal is to get students to see this at a societal level. If instructors do this right—if we get to the point where students accept that this is the reality—that the gaps are really this huge and are far beyond individual action and control—we then reach a difficult question, "What do we do about it?" This is a tough question. My goal, though, is try to finish with answers to this question when teaching on the topic of economic inequality and race. If students are asking this question, or, at least, are open to me asking them this question, then we have accomplished something. A discussion of how to solve a problem requires, first, acknowledging the problem exists. This is when I feel we have accomplished something. If we reach this point in the conversation, I believe most students have accepted the facts and statistics presented about racial inequality and accept that the cause of the problem is not simply at the individual level. This final discussion about solutions is not as much about finding the actual solution, but rather it helps solidify the idea that the problems are well beyond the scope of the individual.

When we discuss solutions, I always ask my students to brainstorm and tell me what they think, rather than give my ideas. I think this is important. Even when they ask what I think or what I would do, I usually refuse. It's their class, not mine, and I want to know what they think. As students start to provide possible solutions, I think it is important not to judge. Some ideas are better than others, but that is not the point. The discussion itself is the goal, not the outcomes. Inevitably, the discussion comes around to redistribution of wealth in some form. Students realize they are seriously talking about redistribution policies and there are people they know who would likely have a negative knee-jerk reaction about, if mentioned in another context. Given the historical and structural factors that concentrated wealth to some groups, however, a policy or law to spread this wealth around to those who have not benefitted seems a little less radical. We often talk in practical terms about how redistribution might occur. The state could raise taxes to redistribute wealth or could flat-out take wealth from those who have it. The first option usually sounds better to most of my students. We now are talking about the real possibility of increasing taxes on those who have benefited from systems of advantage to help those who have been excluded from these systems. To be clear, my goal is not to convert students to any particular way of thinking. But, if we can help students see from a sociological perspective that we do not have a level playing field—that the current system is inherently unfair—then it opens the possibility in our students' minds for a wider range of possible policies and solutions.

It is our job to teach students about inequality and help them understand how systems of inequality have evolved over time. We need to help students understand that individualism, hard work and effort alone cannot explain the disparities between groups we see in our society today. The discussion of possible corrective policies and solutions at a broad level is important, but students also ask what they can do personally about this. What can they do at an individual level about these problems? Here is where I end. While we may not easily solve these problems at a societal level, they can choose to act differently in their own lives. If they are interviewing job candidates in the future, they can ask, "Are all candidates being treated fairly?" If a co-worker or friend assumes someone who is poor deserves to be where they are, will you say something? If one hears racist comments will he/she speak out? Students have the power to speak out at an individual level, especially those in positions of relative power and advantage. It is meaningful when someone in a position of privilege speaks out against prejudice or discrimination. This will not solve all the problems we discuss, but individual action, one person at a time, does make a difference. Our job is to provide students with the knowledge and information they need to understand our world. What they do with that knowledge is ultimately up to them.

References

Bertrand, M., & Mullainathan, S. (2004). Are Emily and Greg more employable than Lakisha and Jamal? A field experiment on labor market discrimination. *The American Economic Review, 94* (4), 991–1013.

Kochhar, R. (2014). Wealth inequality has widened along racial, ethnic lines since end of Great Recession. http://www.pewresearch.org/facttank/2014/12/12/racialwealthgapsgreatrecession/. Retrieved January 26, 2017.

Oliver, M. L., & Shapiro, T. (1995). *Black wealth/white wealth: A new perspective on racial inequality*. New York: Routledge.

Pager, D. (2003). The mark of a criminal record. *American Journal of Sociology, 108*(5), 937–975.

Shapiro, T. M. (2012). Transformative assets, the racial wealth gap and the American Dream. In C. A. Gallagher (Ed.), *Rethinking the color line* (pp. 49–52). New York: McGraw Hill.

The House We Live In [DVD]. (2003). *Race—The power of an illusion, episode 3*. San Francisco: California Newsreel.

Irreversible Punishment: Teaching About Inequalities in Capital Punishment

Kristine Levan

Author's Reflective Statement

I spent the majority of my life in Texas, a state known for its relatively conservative identity. One of the features of the state's conservative culture is its greater reliance on capital punishment in comparison with other states. Despite this reliance, many Texas residents (and residents of other states) are not well informed on the laws and parameters surrounding capital punishment eligibility or the disproportionate use of it against those who are economically disadvantaged. I hold a deep interest in understanding the systems in place that divvy out the most extreme punishments, as well as the formal systems and individuals that both support and oppose this form of punishment. Moreover, from a pedagogical standpoint, I am interested in conveying the inherent flaws in the existing system to students while allowing them to reach their own conclusions on the applicability and utility of capital punishment in comparison with other forms of punishment.

Introduction

Teaching about capital punishment can be a challenging endeavor. The climate for capital punishment is dynamic and dependent on multiple factors. High profile cases, either on the state or federal level, can have a substantial impact on support or opposition to capital punishment. Issues related to potential innocence and executions, particularly egregious crimes, and stories of botched executions continue to keep a public focus on this ultimate punishment. Furthermore, the persistent and

---

K. Levan (✉)
University of Idaho, Moscow, ID, USA
e-mail: klevan@uidaho.edu

K. Haltinner and L. Hormel (eds.), *Teaching Economic Inequality and Capitalism in Contemporary America*, https://doi.org/10.1007/978-3-319-71141-6_19

egregious inequality inherent in the decision-making process has a profound effect on public opinion.

Capital punishment is a subject about which most individuals have preconceived notions—and college students are no exception. Teaching various courses (including introductory level criminology and criminal justice, introduction to corrections, criminology, senior capstone, and inequalities in criminal justice) in degree programs at different universities across four regions (the South, Midwest, New England, and Pacific Northwest), allows me to have a broad perspective for pedagogical techniques on this topic, which I present in this chapter.

This chapter offers a series of methods and activities to engage students in discussions related to the unequal distribution of the death penalty. Depending on the course topics, these may be used as isolated activities, or as a progressive series of activities to allow a greater understanding of the disparities inherent with the death penalty. The first activity, "the reflection exercise" should always be used as an initial activity; I often consider this an icebreaker to the material. The second, "worst of the worst" exercise, is a likely extension as it allows students to compare the real-world application of capital punishment cases with personal beliefs of who is the most deserving of the punishment. The natural progression of a course will often lead to discussions for which the "geographical differences" and "O. J. Simpson" activities will easily be adapted. Finally, I present possibilities for guest speakers to consider in a course discussion capital punishment. Case studies and guest speakers, such as the ones presented here, should be included as pedagogical tools when discussing capital punishment to illustrate necessary points and provide meaningful examples.

Reflection Exercise

Controversial topics—including the issue of capital punishment—tend to elicit strong opinions, even if an individual is generally uninformed on the topic. As I prepare my students to engage in dialog on capital punishment, I ask them to take out a sheet paper. Not identifying themselves on this paper, I ask them to answer the following: "Do you, in general, favor or oppose capital punishment? Tell me why you feel this way." I reiterate to students there is no correct or incorrect answer. After several minutes have passed, I ask for those who are comfortable to share as much as they are comfortable sharing in an open forum. I draw columns on the board to allow students to view both the positives and negatives of capital punishment, and engage students in discussion on these various viewpoints.

Although this is an opinion-based reflection exercise, I generally find students are more open to conversations with one another and with me once they understand how others are framing their discussion. This exercise can be completed in a range of classes, and I have used this to frame conversations in topics courses focusing on capital punishment, as well as more survey oriented courses on corrections. The key point with this exercise is to engage students in this discussion prior to beginning readings or discussions on capital punishment. I also, then, follow this up at the end of the semester (or individual module on capital punishment) asking how discussions, readings, and activities informed students' viewpoints on capital punishment.

"The Worst of the Worst" Exercise

After students begin thinking about their opinions on capital punishment and a dialogue is started, I begin to deepen student analysis. One way of doing this is through, what I call, "The Worst of the Worst Exercise". This activity helps students examine how the death penalty is applied in practice.

To begin, I ask students to describe who they believe is the most "deserving" of capital punishment. I use "deserving" here to relate to (a) Williams' (2012) discussion throughout his text on Supreme Court decisions, and (b) the idea behind "just deserts" as it relates to how, as a justice system, we determine and mete out appropriate punishments based on concepts related to intent, malice and premeditation.

Inevitably, the list students develop includes offenders such as serial killers or mass murderers, and those who kidnap and murder young children. As a class, we deem this our "worst of the worst" list. Students will generally share a consensus that, regardless of beliefs on capital punishment, these are the most egregious of all murders and of all crimes, and should be eligible to receive the harshest punishment available.

The second part of this exercise can (and should, if possible) be done in smaller groups. Students are asked to find online examples of recent executions, and record information on the specific type of offense (such as felony murder, multiple murder, or murder of a law enforcement officer), as well as individual characteristics of the offender (e.g., sex, race, ethnicity, or age). If available, I also have them collect information on the victim(s). The class reconvenes and we collectively begin to illustrate the current state of capital punishment and those who have been executed in comparison with our "worst of the worst" list. Often, the lists have discrepancies and illustrate the point that what we expect is not always what is put into practice as policy. For example, while students expect to find the bulk of executions connected to infamous serial murderers, such as Henry Lee Lucas or Ted Bundy, instead they find cases that range in circumstances. While there are certainly some infamous and egregious cases on the list, there are also others who were not the ones convicted of murder. For instance, take the case of Robert Thompson. Executed in 2009, Thompson shot a convenience store clerk, who ultimately survived. Another clerk fired shots at Thompson and co-defendant Sammy Butler. Butler, who killed the second clerk, was sentenced to life in prison, though Thompson received capital punishment (Death Penalty Information Center).

Another point of illustration is on the glaring differences between how poor, minority individuals are treated as victims versus how the system treats them as offenders (Barak et al. 2015). Though an African American male is more likely to be executed, the criminal justice system is less likely to send the murderer of an African American male to the execution chamber. In 2013, 42% of those sentenced to death were African American (Snell 2014), a percentage that is grossly disproportionate to the number of African American individuals in the United States.

Instructors should then present information on Supreme Court rulings related to inequalities in the dissemination of capital punishment. I talk to my students about Furman v. Georgia and Gregg v. Georgia in this context. The landmark Furman v. Georgia (1972) decision pointed to heavy racial disparities in how capital punishment was practiced. Revisions were mandated to state systems to correct these disparities over the next few years, and the Supreme Court determined they were rectified as indicated in the Gregg decision (1976). Gregg v. Georgia (1976) is considered the turning point after Furman v. Georgia (1972). While the Furman case placed a nationwide moratorium on executions, the Gregg case specified the safeguards for which states needed to implement for capital punishment to be constitutionally sound. For example, states needed to ensure bifurcated trials, mandatory review of all capital cases, and specific mitigating and aggravating factors. However, since 1976, almost 80% of executions have occurred against those convicted of murdering a white victim (Bohm 2013). The continued disparity along racial and economic status lines illustrates that the safeguards are not entirely effective in preventing systemic discrimination.

As students collect information on individual cases throughout this class exercise, discrepancies often become readily apparent. The individuals receiving capital punishment are often not the most egregious. Despite the changes made in the system since the Furman and Gregg decisions, racial, ethnic, and economic bias continues to plague the capital punishment decision-making process.

Geographical Discrepancies

This activity seeks to help students understand geographical variance in the application and equity of capital punishment employment. In my experience, it usually fits best midway through a course on capital crimes and helps students see both the inconsistency with which capital punishment is enacted and the reasons for which this discrepancy exists.

Among the most important determinants of whether an individual is both eligible for and will receive capital punishment is the state and the jurisdiction in which they commit the offense. Displaying data on executions is helpful here. Due to the major overhaul from the Gregg decision, numbers are included post-1976. As indicated, Texas has executed the greatest number of people. We then begin class discussion speculating about why some states use capital punishment with more frequency. Particularly noteworthy are the parameters in which someone is qualified for capital punishment. By way of example, in Texas, there are nine parameters; historically, other states have more parameters and have had fewer executions (see text below for exact wording from Texas Penal Code).

Texas Penal Code § 19.03: Capital Murder

(a) A person commits an offense if the person commits murder as defined under Section 19.02 (b)(1) and:

(1) the person murders a peace officer or fireman who is acting in the lawful discharge of an official duty and who the person knows is a peace officer or fireman;
(2) the person intentionally commits the murder in the course of committing or attempting to commit kidnapping, burglary, robbery, aggravated sexual assault, arson, obstruction or retaliation, or terroristic threat under Section 22.07(a)(1), (3), (4), (5), or (6);
(3) the person commits the murder for remuneration or the promise of remuneration or employs another to commit the murder for remuneration or the promise of remuneration;
(4) the person commits the murder while escaping or attempting to escape from a penal institution;
(5) the person, while incarcerated in a penal institution, murders another:
(A) who is employed in the operation of the penal institution; or
(B) with the intent to establish, maintain, or participate in a combination or in the profits of a combination;
(6) the person:
(A) while incarcerated for an offense under this section or Section 19.02, murders another; or
(B) while serving a sentence of life imprisonment or a term of 99 years for an offense under Section 20.04, 22.021, or 29.03, murders another;
(7) the person murders more than one person:
(A) during the same criminal transaction; or
(B) during different criminal transactions but the murders are committed pursuant to the same scheme or course of conduct;
(8) the person murders an individual under 10 years of age; or
(9) the person murders another person in retaliation for or on account of the service or status of the other person as a judge or justice of the supreme court, the court of criminal appeals, a court of appeals, a district court, a criminal district court, a constitutional county court, a statutory county court, a justice court, or a municipal court.

Another exercise I conduct with students is to test their knowledge on state laws (if their state of residency has a capital punishment statute). I ask them if they can list the parameters in which someone is eligible for capital punishment. After discussing the local context, I also present what I consider to be the most notorious example of justice as determined by geographic location: Harris County, Texas. A combination of overzealous prosecution and underfunded defense attorneys contributes to this county contributing disproportionately to death penalty cases nationwide. The eight counties, including Harris County, who have disproportionate capital punishment outcomes also have disproportionate minority representation within the capital punishment sentences handed down: 69% are individuals of color, and 41% are African American (Rogers 2016).

By discussing issues related to these geographical disparities, students gain a greater understanding of the complex issues related to the intersectionality of location

Table 1 State comparisons of executions (1976–2016) *Source* Compiled from the Death Penalty Information Center State-by-State database

State	Executions since 1976
Texas	538
Oklahoma	112
Virginia	111
Florida	92
Missouri	87
Georgia	69
Alabama	58
Ohio	53
North Carolina	43
South Carolina	43
Arizona	37
Louisiana	28
Arkansas	27
Mississippi	21
Indiana	20
Delaware	16
California	13
Illinois	12
Nevada	12
Utah	7
Tennessee	6
Maryland	5
Washington	5
Idaho	3
Kentucky	3
Montana	3
Pennsylvania	3
South Dakota	3
US Government	3
Oregon	2
Colorado	1
Connecticut	1
New Mexico	1
Wyoming	1

and demographic factors. This discussion moves past the statutes for each state; statutes are merely a starting point for someone to qualify for capital punishment. The culture of capital punishment within the state and jurisdiction also must allow for the acceptance of the death penalty. After 1976, when the nationwide moratorium was lifted, we see that many states that technically have statutes for capital punishment have either opted not to use it, or have done so sparingly (Table 1).

Ultimately, those accused of similar offenses should be given the same treatment, regardless of the state in which the offense was committed. However, the reality is that those residing in states that are willing to invest more taxpayer money into the capital punishment system are more at risk to fall victim to a flawed system of punishment, especially if they are economically disadvantaged. This holds true if they are simply accused of capital murder, even if they are not guilty of the crime.

OJ Simpson: A Case Study

Using a famous or celebrity-based case can also help students weave together the various concepts and themes related to capital punishment and inequality in the criminal justice system. In my class, I often use this activity centered around the case of O.J. Simpson to help students start to see these intersecting factors operate in concert.

Although OJ Simpson's trial took place over two decades ago in 1995, university students are still relatively well-versed in many of the details of the crime and the accusations made against Simpson. Rather than asking them to suspend judgment on whether they personally believe him to be innocent or guilty, instead I ask: "What if the defendant had been a different African American male accused of this crime? How might this case have been judged differently?" Rather than deal with a hypothetical situation, I then compare OJ Simpson's case to that of Demetrie Mayfield. As Costanzo (1997) explains,

> Mayfield was accused of murdering a woman friend and a man who (like Ronald Goldman) was apparently in the wrong place at the wrong time. Mayfield's attorney spent a total of forty hours preparing for the trial. His only real interview with the defendant took place the morning before the trial began (p. 74).

Mayfield was originally sentenced to death in California. Eventually, the U.S. Court of Appeals overturned his death sentence due to "deficient" counsel, and that he "suffered prejudice as a result" of inadequate defense representation (U.S. Court of Appeals, 9th Circuit). He is now serving a life sentence in prison.

Comparing the facts in these two cases, there are many apparent similarities, including both victim and offender characteristics and geographic location. But Mayfield was an unknown African American male prior to this crime. He did not receive the media attention or publicity that Simpson garnered. On a related and perhaps more important point, he did not have the "Dream Team" of attorneys that Simpson could afford. Simpson's defense costs have been estimated to be between

$4 M and $6 M (Costanzo 1997). As Reiman and Leighton (2010) explain there are really "two transmission belts of justice: one for the poor, and one for the affluent" (p. 129). Few examples so perfectly illustrate the discrepancies between classes as these two extreme cases. Simpson and Mayfield's cases were processed using different transmission belts.

I then demonstrate to students that, if a defendant is indigent, they will either be assigned a public defender, a court-appointed lawyer, or a contract lawyer, to represent them at their initial trial (Bohm 2013). Bohm (2013) provides an example of death penalty defense attorneys in one state being paid a flat fee of $15,000 per case. One attorney explains that once you divide what sounds like a lot of money—$15,000—by the approximately 800 h of work on the case, the usual public defender is only earning $18.75 per hour. The normal billing rate this attorney would ordinarily charge is $120 per hour (p. 92). This example shows students the role unequal compensation for public defense can play for low-income defendants.

In class we also discuss how, during postconviction proceedings, indigent defendants may take different routes, depending on whether they are at the federal or state level. At the federal level, they can either use attorneys provided from the private bar (which is limited to $5000 in fees) or use public defender organizations, which are grant funded (Bohm 2013). Florida was the first state to create a state level Postconviction Defender Organization in 1985. Though (and perhaps because) it was successful, it was replaced with Capital Collateral Regional Counsels (Bohm 2013). Similar strains on resources are experienced at the post-conviction stage as during the trial stage. Underfunding and understaffing can prevent those with good intentions from being able to zealously defend these individuals. If more money was earmarked for this type of assistance, there would be more effort that could be dedicated to defense, and the possibilities of irreversible errors likely reduced (Bohm 2013).

As Williams (2012) observes, the quality of the defense counsel determines the outcome of capital punishment. Issues ranging from sleeping defense attorneys to those who fail to meet filing deadlines have led to defendants receiving inadequate defense services (p. 17). When combining the lack of quality defense with well-resourced, overzealous prosecutors, it seems many indigent defendants are beginning their trials with a substantial disadvantage.

Many students are quick to identify the similarities in OJ Simpson's case with other similarly situated defendants. This high profile example provides an illustration of economic discrepancy that most can identify. By using a real world case study, we can discuss issues with adequate counsel and use this as a comparison case.

Guest Speakers

The activity that seems to resonate with students the most with respect to capital punishment is bringing in relevant and engaging guest speakers. Depending on the location of the university, guest speakers may include prosecutors, defense attorneys, expert witnesses, or others involved in this type of case. Individuals working within the system who have experience with death penalty cases can provide unique and applied insight on individual cases and the capital punishment system.

The most rewarding activity I have personally encountered with students on this front is an event organized in conjunction with an abolition group while I was a faculty member in New England. Organized by our student criminal justice organization group and me (as their faculty advisor), we arranged for a former death row inmate in Arizona, Ray Krone, now exonerated, to speak on campus. It was an extremely well-attended event, with community members, faculty, staff, and students in the audience. The audience listened while he explained how he was wrongfully accused and convicted, and spent over a decade in prison for a murder he did not commit. His family endured additional financial burden as they continued to fight these allegations.

Ray Krone's case and presentation focused mainly on overzealous prosecutors and how issues within the system can lead to wrongful convictions. In 1992, he was tried and sentenced to death. In 1996, he was given a new trial, but was sentenced to life in prison. In 2002, Krone's innocence was proven by DNA and he was exonerated of all charges (The Innocence Project). As he so aptly discusses in an op-ed piece (Krone 2008):

> In 2002, through the tireless work of my attorneys, I was the 100th person to be exonerated and released from death row since the death penalty was reinstated in the United States. Despite DNA evidence that exonerated me, it took years before the prosecution grudgingly acknowledged it had no case against me. If it had been up to the state of Arizona, I'd be dead today. Who knows how many more innocent people sit on death row today, guilty of nothing more than the fact that they couldn't afford a lawyer? And can anyone honestly say with certainty that of the nearly 1100 people who have been executed in the past 30 years, not a single one wasn't innocent? As my story illustrates, even with DNA testing there will always be a chance an innocent person will be sentenced to death and executed.

Though this guest speaker was not an activity specifically designed for class, many of my students attended. Some students in the Senior Capstone course attended this talk and chose to write an optional response paper on the event. In their response papers, a few indicated the experience had perhaps a greater impact on them than any other event they had attended while enrolled in college. Not only had this speaker illustrated issues related to innocence and wrongful convictions, but also the devastating impact that capital punishment has (emotionally, physically, and financially) on all parties involved in the process.

Students obtaining degrees in Criminology, Criminal Justice, or Sociology with the goal of working in the criminal justice system as a career need exposure to individuals who have experienced the system in this manner. Not only does this provide perspective on portions of the system that are less visible to us as a public (prisons and capital punishment), but it also depicts a system in need of change. Throughout his discussion the speaker was able to illustrate issues with fairness and income inequality that cannot be easily conveyed in a classroom.

Implications of Discussions on Capital Punishment

Justice Thurgood Marshall famously believed that as the general public garners more knowledge about the death penalty, fewer will support its use, with the exception of those who hold strong supporting beliefs. As he argues,

> While a public opinion poll obviously is of some assistance in indicating public acceptance or rejection of a specific penalty, its utility cannot be very great. This is because whether or not a punishment is cruel and unusual depends, not on whether its mere mention "shocks the conscience and sense of justice of the people," but on whether people who were fully informed as to the purposes of the penalty and its liabilities would find the penalty shocking, unjust, and unacceptable. In other words, the question with which we must deal is not whether a substantial proportion of American citizens would today, if polled, opine that capital punishment is barbarously cruel, but whether they would find it to be so in the light of all information presently available (Furman v. Georgia 1972, 408, US 238, 362).

Considering the Marshall Hypothesis, university students (and others) who fully support capital punishment, once exposed to knowledge about the inequalities associated with capital punishment, should theoretically shift opinions after embarking on a semester (or a degree program) that illustrates such inadequacies. You might find, then, that your students' feelings about this topic evolve over the duration of your course.

We also know that opinions on capital punishment tend to ebb and flow. Over time, student opinions may shift to more closely reflect their original positions (Bohm and Vogel 2004). It is likely that the knowledge acquired from one course or a series of courses is inadequate to elicit lasting impressions of the inherent discrepancies of capital punishment—making our jobs as educators even more important. In my experience, the activities presented in this chapter have been effective in helping students understand the issues of inequality wrapped up in the use of the death penalty.

Conclusion

Ultimately, many students are left wondering who really benefits from the use of capital punishment. With the questionable findings on issues related to feelings of closure and retribution (see e.g. Costanzo 1997; Bohm 2013), we cannot state that all, or even most, of the families and loved ones of victims find solace or gain in the use of capital punishment. Taxpayers are footing much of the bill, and even public opinion is shifting away from endorsement of the death penalty.

Gideon v. Wainwright (1963) held that states must provide indigent defendants counsel. Even with a system meant to safeguard against discrimination, the system is still fraught with bias. In a system where the affluent defendants are able to afford better defense, they will be poised for success, while the poor defendants less likely so. This is true for all potential sentences, but no sentence is as immobilizing or permanent as capital punishment.

Depending on the individual background of each student, some enter our classrooms believing that equal justice is available to all, regardless of race, ethnicity, or economic status. This is an ideal that the United States criminal justice system, as is currently structured, cannot accomplish. Some are able to afford the highest quality defense attorney who can focus their attention on their client's defense. Others are appointed counsel who can scarcely keep pace with their caseloads. Both groups will be facing the same obstacles in court, and one is at a significant disadvantage. When also factoring in geographic location and the culture of capital punishment in some areas, the discrepancies become more pronounced. As students learn the complications associated with the decision-making process, some become more hesitant to impose an across-the-board sanction of capital punishment for all cases that meet the minimum specifications.

Defendants who are not zealously represented are at a greater risk of falling victim to discrimination based on class, race, gender, or myriad of factors. Helping students to understand the consequences of inadequate representation, overzealous prosecution, and other factors within the criminal justice system can allow them to visualize how this potentially plays into a larger system of inadequacies and discrepancies.

References

Barak, G., Leighton, P., & Cotton, A. (2015). *Class, race, gender and crime: The social realities of justice in America* (4th ed.). Lanham: Rowman and Littlefield.

Bohm, R. M. (2013). *Capital punishment's collateral damage*. Durham, NC: Carolina Academic Press.

Bohm, R. M., & Vogel, B. L. (2004). More than ten years after: The long-term stability of informed death penalty opinions. *Journal of Criminal Justice, 32,* 307–327.

Costanzo, M. (1997). *Just revenge: Costs and consequences of the death penalty*. New York: St. Martin's Press.

Furman v. Georgia, 408 U.S. 238 (1972).

Gideon v. Wainwright, 372 U.S. 335 (1963).

Gregg v. Georgia, 428 US 153 (1976).

Krone, R. The Innocence Project. http://www.innocenceproject.org/cases/ray-krone/. Accessed 27 March 2017.

Krone, R. (2008, January 14). Lethal injection is the wrong debate. *San Francisco Chronicle.* http://www.sfgate.com/opinion/article/Lethal-injection-is-the-wrong-debate-3298189.php. Accessed 27 March 2017.

Mayfield v. Woodford, U.S. Court of Appeals, 9th Circuit (2001).

Reiman, J., & Leighton, P. (2010). *The rich get richer and the poor get prison: Ideology, class and criminal justice* (9th ed). Boston: Allyn and Bacon.

Rogers, B. (2016). Harris County stands out for death penalty cases, study finds. *The Houston Chronicle*. http://www.houstonchronicle.com/news/houston-texas/houston/article/Harris-County-stands-out-for-death-penalty-cases-9187154.php. Accessed 22 December 2016.

Snell, T. L. (2014). Capital punishment, 2013—Statistical tables. *Bureau of Justice Statistics*. NCJ 248448 Department of Justice. https://www.bjs.gov/content/pub/pdf/cp13st.pdf. Accessed 27 March 2017.

State by State Database. Texas. *Death Penalty Information Center*. http://www.deathpenaltyinfo.org/state_by_state. Accessed 27 March 2017.

Those Executed Who Did Not Directly Kill The Victim. Death Penalty Information Center. https://deathpenaltyinfo.org/those-executed-who-did-not-directly-kill-victim Accessed 1 October 2017.

Texas Penal Code § 19.03.

Williams, K. (2012). *Most deserving of death: An analysis of the Supreme Court's death penalty jurisprudence*. Farnham Surrey: Ashgate.

Making Room for a Postcolonial Critique in the Introductory STS Curriculum

Dilshani Sarathchandra

Author's Reflexive Statement

"In Wasgamuwa, our farmers remain in perpetual debt, mostly due to HEC-induced crop losses [human-elephant conflict] and the low market value of rice. Rice has a high water dependency, which poses significant challenges to cultivation during periods of drought. To alleviate some of the hardships faced by Sri Lankan farmers, my organization initiated the *Project Orange Elephant*. At the pilot stage, we introduced two marginal villagers and farmers to a special variety of cash-crop orange (i.e., *Bibile* sweet orange), which commands a high value in the open market and can be used to produce concentrated beverages. Mostly importantly, wild elephants don't eat these oranges. As a result we were able to investigate two of our long-term conservation objectives: generating extra income for small-scale farmers, and reducing further clearance of elephant habitats in bordering villages. We have collected promising data that indicate the beginnings of an incentive-based, sustainable conservation project."

The above excerpt (included with permission) is taken from one of my recent email correspondences with a colleague (Chandima Fernando; *Sri Lanka Wildlife Conservation Society*). A conservation biologist by profession, trained in Australia and New Zealand, Chandima is now based in Sri Lanka, working with some of the most socially and economically marginalized communities in the country.

Foundational to my colleague's description above, is a 'new norm' in contemporary science: a science that would not be possible without the transnational movement of people and knowledge, and the postcolonial political context within which it gets constructed, distributed, and consumed. At the same time, this new science and its associated norms does pose an epistemic challenge to the traditional ethos of science (e.g., Merton 1942).

D. Sarathchandra (✉)
University of Idaho, Moscow, USA
e-mail: dilshanis@uidaho.edu

K. Haltinner and L. Hormel (eds.), *Teaching Economic Inequality and Capitalism in Contemporary America*, https://doi.org/10.1007/978-3-319-71141-6_20

Descriptions such as the above are abundant in accounts of contemporary collaborative scientific work. And, yet, often in Western teachings of science and science studies, instructors seem to shy away from critiquing the traditional ethos of science and the largely West-centric approaches to thinking about scientific rationality. It is as if fully acknowledging the context dependence of science would somehow weaken our scientific enterprise. Due to this hesitancy, we seem to be missing an opportunity to fully grapple with the complex ways in which inequities continue to shape scientific knowledge.

To some extent, the development of the interdisciplinary field of Science and Technology Studies (STS) can be viewed as a response to this critique. Since its inception in the 1930s, STS has established itself as a dynamic interdisciplinary field, combining expertise of historians, philosophers, sociologists, anthropologists and others, to examine the various 'social processes' of science.

For undergraduates who are interested in the intersection of science, technology and society, an *Introduction to STS* course offers an entry point to investigate science in the social context. An introductory course familiarizes students with STS concepts by exposing them to theoretical underpinnings, methodological challenges, and empirical findings related to STS. However, when teaching STS, early introductory courses (and sometimes even STS programs and departments) have often treated Western ideals of scientific rationality and objectivity as fairly unproblematic and universal (Harding 2011). They demonstrate little explicit engagement with how economic inequalities shape the practice and consumption of science.

While the recent turn to "postcolonial technoscience" has made it more acceptable to discuss "postcolonialism" in social science and humanities departments in the United States, according to Harding (2011), it has been much harder to introduce postcolonial issues to the study of STS in U.S. universities. Some of the resistance to institutionalizing a postcolonial critique in higher education in the West comes from the notion that such institutionalization might challenge the claims to universally valid knowledge, achievements, and consequent political entitlement of the U.S. and the West.

The predominantly Euro/West-centric approach to teaching (and learning) STS is unfortunate at a time when most U.S. campuses are transforming themselves into global campuses. Over the past few decades we have seen an exponential growth in the number of 'Third World' students and faculty entering U.S. higher education institutions, as well as U.S.-born students and faculty traveling to the 'Third World' for scholarly as well as cultural investigation. These demographic changes are leading to accelerations in research and scholarship that cuts across geographic and intellectual divides between the West and the rest (Harding 2011).

As a result, there is a need for developing a form of education that strengthens our students' understandings of how global politics, economics, and social relations work. Instructors of introductory STS courses should be cognizant of global transformations in STS and encourage students to explore the regulatory ideals of Western science in tandem with global standpoints and postcolonial criticisms.

At a personal level, such an integrative approach to teaching STS is important to me as someone who grew up in a post-colonial (and now post-conflict) country, Sri Lanka, where we continue to struggle with ethnic tensions rooted in a legacy of colonialism. Additionally, in my current position as an academic at a rural Northwest university (where my students tend to be mostly American, white, and first-generation) I feel a deep sense of responsibility to help students navigate the global implications of their various social relations.

In this chapter, I argue that by better aligning new developments in STS (e.g., postcolonial technoscience) with how we teach STS in the undergraduate curriculum, we can help students understand the ways in which unequal relations are developed and reinforced through scientific knowledge and technological developments. Consequently, I suggest that incorporating a postcolonial critique into STS can better prepare U.S. students to face the (often unknown and unseen) challenges of a changing global order. I begin with a brief summary of recent developments in STS and its embrace of postcolonial studies.

STS Over the Decades

Science and technology are important driving forces of today's 'postindustrial' (Hage and Powers 1992) social order: a social order in which we seem to have moved away from a system based on heavy industry (i.e., capital and labor) to a system where 'knowledge' acts as the primary productive force (Knorr-Cetina 2005). In this 'knowledge society,' science and technology has restructured many facets of our contemporary lives, including changes in the division of labor, development of specialized occupations, emergence of new enterprises, and measures of sustained growth (Knorr-Cetina 2005, p. 546).

STS posits a challenge to the above 'knowledge society' model that views science purely from a "social impact perspective" (Knorr-Cetina 2005, p. 547). On the contrary, STS seeks to examine not only the impacts of science and technology on society, but also what constitutes scientific knowledge. STS asks how the technical core of scientific knowledge comes to its existence. Within this intellectual inquiry, several robust themes have emerged, including (1) the deep embedding of science and technology in society as social institutions, and (2) the creation of STS-specific understandings of scientific innovations.

The early history of STS in the United States was dominated by *Sociology of Science*, which dates back to the 1930s, and was led by social-structural and institutional analysis (e.g., Merton 1942, 1968). The subsequent development of STS was a result of a collective move away from the institutional analysis of scientific organizations and groups to a more comprehensive analysis of the "cognitive contents" of science (Shapin 1995). With the new turn towards STS, social scientists were now able to demonstrate how social science methods could be applied to the technical core of science, making the content and practice of science open to sociological examination. Natural science was no longer 'exempt' from social analysis.

Since the 1970s, a number of research trajectories have emerged and flourished within STS, including *postcolonial technoscience* that examines changing political economies and their effects on science and society. As a STS subfield, *postcolonial technoscience* consists of many avenues and opportunities to engage students in a critical examination of economic inequalities (both locally and globally). In this chapter, I identify a few of those opportune points where political economy intersects with science/knowledge, and discuss how incorporating a postcolonial critique in the Introductory STS curriculum can assist in our teaching of economic inequality and capitalism.

Political Economies of Knowledge

Because STS does not distinguish epistemic processes from the political and economic contexts within which they occur, it constitutes a unique vocabulary and a set of analytical tools to investigate today's political economies of knowledge (i.e., how knowledge is produced, distributed, and consumed). Additionally, as mentioned above, STS has developed a critique of the 'knowledge economy' model that treats knowledge purely as a resource to be owned and controlled. While traditional *HPS of Science* (History, Philosophy, and Sociology of Science) often frame science as "a free market of knowledge," the new STS scholarship reveals cultures, practices, individuals, and institutional gatekeepers, who are responsive to a variety of demands and forces, and regulate contemporary knowledge markets (Sismondo 2010, p. 190). As such, today's scientific knowledge drives a variety of internal and external factors, beyond a simple desire of the public for more information.

Several branches of STS scholarship have explicitly adopted a 'political economy' framework to examine the intersection of science, technology, and society. Examples include recent research on commercialization of biological material, which not only examine the commercial potential of "tissue economies" (Waldby and Mitchell 2006), but also confront and bring to light the "exploitations of research subjects" within these seemingly "value-neutral" processes of knowledge production.

Similar efforts to make frameworks of political economy explicit within STS (Sismondo 2010) include, for example, Kaushik Rajan's widely acclaimed 2006 book *Biocapital: The Constitution of Postgenomic Life*. Making a valuable contribution to both STS and political economy literature, *Biocapital* develops an ethnography of genomic research and drug development marketplaces in the Unites States and India, masterfully weaving a thread through not only methods of research, but also the associated regulatory, financing, and marketing aspects of these new technologies. Through this, *Biocapital* illuminates the global flows of knowledge, capital, and people, demonstrating how life sciences have become simultaneous producers of "epistemic value" and "economic value" in the late twentieth and early twenty-first century (Rajan 2006).

In another related line of research, STS scholars have examined the 'academic capitalism model' that was developed in the 1980s, parallel to the increased commercialization of U.S. university research which was triggered by the passage of the Bayh-Dole Act (this act paved way to university researchers to patent research funded by the federal government). Many in the STS community have demonstrated how this change has increased the rate of UIRs (University-Industry Relationships) and even University-Industry-Government interactions. Overall, STS accounts of commercialization elucidate how we are asking, and sometimes demanding, that university science explicitly contributes to economic growth (potentially further disrupting the Mertonian ethos of science, if there ever existed one).

Other notable examples include Daniel Kleinman's 2003 book *Impure Cultures: University Biology and the World of Commerce*, which explores the co-creation of academic culture and commercial culture through a blurring of the boundaries between university biology and commerce. Using data gathered through participant observation at a U.S. Plant Pathology laboratory, Kleinman examines not only direct UIRs, but also indirect and pervasive influences of the world of commerce on academic science. Overall, the scholarship in political economies of knowledge exemplifies the intersection of science and capital, focusing on how commercialized research has converted science from "commons" to "anti-commons," where "rights holders may impose excessive transaction costs or make the acquisition of licenses and other rights too burdensome to permit the pursuit of scientifically and socially worthwhile research" (Walsh et al. 2005).

The Turn Towards Postcolonial Technoscience

While the scholarly agendas described above tackle many issues surrounding political economies of knowledge, in some ways they remain limited due to the centering of attention on science in a Euro-Western context. In contrast, the relatively new branch of *postcolonial technoscience* has been gaining traction by developing a critique of the Western hegemony in science studies, and examining new ways to study the changing political economies of capitalism and science in the global context. In this work, the term "postcolonial" is taken to mean not only new configurations of technoscience (such as the increased transnational movement of people, practices, knowledge, and technologies), but also new and critical methods of identifying them (Anderson 2002).

Although much has been written about the interconnections between science, technology, and global development, the field of STS has had limited engagement with these topics until recently. The lukewarm response of STS to postcolonial studies changed around the year 2000 with the rise of *postcolonial technoscience*, which began to explicitly address the ways in which science and technology is used to legitimize colonialism in its various forms.

In 2002, a special issue of *Social Studies of Science* (a leading international journal in science studies) focused on identifying the different ways to combine STS scholarship with postcolonial studies. In the introduction to this issue, Anderson (2002, p. 643) argued that many ideas about our differences, such as 'traditional' and 'modern' are "enacted and distributed in the performance of technoscience." A combined research effort (STS + postcolonial studies) would allow us to effectively challenge these various dichotomies (e.g., global/local, first-world/third-world, Western/Indigenous, modern/traditional, developed/underdeveloped, big-science/small-science) that have been produced through the hegemonic claims of colonial regimes, often in the service of corporate globalization. As such, Anderson (2002) frames *postcolonial technoscience* as a direct response to concerns about the Western hegemony and commodification of science in the service of corporate capitalism.

Additionally, postcolonial theory has often challenged the simplistic assumptions of objectivity and universal applicability of Western knowledge, calling into question the various "epistemic violences" committed against "alternative local knowledges." Therefore, Anderson (2002, p. 647) argues, "an engagement of science studies and postcolonial theory would not simply provide us with instances of Western science and technology in different settings—potentially it might even 'colonize' and destabilize conventional accounts of Western technoscience at 'home'." In other words, a postcolonial study of science and technology might offer new and more nuanced answers to critical questions of political economies of knowledge, and perhaps even develop new analytic tools that do not privilege specific forms of knowledge (e.g. Western technoscience) or specific localities (e.g. first-world).

More recently, *postcolonial technoscience* has built up steam within STS, with research originating from the core to the periphery and vise versa, building on and expanding both the more traditional, institutional analysis of *sociology of science*, and the constructivist analysis of *sociology of scientific knowledge*. Several of these research agendas grapple directly with questions about fast-changing political economies of knowledge. Just in the Special issue mentioned above, research ranged from Uranium mining in Africa (Hecht 2002: power relations in science and technology are highly localized) to the colonial context of space exploration (Redfield 2002: colonization impulses determine who gets to 'provincialize' even the outer space). A range of similar examples shows that postcolonial STS has been particularly successful in "displaying the locality of science and technology, and the consequent conflicts and other relations between localized science and technology" (Sismondo 2010, p. 196).

A more recent special issue of *Social Studies of Science* (Volume 43, 2013) addressed the intersection of indigenous bodies/knowledge and *postcolonial technoscience*. Topics ranged from how Australian indigenous DNA evolved from 'lab materials' to 'sacred objects' to 'political time bombs' through postcolonial politics (Kowal 2013), to how Peruvian indigenous identities emerged through the intersection of globalized population genome research and localized political strategies (Kent 2013).

Furthermore, Harding's 2011 book *The Postcolonial Science and Technology Studies Reader* covers many relevant topics, from theorizing postcolonial technoscience to navigating "other culture science" in an era of massive globalization: topics covered include federal science, Islamic science, indigenous science, civil science, and knowledge mining through technology. In further research, Prasad (2016) has demonstrated the continued Euro/West-centrism in scientific practices and lay imaginaries.

The establishment and institutionalization of several journals and academic/professional conferences also exemplify the rising influence of postcolonial interventions within STS. For instance, the journal *East Asian Science, Technology, and Society*, sponsored by the Taiwanese Ministry of Science and Technology, explicitly aims to publish "research on how society and culture in East Asia interact with science, technology, and medicine" (https://www.dukeupress.edu/East-Asian-Science-Technology-and-Society/). The 4S/EASST conference aims to brings together the 4S (*Society for the Social Studies of Science*) STS scholars in contact with Latin American STS scholars (ESOCITE) to "demystify the neutrality of knowledge and to show that 'mainstream' knowledge does not imply or guarantee social utility" (http://www.4sonline.org/meeting/14#E).

Overall, above examples illustrate that, while a relatively new branch, *postcolonial technoscience* has already made important contributions to the interdisciplinary field of STS and provided us with vocabulary and analytical tools to better examine the power relations and inequities between Western and non-Western knowledges. Consequently, the need for applying a postcolonial critique into the introductory STS curriculum has become evident over the past few years.

Embedding a Postcolonial Critique in the Introductory STS Curriculum

Although there is widespread agreement that the development of nations depends on science and technology to a large extent (Sismondo 2010), early STS scholarship was less willing to explicitly address these issues at a global scale. As a consequence, the way we teach STS, particularly at the introductory level, has often overlooked an area of STS scholarship that consists of many opportunities to teach students economic inequality, globalization, and capitalism through a science studies lens. While attempts to integrate postcolonial studies into STS scholarship have been on the rise, similar efforts to integrate a postcolonial critique into our STS curriculum have been meager.

My analysis of 58 open-access undergraduate STS syllabi on *Society for the Social Studies of Science* web archives revealed only four course syllabi that explicitly mentioned the term "postcolonial" or consisted of readings related to this growing field of research. The dearth of engagement with these issues could be partly a reflection of the pipeline of postcolonial research in STS rather than a conscious omission: much of the important research efforts in this area have occurred over the past decade and a half.

A similar trend can be seen when looking at popular STS handbooks as well. While early handbooks only made cursory references to issues of state, government, capital, globalization and international relations (e.g., Jasanoff et al. 1995), more recent handbooks tackle postcolonial issues much more directly. For example, the 2007 *Handbook of Science and Technology Studies* (edited by Hackett, Amsterdamska, and Bijker) covers a range of topics that combines STS and postcolonial studies, including chapters entitled "postcolonial studies of technoscience" "practices, people, and places" "the commercialization of science and the response of STS" and "boundaries and relationships between university and industry." The newest STS handbook (Felt et al. 2016, 4th edition) goes further by covering topics such as "science and democracy" "structural inequality and the politics of science and technology" and "feminism, postcolonialism, technoscience."

A comprehensive STS/*postcolonial technoscience* curriculum can provide students with many instances where they can identify inequities within local and global systems of knowledge and power. Examples include examinations of, (1) relationships between science in the "centers" and science in the "peripheries"; (2) mechanisms of maintaining stratification through scientific knowledge and technological advances; (3) increased transnational flow of information, people, knowledge, and their implications; (4) movements of tacit knowledge between nation states and cultures; (5) co-construction of science and politics; (6) commodification and commercialization of biological materials and technoscientific knowledge; (7) unequal treatment of Western and non-Western knowledge; (8) autonomy and legitimacy of knowledge from marginal communities; (9) implications of big data and democratization of science; (10) 'bioprospecting' and the continued exploitation of local bodies/knowledge; and (11) postcolonial politics in reshaping global intellectual property regimes. That STS engages in a seemingly deliberate effort to extend tools of social analysis to the natural sciences means it is imperative that we apply the same tools to our teaching of STS. Only then would we be able to fully demonstrate how science and technology act as key systems of knowledge production, often forging and sustaining unequal global relations, both implicitly and explicitly.

All in all, viewing science and technology as "context-specific forms of knowledge and practice that interact with a set of globally distributed social interest" (Shrum and Shenhav 1995, p. 631), in other words, making room to think of science and technology as entities situated in material spaces and extant power structures, is likely to not only increase our students' ability to critically analyze the intersection of science, technology, and development, but also to better grasp the pervasive influences of inequity and capitalism in how they shape humanity's most–treasured cumulative knowledge pool.

References

Anderson, W. (2002). Introduction: Postcolonial technoscience. *Social Studies of Science, 32,* 643–658.

Felt, U., Fouche, R., Miller, C. A., & Smith-Doerr, L. (2016). *The handbook of science and technology studies* (4th ed.). Cambridge, MA: MIT Press.

Hage, J., & Powers, C. H. (1992). *Post-industrial lives: Roles and relationships in the 21st century*. Newbury Park, CA: Sage.

Harding, S. (2011). *The postcolonial science and technology studies reader*. Durham, NC: Duke University Press.

Hecht, G. (2002). Rupture-talk in the nuclear age: Conjugating colonial power in Africa. *Social Studies of Science, 32,* 691–727.

Jasanoff, S., Markle, G. E., Peterson, J. C., & Pinch, T. (1995). *Handbook of science and technology studies*. New York: SAGE.

Kent, M. (2013). The importance of being Uros: Indigenous identity politics in the genomic age. *Social Studies of Science, 43,* 534–556.

Kleinman, D. L. (2003). *Impure cultures: How does the world of Commerce shape the everyday practices of Academic Biology*. Madison, WI: The University of Wisconsin Press.

Knorr-Cetina, K. D. (2005). Science, technology, and their implications. In C. Calhoun, C. Rojek & B. Turner (Eds.), *The Sage handbook of Sociology* (pp. 546–560). Thousand Oaks: Sage.

Kowal, E. (2013). Orphan DNA: Indigenous samples, ethical biovalue and postcolonial science. *Social Studies of Science, 43,* 577–597.

Merton, R. K. (1942). The normative structure of science. In *The Sociology of Science: Theoretical and empirical investigations* (pp. 267–278). Chicago: University of Chicago Press.

Merton, R. K. (1968). The Matthew Effect in science. *Science, 159,* 56–63.

Prasad, A. (2016). Discursive contextures of science: Euro/West-centrism and science and technology studies. *Engaging Science, Technology, and Society, 2,* 193–207.

Rajan, K. S. (2006). *Biocapital: The constituion of postgenomic life*. Durham, NC: Duke University Press.

Redfield, P. (2002). The half-life of empire in outer space. *Social Studies of Science, 32,* 791–825.

Shapin, S. (1995). Here and everywhere: Sociology of scientific knowledge. *Annual Review of Sociology, 21,* 289–321.

Shrum, W., & Shenhav, Y. (1995). Science and technology in less developed countries. In Jasanoff et al. (Eds.), *Handbook of Science and Technology Studies* (pp. 627–651). Thousand Oaks: Sage.

Sismondo, S. (2010). *An introduction to science and technology studies*. UK: Wiley-Blackwell.

Waldby, C., & Mitchell, R. (2006). *Tissue economies: Blood, organs, and cell lines in late capitalism*. Durham, NC: Duke University Press.

Walsh, J. P., Cho, C., & Cohen, W. M. (2005). View from the bench: Patents and material transfers. *Science, 309,* 2002–2003.

Utilizing Social Science Theories, Findings, and Comparative Analyses to Create a Framework for Understanding Economic Inequality"

Derek J. Robey and Jason P. Robey

Authors' Reflexive Statement

We are brothers who grew up in a large upper-middle-class family in a rural Minnesota town that was racially, religiously, and economically homogenous. In this context, we rarely had to consider systems of inequality nor how our upper-middle-class background shaped our experiences and afforded us tangible advantages in several social domains. Our relative socioeconomic advantage made postsecondary education accessible and affordable, provided high quality healthcare throughout our youth, and, above all, offered us a sense of security and stability that was indispensable to our growth and development.

Our socioeconomic privilege also framed out understanding of economic opportunity and equality in the United States. Like many young people, we were inundated with media images of poverty-stricken families in distant nations and commercial solicitations for monetary support from large charitable organizations. Though we knew of local families struggling to pay medical bills or in need of assistance for other major expenses, abject poverty and drastic economic hardships seemed not to affect American families. This naivety was coupled with a strong belief that any person could achieve the American Dream and that the United States was "a land of opportunity" for all.

Our naïve conception of socioeconomic inequality, poverty, and financial hardship in the United States, common among white middle- or upper-middle-class Americans, remained largely unchallenged before we enrolled at a large state university in a major metropolitan area. Here we met students from diverse social

D. J. Robey (✉)
Harvard University, Cambridge, USA
e-mail: derekrobey@g.harvard.edu

J. P. Robey
University of Wisconsin-Madison, Madison, USA
e-mail: jprobey@wisc.edu

K. Haltinner and L. Hormel (eds.), *Teaching Economic Inequality and Capitalism in Contemporary America*, https://doi.org/10.1007/978-3-319-71141-6_21

class backgrounds and studied issues of inequality with regard to race, religion, gender, and socioeconomic class through social science coursework. We know firsthand the value and importance of quality instruction in training students to think critically about the world around them, analyze the social systems and processes that give rise to inequality, and imagine policy interventions for redressing unequal access to opportunities.

Our sociological training provided us with the tools and knowledge necessary for better understanding the deeply entrenched socioeconomic disparities in the United States, a reality our relative economic advantage had shielded us from confronting. From our perspective, students should learn inequality can be conceptualized and understood in several ways. For this reason, we outline below multiple frameworks for understanding socioeconomic inequality—absolute or relative mobility, expanding disparities between the rich and poor, and measures of poverty or resource deprivation—and the systems responsible for producing and reproducing these disparities. Additionally, assessing the prevailing belief that the United States is a land of equality in comparison to other nations should be a primary goal of social science instruction. To this end, we propose comparative analyses rooted in empirical research are instrumental for critiquing the myth of meritocracy in the classroom.

Introduction

Teaching undergraduates about economic inequality in the United States requires instructors possess a vast and diverse set of pedagogical tools capable of challenging students to think analytically and critically about substantive issues. Thus, in this chapter, we argue instructors should use empirical social science research and analytical comparisons to construct a framework in which students can:

(1) question the hegemony of socioeconomic inequality;
(2) conceptualize and operationalize inequality in a variety of ways;
(3) compare levels of inequality and asymmetrical rates of mobility across contexts;
(4) describe the impact of high levels of economic inequality on those across the social class spectrum.

We draw upon literatures from multiple social science disciplines to provide support for this perspective. By consolidating the literature and putting distinct research focuses in conversation with one another, instructors can challenge their students to think more deeply about how issues of inequality are related. A narrow US-centric perspective limits students' abilities to identify causal mechanisms of economic inequality, consider the historical development of socioeconomic inequality, imagine possible futures or alternatives, and understand the importance of redressing systems of stratification. Our hope is this chapter provides instructors with the empirical research, theoretical framework, and instructional guidance necessary to construct an engaging syllabus, articulate these issues in the classroom, facilitate an engaging conversation in the classroom, and develop students' abilities to critically examine economic inequality. Certainly, these tactics alone are not the only effective method for achieving these goals, but instructors should strongly consider utilizing such a framework in the classroom because it forces students to consider the fundamental characteristics and features of social inequality. Finally, we provide the outline of an activity instructors can use in the classroom to stimulate discussion on these topics.

Challenging Hegemony

Gramsci's (1971) concept of hegemony—in which the upper class controls the dominant ideas, values, and worldview available in the cultural milieu in ways that are advantageous to their own interests—is a particularly useful concept with which to engage students as they begin to explore the realities of economic inequality in the United States. As Burawoy (2012) notes, hegemony is normalized through civic cultural institutions such as the media and schools. In this way, elites are able to manufacture consent among non-elites (our students) and justify economic structures through a logic of rational self-interests. Gramsci (1971) argues this cultural hegemony makes it difficult or impossible to question the existing capitalist order and imagine alternative economic systems. Thus, for students to fully examine and understand economic inequality, instructors must support students' abilities to overcome hegemonic forces that constrain thought and dissuade them from questioning the systems in which they are embedded. An analytical comparative framework that utilizes empirical research is well-suited to challenging the cultural hegemony that legitimize economic structures and inequality in the United States.

One hegemonic belief prevalent among students (and others) in the United States is the notion that certain levels of inequality is inevitable, natural, or even desirable. This argument has dominated the national conversation several times in various forms. For example, in the 1990s, Herrnstein and Murray (1994) published *The Bell Curve: Intelligence and Class Structure in American Life.* In it, the authors argue that inherited intelligence is unequally distributed among the population and highly predictive of one's attained socioeconomic status as an adult. The authors claim that natural intellectual disparities are driving gaps between the rich and poor and that future public policy debates should recognize that intelligence is largely immune to program interventions. Though *The Bell Curve* is only one example, similar arguments are pervasive and legitimate or naturalize existing levels of inequality.

How then can we as instructors effectively challenge our students to think critically and question strongly entrenched beliefs? We argue instructors should develop a repertoire of high quality empirical research that challenge culturally hegemonic worldviews. For example, in response to *The Bell Curve*, many social scientists critique Herrnstein and Murray's arguments through in-depth analyses of the data and methodology. Fischer et al. (1996) explicitly state they are challenging "a philosophy ages old: Human misery is natural and beyond human redemption; inequality is fated; and people deserve, by virtue of their native talents, the positions they have in society." They demonstrate that Herrnstein and Murray (1994) greatly overestimated the potential causal effect of natural intelligence on socioeconomic attainment and underestimated the effect of various ascribed social statuses (socioeconomic status of parents, race, and gender among others). Other subsequent studies made similar conclusions. Fischer et al. (1996) further argue that U.S. social policy and cultural norms create and legitimate the level of inequality that exists in the United States, in direct contrast with the notion that inequality is natural and inevitable.

What implications does this have for teaching undergraduate students? If, as Fischer et al. assert, levels of inequality are not inherent or inevitable, we are forced to consider the factors that shape and predict the amount of inequality present in any particular society. Unsurprisingly, social scientists have identified a vast array of structural determinants of the level of inequality in society. Though this chapter does not fully detail the many ways economic inequality is shaped by various social institutions or structures, instructors may look to the following substantive areas. Several scholars have noted a shifting occupational structure and between-occupation dispersion of wages as a driving force behind economic inequality (Mouw and Kalleberg 2010; Kalleberg 2009; Weeden 2002; Hout 1988). The increasing importance of a college education, rising wage returns to skilled labor, and vast disparities in educational attainment have also been proposed as mechanisms driving economic inequality (Lucas 2001; Reardon 2011; Armstrong and Hamilton 2013). Unsurprisingly, social policy and the existence of social assistance programs is highly predictive of levels of economic inequality (Brady and Burroway 2012; Korpi and Palme 1998; Katznelson 2005). Structural features like the family, neighborhoods, social capital, culture, the criminal justice system, racial and ethnic background, gender identity, and many others are, of course, also critically important to understanding economic inequality.

The aforementioned journal articles and books will help students identify underlying mechanisms producing and reproducing socioeconomic inequality, but instructors can also use them to invite students to question hegemonic beliefs. This first requires instructors generate a list of beliefs student have about equality, opportunity, socioeconomic class in the United States. Students are often hesitant to express such beliefs so it is helpful to come prepared with examples to get the conversation started. For example: the United States is fundamentally a meritocracy where any person can achieve their dreams; education makes it possible for any person to improve their condition in life; the United States used to be highly unequal, but that is not true anymore.

Having generated a list of hegemonic beliefs, instructors should then use empirical research to invite students to interrogate whether these beliefs hold up to academic scrutiny. If inequality is inevitable or rooted in individualistic explanations, why do measures of inequality vary across time and space as occupational structures change? If education is "the great equalizer" as many believe, why does the socioeconomic status of the parents predict the educational attainment of the child so well? Too often, as instructors, we have students read empirical pieces without facilitating the questions or discussions necessary to interrogate pervasive beliefs about meritocracy and equality in the United States.

Though empirical studies are instrumental for challenging deeply entrenched beliefs and worldviews, focusing solely on the United States limits their effectiveness in contextualizing systems of economic inequality. For this reason, we construct a framework for exploring issues of inequality—how to conceptualize inequality, compare levels of inequality across contexts, and identify the consequences of high levels of inequality.

Conceptualizing Inequality

Before discussing how comparing levels of inequality across contexts is important for student learning, it is necessary to discuss the multiple ways inequality can be conceptualized and understood in the social sciences. Though there is considerable variation and certainly no consensus in the discipline, social scientists generally discuss inequality through one of three frameworks: (1) unequal distribution of financial or economic resources, (2) unequal access to opportunities and possibility for mobility, and (3) relational poverty. Next, we briefly outline the basic assumptions for each, with the hope that instructors can use these to expand how students understand inequality in the United States. The activity outlined at the end provides an in-classroom technique for visualizing these frameworks for understanding inequality.

Socioeconomic Resource Distribution

The unequal resource distribution paradigm focuses on the unequal distribution of, access to, and control over socioeconomic resources. Marx's classic theoretical framework argues inequality is rooted in a bifurcated class system based on a person's relation to the ownership of the means of capitalist production (Grusky and Szelenyi 2011). Though contemporary scholars focus less explicitly the means of production, the unequal distribution of tangible financial and economic resources remain the primary concern of many inequality scholars. The dominant focus for many years has been income and wage inequality (see Fernandez 2001; Piketty and Saez 2003; Kalleberg 2009; Mouw and Kalleberg 2010). Though income inequality is a dominant paradigm, there has been a recent trend toward measuring wealth inequality (Spilerman 2000; Oliver and Shapiro 2006; Killewald 2013).

Scholars in this tradition argue that focusing solely on the unequal distribution of income limits our ability to understand how inequality functions in society. Wealth is a crucial factor in the cumulative advantage and disadvantage within and across generations. Still others suggest neither income nor wealth is adequate for understanding economic inequality. For example, Sen (1997) argues a narrow focus on concrete financial resources ignores the intangible aspects that contribute to a holistic economic well-being. His "capabilities perspective" contends analyses should consider instead how people use the tangible resources at their disposable to execute functions they need for survival and desire.

How can instructors use this in the classroom? This framework is often the most intuitive for undergraduate students. Though it is easy to visualize and understand that some people have more and others have less, it is less immediately clear to undergraduate students how the level of disparity or inequality might vary across contexts. The activity outlined at the end of this chapter will help illuminate this reality. Still, instructors should push their students to think more deeply by asking probing questions. What unit of analysis—individuals or families—does it make the most sense to compare? How might wealth and income inequality matter in different or similar ways? What is missing by a narrow focus solely on financial resources that are easily quantified? Should we also consider social, cultural, and human capital disparities? To what extent and how are these resource disparities connected? Instructors should also invite students to assess whether or not the existence of vast socioeconomic resource inequality undermines any of their fundamental or hegemonic beliefs about the United States.

The equal or unequal distribution of socioeconomic resources can be estimated using a number of different formulations. The most well-known calculation is the Gini coefficient, a measure of the statistical dispersion of the income or wealth among a nation's residents. While assessing trends in the Gini coefficient (or similar measures) over time will provide a sense of whether or not the distribution of resources is becoming more or less equal, it does little to convey how flexible the socioeconomic class structure is or how easy it is for an individual to attain a certain socioeconomic status in the United States. For this, one must turn to another paradigm for understanding inequality: the mobility framework.

Social Mobility

The mobility framework understands and measures inequality through a comparison of the rates of intergenerational transmission of socioeconomic status from one generation to the next. Put another way, the mobility literature assesses the likelihood that a person born into a family with a particular socioeconomic status will attain a different socioeconomic status as an adult. Importantly, scholars in this tradition consider rates of both upward and downward mobility. Erikson and Goldthorpe (2002) note that, in a similar vein to the unequal resource distribution tradition, mobility scholars operationalize and measure the concepts in various ways. For example, they argue that economists measure the intergenerational transmission of income and wealth. On the other hand, sociologists primarily use a categorical and class-based measure of mobility. This can be done using crude distinctions like upper class, middle class, working class, and poor. However, the authors also describe how categories can be constructed based on occupational positions and employer relations. Studies using mobility measures are often understood as a measure of the equality of opportunity and life chances in a given society.

In addition to an empirical analysis, Breen (2004) provides an important distinction between two different types of mobility that social scientists can measure and analyze. The first is called absolute mobility. This measures the rate of individuals in a society who moved from one class origin position based on their parents' socioeconomic status to a different class destination position as an adult. Importantly, this could be upward or downward mobility. The second type of mobility is called relative mobility. Social scientists measure this by using contingency tables to compare the relative chances of being in a particular social class destination as an adult based on their class origin position. For example, it would measure someone's chance of being in the top income quintile as an adult if their class origin was in the bottom quintile in comparison to their chance of ending up in the same social class destination if their class origin began in the top quintile. For this reason, relative mobility is often seen as a better indicator of societal equality of opportunities.

Of course, we do not expect instructors will have students calculate mobility rates or construct contingency tables in the classroom. Instead, instructors can spend time in classroom facilitating a discussion on how social mobility (or immobility as the case may be) relates to established hegemonic beliefs. For this, look to empirical research in section three of this chapter (Comparing Inequality Across Contexts). The chapter described at the end of this chapter also provides a helpful visualization technique for understanding social mobility.

The mobility and resource distribution paradigms both offer considerable advantages and benefits for helping students understand inequality. Both look holistically at the entire spectrum of socioeconomic positions and statuses which people in a particular society occupy. However, a singular focus on the either the asymmetrical mobility rates or absolute dispersion of resource distributions fails to capture how one's position in the class hierarchy shapes his or her lived reality. For this, we turn to a third and final (for the purposes of this chapter) perspective on socioeconomic inequality.

Relational Poverty

The relational poverty framework focuses explicitly on how socioeconomic inequality shapes the life chances and opportunities of the most disadvantaged members of society. Jencks et al. (1972) make a very important point: poverty is relative. Poverty is defined and understood by assessing how one's economic well-being compares to the economic well-being of others in the society in which they live. They define poverty as the condition in which a person or family is unable to meet their basic needs for food, shelter, and other necessary goods or services.

Importantly, the financial resources necessary to meet one's basic needs vary across societies and the proportion of individuals below the poverty line varies, too. For students to understand inequality, a relational poverty framework centers their attention on whether or not individuals are able to meet their basic needs in a particular context.

Why does this matter for undergraduate instructors? Many undergraduate students come into the classroom with a belief that very few people are truly poor in the United States. They argue that because low-income families have refrigerators and televisions—items many around the world or in previous generations did not have access to—they cannot truly be poor. A relational poverty framework challenges to think about how inequality is relational and consider how many families struggle to meet their basic economic needs. Playspent (playspent.org) is an online activity that simulates the difficult choices low-income individuals routinely make as they decide how to spend their limited financial resources. It is also a useful instructional tool to help students better understand the relational poverty framework.

Comparing Inequality Across Contexts

In order to understand economic inequality on an empirical level students must be familiar with its common measures and the range of those statistics transnationally. Economic inequality is often measured using the relative distributions of income or wealth in a society. One commonly used measurement of this distribution is the Gini coefficient or Gini index, where a perfectly equal society (everyone has exactly the same income) has a Gini coefficient of 0 and a perfectly unequal society (one individual has all of the income and everyone else has no income) has a Gini coefficient of 1 or 100% (Gini 1921; *for a current database see* the websites of the World Bank or Central Intelligence Agency). Another common measure of inequality is the rate of poverty or the percentage of individuals who fall below a certain socially constructed level of income deemed necessary for living. These measures and many others refer to the current position of an individual within the social distribution of economic well-being. However, it is also informative to measure an individual's ability to improve (or worsen) their economic situation, which we refer to as economic or social mobility. Once students have a deeper understanding of the strengths and weakness of the various measures, they have the foundation to understanding the range of economic inequality that exists in the social world.

Perhaps the simplest way to demonstrate the levels of inequality across countries is with the list of countries ranked by Gini coefficients, where the five most unequal countries are Lesotho, South Africa, Central African Republic, Micronesia, and Haiti while the most equal countries are Slovenia, Ukraine, Denmark, Sweden, and Czechia (CIA 2016). Students will likely be unfamiliar with this list, which could be used to challenge their critical thinking skills from previous lessons on economic inequality. Instructors could challenge students to guess the most equal and unequal countries and estimate their Gini coefficients. If the students do not list the United States in their list of the most equal or unequal countries, challenge them to estimate its position on the list.

Another measurement tool for inequality is the level of poverty, which may be more familiar to students, but is still informative. One particular measure of poverty, that may be less familiar to students, is the rate of poverty among single mother households, as measured by the household's employment, education, and age composition. Across 18 affluent Western countries, the United States has the highest levels of poverty for single mother households (Brady and Burroway 2012). In discussions of poverty, it is also important to emphasize the difference between relative poverty (how my income compares to others in my society) versus absolute poverty (a simple measure of my material possessions).

The most dynamic measure of economic inequality is social mobility. Conceptually, social mobility is essential in teaching economic inequality because it complicates the ideal of meritocracy in society. That is, those who work hard should be rewarded with the appropriate economic value and social status. However, social mobility research demonstrates that an individual's likelihood to improve their social position varies greatly across social contexts. Numerous scholarly articles have explored the variations of economic mobility transnationally (Solon 1992, 2002; Torche 2014; Breen 2004; Erikson and Goldthorpe 2002). In particular, Gary Solon compiles previous works to suggest that the United States and United Kingdom have less mobility than Canada, Finland, and Sweden (Solon 2002). Challenge students to position the United States relative to these countries in terms of mobility measures.

Educating students about the various measures of inequality provides the foundation for their own interpretations of economic inequality, especially in a transnational context. It challenges students to realize economic inequality, however we measure it, varies greatly across social contexts and a certain level of inequality is not inevitable. Lastly, a discussion of varying levels of economic mobility will challenge the achievement ideology of the American dream by forcing students to realize that the United States is both less equal and less mobile than other countries.

Consequences of Inequality

Even after all of the above instruction, students, especially the most privileged students, may still ask "so what?" There are other economic models, various levels of inequality and rates of mobility, and inequality is driven by economic circumstances, but how does all of this affect the relatively privileged students who already sit atop the social hierarchy? In response, instructors would benefit from transnational comparisons of various social characteristics based on the levels of inequality.

Hundreds of studies have explored the relationship between societal levels of economic inequality and various measures of social well-being. The majority of these studies find that countries with greater economic inequality are worse off in several measurable social characteristics including: life expectancy, mental illness, violence, imprisonment, lack of trust, racial discrimination, status of women, teenage pregnancy, obesity, drug abuse, and educational achievement (*for a comprehensive review of this literature see* Wilkinson and Pickett 2009; Wilkinson 2005). In the United States, many of these findings hold true when comparing at the state level, where states with higher economic inequality fare worse in these measures of social well-being. In all of these ways, there is a positive correlation between the increasing level of economic inequality in a society and higher prevalence of social problems.

Students confronted with this information may counter that the egalitarian countries tend to be wealthier or that these countries simply have fewer poor people. This argument is refuted by analyses of the same social characteristics with relation to a country's average income or Gross National Product. Most of the social characteristics listed above have no correlation with the average income of a country and the few characteristics that are correlated have greater correlations with the level of economic inequality (*for a comprehensive review of this literature see* Wilkinson and Pickett 2009; Wilkinson 2005). Thus, the prevalence of social problems in a country is explained more by the social position relative to their social context rather than the absolute social position. In other words, a poorer egalitarian society can outperform a wealthier unequal society in a variety of measures.

The most astute students may note that none of this data demonstrates how economic inequality affects the most affluent members of a society. Numerous studies demonstrate that every social class benefits from economic equality. In particular, there are two studies that compare the rates of infant deaths and working-age men between Sweden (a very egalitarian country) and England and Wales (countries with modest levels of inequality). Across every social class, the individuals in Sweden have lower infant mortality and death rates (Leon et al. 1992; Vagero and Lundberg 1989; *see also* Wilkinson and Pickett 2009). When comparing England to the even more unequal society of the United States, England had lower morbidity rates for various diseases across every social class (Banks et al. 2006). Once again, these trends hold true in comparisons of the individual states in the United States (Subramanian and Kawachi 2006; Wolfson et al. 1999). The adverse effects of high levels of inequality are most easily recognizable through a transnational comparative lens. Using the empirical studies outlined above, instructors will be able to challenge their students to think critically about socioeconomic inequality in the United States.

Conclusion

As demonstrated in the preceding passages, socioeconomic inequality in the United States is a multi-faceted and intricately complex phenomenon. Helping students unpack, understand, and critically examine systems of inequality requires a vast repertoire of skills, frameworks, and approaches. We have outlined a theoretical and empirical framework with analytical comparisons that instructors can use in the classroom to develop their students' abilities to understand and critically examine systems of economic inequality.

References

Armstrong, E., & Hamilton, L. T. (2013). *Paying for the party: How college maintains inequality*. Cambridge, MA: Harvard University Press.
Banks, J., Marmot, M., Oldfield, Z., & Smith, J. P. (2006). Disease and disadvantage in the United States and in England. *JAMA, 295*(17), 2037–2045.
Brady, D., & Burroway, R. (2012). Targeting, universalism, and single-mother poverty: A multilevel analysis across 18 affluent democracies. *Demography, 49,* 719–746.
Breen, R. (Ed.). (2004). *Social mobility in Europe*. Oxford: Oxford University Press.
Burawoy, M. (2012). The roots of domination: Beyond Bourdieu and Gramsci. *Sociology, 46*(2), 187–206.
Central Intelligence Agency. (2017). The World Factbook. https://www.cia.gov/library/publications/the-world-factbook/rankorder/2172rank.html.
Erikson, R., & Goldthorpe, J. H. (2002). Intergenerational inequality: A sociological perspective. *Journal of Economic Perspectives, 16*(3), 31–44.
Fernandez, R. M. (2001). Skill-biased technological change and wage inequality: Evidence from a plant retooling. *American Journal of Sociology, 107,* 273–320.
Fischer, C. S., Hout, M., Jankowski, M. S., Lucas, S. R., Swidler, A., & Vos, K. (1996). *Inequality by design: Cracking the bell curve myth*. Princeton, NJ: Princeton University Press.
Gini, C. (1921). Measurement of inequality of incomes. *The Economic Journal, 31*(121), 124–126.
Grusky, D., & Szelenyi, S. (2011). *The inequality reader: Contemporary and foundational readings in race, class, and gender*. Boulder, CO: Westview Press.
Gramsci, A. (1971). *Selections from the prison notebooks*. New York: International Publishers.
Herrnstein, R. J., & Murray, C. (1994). *The Bell Curve: Intelligence and Class Structure in American Life*. New York: Free Press.
Hout, M. (1988). More universalism, less structural mobility: The American occupational structure in the 1980s. *American Journal of Sociology, 93,* 1358–1400.
Jencks, C., Smith, M., Acland, H., Bane, M. J., Cohen, D., Gintis, H., et al. (1972). *Inequality: A reassessment of the effect of family and schooling in America*. New York: Basic Books.
Kalleberg, A. L. (2009). Precarious work, insecure workers: Employment relations in transition. *American Sociological Review, 74*(1), 1–22.
Katznelson, I. (2005). *When affirmative action was white: An untold history of racial inequality in twentieth-century America*. New York: W.W. Norton and Company.
Killewald, A. (2013). Return to *being black, living in the red*: A race gap in wealth that goes beyond social origins. *Demography, 50*(4), 1177–1195.
Korpi, W., & Palme, J. (1998). The paradox of redistribution and strategies of equality: Welfare state institutions, inequality, and poverty in the western countries. *American Sociological Review, 63,* 661–687.

Leon, D. A., Vågerö, D., & Olausson, P. (1992). Social class differences in infant mortality in Sweden: Comparison with England and Wales. *BMJ, 305*(6855), 687–691.
Lucas, S. R. (2001). Effectively maintained inequality: Education transitions, track mobility, and social background effects. *American Journal of Sociology, 106,* 1642–1690.
Mouw, T., & Kalleberg, A. L. (2010). Occupations and the structure of wage inequality in the United States, 1980s to 2000s. *American Sociological Review, 75,* 402–431.
Oliver, M., & Shapiro, T. (2006). *Black wealth/white wealth: A new perspective on racial inequality* (2nd ed.). New York: Routledge.
Piketty, T., & Saez, E. (2003). Income inequality in the United States, 1913–1998. *Quarterly Journal of Economics, 118,* 1–39.
Reardon, S. F. (2011). The widening academic achievement gap between the rich and the poor: New evidence and possible explanations. In Greg J. Duncan & Richard J. Murnane (Eds.), *Whither Opportunity? Rising Inequality, Schools, and Children's Life Chances*. New York: Russell Sage Foundation.
Sen, A. K. (1997). From income inequality to economic inequality. *Southern Economic Journal, 64*(2), 383–401.
Solon, G. (1992). Intergenerational income mobility in the United States. *American Economic Review, 82,* 393–408.
Solon, G. (2002). Cross-country differences in intergenerational earnings mobility. *The Journal of Economic Perspectives., 16*(3), 59–66.
Spilerman, S. (2000). Wealth and stratification processes. *Annual Review of Sociology, 26,* 497–524.
Subramanian, S. V., & Kawachi, I. (2006). Whose health is affected by income inequality? A multilevel interaction analysis of contemporaneous and lagged effects of state income inequality on individual self-rated health in the United States. *Health Place, 12*(2), 141–156.
Torche, F. (2014). Intergenerational mobility and inequality: The Latin American case. *Annual Review of Sociology, 40,* 619–642.
Vagerö, D., & Lundberg, O. (1989). Health inequalities in Britain and Sweden. *The Lancet, 334* (8653), 35–36.
Wilkinson, R. G. (2005). *The impact of inequality: How to make sick societies healthier*. New York City: The New Press.
Wilkinson, R. G., & Pickett, K. E. (2009). Income inequality and social dysfunction. *Annual Review of Sociology, 35,* 493–511.
Weeden, K. A. (2002). Why do some occupations pay more than others? Social closure and earnings inequality in the United States. *American Journal of Sociology, 108,* 55–101.
Wolfson, M., Kaplan, G., Lynch, J., Ross, N., & Backlund, E. (1999). Relation between income inequality and mortality: Empirical demonstration. *BMJ, 319*(7215), 953–957.

Part V
Capitalism and Higher Education: Constraints and Opportunities

Capitalism and the Cost of Textbooks: The Possibilities of Open Source Materials

Annie Gaines

Author's Reflexive Statement

Although I was a part of an upper middle class family in my youth, it wasn't until my family became a single-parent one that I began to notice the socio-economic hierarchical class structure around me and the social value placed on wealth. Living in rural Oregon, most of our neighbors were lower middle class or near poverty. Because of our financial standing, I held several part-time jobs during high school in order to afford college, and the pressure to succeed academically in order to get the scholarships and loans I'd need to attend college was nearly overwhelming. The additional cost of $400 a quarter for textbooks felt like a slap in the face.

Textbook Affordability Is a Problem

Textbooks and course materials are essential tools in higher education, yet these important educational resources remain unaffordable for many students. Textbook prices have increased three times the rate of inflation since 1978 (Perry 2012), and the impact on students is well documented (Senak 2014, 2015, 2016). The average student at a four-year public university was expected to pay an average of $1298 for textbooks and course materials for the 2015–2016 academic year (College Board 2016). And the cost of textbooks for two-year community colleges make up 30% of the total cost of a college degree. As a result of these high textbook costs, 66% of students surveyed by Florida Virtual Campus in 2016 did not purchase the required textbook, and nearly 50% of students reported regularly taking fewer courses (Florida Virtual Campus 2016) (Fig. 1).

A. Gaines (✉)
University of Idaho, Moscow, USA
e-mail: againes@uidaho.edu

K. Haltinner and L. Hormel (eds.), *Teaching Economic Inequality and Capitalism in Contemporary America*, https://doi.org/10.1007/978-3-319-71141-6_22

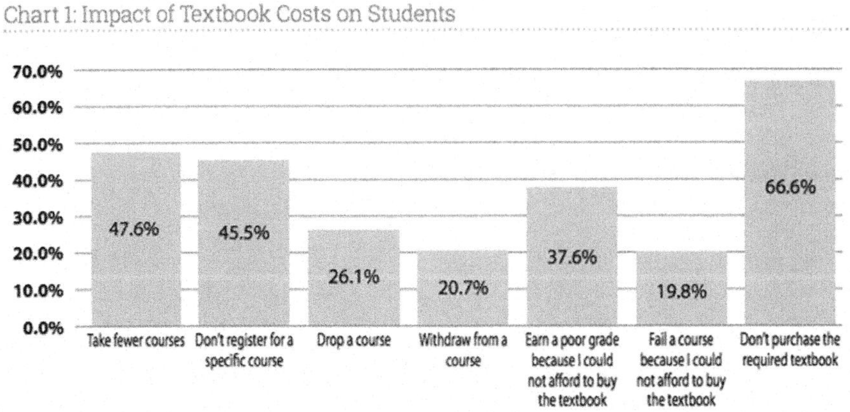

Fig. 1 Florida Virtual Campus (2016). 2016 Florida Student Textbook & Course Materials Survey. Tallahassee, FL. (CC BY)

Academic publishers continue to profit from education by regularly releasing new editions and packaging books with extra software or online access codes that keep the costs of the materials rising (Wischenbart 2014). The additional cost of textbooks can be overwhelming for many low- and middle-income students and families already struggling to afford tuition and fees, and many students have no choice but to go without their textbooks and risk poor academic performance in their courses.

Over the last 30 years, the average tuition at a public four-year university has more than tripled, far over inflation (Jackson 2015). As a result, more students than ever rely on student loans to pay for their college education. Today, 71% of students earning a bachelor's degree graduate with debt, and those debts are, on average,

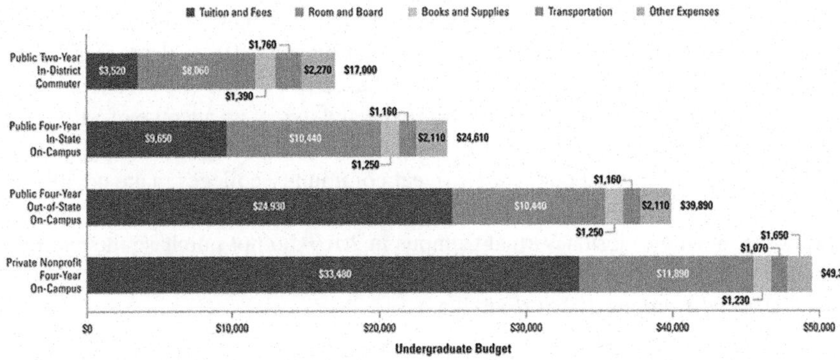

Fig. 2 Average estimated full-time undergraduate budgets (enrollment-weighted) by sector, 2016–17. *Source* https://trends.collegeboard.org/college-pricing/figures-tables/average-estimated-undergraduate-budgets-2016-17

around $30,000 per student (TICAS 2016). This lack of affordability means students from low- and middle-income families are far less likely to pursue a college education, even though it would be a massive benefit to them in the future (Fig. 2).

Open Is a Solution

Over the past several years, an alternative to the traditional commercial textbook system has developed and rapidly expanded—open educational resources.

Open educational resources (OER) include any educational resource that is openly available for use by students and educators without any need to pay for a license or royalties. Open educational resources may be considered a tangent of the open source movement (Brown and Adler 2008), a movement that supports the use of open-source licenses for some or all software. Moving beyond collaboratively edited software code, open educational resources can include syllabi, textbooks, course materials, video and audio, software, applications, along with any other materials that are designed for use in teaching and learning (UNESCO 2002).

The underlying structure of open educational resources, the thing that makes them accessible and free to use and share, is a broad spectrum of frameworks and licenses. The best known of these are the Creative Commons licenses, which provide a simple, standardized way for creators to give permission to share and use their work on the conditions of their choice.

Open textbooks are a type of open educational resource that is peer-reviewed and faculty-written, packaged and structured to align with a course. Many of the first open textbooks available online were created for the most common high-enrollment courses including introductory psychology, biology, and statistics. Additionally, open textbooks have gained attention from governments, including the state of Washington and the state of California (Volmer 2012) as well as the province of British Columbia (Jhangiani et al. 2016). And, it makes sense for governments to fund opportunities to lower the cost of course materials, as billions of scholarship dollars each year go to textbooks.

Open educational resources and open textbooks are most commonly highlighted as alternatives to traditional textbooks for their low cost and accessibility benefits, however, these materials may also enhance student retention and performance. Some evidence suggests that when an open textbook is carefully adapted to suit a particular program it can "increase interactivity and enhance teaching and learning for readers" (Petrides et al. 2011; Jhangiani 2014).

What follows is a summary of faculty and student perceptions and reactions to open educational resources or open textbooks in the classroom.

Overview of Faculty Perceptions

Cost reduction for students is often the most significant factor influencing faculty adoption of open textbooks. In fact, some faculty indicate that the cost of textbooks was a determining factor in the success of their students, as sometimes the cost results in a barrier to accessing these materials. Open textbooks and open educational resources are a logical choice for those faculty looking to reduce costs for their students, as many studies have shown significant savings in courses that adopted OER (e.g., Wiley et al. 2012 and Hilton et al. 2014).

Belikov and Bodily (2016) find that faculty place the highest importance on cost and pedagogical benefits for their students when considering adopting OER, and faculty express that they were willing to spend time to seek out and evaluate open resources. Petrides et al. (2011) find a range of reasons faculty might be motivated to use OER, including student cost savings, a feeling of personal responsibility toward their students, and increasing access and ease of use. One motivating factor for faculty was equal access to materials on day one:

> I like the fact that on day one of the class everyone has the book. With regular textbooks there's hemming and hawing, students will say: 'I don't have the book, it hasn't arrived at the bookstore yet.' (Petrides et al. 2011, p. 43)

Additionally, Pitt (2016) argues that immediate access to course materials is a great benefit to both students and faculty, and allows every student to participate in their preferred way. One educator using OER describes this type of teaching environment:

> The availability of OpenStax textbooks online has allowed me to give more responsibility to my students. They cannot use the excuse that they left their book at home. The textbook is always available and with our class web page, their assignments and handouts are also always available. Easy home access has given us more time to spend working on problems collaboratively in class. In the past when assigning problems as homework, if the student were to get stuck, he/she was stuck. Now, working collaboratively, students answer each other's questions and I am there to help as well. (p. 148)

Bliss et al. (2013) argue that 90% of instructors surveyed report that, when using OER, their students are equally prepared (60%) or more prepared (30%) than students in previous semesters using traditional textbooks. Pitt (2016) finds that educators using OER report increased student participation as a result of using OER in their classes. In fact, most educators feel that OER use in the classroom develops learners' increased independence and self-reliance, allows teachers to better accommodate diverse learners' needs, and increased learners' satisfaction with the learning experience (Pitt 2016).

After engaging with OER Pitt (2016) finds there are two main impacts reported by educators on their teaching practice: around 30% of educators report that using OER makes teaching easier, and around 25% of respondents report that using OER enables innovation or changes their pedagogical approach.

Robinson et al. ((2014) argue that copyrighted materials, including textbooks, directly contribute to the "deskilling of teachers and the sense that the curriculum is beyond their control." Since open educational resources are openly licensed, however, educators can use as much or as little of the book as they like and modify or integrate other resources as needed. Pitt (2016) confirms that openly licensed materials allow educators to take back some of the control which was perceived as lacking. One educator describes the experience of using open textbooks as liberating:

> I am teaching the way I want to teach, in the order and flow that I want. I am free of any text book. The book is a resource… the book no longer drives the course. I produce the curriculum. The book is my servant. I am not its servant. (p. 148)

Pitt (2016) also finds that 95% of educators are more likely to recommend open educational resources to fellow educators as a result of using them. Additionally, Bliss et al. (2013) report that all instructors indicate they would be very likely to use open texts in future courses. Belikov and Bodily (2016) find that 55% of faculty felt the OER was the same quality as traditional resources, and 35% said the OER was better.

Overview of Student Perceptions

Overall, student opinions of open textbooks are high. This is at least partially because of the dramatic cost difference between traditionally published textbooks (which can be upwards of $300 each) and the free or low-cost open textbooks. Additionally, students responded positively to using open textbooks and OER.

Bliss et al. (2013) report that many students feel they are better able to learn with an online book, and some teachers feel that technology helps their students become more interested and engaged in the course material. Many students mention the built-in search functionality in online textbooks, as well as ease of browsing (Bliss et al. 2013). In another study, Bliss et al. (2013) find that students value the interactive and searchable nature of the OER text, and consider their OER text to be easier to understand and better organized than previously used traditional textbooks. Many students are particularly interested in embedded videos, quizzes, visuals and other study guides in the OER (Bliss et al. 2013).

On quality, Bliss et al. (2013) find that students believe the open textbooks to be of high quality: 56% of students rate the OER used in their course as having the same quality as textbooks in other courses, and 41% report the OER was better quality. Belikov and Bodily (2016) also find that approximately half of students surveyed consider the open educational resources used in their course to be the same quality as traditional textbooks, and 40% perceive the OER as better than traditional resources. Although most often educators appreciate the ability to customize and align course materials to their courses, students also note that better alignment with course goals and up-to-date content made the OER a better choice for them than the traditional textbook.

Research shows that students prefer open textbooks, and will seek out courses that use them in the future. Bliss et al. (2013) report that the majority of students exposed to OER in a course would be likely to register for a future course that uses OER. In 2016, Belikov and Bodily found that a majority of students surveyed (65%) prefer using an open textbook and they attribute this preference to cost and ease of use.

Discussion of Barriers and Solutions

Although open educational resources and open textbooks can sometimes seem like the obvious solution to all problems relating to textbooks, it is clear that this isn't the case. Aside from the time taken to prepare a course, issues with the Internet and new technology can be problematic for both educators and students. However, the most prominent issue with OER is a lack of information.

As with any new teaching material, it takes time for educators to familiarize themselves and prepare their courses. However, according to Bliss et al. (2013), most faculty surveyed (82%) spend somewhat more or much more time preparing to teach with open educational resources compared to traditional textbooks they have previously used. This hidden cost of implementation was also noted by Bliss et al. (2013) and Belikov and Bodily (2016).

Among students, a small number had a negative perception of OER. Bliss et al. (2013) find that 10% of students surveyed dislike OER. Those students report low visual appeal, web site issues, online navigation problems, general text uselessness, note-taking limitations, Internet access issues, and low readability. Additionally, Bliss et al. (2013) find that several teachers believe technology to be a barrier to instruction and learning rather than a benefit. This discrepancy between students and educators delighting in new technology and struggling with it indicates the digital divide van Dijk and Hacker (2011) is still a prominent barrier in education.

Some barriers prove there is a significant amount of awareness raising to be done with OER. Belikov and Bodily (2016) find that most faculty would like more information on OER, including what OER is or entails, how to release their materials using open licenses, and where to find reliable OER.

Open Pedagogy in Practice

> Open textbooks save money, which matters deeply to our students. But they can also create a new relationship between learners and course content, and if teachers choose to acknowledge and enable this, it can have a profound effect on the whole fabric of the course. Jumping into the "open" part of the open textbook means opening our eyes to the real hazards and challenges of connecting our courses to a wider public. (DeRosa 2016)

Using open educational resources, in addition to being a useful way for faculty to make their course materials more accessible and affordable to their students, can also be a gateway into changing the way faculty teach. Wiley (2015, 2016) writes extensively on the subject of open pedagogy, and defines it as a set of teaching and learning practices that are only possible or practical through the free access and permissions characteristic of open educational resources. The following examples illustrate how using open educational resources can lead to open pedagogy.

Robin DeRosa, a professor at Plymouth State University, began an open textbook project in order to save her students $85 on an anthology of American literature, but wound up dramatically changing her perspective and teaching pedagogy. DeRosa and her students created *The Open Anthology of Earlier American Literature*, an OER anthology of public domain texts with student created introductions to each piece of literature. Students also completed editorial work on the primary documents, such as modernizing spelling, and produced short films, discussion questions, and assignments related to the primary texts (DeRosa 2016).

Rather than using disposable assignments, DeRosa engaged her students by using class assignments to build on and add to the open textbook, and her students were thrilled. As DeRosa says, "the idea that they were creating something that would be read/used by a different cohort of students a few months later was a truly novel and thrilling concept." DeRosa found that when students were able to contribute to the textbook in their own words and to make editorial decisions about what kinds of materials and discussions to include, they seemed more connected to the textbook and more willing to engage with it (DeRosa 2016).

DeRosa's student work in *The Open Anthology of Earlier American Literature* is a great example of a 'renewable assignment,' an assignment in which the student's work adds value to the world, resulting in meaningful and valuable artifacts that enable future work (Wiley 2016). Confirming DeRosa's findings, Wiley found that students invest significantly more time and effort into renewable assignments, and enjoy doing them more than a disposable assignment (Wiley 2015).

Another example of renewable assignments includes those completed by students in the University of British Columbia's course 'Murder, Madness, and Mayhem: Latin American Literature in Translation.' Motivated in part to encourage students to re-read and reflect upon their own work and to engage in a real world project with tangible and public effects, the Murder, Madness, and Mayhem project set out to bring a selection of Wikipedia articles on Latin American literature to featured article status (Beasley-Murray 2008). Wikipedia's editors consider featured articles the best Wikipedia has to offer, and these articles must go through a peer-review process to assess accuracy, neutrality, completeness, and style (Wikipedia 2017).

In an essay describing the experience, Beasley-Murray found the assignment improved students' research skills and familiarity with writing for a public audience. Wikipedia, he says, does not encourage the kind of persuasive writing usually sought for in a university setting, but it can be a great exercise in critical thinking and research (Beasley-Murray 2008).

In another example of incorporating open educational resources and an open pedagogy into the classroom, a chemistry professor at North Carolina State University collaborated with students to create a series of short videos to replace an organic chemistry lab technique textbook. These lab videos, created by students and for students, were more effective than in-person instruction from a teaching assistant – an average of 17% more students correctly answered questions about laboratory procedure after watching the video compared to a TA lecture (Jordan et al. 2016).

Conclusion

Even though the textbook is the most prominent curriculum delivery method in schools in the United States (Jobrack 2011), its ubiquity is beginning to be questioned. Between skyrocketing costs and the nearly unethical behavior of academic publishers looking to profit off of students, traditional textbooks are quickly becoming too expensive for the average student.

Open educational resources present an alternative to the traditional textbook, one that not only has the ability to save students a significant amount of money and increase access to education, but also has the potential to open up the practice of teaching. Open textbooks and open educational resources have a positive impact on both students and teachers. Bell hooks writes that "the classroom remains the most radical space of possibility in the academy" (Hooks 1994). Why not use this radical space to test new curriculum delivery methods?

Literature Cited

Beasley-Murray, J. (2008). *Was introducing Wikipedia to the classroom an act of madness leading only to mayhem if not murder?* [*Essay*]. Retrieved from https://en.wikipedia.org/wiki/User:Jbmurray/Madness.

Belikov, O. M., & Bodily, R. (2016). Incentives and barriers to OER adoption: A qualitative analysis of faculty perceptions. *Open Praxis, 8*(3), 235–246.

Bliss, T. J., Hilton, J., Wiley, D., & Thanos, K. (2013). The cost and quality of open textbooks: Perceptions of community college faculty and students. *First Monday, 18*(1).

Bliss, T. J., Robinson, T. J., Hilton, J., & Wiley, D. A. (2013). An OER COUP: College teacher and student perceptions of open educational resources. *Journal of Interactive Media in Education*.

Brown, J. S. & Adler, R. P. (2008, January–February). Minds on fire: Open education, the long tail, and learning 2.0. *EDUCAUSE Review, 43*(1), 16–20, 22, 24, 26, 28, 30, 32.

College Board. (2016). *Average estimated undergraduate budgets, 2016–17*. Retrieved from https://trends.collegeboard.org/college-pricing/figures-tables/average-estimated-undergraduate-budgets-2016-17.

Creative Commons. (2017). *What we do*. Retrieved from https://creativecommons.org/about/.

DeRosa, R. (2016, June 24). *My open textbook: pedagogy and practice* [*Blog post*]. Retrieved from http://umwdtlt.com/open-textbook-pedagogy-practice/.

Florida Virtual Campus. (2016). *2016 student textbook and course materials survey*. Tallahassee, FL.

Hendricks, C. (2015, October 29). *Renewable assignments: Student work adding value to the world* [*Blog post*]. Retrieved from http://flexible.learning.ubc.ca/news-events/renewable-assignments-student-work-adding-value-to-the-world/.

Hilton, J., Robinson, T., Wiley, D., & Ackerman, J. (2014). Cost-savings achieved in two semesters through the adoption of open educational resources. *The International Review of Research in Open and Distributed Learning*.

Hooks, B. (1994). *Teaching to transgress: Education as the practice of freedom.* New York: Routledge.

Jackson, A. (2015). *This chart shows how quickly college tuition has skyrocketed since 1980*. Retrieved from http://www.businessinsider.com/this-chart-shows-how-quickly-college-tuition-has-skyrocketed-since-1980-2015-7.

Jhangiani, R. S. (2014). *A faculty perspective on open textbooks* [*Blog post*]. Retrieved from https://thatpsychprof.com/2014/04/.

Jhangiani, R. S., Pitt, R., Hendricks, C., Key, J., & Lalonde, C. (2016). *Exploring faculty use of open educational resources at British Columbia post-secondary institutions. BCcampus research report*. Victoria, B.C.: BCcampus.

Jobrack, B. (2011). *Tyranny of the textbook: An insider exposes how educational materials undermine reforms*. Lanham, MD: Rowman & Littlefield.

Jordan, J. T., Box, M. C., Eguren, K. E., Parker, T. A., Saraldi-Gallardo, V. M., Wolfe, M. I., et al. (2016). Effectiveness of student-generated video as a teaching tool for an instrumental technique in the organic chemistry laboratory. *Journal of Chemical Education, 93,* 141–145. https://doi.org/10.1021/acs.jchemed.5b00354.

Perry, M. J. (2012). *The college textbook bubble and how the "open educational resources" movement is going up against the textbook cartel*. Retrieved from http://www.aei.org/publication/the-college-textbook-bubble-and-how-the-open-educational-resources-movement-is-going-up-against-the-textbook-cartel/.

Petrides, L., Jimes, C., Middleton-Detzner, C., Walling, J., & Weiss, S. (2011). Open textbook adoption and use: Implications for teachers and learners. *Open Learning, 26*(1), 39–49.

Pitt, R. (2016). Mainstreaming open textbooks: Educator perspectives on the impact of OpenStax College open textbooks. *International Review of Research in Open and Distributed Learning, 16*(4), 133–155.

Robinson, T. J., Fischer, L., Wiley, D., & Hilton, J. (2014). The impact of open textbooks on secondary science learning outcomes. *Educational Researcher, 43*(7), 341–351.

Senak, E. (2014). *Fixing the broken textbook market: How students respond to high textbook costs and demand alternatives*. Washington, D.C.: Student PIRGS. Retrieved from http://www.uspirg.org/reports/usp/fixing-broken-textbook-market.

Senack, E. (2015). *Open textbooks: The billion dollar solution. The Student PIRGs*. Retrieved from: http://studentpirgs.org/reports/sp/open-textbooks-billion-dollar-solution.

Senak, E. (2016). *Covering the cost: Why we can no longer afford to ignore high textbook prices*. Washington, D.C.: Student PIRGS. Retrieved from http://www.uspirg.org/reports/usp/covering-cost.

The Institute for College Access & Success (TICAS). (2016). *Student debt and the class of 2015*. http://ticas.org/sites/default/files/pub_files/classof2015.pdf.

UNESCO. (2002). *Forum on the impact of open courseware for higher education in developing countries. Final report*. Retrieved from www.unesco.org/iiep/eng/focus/opensrc/PDF/OERForumFinalReport.pdf.

Van Dijk, J., & Hacker, K. (2011). The digital divide as a complex and dynamic phenomenon. *The Information Society, 19*(4), 315–326.

Volmer, T. (2012, September 27). *California passes groundbreaking open textbook legislation* [*blog post*]. Retrieved from https://creativecommons.org/2012/09/27/california-passes-groundbreaking-open-textbook-legislation/.

Wikipedia. (2017). *Wikipedia: Featured articles*. Retrieved from https://en.wikipedia.org/wiki/Wikipedia:Featured_articles.

Wikipedia staff. (2008, April 14). "*Interview with the team behind one of the 2000th featured articles*." *Wikipedia Signpost*. Retrieved from https://en.wikipedia.org/wiki/Wikipedia:Wikipedia_Signpost/2008-04-14/2000th_FA.

Wiley, D., Hilton, J., Ellington, S., & Hall, T. (2012). A preliminary examination of the cost savings and learning impacts of using open textbooks in middle and high school science classes. *The International Review of Research In Open and Distributed Learning, 13*(3), 262–276.

Wiley, D. A. (2015, December 3). *Reflections on open education and the path forward* [*Blog post*]. Retrieved from https://opencontent.org/blog/archives/4082.

Wiley, D. A. (2016, July 7). *Toward renewable assessments* [*Blog post*]. Retrieved from https://opencontent.org/blog/archives/4691.

Wischenbart, R. (2014). *The global ranking of the publishing industry 2014. Livres Hebdo*. Retrieved from: http://www.wischenbart.com/upload/Global-Ranking-of-thePublishing-Industry_2014_Analysis.pdf.

Writing Against Ideology: Exploring Strategies that Resist Assessment Orthodoxy in the Classroom

Joshua Olsberg and Raphi Rechitsky

Authors' Reflexive Statements

Joshua Olsberg is a first-generation Cuban-American and first-generation college student. Rechitsky came to the United States at a young age, also an expatriate of state socialism, of Soviet Ukraine. Both benefited from upward mobility of our families as a result of our state status as prized exiles during the Cold War, rather than unwelcome, "illegal" immigrants. Olsberg remembers realizing the extent to which the space he was in was a privileged one, and observing the profound inequities in education propelled that propelled him into graduate work and teaching. Rechitsky came to observe a contrast in the ideology and lifeworld, in his family's earnest beliefs in American meritocracy clashing with lived reality of struggles with work in a changing labor market. In graduate school, both authors grew increasingly committed to the transformative power of critical theory and critical pedagogy. Both authors have experienced teaching at both large research Universities and private liberal arts universities. However, it was not until coming teach at our current position, at an open-enrollment institution serving primarily nontraditional working class students, that we came to such a sharp critique of market-driven higher education models. We saw how much our students struggled to critically reflect on course content, and that writing assignments proved daunting and frustrating. Thus, we took up a seed grant service opportunity (offered by our college) to improve our teaching practice by focusing on writing.

In 2015, we observed how the administration of our growing private university introduced plans to implement another emerging policy trend in education policy of

J. Olsberg (✉) · R. Rechitsky
National University, San Diego, USA
e-mail: jolsberg@nu.edu

R. Rechitsky
e-mail: rrechitsky@nu.edu

K. Haltinner and L. Hormel (eds.), *Teaching Economic Inequality and Capitalism in Contemporary America*, https://doi.org/10.1007/978-3-319-71141-6_23

so-called “precision learning.” A cousin of competency-based education, this effort sought to move the university away from subject-matter coursework in scholarly fields and towards the assessment of a plethora of skill-based “competencies.” Originally developed for vocational and then primary education in the 1980s, precision learning was originally designed as a teaching method to customize and individualize student learning to match existing strengths and interests of their institutions (White 1986; Koorland et al. 1990). Yet, precision learning increasingly represents an artifact of contemporary hyper-assessment culture in higher education, which seeks to undo liberal arts principles of education as part of the scientific enterprise, and represents but one recent manifestation of neoliberal rationalization (see Neem 2013).

A consequential component of any alternatives to assessment orthodoxy, we urge, must engage students in writing as an iterative process centered around critical thinking. Understanding the way students approach writing and critical thinking activities is vital to constructing them in a useful manner, and augmenting existing pedagogical practices to be more attuned to not only each student’s particular needs and skills, as well as their collective experiences under capitalism. In the pages that follow, we explore three activities as interventions we believe address problems facing especially working class and first generation students, seeking to also understand and unpack the depth of student responses to activities that challenge them. We start with a reflexive question: how do we judge the efficacy of teaching interventions when we seek to separate ourselves from conventional capitalist modes of teaching assessment?

Introduction

A cursory glance at the typical university website offers images that have become familiar to those of us working in higher education: colorful pictures of smiling students, attached to words like investment, choice, success, and so on. Our students come to our classrooms with expectations molded by such images. The corporatization of higher education since the late 1980s, and recent federal policy promoting initiatives such as “competency-based education,” set expectations of education not only as a capitalist project (e.g., Neem 2013), but also as a pedagogical process.

Even as market value may be assigned to the liberal arts, business-driven discourse promoting market-ready degrees implies that the value of education is measured solely by the presumed subsequent increase in income and professional status cashed-in for a degree. This transactional vision of education not only obscures exploitation inherent in all paid labor, but denigrates the value of science and self-discovery integral to a civic vision of higher education. Lost in the market-ready vision of education are not only the harsh realities of the labor market, but also the very Greek root of the word scholar, as one who seeks to live with ease in the collectivity of a demos, as a result of scrupulous study. Instead, the student as scholar is replaced with a model of the student as Horatio Alger, who heroically finishes their degree–that is as efficiently and painlessly as possible–in hopes of cashing in on American dreams of a life of plenty.

The entrenchment of a market-based value of education calls for teaching strategies that encourage critical thought as well as the means by which it can be expressed. This essay addresses a central challenge instructors face, to practice a kind of pedagogy that uncovers the social forces reproducing the myth of meritocracy under capitalism, without succumbing to the logics of neoliberal rationalization enforced with assessment orthodoxy. In what ways do the political and economic modalities of spaces of assessment in higher education mediate the teacher-student relationship and impact possibilities for consciousness? How do we find ways to reveal the emancipatory potential of critical thinking to our students as the system increasingly curtails its use?

Inequality and ideology leave many students, particularly those that are working class or first generation, arriving to college ill-prepared to engage in critical thinking about the social conditions that structure their life experiences. Furthermore, students are often deprived of training necessary to begin transforming real and existing critical observations into carefully constructed and intellectually sound writing. Dominant assessment practices in education, on one hand, and the culture of advanced capitalism, on the other hand, shape student perceptions of themselves and possibilities for learning, and the capacity to interpret information they encounter daily as students as well as workers and consumers.

In this essay, we discuss approaches to teaching and critical thinking and writing about and under capitalism, while exploring three different kinds of writing-based activities that depart from trends toward hyper-assessment in higher education in the United States. For two terms in 2015 and 2016, we devised three different types of writing activities in core courses in sociology and interdisciplinary studies. The activities included interactive, argumentative, and essay revision types of writing. We implemented these activities in core curriculum and introductory courses in two different undergraduate programs.

We first review critical theories and studies of about writing and pedagogy about capitalism and inequality, and reflect on our personal and professional standpoint within higher education. We then detail three types of writing-based activities: interactive reflections, timed-writing, and peer revision. Finally, we discuss the implications of these activities on the scholarship of pedagogy and the significance of student reactions to these activities.

Teaching About Capitalism, Writing Under Capitalism

Agger (1989) defines the problem of writing and thinking critically in what he calls "Fast Capitalism" as one in which critique (the result of critical thinking becoming actuated as writing) is no longer effective because it fails to achieve necessary distance from the object it seeks to analyze. We all find difficulty in writing meaningful critiques of capitalism because capital has co-opted the act of critique into its rubric of everyday activities. In the classroom, students often struggle to do more than reproduce fragments of doxic political discourse such as the 'American Dream' myth. Ideology may cloud the process of accessing and assessing empirical evidence, curtailing the agency students already carry to analyze their lifeworlds from a critical perspective. Here, writing becomes an act of reproducing hegemonic narratives about the myth of American meritocracy rather than an emancipatory form of creative labor that critiques one's lifeworld. The role of instructors, then, is to aid students in reconnecting their lifeworld to their writing to regain authorial agency.

The problem of writing and cultivating a critical consciousness are compounded by the one-dimensionality (Marcuse 1964) of education in contemporary capitalist societies. Even well-meaning instructors are often inundated with the rationalization of the education system under advanced capitalism, their lesson plans held captive by assessment imperatives of the modern culture industry of producing marketable flexible labor. In this context, working class students' capacities to sustain critical ideas that might undermine the capitalist system through writing practice are absorbed in the system's, "supreme promise [of] an ever-more-comfortable life for an ever-growing number of people who… cannot imagine a qualitatively different universe of discourse and action" (Marcuse 1964, p. 23). Any model of education that precludes the possibility of seeing beyond the parameters of the system is authoritarian in nature.

Freire (1970) criticized authoritarian "banking models" of education that placed power in an all-seeing instructor. Instead critical thinking needs to be prioritized in terms of a liberatory education in a process that levels power relations in the classroom between student and teacher. This became the precept rather than the outcome of any kind assessment of student success—here class-consciousness. A Freirian approach provides a way forward to centering critical thinking and writing across the education process instead of around currently popular models of assessment as means-based testing. Freire (1970, pp. 57–64) insists that critical pedagogy must challenge dominant "banking" models of teacher-student relationships where knowledge is but "a gift bestowed upon" an "ignorant" student by an "all-knowing" teacher. He advises that this tendency encourages educators in, "[r]ationalizing [their] guilt through paternalistic treatment of the oppressed. Instead, he urges that in teaching *with* working class students, "solidarity requires that one enter into the situation of those with whom one is [in] solidarity; it is a radical posture." (Freire 1970, p. 34). Following the Freirian model of pedagogy, strategies that may be most successful are those that see the dialectical relationship between teaching capitalism within the classroom and teaching about capitalism beyond its walls, those that can both compel agentic knowledge production coming from students' common experiences "in here," but also not limited to them by challenging students to tease out the social forces endemic to capitalism "out there."

We see student challenges with writing as symptomatic of these fault lines, and what has been widely described as a hidden curriculum (e.g., Margolis 2001) that de-prioritizes critical thinking for working class students before they arrive in college. Challenging the diffusion of a hidden curriculum into higher education still demands that social science instructors directly and systematically address writing and critical thinking concerns, even as they are presenting the core concepts particular to their disciplines. Institutions of higher education increasingly represent the front line in this struggle over the transformation of higher education (Neem 2013). The forces of corporatization have accelerated and spread to educational practices themselves (Schrecker 2010). Especially since the great recession of 2008, both the "audit culture" and discourse of assessment (Taubman 2010) have advanced from high-stakes testing in primary schools to reorganize the college classroom itself.

Assessment orthodoxy has facilitated a neoliberal rationalization of the classroom in a way that has resulted in the advance of what Freire criticized as a banking model, now into what we call a *speculative model* of education. Consequently, students are taught to see education not as a right aimed at developing their capacity to be a citizen, but rather as an individual financial investment, where skills become an abstraction through which each seek returns in an ever-changing labor market. Moleswoth et al. (2009) see parallels in the British university system, noting the transition in which students now seek to *have a degree, rather than be learners*. As Newsom (2004) points out, this makes the project of implementing critical pedagogical practices more difficult than ever–the speculative model promises to emancipate students via the mechanism of consumptive choice within their educational experience, all the while through standardization of teaching it actually limits the extent to which education is student-centered. In this guise, an educator is reduced to a transferer of information and human capital, facilitating a smooth and predictable learning experience for the student-investor. On the one hand, we recognize that an educator is faced with the choice to either, "perpetuate the institutional structures and people who hold power in the structure, or to be critical of the institution and those who hold power as a means to lessen oppression." (Breunig 2005) On the other hand, even having the ability to make that choice seems less likely, as our methods of delivering course content and assessing learning become more constrained. Our teaching approach looks for a diverse set of writing-based activities to disrupt this speculative model of education, exploring an alternative to assessment orthodoxy.

Three Different Types of Writing Activities

This essay was motivated by a small study in service of a pilot teaching project looking to assess changes in student writing with innovative activities. After a review of literature on assessment orthodoxy, however, we instead decided to challenge this approach by preparing a symbiotic range of writing activities, as opposed to threading the needle of precision, and seek to determine the relative value of one kind of activity over another.

The sample activities we present include three types of exercises related to interactive, argumentative/analytic, and revision-based writing activities. The first entails the use of short writing assignments as an expansion of activities simulating and discussing inequality through active or experiential learning. Second, argumentative/analytic essays ask students to write critically about current events. A third type of activity involves the incorporation of multiple editing and peer-review sessions ahead of major term papers. Its aim is to allow students to carefully formulate strategies for robust substantive revision based on collective and guided small group discussion of written work.

We explore the efficacy of these three teaching strategies in the following pages, with consideration to the following three goals priorities for critical thinking and writing:

1. Understand the logic behind social reasoning and the scientific method behind the use of evidence and source materials,
2. Develop arguments with attention to peers and target audience,
3. Explore their voice as writers with an identified and reflexive contribution to an existing conversation.

Interactive Simulation and Writing Reflection

The first of three activities we use is an interactive simulation of socioeconomic inequality, combined with a guided writing reflection. The motivation for using an interactive activity is, as Hilligoss (1992) found, comes from our assumption that working class students perform better in classrooms where interactive teaching methods are utilized, as compared to classrooms using a traditional lecture format. Specifically, inequality simulations illustrate the uneven distribution of resources reflected in capitalist societies by demonstrating the mechanisms reproducing social structure. A more in-depth debrief following interactive activities, we presume, enables students to better-reflect on structural inequality and link it to their own lifeworld, as well as the mechanisms reproducing differential life chances.

We elected to use Coghlan' and Huggins' (2004) "Stratification Monopoly" simulation. We opted to develop this widely-used activity, choosing it from a range of other inequality simulations published in the journal *Teaching Sociology* and other sources like "The Society Pages" (Coghlan and Huggins 2004; Groves et al. 1996; Jessup 2001; Giuffre and Paxton 1997). Coghlan and Huggins' (2004) simulation is especially useful for our purposes since it both claims to be an "effective tool for demonstrating the structural nature of social inequality" (177), and since this efficacy is said to be based on feedback from students themselves. However, we suppose that Coghlan and Huggins' activity design could be more effective at developing critical thinking if a more robust writing assignment can be combined with the interactive activity.

To tap into connections to students' life experience beyond the classroom, we develop this simulation to include a lengthy writing reflection. But, first, we set up the "Stratification Monopoly" activity per Coghlan and Huggins' instructions

(2004, pp. 179–182). Re-designing several standard Monopoly board games, starting assets and income for "passing go" are distributed differently for each of the five players, proportionally to actual quintiles in the U.S. wealth and income distribution. After playing this game for thirty-minutes, students compare their final assets to their starting position. They then debrief with a short worksheet built into the debrief of the activity itself (see Coghlan and Huggins 2004, Appendix A and B). In our version of the assignment, we introduce an additional writing activity to allow students time to reflect on the significance of their observations.

We first were surprised about the extent to which our students enthusiastically engaged in the activity with a curiosity rarely unseen in other coursework. Previously accustomed to rigid top-down educational settings, we observed how our working class students appreciated both the interactive and hands-off character of a simulation with much intrigue. In mid-term and final evaluations, students remembered and even went on to praise this activity and its lessons as most impactful on their learning. One student described the simulation as "clever and enjoyable," while another alluded to its "creativity," explaining that it helped them get to know their classmates much better. We believe that its self-interested engagement, rooted in working class experience that makes possible the surprise students go on to express about the difficulties for upward social mobility in the simulation.

Nevertheless, after some minutes of completing the short accompanying assignment, the debriefing began with two vocal students passionately repeating the meritocratic tenants of American capitalism. They pointed to the importance of "hard work" for the one observed instance of upward mobility among twenty of their peers playing the game. Other students moderated those thoughts, but remained reticent to give a structural explanation of the impact of the initial wealth distribution; "luck had something to do with it, too," a third student added.

To advance the lesson, the class was then instructed to begin an additional part to the assignment, a fifteen-minute writing activity. Students wrote a 300-word essay. First asked to reflect on their observations on the worksheet, students start with a thesis that would represent a reasonable conclusion explaining the outcome of the game. We found that it is only after this writing reflection, that we a more critical discussion emerged. Mobilized by the observations in an interactive activity, but now also having reflected on these observations through writing, students stepped into identify the primacy of structure in the simulation for explaining a largely unchanged wealth distribution. One student noted how the "rich got richer" from rent on properties "at the expense of the poor getting poorer." Two students representing the poorest quintile noted their declining enthusiasm, linking this to a homework reading criticizing the culture of poverty thesis (Gans 1990). This brought the class into a discussion of the culture of capitalism, as encouraged by cutthroat competition in the game (this is why nobody changed the rules to redistribute wealth, one student pointed out). In their short essays all but one student argued—many quite passionately—about the importance of wealth distribution for perpetuating social inequality and social problems. Others ostensibly identified the divergence of life chances through the game itself, for players with different needs for rent paid and chance cards drawn during the game.

Asking students to write reflective essays soon after simulations improved student capacity to critically analyze observations they had previously struggled to articulate. Such reflection essays, when combined with simulations develop authorial agency by demanding students construct a clear thesis deduced from a set of their own observations. In a reflection writing activity, observation and logic, rather than ethics alone, motivates students to reflect on the social problems engendered by structural inequality.

Timed Analytic Essays

Given that market-driven constraints under which educational institutions operate often deny working class students the means of effectively critiquing the social conditions in which they operate, we sought to create an intervention that pushed students to analyze those conditions while also reflecting upon the uses of writing in leveling critique. These timed analytic essays were given in-class in the second and fourth week of the course. Students were informed ahead of time that they would be completing an in-class essay, and that they could use their laptops to help them find appropriate sources, but that is all the information they had prior to arriving to class that day. When students asked if they should include particular course materials in their response, they were told to use their best judgment and rely upon building their argument with the most reliable peer-reviewed sources. They were given 60 min to complete the essay. They were prompted to read a brief news article (around 750 words), and asked to write an op-ed to their local newspaper in response to the article informed by the terms and concepts taught in class (see appendix). The news articles all had something to do with the rise of mass surveillance and governmental use of digital technology as a means of extending its power—central themes in the course.

Though the 'Letter to the Editor' format of the assignment is not the typical way that academic writing is done, we sought to simulate the conditions under which students would encounter current affairs covered in news media in their daily life, and asked them to produce an evidence-based argument in response to that content. Most of us have only a small amount of time each day outside of work and family activities, and in that time we must encounter the world refracted through various forms of media, determine the veracity of that content, and formulate our opinions in short order.

We believe that engaging in this outward facing style of critical analysis is profoundly important to working class students, and represents an opportunity for them to understand the value of applying otherwise abstract theoretical thinking. With that in mind, after the students completed and submitted their essays the class would take a brief break, then come back to discuss the assignment. The discussion ranged from specific strategies students used to answer the question to general discussions about writing and critical thinking. The instructor allowed students to take the time to reflect upon how building an argument using evidence changed their approach to writing, but also to simply vent their frustrations regarding the painstaking nature of scientific thought.

Some students were successful in at least building the foundation of a critical analysis on the subject. For example one student was able to make several important connections in her analysis of NSA surveillance and the revelations made by Edward Snowden. In her response she:

1. Correctly identified that the Fourth Amendment was a key legal document in regards to the case,
2. Incorporated the relevance of the concept of the panopticon (even including a quote from a Republican congressman who stated that Jeremy Bentham would be a top government consultant were he alive today).

And identified a general trend towards increased surveillance of people's consumptive practices by private corporations as being an important consideration in formulating one's position on the issue.

Often, students seemed reticent (particularly on the first of the two timed analytic essays) to attempt to utilize terms and concepts from the course to articulate their perspectives. One student cited two peer-reviewed sources that discussed the relevance of the panopticon to the issue of surveillance, but she did not elaborate on the idea in her own terms: the citations were left more or less unattended.

Some students had trouble moving beyond the realm of their own personal experiences to a broader view on the issue. One student responded by writing almost exclusively on her negative emotional response to the article, but did not incorporate peer-reviewed research. She only briefly touched upon our class readings in Foucault at the end of her essay, but in a way generally disconnected from the rest of the response. Interestingly, the feedback from the instructor and discussion of academic writing seemed to make an impact between the first and second versions of this assignment. She was far more successful in utilizing relevant peer-reviewed research the second time, and her opinion was built through the facts she presented.

Term Paper Revisions

While interactive and timed writing activities tone existing interest in critical thinking and short writing formats, an extensive and shared writing assignment develops capacity towards more complex forms of writing by encouraging students to work together. While the first two assignments' focus on inequality under capitalism, this assignment takes the pedagogical method of collective work as the innovation, modeling scientific peer review as a process that enlists students in collaboration they are too-often discouraged from under banking models of education.

The classes in which we piloted various interventions featured lengthy and involved peer-editing sessions. We oriented these activities primarily on the distinction between *Higher Order Concerns* and *Lower Order Concerns* in editing, as defined by the Purdue Online Writing Lab. Purdue OWL prompts students to move beyond proofreading for grammar, and begin seeing editing as a process in which the student should engage the logic, scope, and purpose of written work, teaching students how to improve essays in four discrete areas of *thesis, audience, organization, and development*. The following two versions of our revision activity give two assignment structures for this tool, which go beyond a simplistic pair-and-share format, and develop a rigorous form of collaboration in a semester-long writing assignment.

Olsberg's Revision Assignment

Our editing sessions generally involve firm ground rules meant to keep the students focused on Higher Order Concerns, though we have tried a few variations on the precise format. An example of some of the typical ground rules would be:

- no nice comments, only critique will help your partner improve
- no comments about the flow of the paper, focus on whether the paper addresses the assignment parameters
- no discussion spelling, grammar, or other Lower Order Concerns
- pay close attention to the sources your classmate used and from where they come (they should be peer-reviewed).

We try to make these rules as explicit as possible primarily because we have often found our students be reticent to critique of their classmates' work. We believe this to be because students do not have a clear understanding of strategies for editing academic writing, and therefore do not see themselves as having the authority to offer specific critiques. Giving attention and time to discussing editing strategies and a mandate to be critical rather than overly courteous is meant to empower students to engage the writing process as scholars typically do, something we hope will allow them to develop a sense of themselves as intellectuals.

Once the initial session is complete, we reconvene as a class and discuss the feedback partners give one another, reflect upon how the feedback is useful in addressing Higher Order Concerns, and conceive of strategies for editing moving forward. Often, these group sessions reveal that students are conducting research along similar lines and spark dialogues about approaches to studying certain topic and various disciplinary perspectives. Some student comments reflect a sense of personal growth and accomplishment which stemmed in part from such discussions. One student said, "I'm very proud of the work I turned in and I know that I did the best I could. I am especially proud of my research paper. I learned a lot, too. A lot of discussions we had in class sparked curiosity in things I never really thought to think about before." This particular student admitted that he lacked confidence in his writing, but seeing other students' work and coming to better understand that writing is an ongoing and often difficult process helped him to see he was not alone in his struggles. During one of the post-editing discussions, the instructor showed students early iterations of what eventually became a published academic article, describing his own struggles—the students seemed to appreciate that even professional scholars experience misgivings similar to their own.

We believe that this approach to teaching writing, which incorporates into the activity a meta-discussion on the value of editing and a reflection upon the connections between thinking, writing and editing, encourages ownership of the written work on the part of the student.

Rechitsky's Revision Assignment

Another version of the revision assignment may focus on peer review as part of a multi-step term paper. At the start of two different core curriculum sociology courses, students are provided more detailed instructions than can be relayed here for writing a term paper across an accelerated ten-week term:

Part 1: Topic Statement, Due: Week 2

Part 2: Outline, Due: Week 3

Part 3: Full Draft, Due: Week 6

Part 4: Peer Review, Due: Week 7

Part 5: Revised Draft, Due: Week 10

Gauging the range of writing abilities, the first three parts of the assignment guide students to a substantive focus of the paper in a given course. Students are warned that their draft must be a complete paper, and represent their best work. Though much of the writing is completed as homework, the in-class work of the fourth part of the assignment is central, and takes about thirty to forty five minutes across two consecutive class sessions. During the first class session, students come to class not only with another copy of a full draft of their paper they turned in days earlier to the instructor, but also having exchanged those papers with a peer. This class begins with an overview of the peer review process in the academy, and an exchange of papers with a peer working on a paper with a similar subfield. Students then read a handout about detecting *higher order concerns* in writing. Each student spends ten to fifteen minutes reviewing their peer's paper, devising four specific questions that ask for clarification from their peer, one question in each of the four higher order concerns. Next, students spend another ten to fifteen minutes in a pair-and-share discussion interviewing their peer using the questions they have formulated, seeking clarification about the peer's paper that they have now read twice. Students are also instructed to take notes about their peer's answers during the interview.

The instructor may also take this opportunity to circulate around the room to hear student responses reflecting on their own draft writing.

Before the second class of peer review, students complete a formal assignment for homework. Given instructions about how to mark their peer's paper, they are asked to use what they learned in their peer interview, and in reading of their paper, towards writing a 300–500 page peer review identifying examples of key Higher Order Concerns. This assignment is turned into both their peer and the instructor at the next class period, when students read their peer's review, and go on to write a brief self-assessment of their own draft after reading their peer's review, as to help plan for revisions for their own work towards part five of the assignment. Finally, in a feedback session, students are asked to evaluate what they learned about the process of revision. This feedback reinforces the lessons for developing writing skills based both on the instructor's feedback they should have reviewed, as well as the feedback provided by their peers.

For term papers, we observed how students' first express frustration with the revision dimension of the assignment. However, in feedback sessions, we have learned that students come to articulate a deep appreciation for the opportunity to reflect on their writing in real time with a peer engaged in the substantive dimensions of their work. Students go on with inspiration to the process of write a longer and more developed final draft, addressing instructor and some peer suggestions.

Student Responses to Rigorous Writing

The next section is a reflection about how students respond to rigorous activities with an increased emphasis on writing, critical thinking, and editing. While some students have reacted with mere frustration of increased rigor of writing, others have acknowledged the value of struggling to improve skills and capacities. We acknowledge, as recent research has shown, that student evaluations do not reflect student learning (Stark and Freishtat 2014). However, we suppose that we should take seriously the challenges students expressed, understanding them as variegated types of intellectual struggle in the context of higher education under advanced capitalism.

We found two types of struggle expressed by students after their writing. On one hand, frustration first arises out of the expectations of a market-driven model of education. In focusing on the pushing students through to the degree in the shortest duration possible, this model intrinsically eschews any notion of challenge and development as necessary to education, with students' expectations aligning the means to those goals through that logic. So when students are challenged with new ways of thinking and writing, in particular, they often lash back, something we see on instructor evaluations and other feedback on more advanced yet otherwise typical courses: "I understand what it means to be in an upper level class, but the homework's [sic] are simply too much." A student in a lower-division course similarly announced, "I think the instructor's workload was ridiculous in many ways because as a full time working parent it was hard to just sit down and read this material and write out a online journal that was going to be critiqued. I am glad that its [sic] just over." The source of frustration with workload may be both a reaction to higher expectations in the context of (1) low workload expectations promoted by our institution, but also (2) the broader context of a market-based model of education where students seek the straightest (most struggle-free) path to a degree. After all, the rigor of the writing assignments pushes students to acquire writing skills working class students may be still developing, or had even been taught to resist. Many seek out fast degree programs such as provided by our Universities as nontraditional students, with education on the side of family and careers: "the workload was unmanageable…I understand the point of each assignment but I was under the impression that National was formatted for students who also work or have families." Frustrated as well as constructive comments from students reflected the challenges of a standard college workload, but combined with high personal grade and high institutional expectations of time-to-degree.

However, it is just as notable how similarly such students instead came to perceive their challenges with writing, instead, as a *positive struggle* rather than a negative one. Reflective of such positive struggle, a student from one of the early courses in which we piloted our new approach had this to say:

> I wanted to take the opportunity to say thank you. Looking back on the course, I feel that I may have come off a bit over dramatic on my struggling through the course. It probably came across too in my course evaluation. While, I did struggle, I feel it was a struggle in a positive way. I'm very proud of the work I turned in and I know that I did the best I could.

Some of the same students begin to see the value of challenges to critical thinking through writing, undermining the struggle-free version of learning encouraged by education under capitalism. In a final self-evaluation, one student wrote, "the theory paper was difficult…I never compared theories and required a lot of rewriting. Still, I believe that I have written a paper that explains what I was trying to convey." Students proud of their work product due to the process of education are further inspired by positive struggle. Regardless, instructors should be mindful of how students see our role as either adding to a negative struggle or enthusiastically encouraging and supporting them to a positive struggle. Another comment from a student evaluation alluded to this agency of the instructor in this dynamic:

> Out of all the courses I have taken from National University this one has been the most challenging. This course taught me a lot more than what I expected. The research project was time consuming and a bit stressful. The professor was very enthusiastic and his comments on our papers were very helpful.

This student clearly alluded to struggling, but acknowledged that the instructor's approach and specific feedback on written assignments helped them to push through the process. If students see the instructor as challenging yet supportive, they may be less likely to simply accept failure, and potentially see struggle is often a path to success in learning. Rather than rubric-driven prescription driving the design of writing activities, a closer look at feedback than student evaluations can show reveals that students can and do make choices as they undertake their written work, understanding that these decisions are what gives them ownership of their intellectual activities, something that justifies their struggle and long hours of revision.

Discussion

Though they may apply to a range of fields of study, the three kinds of writing activities detailed in this essay sought to illustrate the wide range of pedagogical strategies available for instruction both about and for teaching under capitalism. First, we suggest interactive writing, extended reflections following game simulations empowers students to relate their experiences in the classroom to the reproduction of inequality in their life, and do so in a way that moves beyond the alienation of commodified, top-down education they tend to experience in traditional classroom settings. Second, timed argumentative writing in short analytic essays seek to replicate the rapidity with which students must be able to critically process information given the dearth of free time fast capitalism affords. The ability to reflect and then pass informed judgment on information encountered in daily life is a crucial part of the practice of citizenship central to the goals of a liberal arts education. In a third writing activity, the term paper revision enlists instructors in guiding students to develop their writing capacities in concert with their peers, by encouraging and guiding collective study of writing between students rather than over correcting for academic dishonesty and punishing all forms of collaboration. We have argued that dominant assessment practices in education on one hand and the culture of advanced capitalism on the other hand shape student perceptions of themselves and possibilities for learning. We suggest teaching strategies that use a broad range of critical writing activities rather than a uniform assignment calculable with assessment orthodoxy as best suited to develop critical thinking in a way that can challenge ideology under a "speculative model" of education under late capitalism.

This essay contributes to pedagogical and institutional discussions about higher education, with the activities proposed in a way that challenges the dominant tenets of modern higher education, particularly in the United States. By presenting activities that demand critical thought through writing, we have sought to challenge the assessment-driven model of pedagogy that results from viewing education as a commodity of ready-made degrees, high-stakes testing, and measured by grades and evaluation rather than development of whole citizens. We have taken the position that assessment orthodoxy acts as a regressive tendency, ensuring that education is bound within the confines of the classroom and the rhetoric of market-readiness. This essay sought to push back on assessment-centric efforts at designing activities, towards a different kind of change in the institutional practices of Universities facing the tide of rising corporatization. The implication is that in viewing the goal of education as a process that instead produces critical thinkers, there can be no silver bullet to knowledge introduced to be bestowed upon passive learners, but rather a pedagogy that values students' experiences and skills. We hope the alternatives we provide will help teacher-scholars better-understand a sample of the array of pedagogical approaches that allow students to develop an ability to think critically about capitalism, and effectively communicate the powerful ideas about economic inequality yielded by critical theory.

The role of a reflexive teacher in the pedagogical process is not to distance oneself from working class students by consciously stressing their own social privilege. Yet, neither is it the goal of a reflexive teacher to unconsciously reify the model of educator as judge or jury of student work, reproducing the banking model of education. Rather, critical thinking emerges when the instructor acts as a facilitator of a range of types of writing activities that allow students to both deliberate and express themselves. As such, teacher-activists inspire organic intellectual students who can relate to their peer's experiences under capitalism, advancing their critical thinking and writing practice in a way that peel back ideology, collectively uncovering the relational character of structure and agency in their daily life. To some extent, assessment requires specifying teaching strategies with an aim towards refining and improvement. Yet, at the same time, a critical pedagogy must resist the hegemonic culture of assessment as primary in education policy by connecting a range of types of activities to students' wide array of common experiences under capitalism and the diverse learning needs they engender. Deploying a wide breadth of teaching strategies not only caters to psychological approaches advising a diversity of learning styles. Future studies must continue to examine the extent to which current pedagogical practices either reinforce or challenge the tenets of both inequality under capitalism and the speculative model of education it engenders.

References

Agger, B. (1989). *Fast capitalism: A critical theory of significance*. Urbana-Champaign: University of Illinois Press.

Breunig, M. (2005). Turning experiential education and critical pedagogy theory into practice. *Journal of Experiential Education, 28*(2), 106–122.

Coghlan, C. L., & Huggins, D. W. (2004). "That's not fair!": A simulation exercise in social stratification and structural inequality. *Teaching Sociology, 32*(2), 177–187.

Freire, P. (1970). Pedagogy of the oppressed. New York, NY: Bloomsbury Publishing.

Gans, H. 2014[1990]. Deconstructing the underclass. In: P. S. Rothenberg &K. S Mayhew (Eds.), *Race class and gender in the United States* (9th edn, pp. 104–110). Worth Publishers.

Giuffre, K. & Paxton, P. (1997). Building social networks. *Teaching Sociology, 24*(3), 207–213.

Groves, J., Warren, C., & Witschger, J. (1996). Reversal of fortune: A simulation game for teaching inequality. *Teaching Sociology, 24*(4), 364–371.

Hilligoss, T. (1992). Demystifying "Classroom Chemistry": The role of the interactive learning model. *Teaching Sociology, 20*(1), 12.

Jessup, M. M. (2001). Sociopoly: Life on the boardwalk. *Teaching Sociology, 29*(1), 102

Koorland, M., Keel, M., & Ueberhorst, P. (1990). Setting aims for precision learning. *Teaching Exceptional Children, 22*(3), 64–66.

Marcuse, H. (1964). *One-dimensional man*. Boston: Beacon Press.

Margolis, E. (2001). *The hidden curriculum in higher education*. Psychology Press.
Moleswoth, M., Nixon, E., & Scullion, R. (2009). Having, being and higher education: The marketisation of the university and the transformation of the student into consumer. *Teaching in Higher Education, 3,* 277–287.
Neem, J. (2013). Experience matters: Why competency-based education will not replace seat time. *Liberal Education, 99*(4).
Newsom, J. (2004). Disrupting the 'student as consumer' model: The new emancipatory project. *International Relations, 18*(2), 227–239.
Schrecker, E. (2010). *The lost soul of higher education: Corporatization, the assault on academic freedom, and the end of the American university*. New York: The New Press.
Stark, P. B., & Freishtat, R. (2014). An evaluation of course evaluations. *ScienceOpen Research, 9,* 2014.
Taubman, P. M. (2010). *Teaching by numbers: Deconstructing the discourse of standards and accountability in education*. New York: Routledge.
White, O. R. (1986). Precision teaching—Precision learning. *Exceptional Children, 52*(6), 522–534.

Lessons on Inequality and Capitalism: Perspectives from a Community College

Peter J. Wruck

Author's Reflexive Statement

Many books on teaching in higher education pay little attention to the specific challenges facing instructors in the institutions that serve a majority of undergraduates in the United States—community colleges. When I got my first job teaching as an adjunct at a community college, and given that I was still a graduate student at the University of Minnesota, I decided that I would transfer all of my curricula and teaching strategies from the four-year institution to the two-year institution. My logic in doing so was that students at the two-year level deserve courses that were just as rigorous, in-depth, and thought-provoking as those at the four-year level. While I still hold those beliefs today, what I soon learned was that, while the rigor and content transferred easily, the teaching strategies that I employed did not. I made the fatal error that many new community college adjuncts make; I assumed that my students would more or less be similar to those at the university. This was due to two factors: my own inexperience with the student makeup of community colleges and the fact that my graduate program had done little to prepare me for teaching. Moreover, my graduate program entirely focused on teaching students at four-year institutions—not community colleges.

Part of what I valued—and continue to value—about working at community colleges is that my status-informed assumptions about the nature of education and society are themselves continuously challenged. Unlike at the public and private universities where I taught earlier, I had students in the same class ranging from (mostly white) accelerated high school students from wealthy backgrounds to (mostly people of color) English language learning refugees to single parents receiving TANF benefits to former felons to students with substantial disabilities—all in the same classroom. One quickly learns that sweeping statements about the

P. J. Wruck (✉)
Gavilan College, Gilroy, USA
e-mail: pwruck@gavilan.edu

K. Haltinner and L. Hormel (eds.), *Teaching Economic Inequality and Capitalism in Contemporary America*, https://doi.org/10.1007/978-3-319-71141-6_24

nature of society and its structure are far more likely to be challenged during a lecture at a community college than they are at a university. Moreover, I quickly learned that my students at the community college had far more diverse life histories that informed their views than the typical fresh-from-high-school university student. This, quite clearly, leads to students having a wealth of experiential knowledge to contribute to the course, in ways that students in more homogenous settings may not. All of these factors influenced the major changes I was forced to make both in my own assumptions and biases and in how I would approach the same in my students.

My own socioeconomic history and my interest in inequality began at a relatively early age. With parents who were always concerned about social justice, I was exposed to the ideas surrounding inequality relatively early on. However, growing up in a middle (and later, upper-middle) class background insulated me from many of the realities facing those who are lower on the socioeconomic spectrum. I gained firsthand experience with inequality through two major life events. The first was being a part of a desegregation initiative that bused me across the city to a different elementary school while living in a major city, and then moving to an almost entirely white and affluent school district when my family relocated to the suburbs. The second was a trip through rural northern Mexico taken with my grandmother when I was in junior high school. While I could go into great detail about specific incidents in both of these events that very much sparked my own attention to inequality, for the sake of parsimony I will merely state that through exposure to diversity, powerful poverty and dramatic inequality, differential treatment by authorities, the role of religion, and the differences in family life that I observed, I knew sociology was something I wanted to pursue by the time I was in high school. Choosing to work at a community college was simply the next progression in this type of work for me. I certainly didn't "settle" for a community college; I chose it. The perception among certain academics that some of us "settle" for work at community colleges—where the focus is on teaching and social justice rather than on research—is not only wrong, it is itself rooted in class- and race-based bias. This background, coupled with experience in the community college setting, have led me to the following lessons.

Academic Preparedness

While teaching at the university level, I was generally able to assume a certain level of academic preparation and preparedness on the part of my students. In general, my students had a basic idea of how to form an argument, critically think, write an undergraduate paper, and effectively take an exam. Even if these skills were very rough, or in some cases in need of some serious help and development, the fundamentals were generally there. At the community college, I learned fast that I could not take this for granted. They key difference is that community colleges are —almost entirely—open access. Even after passing required remediation—itself fraught with stratification implications—many students simply are not in a position to write or test successfully in a college-level course. In many cases, this is because remedial English courses focus in large part on the basic mechanics of writing sentences, paragraphs, and essays—not holistic research paper writing.

Thus, I changed my assumption. I knew that my students were equally capable as those I had taught at the university, but I needed to evaluate them in different ways in order to accurately assess the effort put into the course and the learning that resulted from this effort. For example, I started weighting my syllabus far more heavily on participation in small- and large-group discussions. This sometimes made up one third of the final grade. During these activities, I circulated around the room and actively participated in the discussions. In addition, I was more fully able to determine who had and had not done the reading. This was all the more important as faculty impressions of and student self-reports of their time spent on material outside of class are typically very divergent (c.f. national CCSSE and CCFSSE results). Recognizing that my own writing informs my background, I also tried to write my exam questions to avoid cultural biases. I avoided colloquialisms, situational examples that were class-based, and tried to draw a variety of class experiences into practical application questions to challenging students from all backgrounds. In addition, writing assignments were either entirely factual-content based or asked students to use their own life experience as a reference point. In doing so, I avoided assignments or projects that made assumptions about the frame of reference that students would have towards the content and allowed their own experience to shape their framing of their argument.

After identifying the different levels of preparedness in class, coupled with some selected results from papers and exams, I was able to refer students to appropriate support programs and/or meet with them individually to help scaffold their success in my courses.

Diversity of Life History

I will never forget the first time I had a university student say during class that being poor in the United States "wasn't such a bad deal—I mean, you can make a pretty good living off of all of those welfare programs. You even get an Obamaphone." While I literally had to assume that students at the university (in this case, a private one) did not necessarily understand that being poor was, in fact, not a desirable or easy position to be in, at the community college I had an entirely different experience with the same topic. To be frank, my community college students were far more likely to come from impoverished and disadvantaged backgrounds, and those experiences colored their receptiveness to being taught about the concept of economic inequality from a middle class academic like me.

At the university, I typically spent large amounts of time laying out what the academic research on the effects of poverty are, how it influences life changes independent of "self-motivation," and what the actual realities of poverty alleviation programs really are—including dispelling a variety of myths about public assistance. No, being poor isn't actually fun. Yes, most people in poverty are highly motivated and honest. Students typically reacted well to the content, and often we ended up with a discussion about how the discourse about these things in and of themselves was a challenge facing Americans. During my first course at the community college, I presented the material in the exact same manner and received a drastically different response. Students didn't need to be told that poverty was indeed bad. Rather, they responded totally differently. Responses typically fell into several categories:

(A) *The resentful opponent.* Every class typically had at least one student who would mention someone they personally knew—a family member, a neighbor, a friend—who they perceived as a "welfare cheat." They would then use this as proof positive that public assistance should be cut. Interestingly, I never had a university student express to me that they *personally* knew someone who was receiving some form of benefits.
(B) *The bootstrap tailor.* Just like at the university, every class also had the student who would bring up the classic bootstraps explanation for personal success. Unlike my experiences at the university, however, there was almost always another student willing to challenge that point of view without my prodding.
(C) *The determined sideliner.* I knew for a fact that many of my students were very poor, homeless, or receiving public assistance. This is because they often needed my signature on various forms proving that they were in class and making satisfactory progress in order to continue to receive various benefits. However, given the stigma attached with public assistance, and given the viewpoints vocalized by the previous two categories, these students were often silent during discussions. Thus, it was all the more important that I create both a safe space for all students to participate while also ensuring that all viewpoints were heard—even if I had to share them. This was made all the more difficult due to my tendency to prefer not to presume to speak for someone's experiences, but rather with them.
(D) *The observer.* A majority of students were rather passive receptacles to the content. While interested, they didn't much engage in discussion given the vociferousness of the aforementioned groups.

Why does this categorization matter? The answer is simple. Even more than at the university (in my opinion), setting the ground rules for discussion before exploring the topic was critical. Students from various backgrounds could feel downright threatened, devalued, or dehumanized by the statements of other students making broad generalizations about the nature of those in poverty. Thus, I always set the class the following ground rules:

(A) Even during class discussion, if you're going to make a generalized point, be prepared for me to challenge you to cite hard material to back up your claim. Otherwise, avoid the generalizable claims. Stick to the course material and what you objectively know.

(B) Do not denigrate or ignore the lived experience of anyone in class. All viewpoints are welcome, and if someone chooses to share a personal story, it's often out of a sense of pride and courage. Value and respect your classmates.
(C) Be respectful in your conversations. It should never get personal.
(D) Leave the vague horror stories out of it. The public discourse is full of poverty-related horror stories. Unless it's something you have first-hand knowledge of, it's best to not bring it into the classroom.

There are also decidedly some major advantages to having such a diversity of lived experience in the classroom. Particularly at the private university, virtually all of my students were from middle class backgrounds and above. This made for relatively boring discussions that lent themselves much more to the course content. Contrast that with the community college, where I had students from more backgrounds and life stories than I could imagine. They key is to harness those students who the instructor knows are willing to share and draw out their stories to bring a clear illustration to the academic point he/she/they're trying to make—but never calling on them by name so as to not label to the student, isolate the student, tacitly ask a student to speak for "all _____," violate confidentiality, or force the student to share life experience they don't wish to be shared. I would often ask if anyone had any concrete examples of a given concept—and even though I knew some students did have such examples from their personal lives, I'd never call on anyone specifically. I always left it open as a general question so those who were willing to share would do so.

For example, from discussions in office hours and in previous classes, I knew that one student had been homeless and had a violent and drug-related felony record. He spoke at length with me about the implications of his background on his socioeconomic outlook, and I asked him if he would be comfortable sharing his experiences in class with others as brief examples might be appropriate (while making it clear that his choice would have no bearing on his grade). His response? "Hell yes—some of those kids really need some help painting the fucking picture".

Do More Listening Than Talking

Due to the lack of personal experience with much inequality among my university students, I found that I often did far more talking than I did listening. Often, my students either personally knew about or had experience with wealth and/or the wealthy, but few had the same degree of experience with the poor. The opposite was true when I was teaching at the community college. Because my students spanned the entire spectrum within the single classroom, there was experience to share by and with everyone. Thus, I often set up a topic for discussion and let the class go, whereas at the university this strategy rarely worked.

Be Prepared to Be Far More Adaptive

This point isn't about teaching economic inequality per se, but rather having to be adaptive in your teaching as a result of the existence if stratification in society. While teaching at the university, the worst issue that a student went through (that I knew about) was the death—from natural causes—of a family member. While tragic, and requiring accommodations, for me this felt like a normal part of teaching. I had students at the community college who were evicted and living in their cars while trying to pass their classes, had been victims of domestic violence, had friends murdered, and had been arrested or incarcerated, all while enrolled in my classes. One of the most creative set of accommodations that I made was for a student, incarcerated on a technical parole violation, to be able to complete the course through a supervised release program via the local sheriff's department. This required me to adapt a variety of course requirements, since he couldn't do a research paper from jail, he couldn't type his paper, he needed a textbook without hard covers, and the time of the final exam fell outside the hours that the sheriff would allow him to come to campus. I didn't want anything to stand in the way of his passing the course. In this experience, I learned another key lesson: be prepared to meet the student where they need to be met, not the other way around.

Encourage the Student to Make the Hard Choice

Similar to my last point, this is less to do with teaching the content and more to do with adaptive teaching as a result of stratification. Often, students need to be encouraged to make the hard choice to withdraw from a class rather than fail it. I always made clear to the student that this wasn't a personal reflection on them—indeed, their desire to finish out the course is testament to their intentions—but rather, a defense against the tyranny of the GPA (see Chapter VII by Backer). Later, during the registration period, I also typically would personally reach out to the student to encourage them to retake the course with me in the following term.

Remember the Broader Implications

As I've moved into community college administration, one of the things that has struck me is just how much economic inequality plays into our goal setting, planning, and decision-making. As I alluded to earlier, with very rare exceptions, we are institutions without research requirements for faculty and solely focus on student experience and student success. For instructors considering a career in any kind of administration—community college or otherwise—remember the following lessons that I've learned along the way.

No matter what you think, *every* choice you make at the university or college has an equity implication for students and economic inequality. Even something as simple as when you schedule a class has an economic inequality/equity implication. The fact that a certain time works better for your advisee meetings or that committee you're on or to beat rush hour or keep Fridays free for writing time, while important implications for you, also have ramifications for students. Students with work responsibilities are less likely to be able to take daytime classes and more likely to want Friday and weekend classes. Students with children may not be able to take nighttime classes. Students in the criminal justice system may only be able to take midday classes. And the list goes on. So, before you lay out the schedule of classes for your students to take in your major area, have you mapped out whether or not a hypothetical daytime or nighttime student could actually graduate on time based upon when you offer your courses? What accommodations might you be able to make to facilitate completion for all students? Will taking on that journal editorship mean that no one in your department can teach a certain course for two years? How often can students see an advisor, and can they do so when they need to rather than during selected office hours?

The same holds true for things like degree requirements or internships. For example, since criminal records are inexorably tied to economics in our nation, they could easily prevent a student from getting the required internship or service-learning site that they want. One technique that can alleviate this problem without giving students the preverbal scarlet letter is to note in the list of options which sites require a background check and which do not and then giving students the choice of anything on the list.

Another question that institutions need to continue to ask themselves is what the implications of remediation and time to degree are on the economic circumstances of students. The longer a student is out of the labor force, the longer they are both accumulating student debt and not accumulating pay. For some students this is by choice—the exploration of many domains of knowledge offered by the classical liberal arts education is priceless. For many, however, this is a curse—or even a barrier. Working class and impoverished students are often in school to get a degree for a specific purpose, and time to degree only complicates their lifetime earnings.

Remediation is highly tied to the preceding paragraph. Increasingly, national evidence suggests that far too many students are placed at remedial levels of education when not necessarily appropriate. This is giving rise to the "multiple measures" placement movement, rather than a focus on a single high-stakes placement test (c.f. work in California by the RP Group on Multiple Measures Assessment). Again, remediation is tied to stratification: students' economic circumstances are tied to their likelihood of testing into remedial coursework. This lengthens time to degree and increases the likelihood of failing to complete (thus compounding the aforementioned penalties with no earned degree). Thus, faculty must ask: what is the institution doing to ensure that students are appropriately placed such that they are not incurring an economic and social penalty by undergoing needless non-college level coursework?

Taken in total, this essay has introduced a number of teaching and administrative related challenges as they pertain to economic inequality—both at the community college and otherwise. Higher education is, for many, the gateway to a solid footing into the middle class. For many students, community colleges are the only means of getting there. In educating more than half of undergraduates, and in some states educating the vast majority of those who ultimately go on to earn a bachelor's degree, community colleges are a major component in the ultimate goal of both teaching about and ultimately helping to alleviate economic inequality in America.

Capitalism, Racism, and the Neoliberal University: The Case of the University of Missouri (Mizzou)

Rose M. Brewer

Setting the Context for Teaching: Black Student Resistance and Racial Capitalism

Capitalism has always been deeply intertwined with racism in white supremacist societies. In the United States, in particular, as the political economy changed from industrial to its current neoliberal form, a racist structure was placed at the center of the nation's capitalist system. Recent events (including the removal of the University President by Black student activists) at the University of Missouri provide the possibility of radical liberatory education on 21st century neoliberal racial capitalism in our classrooms. This case study is relevant, useful, and, I argue, essential for teachers who educate on issues of global capitalism to include in their courses. Thus, this chapter examines the Black student struggles at the University of Missouri drawing upon an understanding of the radical Black Studies tradition, to help instructors apply this topic to their epistemology and personal ontology.

The case at hand is that of widespread Black activism in the wake of the 2015 murder of Michael Brown. However, the seeds of resistance are enmeshed in a deeper and longer history of the state of Missouri and the University campus: there were long-standing Black student grievances about racism that had been ignored by the institution. These acts included overt racist acts directed at the Black president of the Missouri Student Association, Payton Head, who, for example, reported being called the "n-word" repeatedly by a passenger in a truck. There was no response to this, or to other racist incidents (including racist graffiti, interpersonal incidents, and much more), by the University.

It was the foot dragging of the President in addressing these and other issues that boiled under the surface, a fire that was catalyzed by the murder of Michael Brown

R. M. Brewer (✉)
University of Minnesota-Twin Cities, Minneapolis, USA
e-mail: brewe001@umn.edu

K. Haltinner and L. Hormel (eds.), *Teaching Economic Inequality and Capitalism in Contemporary America*, https://doi.org/10.1007/978-3-319-71141-6_25

by police officer Darren Wilson in Ferguson. Following Brown's murder, students organized and, under the name "Student 1-9-5-0", coalesced a list of demands to improve the University of Missouri, challenging its racist neo-liberal practices. These demands are as follows:

I. We demand that the University of Missouri System President, Tim Wolfe, writes a handwritten apology to the Concerned Student 1-9-5-0 demonstrators and holds a press conference in the Mizzou Student Center reading the letter. In the letter and at the press conference, Tim Wolfe must acknowledge his white male privilege, recognize that systems of oppression exist, and provide a verbal commitment to fulfilling Concerned Student 1-9-5-0 demands. We want Tim Wolfe to admit to his gross negligence, allowing his driver to hit one of the demonstrators, consenting to the physical violence of bystanders, and lastly refusing to intervene when Columbia Police Department used excessive force with demonstrators.
II. We demand the immediate removal of Tim Wolfe as UM system president. After his removal a new amendment to UM system policies must be established to have all future UM system president and Chancellor positions be selected by a collective of students, staff, and faculty of diverse backgrounds.
III. We demand that the University of Missouri meets the Legion of Black Collegians' demands that were presented in 1969 for the betterment of the black community.
IV. We demand that the University of Missouri creates and enforces comprehensive racial awareness and inclusion curriculum throughout all campus departments and units, mandatory for all students, faculty, staff, and administration. This curriculum must be vetted, maintained, and overseen by a board comprised of students, staff, and faculty of color.
V. We demand that by the academic year 2017–2018, the University of Missouri increases the percentage of black faculty and staff campus-wide to 10%.
VI. We demand that the University of Missouri composes a strategic 10 year plan by May 1, 2016 that will increase retention rates for marginalized students, sustain diversity curriculum and training, and promote a more safe and inclusive campus.
VII. We demand that the University of Missouri increases funding and resources for the University of Missouri Counseling Center for the purpose of hiring additional mental health professionals—particularly those of color, boosting mental health outreach and programming across campus, increasing campus-wide awareness and visibility of the counseling center, and reducing lengthy wait times for prospective clients.
VIII. We demand that the University of Missouri increases funding, resources, and personnel for the social justices centers on campus for the purpose of hiring additional professionals, particularly those of color, boosting outreach and programming across campus, and increasing campus-wide awareness and visibility.

In the end, Black students—prominently joined by Black Missouri football players, a population often exploited by the neoliberal university—succeeded in bringing down the University President and producing important changes at the University. Though largely invisible in discussions of the upheaval, the curricular emphasis of Demand IV is noteworthy: in addition to structural change at the university, students were seeking to decolonize knowledge.

Beyond the demand for change at the University of Missouri specifically, Concerned Student 1-9-5-0 joined with over a 100 other Black student groups from around the country to issue a National Demand Manifesto (Black Student Manifesto) demanding national change in campus climates and practices for Black students on campuses. This Manifesto directly links 21st century Black resistance to the corporatization and 21st century racialization of the university as well as to an older legacy of Black student struggle: the 1960s fight for Black Studies. As a member of the national collective of Black students, Concerned Student 1-9-5-0 asserted three national demands:

1. We demand, at the minimum, Black students and Black faculty to be reflected by the national percentage of Black folk in the state and the country.
2. We demand free tuition for Black and indigenous students.
3. We demand a divestment from prisons and an investment in community.

Free tuition strikes at the heart of the neoliberal mandate of 21st century higher education, a mandate saddling students with enormous debt. This demand coalesces with the international demands of Black students in South Africa, #FeesMustFall, who call for no tuition and free public higher education (Heffernan and Nieftagodien 2016).

Critical to this analysis, and understanding the actions and demands of Concerned Student 1-9-5-0, is the racial history of the Missouri. Capitalism in Missouri, and in many other states and the nation as a whole, emerged in and through racial slavery. Racial exclusions in Missouri continued through the Jim Crow era, and are rearticulated in the neoliberal shifts in higher education of the recent past. The othering of the Black Missouri population, who had no access to the University until the 1950 court-ordered desegregation of the institution, is critical because of persistent racial exclusion in the state. The convergence of institutionalized racism, a corporatized academy, and Black student resistance rocked the campus and the nation in 2015. In this chapter, I use this case study to analyze the broader story of racial capitalism and neoliberalism in the U.S. corporatized university today and highlight Black Studies as a place for liberatory change (Cha-Jua 2000; Marable 1984, 2000).

Capitalism, the State of Missouri and Racism

It is in the context of racial capitalism that we teach. It is in the pedagogy of the university classroom that the political economy of neoliberalism and its convergence with the long history of white supremacy in the United States haunt our professorial practice. It must be named, rendered visible, and its history lifted—a process that the Black student protestors at Mizzou have modeled. The case of Mizzou, then, is the story of Black student resistance, captured in the demands of those rebelling against racism, classism, and neoliberalism at a major research university in the United States.

These were not the first protests on the campus. The Concerned Student 1-9-5-0 embodied that history in its name: the first Black students were admitted to the University of Missouri in 1950 and Concerned Student 1-9-5-0, of course, referenced this historic shift. Thus, it is through Missouri's racial history and continued racist-exclusionary practices that we can truly understand Black student resistance at Mizzou (the popular name given to the University of Missouri).

Scholars such as Lang (2009) and Gordon (2008) have articulated the Missouri's rabid racial history. They argue that it is no accident that Mizzou would be the site for racial tension and demands for a radical shift in governance. For example, Gordon (2008) argues Missouri has a distinct racist tradition that reflects the history of white supremacy in both the slave holding south and highly segregated north.

Slavery existed on Missouri's western border. Burke (2010) contends that it was as brutal as slavery in the South. Missouri's bondage was small holding slavery: most slave owners in the state held fewer than 10 people (the state held approximately 115,000 enslaved Africans all together). To maintain profitability under these circumstances, "the result was a system of slavery that was economically flexible… Missouri slaveholders regularly employed slaves at non-agricultural tasks and hired out their underemployed workers to their neighbors" (Burke 2017). While different in form from other slave-holding states, the economic foundation of Missouri was built on unfree labor: African slavery. The Civil War would bring an official end to the peculiar institution in the state, but the border state dynamic of Black and white would shape race relations over many decades.

The practices of the Jim Crow south were, also, embedded in Missouri. The enslaved generated wealth for slave-owners and built the state, but were kept impoverished following emancipation. This economic dispossession would play out over the decades, capitalism and racism inextricably linked (DuBois 1990; Cox 1970).

Denial of African American access to the University of Missouri was a major feature of the state's racial apartheid. It would take a protracted court battle by civil rights activists in the state to desegregate the institution. Ultimately, court ruling in 1950 led to University desegregation.

As mentioned, Missouri's racial capitalism also mirrors the circumstances of northern states: namely deep segregation along the lines of racial wealth. The intense segregation of Missouri, especially its cities, is particularly important in this regard. These are sites of extensive concentrated poverty, and the processes of globalization and deindustrialization have hit Black communities hard. In the 1960s and 70s the majority of workers laid off in railroad and manufacturing were African American, and wages were bifurcated by race—a Black wage (Gordon 2008).

Despite these significant and incremental changes, Black's and white's unequal labor force conditions express the state's reliance on racial capitalism, historically and into the current period. Indeed, the core of capitalism is profit seeking largely through labor exploitation. Racial capitalism refers to the interlacing of racism woven into capitalism, a system built on the expropriation of labor to instill competition between workers that ensure some kinds of workers are constantly the cheapest. Black labor has served this role historically. Today, in the U.S. nationally and in Missouri locally, Black labor is expendable domestically and highly exploitable globally. This means that low paid Black wage labor is largely gone. It has been shifted out of the country or mechanized (Brewer 2012). Racial capitalism is intertwined with neoliberalism today. Capital dismantles the social wage, privatizes all that can be privatized, and seeks the cheapest labor globally.

The privatization of higher education is emblematic of this interlacing of racial and capitalist systems of oppression. Those least likely to have access and ability to pay are disproportionately Black. Those students most likely to experience disrespect, accrue debt, exclusion from the core curriculum in terms of knowledge production, and told to "go home, nigger" are the African Americans in the state.

Indeed, segregation was the law of the land in Missouri for several generations and de facto segregation continues. The color bar was broken when now 89-year-old Mr. Gus Ridgel gained admission to Missouri's graduate program in economics in 1950 (Wines 2015). In the spirit of this resistance history, the struggle continues into the 21st century.

In the face of this history and current realities, Black student activists said, "No more!" This is where the struggle for justice intersected with the demand for the critical knowledges of Black experience. Black students at Mizzou and across the nation insist on transforming the Eurocentric curriculum and empowering Black studies even as the neoliberal university asserts the demand for "usable" majors.

The Neo-liberal University

It is important to think of capitalism as a world system with a neoliberal ideological logic and practice (Brewer 2012) advanced by transnational institutions of capital as state practices rooted in privatization and advancement of market supremacy, trade policies rooted in liberalization, an ideology and discourse of the end of racism, and austerity rhetoric and state practices involving the dismantling of public supports from Medicare to Social Security.

Indeed, at the heart of the neoliberal university is the crafting of privatization rather than public resource (Tuchman 2007). Bagakis (2016) contends that: "One aspect of the project of neoliberalism was to reshape the population's understanding of the purpose of public institutions, such as schools and universities to fit the corporate model." Tom Wolfe, the deposed president of Mizzou, was brought to the University of Missouri explicitly for these neoliberal purposes. Indeed, "Wolfe was a corporate executive brought in largely to cut costs in the state system" (Packer 2015).

What happens when implicit loyalty to the market becomes explicit and protestors are wise enough to recognize this capitalist pressure? Given the hunger for national athletic recognition in football and other sports, athletics is part of the prominence lever. The inclusion of Black football players in the protests at Mizzou certainly was instrumental in Black student protester's success. When the football team joined and refused to play until the situation changed, big money was on the table. Protesters used capitalism against itself.

The Long Duree of Black Student Struggle: Black Studies

What has been less visible in this discussion is the continuity of the Mizzou resistance with earlier struggles by Black students. Concerned Student 1-9-5-0 references the demands of 1969 Black student protests of the campus, demands still not fully realized nearly 50 years later. A key continuity in the ongoing struggle is for the university to change the curriculum, employ a greater number of Black faculty and staff, and increase cultural and other resources on the white campus. The demands embody a fundamental critique of the curricular structure and institutionalized inequalities of higher education. Indeed, almost 50 years ago, the struggle for Black Studies in higher education opened up a radical possibility for knowledge transformation in the academy. The student struggles of the late 1960s laid the groundwork for these 21st century demands.

Our pedagogy as 21st century scholars cannot escape the challenges of racial capitalism and student activism today. As the late (Manning 2000, p. 189) asserts in *A Plea that Scholars Act Upon, Not Just Interpret, Events:* "At the heart of black studies is the black intellectual tradition… The black intellectual tradition has also tried to correct the racist stereotypes and assumptions of black genetic or cultural inferiority that unfortunately still exist within much white scholarship." A new generation of Black student activists brought these issues front and center to the University of Missouri and the neoliberal academy in general.

Thus, the challenge for those in higher education today is not to deny but reconnect to a critical sociological perspective that contextualizes the academy as a complicated, globalized, racialized, neoliberal institution. Similar to the conditions in Missouri, the first struggles for Black Studies involved overt resistance with the state, the police, the institutional actors, and demanded the decolonization of knowledge. As Karenga (2010) notes, one of the most important concepts in the general Student Movement of the 1960s, and especially in the Black Student Movement which waged the struggle for Black Studies, was the concept of relevance—in its academic and social dimensions.

By producing persons capable of solving the problems of a contagious American society, Black Studies asserted Academic Excellence and Social Responsibility; failing to do so would make education irrelevant (Karenga 2010). The idea that universities serve the interests of an elite is not a new. And, by the late 1960s the decolonization struggles internationally had begun to influence U.S. activists (Ladner 1972). The development of Ethnic Studies pivoted on this idea of relevant education serving the interests of the people, given the historic exclusivity and Eurocentrism of universities.

By 1966, the Negro Students' Association changed its name to the Black Student Union (BSU), representing a new identity and direction. The term Black folded into itself oppositional identity to denote pride and commitment to liberation. The organization also became involved in San Francisco State's tutorial program for the surrounding community. This and other community service activities signaled the social commitment and service Black studies advocates would place at the center of the academic and social mission of Black Studies (Karenga 2010).

There are lessons to be learned from this history, and its imprint on the National Black Student Demands and the University of Missouri student demands is evident; it is this concern for relevancy that Concerned Student 1-9-5-0. The field of Black Studies since its inception positioned itself as transformational (Marable 2000). This is beyond a "helping" and "aid" enterprise. It pushed beyond the dominant discourses and assumptions about Black inequality. Conceptualizations, such as those reflected in Moynihan's *The Negro Family: The Case for National Action*, (Moynihan 1965) were deeply critiqued (Willie and Reddick 1976). Questions such as, what about the indigenous knowledge(s) of marginalized peoples? What of oppositional histories, the challenges to disciplinary hegemony? What about the history of Black resistance? Sociology for whom? Activist Black scholars raised these questions, illuminating the fact that sociology served the interests of white supremacy and empire (Ladner 1972). These important challenges in the field of Black Studies to the academic status quo embed a legacy central to articulating a critical sociology today. It is a legacy rooted in deep critique and practice, taking seriously indigenous knowledge and resistance in visioning a new society.

W. E. B. DuBois (1990) is also useful here. His observations are helpful when attempting to craft an authentic critical sociology. In *The Souls of Black Folks* DuBois raised the questions: "What does it mean to be defined as a problem?" The particular framing of the "Black Problem" has been the stock and trade frame of the social problems tradition in U.S. sociology. We can extend that DuBoisian interrogation to the persistence of racist scholarship and discourses into this century. DuBois and Black studies activists were correct in placing front-and-center the *inverse* of othering: giving voice to the lived experiences through those who live those experiences. It requires shifting the epistemological lens. Here, it is the deep refusal to be defined, or to define, from without, even in the context of highly determinative structural inequalities. This was the message of Black student struggle at Mizzou.

Concluding Thoughts

The corporate university is deeply implicated in creating, sustaining, and maintaining a set of multiple and entangled social inequalities. Classrooms daily reproduce and rearticulate the intersectionality of gender/sexuality, class, and race inequalities. The fundamental question is, "How do we create and practice a pedagogy radically positioned for movement building and social change?" (Katz-Fishman et al. 2007). Other questions remain including, "What does the neoliberal structure in higher education mean for student learning?" and "What are the lessons of Black Studies and Black student resistance for our teaching?" The University is a microcosm of the larger society. We know this. We also know that the struggle for racial justice on campuses today is at the heart of struggle in higher education. As I have argued, radical Black Studies constitutes a unique contribution to how we conceptualize curricular change today and how we build the critical classroom under neoliberal, racial capitalism. This is what the Black student protestors at Mizzou demanded. They have sharpened our understanding of the pedagogical road ahead.

References

Bagakis, G. (2016). Neoliberalism's decades-long attack on public universities. *Truth-out.org*. Accessed October 1, 2017, http://www.truth-out.org/news/item/37988-neoliberalism-s-decades-long-attack-on-public-universities.

Brewer, R. (2012). Austerity, neoliberalism and black communities. *Souls, 14*(3–4), 227–239.

Burke, D. M. (2010). *On slavery's border: Missouri's small-slaveholding households, 1815-1865*. Athens: The University of Georgia Press.

Burke, D. M. (2017). Slavery on the Western border: Missouri's slave system and its collapse during the Civil War. Civil War on the Western Border: The Missouri-Kansas Conflict, 1854–1865. Accessed October 1, 2017 http://www.civilwaronthewesternborder.org/essay/slavery-western-border-missouri%E2%80%99s-slave-system-and-its-collapse-during-civil-war.

Cha-Jua, S. (2000). *America's first black town Brooklyn, Illinois, 1830–1915*. Urbana: University of Illinois Press.

Cox, O. (1970 [1948]). Caste, class, and race. New York: New York Modern Reader.

DuBois, W. E. B. (1990). The Souls of Black Folks, Reprint. New York: Vintage.

Gordan, C. (2008). *Mapping decline: St. Louis and the fate of the American city*. Philadelphia: University of Pennsylvania Press.

Heffernan, A., & Nieftagodien, N. (2016). *Students must rise: Youth struggle in South Africa before and beyond Soweto '76*. Soweto: Wits University Press.

Karenga, M. (2010). *Introduction to black studies*. Los Angeles: Sankore Press.

Katz-Fishman, W., Brewer, R. M., & Albrecht, L. (2007). *The critical classroom: Education for liberation and movement building*. Atlanta: Project South.

Keller, R. (2016). Concerned Students 1950 renews demands as University of Missouri curators begin presidential search. Columbia Daily Tribune. Accessed October 1, 2017, http://www.columbiatribune.com/article/20160225/News/302259884.

Ladner, J. (Ed.). (1972). *The death of white sociology: Essays on race and culture*. Baltimore: Black Classic Press.

Lang, C. (2009). *Grassroots at the gateway: Class politics and black freedom struggle in St Louis, 1936 to 1975*. Ann Arbor: University of Michigan.

Levine, P. (2015). Deindustrialization and Ferguson. Accessed October 1, 2017. http://peterlevine.ws/?p=14771.

Marable, M. (1984). *Race, reform and rebellion: The second reconstruction in black America, 1945-1982*. Jackson: University Press of Mississippi.

Marable, M. (Ed.). (2000). Dispatches from the ebony tower: Intellectuals confront the African American experience. New York: Columbia University Press.
Moynihan, D. (1965). *The negro family: A case for national action*. Washington, D.C.: United States Office of Planning and Policy Research.
Packer, G. (2015). A hard rain at Mizzou and Yale. The New Yorker. Accessed October 1, 2017, https://www.newyorker.com/news/daily-comment/the-struggles-at-mizzou-and-yale.
Tuchman, G. (2007). *Wannabe U: Inside the corporate university*. Chicago: University of Chicago Press.
Willie, C. V., & Reddick, R. J. (1976). *A new look at black families*. New York: Rowman & Littlefield.
Wines, M. (2015). A real Missouri 'Concerned Student 1950' speaks, at age 89. New York Times. Accessed October 1, 2017, https://www.nytimes.com/2015/11/11/us/an-original-missouri-concerned-student-1950-speaks-at-age-89.html?mcubz=3.

Against the "Institutional Real": The Structural and Cultural Foundations of Corporate Higher Education and the Challenge to Developing Politically Engaged Students

Corey Dolgon

In the mid-1990s, equity researchers at Lehman Brothers cited education as a potentially "hot industry." With schools undergoing serious financial and social challenges, and calls for educational reform increasing, financial strategists concluded that privatization could be positioned as both a solution to real challenges and a formula for making money. Educational Maintenance Organizations (EMOs)—private sector groups providing educational services ranging from school district management to charter school development—would do for education what HMOs had done for health care.

Lehman's "investment thesis" could not be simpler. Their definition of "classic investment opportunity" contends that successful investments depend on the quality of the product—how well one "solves" a problem. But despite mega *failures* throughout the nation, over 20 years of privatization *still* produced billions in profits. EMOs like Edison, Mosaica, and White Hat made investors rich regardless of dismal performances in school district after school district. Lehman's "investment opportunities" obscure capitalism's prime directive—making money. In part, the "problem" for Lehman Brothers and investors was always more about where to profit next than how to "solve" education. By their definition, more profit *is* better. Corporations are hammers and the rest of us nails.

American Colleges and Universities have driven the corporatization bandwagon and I argue that late capitalism's transformation of higher education into profit-seeking and revenue producing industries represents only the latest (and perhaps most complete) hegemonic phase in academia. From the outset, educational institutions reflected and carried out an agenda shaped by America's white, capitalist elite. Often under the ideological cloak of increasing public goods such as democracy, opportunity, and scientific knowledge, schools (especially colleges and

C. Dolgon (✉)
Stonehill College, Easton, USA
e-mail: cdolgon@stonehill.edu

K. Haltinner and L. Hormel (eds.), *Teaching Economic Inequality and Capitalism in Contemporary America*, https://doi.org/10.1007/978-3-319-71141-6_26

universities) have promoted private profit and control under the guise of public interest and reform.

Such ideologies, however, have their contradictions—all hegemonic blocs have their cracks. Thus, many sociologists have argued that educational institutions are not simply reproductive in their practices, but exist as "contested terrain" (Apple 2015; Doane 2003; Ozga 2000; Lagemann 1996). From these analytical perspectives, educational institutions may represent power and wealth from their structural foundations and boards of trustees to their hidden curricula and micro-aggressions, but they also exist as hotbeds of cultural and political tension. Schools, which represent many *different* class and status groups, host multiple and even contradictory efforts to reinforce or upend existing social norms, cultural practices, and power relations. The language of reform—"fixing" education—generally encompasses the varying kinds of impact groups want to have on existing social structures and future political opportunities (Fine et al. 2016; Apple 2004; Petersen 1985).

But to actually "fix" education demands recognizing what we expect from it in the first place. Durkheim argued that education was both the process through which society taught the basic knowledge and values necessary to reproduce dominant social relationships and structures, as well as the place responsible for the discovery, transformation, and coordination of social change (Durkheim 1956; Karabel 1977). In a rapidly changing and increasingly complex and cosmopolitan world, schools evolved as the most effective and important institution for reproducing social stratification, cultural integration, and organic solidarity. By necessity then, American education—as an institution and set of social practices—carries with it two kinds of conflicts and contradictions. Education socializes students into the existing dominant culture and the ruling ideas of the age, yet schools become a terrain on which opposing political and social sensibilities collide. Similarly, schools purport to teach all students the same ideas, facts, figures, and philosophies in order to "democratize" as well as "Americanize" our population. Yet, how can we equalize an already stratified nation when schools so effectively reproduce inequalities? How can we democratize and empower individuals if we force them to deny their history and heritage, identity, and culture? Such paradoxes shape and plague the history of American education.

One aspect of education that has remained present and, as I will argue in this essay, powerfully determinative, is what Stuart Hall called the "institutional real." This term represents the historical, structural, and ideological DNA of higher education that makes significant, progressive institutional change barely possible, and then mostly during periods of mass social movements. And even these changes are immediately susceptible to being recast by the continued pressures of capitalism, patriarchy, and white supremacy. The "institutional real" suggests that progressive programs, policies, and pedagogies become formalized and de-politicized over time as conservatizing forces dig in and fight back (Morton et al. 2012; Beins et al. 2005). Thus, despite radical theorizing, innovative teaching, Affirmative Action, and a diversified curricula that reflected the force of 1960s social movements, corporate restructuring, and ideological ascendancy, hyper-professionalism and the demise of faculty governance, students-as-consumer models, and market-driven curricula, privatization, outsourcing, and the precarity of all campus labor has demonstrated just how hard and fast educational institutions are committed to corporate hegemony (Giroux et al. 2001; Tierney 1994).

In part, this formation comes from the ways in which wealth and power determine the role and function of education—who does or doesn't get access to education and what kinds of education are made available. But these structures and practices also contain social and cultural aspects that legitimize corporate values, reaffirm privileges and entitlements, and sanction whose knowledge counts and for what purposes. While sociologists have effectively argued that education is a "contested terrain," these contests are rarely equal or fair and their outcomes rarely just.

It is crucial for us to recognize the structural and cultural conditions that determine the institutional real in order to challenge them intelligently and effectively. We must put to work our knowledge production and intellectual muster to organize against the conditions of economic inequality, patriarchy, imperialism, and white supremacy while we simultaneously re-envision what a *more* just and equitable society might look like. First, I offer a historical analysis of education's institutional reality and then examine current forces that recast and reinvigorate this institutional real after social and political movements appeared to transform it. I then describe how promising pedagogical practices for democracy and justice—those encompassed by the success of service learning and civic engagement—have themselves been tamed and refashioned by corporatization, neoliberalism, and the customary yet most contemporary aspects of the institutional real. I conclude with some thoughts on how we might continue to teach and act against the institutional real in hopes of radical social change.

Learning Outcomes: A Brief History of American Education and Its "Institutional Real"

From the outset, our national leaders had seriously conflicting ideas about education's potential to empower and disempower. On the one hand, early slave codes from the 18th and 19th century prohibited the teaching of reading and writing to slaves. North Carolina even outlawed "giving or selling books or pamphlets to slaves," explaining, "teaching slaves to read and write, tends to excite dissatisfaction in their minds, and to produce insurrection and rebellion" (Taylor 1925; Bullock 1967; Higginbotham 1978; Williams 2009). Education *could* play a role in liberating people, so Southern lawmakers banned it for Black slaves. Slave codes prohibiting education also helped draw racial distinctions between Blacks and poor whites, giving tangible meaning to the formation of American racism and white supremacy (Saxton 1990; Haney-Lopez 2006; Baptist 2014).

On the other hand, from the early 1800s to the early 1900s, the United States promoted Indian Residential Schools to teach Native Americans how to be

"Americans", not "Indians." Capt. Richard Pratt, founder of the Carlisle School, once reflected on General Sheridan's military campaigns against Native Americans (Adams 1995):

> A great general has said that the only good Indian is a dead one, and that high sanction of his destruction has been an enormous factor in promoting Indian massacres. In a sense, I agree with the sentiment, but only in this: that all the Indian there is in the race should be dead. Kill the Indian in him, and save the man.

To accomplish this task, the government forcibly removed youth from their families and imprisoned them on campuses called "industrial boarding schools." Here girls learned to serve as domestic laborers while boys gained basic agricultural skills—both performing much of the work to keep schools self-sufficient. Federal policies toward Native Americans evolved from violent destruction, displacement, and resettlement to more cultural forms of genocide. So called "civilizing" indigenous peoples required they cast off cultural traditions and beliefs, adopt "individualistic" and "American" values, and they could become obedient workers. According to Indian Commissioner, George Manypenny, assimilation meant Indians learn to say "I" instead of "we," "me" instead of "us," "mine" instead of "ours." Many native communities resisted, though, as significant "tribal opinion saw white education for what it was: an invitation to cultural suicide" (Churchill 2004).

Similar forced assimilation occurred in the Southwest as corporations and regional governments built Chicano boarding schools to house, educate, and train young Mexican women. Not only did business and political leaders hope to create a pliable and effective supply of domestic workers, but policymakers pursued women as the purveyors of cultural values and social practices in their own communities. The next generation of immigrant children could be purged of traditional culture at the same time creating a larger surplus of domestic labor. "Go after the women," wrote educator Alfred White, "and you may save the second generation for America" (Sanchez 1994; Camp 2012).

By the early 20th Century, education as a form of "Americanization" played a large role in the expansion of public schools. Despite three decades of massive immigration from Eastern Europe, Asia, and Mexico, Americanization remained largely about conformity and subservience. Thus, educational policy promoted schools as the institution, "to break up these groups or settlements, to assimilate and amalgamate these people as a part of our American race, and to implant in their children…the Anglo-Saxon conception of righteousness, law and order, and popular government, and to awaken in them a reverence for our democratic institutions…" (Pai and Adler 1997). The "Americanization Movement," according to historian Daniels (2002), "was an organized campaign to insure political loyalty and cultural conformity." Schools not only taught English and Civics, but promoted hygiene and fitness, "middle class values, and discipline more appropriate to the factory than the classroom."

Yet cultural assimilation and creating racialized American identities were not the only goals of early public education. Ultimately, American schools would mirror and buttress the rise of industrial production and monopoly capitalism. Most early support for mass education came from financiers and industrialists who envisioned schools as effective training grounds for teaching an "industrial morality." Early factory owners struggled to transform farm girls, rural immigrants, and independent craftsmen into the efficient and obedient "hands" needed for new factory systems. Far from being concerned with the "intellectual" development of working class youth, manufacturers—and the school boards they selected—espoused the, "object of education" to be more than "mere intellectual instruction." Instead, the primary goal was "a life-long formation of character" composed of "habits" such as: "attention, self-reliance…order and neatness, politeness and courtesy…and [especially] punctuality."

Mid-19th century schools built their classrooms and curricula with the needs of industrial capitalism in mind. Lowell educational reformer, Theodore Edson, even designed "a special clock for classroom use which divided up the school day neatly into thirty-two ten-minute recitation periods" (Bowles and Gintis 1976). The habits of deference and order prepared workers not only with the efficiency and rationalization needed for industrial production, but also the hegemonic mindset and commitment necessary for industrial order. Economist Harry Braverman argued that the triumph of industrial capitalism derived from manufacturers' ability to manage workers by placing the authority and discipline they wanted "under the cap" of the worker himself (Braverman 1974; Gerstle 2002). This "manufactured consent" lay at the heart of educational pioneer, Horace Mann's mission to create dutiful citizens. Mann explained (Bowles and Gintis 1976),

> A stable body politic and a smoothly functioning factory alike required citizens and workers who had embraced and taken as their own the values and objectives of those in authority. Schools might do better than to instill obedience; they might promote self-control (p. 170).

Not only did "educated" workers become more effective, efficient, and obedient, they also saw their own futures linked to the authority and advance of their bosses in the workplace and their leaders in the community. The process of building what Gramsci called the "new industrial worker" would be provided by public education and funded by public money for the benefit of private owners.

Throughout the late 19th and early 20th Century, the same scientific management principles introduced by Frederic Winslow Taylor to heighten industrial efficiency would find their way into schools, too (Rice 1913; Au 2011). Increased rationalization and standardization accompanied the expanding curriculum necessary to train both a burgeoning, yet diverse, industrial workforce as well as a growing professional managerial class of "brain workers." In the mid-1920s, Robert and Helen Lynd (1929) observed classrooms in Muncie, Indiana, and reported,

> The school, like the factory, is a thoroughly regimented world. Immovable seats in orderly rows fix the sphere of activity of each child… Bells divide the day into periods [and] by the third or fourth year practically all movement is forbidden except the marching from one set of seats to another between periods, a brief interval of prescribed exercise daily, and periods of manual training or home economics once or twice a week.

After WWII, education (especially higher education) would once again be called on to establish a conservative, American identity and serve the changing economic and ideological needs of corporate and government leaders. The G.I. Bill sent millions of veterans to rapidly expanding public and private universities to prepare for the new economy (Chomsky et al. 1998; Frydl 2009). Clark Kerr, Chancellor of the University of California-Berkeley, (the pinnacle of America's research institutions and flagship for the nation's largest university system) explained that higher education had been called, "to educate previously unimagined numbers of students; to respond to the expanding claims of national service; to merge its activities with industry as never before." He continued,

> Characteristic of this transformation is the growth of the knowledge industry, which is coming to permeate government and business, and to draw into it more and more people raised to higher and higher levels of skill… [as] knowledge production is growing at about twice the rate of the rest of the economy. What the railroads did for the second half of the last century, and the automobile for the first half of this century, may be done for the second half of this century by the knowledge industry; and that is, to serve as the focal point for national growth (Kerr 2001).

Educational institutions would continue to serve a stratifying function by producing knowledge as a profitable commodity and knowledge workers who were efficient, obedient, and committed to corporate growth and commercial consumption.

The Radicalization and Re-stratification of Higher Education's Institutional Real

But the rapid changes brought forth by post WWII economic and educational expansion also facilitated new student-led social movements against traditional race, class, and gender hierarchies. As Kerr theorized about "multiversities" aligned with corporate capitalism, his own campus at Berkeley exploded with thousands of students staging strikes and taking over buildings to protest newly enacted policies limiting free speech and political engagement. Coming on the heels of McCarthyism, student activism against repression was inspired by southern students fighting Jim Crow (Student Non-Violent Coordinating Committee) and the anti-war, anti-corporate Students for a Democratic Society. On campus after campus radical activists not only declared their opposition to racism, imperialism, and the military-industrial complex, but they demonstrated a physical commitment to direct action as a strategy to attain their goals and protect their rights (Gitlin 1987; Miller 1987).

Postcolonial revolutions abroad inspired expanding anti-racist and anti-imperialist movements at home. Domestic activism and organizing created its own educational frameworks and practices such as SDS's ERAP (Educational Research and Action) projects; SNCC and the Black Panther Party's Freedom Schools; and the Women's Movement's Consciousness Raising groups (Frost

2001; Payne 2008; Evans 1980; Echols 1989). These and other efforts provided new, off-campus classrooms and laboratories, new pedagogies and new knowledge to fuel serious counter-hegemonic politics. Just as educational, though, was the physical act of organizing and protesting, the power of which SNCC leader, McDew (1966), so eloquently described as offering students, "a chance for the word to become flesh." These efforts promoted, "a challenging philosophy—the philosophy of love overcoming hate, of nonviolence conquering violence, of offering oneself as a sacrifice for the cause." Ending Jim Crow in the South, challenging racialized poverty in the North, demanding evacuation from Vietnam all signified a new era of student political efficacy and engagement that would give "The Sixties" a legendary status.

Despite myriad institutional changes and structural and cultural shifts in race relations, gender identities, and challenges to corporate hegemony and militarism, the post WWII period eventually saw the marriage of higher education and industry made even more prominent. While increasingly diverse and liberal, universities' mission to create expert driven knowledge and technology to manage and fuel the prosperity of the growing information-based economy hardly waned. From the 1950s "Atoms for Peace" programs linking scientific research and Cold War supremacy with the dreams of mass consumption, to the 1990s corporate triumphalism and industrial takeover of higher education, capitalism's institutional control over colleges and universities remained hegemonic. Despite various challenges to militarism, racism, and patriarchy, Kerr's vision of the new multiversity directly linked to corporate profits and professional training never lost much legitimacy or steam. Higher education in the 1970s and 1980s would recast student and faculty political activism by professionalizing radical knowledge production, disempowering and degrading faculty leadership and labor, and replacing students' call for political relevancy with paranoia over debt and job market relevancy (Chomsky 1997; Leslie 1993; Dolgon 1998).

Meanwhile, the stagnation in federal funding for research and massive cuts in public monies for higher education resulted in new "partnerships" where corporations funded faculty research and shared in patents and intellectual property rights. In higher education, the Lehman Brothers' investment thesis would look more like corporate mergers and eventually hostile takeovers. Not only did the private sector now shape the research questions scientists asked, but they also profited from the findings, subsequent innovations and other products. Faculty research quickly created "spin-off" companies and teachers and researchers became CEOs overnight. In fact, new majors and curricula were crafted for corporate interests and supported by corporate dollars. By the 1980s and 1990s, privatization and other business philosophies dominated administrative reorganization, institutional governance, and strategic planning in higher education. And by the turn of the 21st century, universities not only "provided knowledge and a trained cadre for private industry," they embraced the language and mimicked the practices of corporations themselves (Giroux 2014; Soley 1995; Aronowitz 2000).

While the primary functions of higher education—research and teaching—still remain, the commodification of knowledge and students, and the industrialization of the academy itself, have resulted in the degradation of both scholarship and pedagogy. Most colleges have tried to increase revenues by bolstering on-line, distance-learning classes and finding innovative ways to capitalize on facilities through conference services and exclusive food and beverage contracts (Tuchman 2011; Washburn 2006; Noble 2003). They have also responded by upscaling dorms, fitness centers, and food services to compete for full tuition paying students while downscaling the status and autonomy of faculty by recruiting part-time labor and speeding up the work process—larger course loads, class sizes, and contact hours. Meanwhile, more and more governance has moved from faculty control to the hands of an increasingly bloated administration. The result, according to Scott (2012), has been the "wreckage of American academia."

As early as the mid-1990s, Bill Readings referred to this devastation as the "University in Ruins." He argued that globalization and late capitalism (read neoliberalism) had dismantled the "nation-state" while post-modernism and anti-colonialism had dismantled a unified, modernist (albeit arrogant and brutal) sense of Culture with a big 'C'. Readings (1996, p. 13) explains:

> The University no longer has to safeguard and propagate national culture, because the nation-state is no longer the major site at which capital reproduces itself… The idea of national culture no longer provides an overarching ideological meaning for what goes on in the University, and, as a result what exactly gets taught or produced as knowledge matters less and less.

Replacing a commitment to national culture and imperialism, universities adopted the language of "excellence." Yet, excellence means nothing except in the language of accounting and assessment, ranking, and competition. Because excellence has no meaning outside of comparison, the raison d'etre of the academy becomes quantitative assessment allowing for pseudo-scientific proof of quality learning, teaching and research, prettier campuses, happier students, and more marketable graduates. All of these suggest the need for cost-effective investments and proven effective outcomes. In the end, the university no longer simply acts like a corporation, it has become a corporation: "The University of Excellence serves nothing other than itself, another corporation in a world of transnationally exchanged capital" (Readings 1984, p. 17).

Administrative growth reflects the increased need to account and measure, plan strategically for efficiency, increase customer satisfaction, cut costs and create something called "excellence." These efforts require higher paying students and lower paid staff. Practically everything gets outsourced from food, health and custodial services, to enrollment management and, ironically, strategic planning itself. Clerical workers once charged with handling logistical tasks are now the first ones fired; their vacancies result in ever mounting administrative burdens for faculty and the few staff that remain. Eventually, more administrators result in faculty and staff doing more work, not less (Ginsburg 2011; White 2000; Tirelli 1997).

Chomsky (2014) suggests that burgeoning layers of administrative and bureaucratic heft represent the necessary cost of control: "If you have to control people, you have to have an administrative force that does it." Corporations have always required more managers to impede the autonomy and resistance of workers. In service economies, managers must handle both employees and consumers, thus becoming more significant to maintaining profits and stability. But Chomsky (2014) also suggests another crucial element for corporate control—the precarity of labor, as this heightened sense of vulnerability serves to reduce workers' expectations for compensation and voice. Thus, the market ideology of contemporary higher education not only permeates the labor process, but also creates a "market McCarthyism" that keeps graduate teaching assistants, adjunct faculty, and most importantly, full-time faculty from complaining or organizing effectively (Chomsky 2014; Schrecker 2010).

Automation has historically helped industry manage workers with threats of obsolescence. Universities adopted these practices as well, employing technologies such as "MOOCs" (Massive Open On-line Course), "courses in a box" and other innovations that encroach on academic freedom and critical pedagogies by rationalizing and standardizing both the process and content of higher education. In 1998, David Noble warned that, "the distribution of digitized course material online, without the participation of professors who develop such material, [may be] justified as an inevitable part of the new "knowledge-based" society…[but] in practice is often coercive… It is not a progressive trend towards a new era at all, but a regressive trend, towards the rather old era of mass production, standardization and purely commercial interests" (p. 120). Almost two decades later, faculty become "content providers" and students "platform users" as quantitative student learning outcomes can be met without the traditional, and increasingly costly, face-to-face, collective dialogues that once characterized teaching.

But the worst victims of such academic carnage may not be faculty and staff; it may be the students themselves. Early entrees into corporatizing higher education promised students a vaunted position as customer. Neoliberalism, however, has degraded the role of consumer, too. ATMs allow us to be our own bank tellers, shoppers now checkout their own groceries, drivers fill their own tanks, and travelers make their own reservations, check their own bags, bring their own food, and in the case of an emergency, remove windows and clear aisles. For students, it's no different. They are expected to register for their own courses, create their own majors, assess their courses and instructors, and navigate the myriad financial aid quagmires necessary to pay tuition. While college faculty have long tried to encourage students as independent learners and critical thinkers, we now dumb down curricula to make students happier while requiring they perform more of the selecting and dispersing of services and evaluating of employees and programs (Koeber et al. 2012; Naidoo and Jamison 2005).

As students navigate the changing demands of higher education, they face increasing emotional and financial obstacles. According to the work of UCLA's Higher Education Research Institute, student stress levels are at an all-time high. In 2017, only about half of all incoming students describe themselves as having an emotional well-being above average or better. This number dropped almost 5% from 2010 and has declined steadily since 1985. Reasons for increased stress are probably many, although students report less time on academics than their predecessors, but exponentially more time spent on social media, extra-curricular activities, and wage work certainly contribute to this dynamic. So, too, does the volatility and hyper-aggressiveness of campus social life (Pryor 2012).

Above all, however, financial insecurities, especially since the fiscal crises of 2007 and 2008, weigh heavily on students. Over half of first year students in public and nonprofit institutions used loans to pay for college, with almost 40% needing $6000 or more. Meanwhile, almost 70% of seniors graduated with debt in 2016, with an average of over $30,000 each. The student loan default rate has doubled in the last decade to over 10% while over 40% of students are either in default or delinquent in their payments. Ross (2014) considers this situation akin to indentured servitude, writing, “In a knowledge economy, when a college degree is considered a passport to a decent livelihood, workforce entrants must go into debt in return for the right to labor. This kind of contract is the essence of indenture” (pp. 10–14). Like developing nations bound to unsupportable World Bank debt, student loans force young people into their own “structural adjustment programs”—choosing majors and careers based on ability to pay back loans, not do meaningful, creative, or autonomous work.

The depressive desperation of students, the degraded and frustrated faculty, hungry caterpillar administrators, and institutions more concerned with enrollment management than critical knowledge production may represent the final whimper in a society searching for some glimmer of possibility, some last gasp before the final demise of education as a contested terrain comes to pass. Yet, within this context, many scholars and teachers committed to a more democratic higher education have found hope and promise in the civic engagement movement. Usually comprised of various “engaged” forms of teaching, research, writing and application, the movement’s founders and framers brought much of their passion and experience from the 1960s and 1970s social movements. They hoped to integrate course content with community action and partnerships. As Stanton, Giles, and Cruz explain in their seminal work (2010): *Service Learning: Pioneers Reflect on its Origins, Practice, and Future*:

> [Founders] were community activists and educators…drawn to the idea that action in communities and structured learning could be combined to provide stronger service and leadership in communities and deeper, more relevant education for students. [They] worked independently and against the grain of what was expected and accepted in communities and the academy. It would take time for them to find each other, conceptualize their work, and institutionalize it as a pedagogy and as a field.

Indeed, we would be hard-pressed to find a more successful progressive movement within higher-education over the past three decades (Saltmarsh and Billig 2010). Almost every college and university has an office or center committed to service learning, civic engagement, or some other incantation and manifestation of the movement.

Still, civic engagement’s triumph has disappointed many of its practitioners despite troves of research and evidence proving its pedagogical merits enhancing course content and encouraging community awareness (Giles and Hatcher 2010).

One major complaint has been the lack of community partner participation in the design and evaluation of projects resulting in an emphasis on students' learning but little attention to the progressive impact on communities (Stoecker 2013; Dolgon et al. 2012). Another complaint notes that institutionalization itself limited the scope and political tenacity of civic engagement—in some ways a betrayal of the founders own social movements experiences and hopes to radically transform higher education. (Dolgon et al. 2012). While some advocates argue that service learning *benefits* from institutionalization (Butin 2010; Saltmarsh 2005) others contend that the forces of formalization and professionalization are exactly what have depoliticized academic feminism, anti-racism, and other "departmentalized" anti-colonial knowledge production once aligned with political movements (Stoecker 2016). What went wrong?

I believe the answer lies in the institutional real conditions and limits that make institutionalization a conservatizing force. The civic engagement movement's triumph has simultaneously capitalized on and been neutralized by higher education's neoliberalization. Ultimately, the movement succeeded on campuses across the nation *because* it neatly fit the needs of a corporate academy's economic and ideological goals. Civic engagement presents an integrated and seemingly compassionate, empathetic, and even democratic pedagogical practice and public relevancy, while NEVER seriously threatening the institutional real power of capitalism and white supremacy. In fact, the movement's advocates hardly acknowledge that higher education's own historical power and fundamental mission played a major role in creating the social problems they portend to address.

The Political Economy of Freddie Gray and an Inconvenient Truth About Higher Ed

A few weeks after Freddie Gray's death at the hands of Baltimore police and the massive protests against police brutality that followed, Johns Hopkins University [JHU] announced that its 21st Century Cities Initiatives program would, "Deploy researchers in wake of Baltimore unrest." Proposing a series of studies on everything from police activity and spikes in abandoned housing and landlord speculation, JHU faculty would conduct research to "help understand what was going on, why [the uprising] happened, and how to engage going forward" (Pearce 2015). But, Baltimore historians and activists had already documented the city's long history of racism, segregation and economic exploitation. From slave port to Jim Crow to its legendary redlining and racist housing policies, white supremacy and economic exploitation not only shaped, but dominated local history and geography. Most notable were the deep, severe pockets of economic and racial gerrymandering that left neighborhoods, especially Gray's hometown of East Baltimore, neglected, poor and under siege.

What makes the city a favorite image of urban dystopia (*Homicide*, *The Corner*, *The Wire*) is the all too real experiences of poor, non-white residents who experience daily the effects of disinvestment, gentrification, privatization, zero tolerance policing and draconian sentencing policies. The especially devastating role of police misconduct came to public light after Gray's death as a U.S. Department of Justice report found the BPD guilty of: (1) making unconstitutional stops, searches, and arrests; (2) using enforcement strategies that produce severe and unjustified disparities in the rates of stops, searches and arrests of African Americans; (3) using excessive force; and (4) retaliating against people engaging in constitutionally-protected expression. The report also cited racist practices in the implementation and enforcing of civil fines and fees—echoing DOJ's report on Ferguson, Missouri and a large literature on similar practices around the U.S. Combined, these forces turned East Baltimore into an economically ignored but highly securitized, segregated community, especially compared to its neighbor, JHU.

In fact, Hopkins played significant roles in the local economic development that *resulted* in the conditions Gray's community experienced. Participating in planning activities and investment strategies, JHU continued its expansion plans and land grabs throughout the 20th and early 21st Centuries. Gomez (2012) documents at least five separate periods during which JHU garnered millions in public and private funding to build not only their medical research and care facilities, but also housing, offices and services. Sometimes JHU drove expansion plans; other times city leaders invited them in. But in all of these elite-driven processes, Black and poor communities were marginalized and displaced. JHU was more than complicit, they actively participated in and benefited from creating the poverty and racism that shaped East Baltimore.

Thus, the notion that JHU social scientists would need "deployment" to help residents better understand the causes of the uprising seems insulting at best. But even worse is JHU's historical amnesia and lack of institutional ownership of its own role in supporting economic exploitation and white supremacy. As Gomez (2012) writes: while JHU's "hospital has grown to be the most prestigious hospital in the nation…the surrounding communities have grown poorer in wealth and health, with some of the most severe indicators of poor health in the state and the country" (p. 34). She continues:

> These inverse relationships, though seemingly disconnected, are not separate in the matrix of power acquiring more power while the disenfranchised continuously lose what little they have; one grows at the expense of the other, widening the gap of rich and poor. The history of race and class segregation and the laws and practices in housing, employment, education and health care established the conditions necessary for creating separate and unequal communities.

This history of JHU complicity and exploitation breathes beneath the neighborhood streets but remains invisible to its own institutional narrative of partnership and service. Gomez (2012) concludes that accepting, "a history of inequality has offered present-day society many blind spots to critically assessing the effects of racism and classism in creating and rebuilding poor communities today" (pp. 34–35).

Nowhere do such blind spots become more acutely visible than in JHU's discussion of civic engagement and service-learning. On their *Hopkins in the Community* webpage, JHU President Daniels proudly announces that, "Johns Hopkins' commitment to our city and our neighbors is not new; it is part of who we are, inherent in our work from clinics to classrooms. And in the wake of the unrest in Baltimore [in spring 2015]—a moment that laid bare harsh and multi-generational inequalities—our work is ever more important." The website itself suggests, "As the city's largest anchor institution, [JHU] feels the constant pull of urban issues. Our faculty, staff, students, and administrators answer the call on a daily basis…from volunteering as tutors in local schools to contributing nearly $5 billion in economic output in the city." In the *Student Outreach Resource Center Annual Report*, the Schools of Public Health, Nursing and Medicine reported that 1528 students volunteered 31,387 hours 2015–2016 at an "estimated economic contribution" of $836,150.

What do such narratives try to tell us about JHU and its engagement? First, the source of local social problems are not JHU's fault, but are "urban issues" that *draw* the university in by necessity. Secondly, given unavoidable challenges, JHU unselfishly shares its resources, thus naturalizing, legitimizing and moralizing its power, wealth and leadership. JHU is not only redeemed by its service, but engagement appears it raison d'etre. Yet, even the "white man's burden" narrative has been neoliberalized and must meet outcome measures. Thus, not only does JHU count student volunteer hours, but it allots a monetary value to them and brags about the financial sums donated through service.

I've written extensively about the serious intellectual and ethical problems of this *very* common practice of counting hours and monetizing service (Dolgon et al. 2017). The hour "data point" is junk science—it cannot be measured or operationalized in any meaningful way or even reasonably compared to any other hour by any other person at any other site. But it's quantitative and as such can be counted and fetishized, monetized and publicized, and turned into grants, awards, and PR. Monetizing it, however makes it bad ethics, not just bad science. After all, if we call it service-learning and argue engaged pedagogy enhances student learning, then shouldn't communities attach a price-tag to their teaching and charge universities. But they never do.

A final issue linking monetization to the neoliberal narrative of civic engagement came as JHU sought increased public support for expansion. JHU lobbied and raised money as it spoke of free medical care and services to the community's poor. With no irony, the very institution whose development played key roles in segregation and poverty promoted expansion to better ameliorate the problems they created. Such is the bold arrogance and inconvenient truth of the modern academy.

Before concluding with some suggestions for what we might do and teach within the powerful structures and cultures of higher education's institutional real, let me acknowledge that JHU is in no way unique in its hypocrisy. I could easily have discussed many colleges and universities who not only benefitted from slavery but participated in its operations: from financing, purchasing, leasing and using slaves, to training student militias to capture runaway slaves and putting down slave rebellions. Or like JHU in Baltimore, I could have discussed Columbia University in Harlem and its long history of development, displacement, and exploitation. The Universities of Chicago, Pennsylvania, Michigan, and many others have similar stories. Most recently, Harvard University received $10 million to study racial poverty and inequality in Boston at the same time that its kitchen workers struck for decent wages and benefits. The academy is rife with these ironies, demonstrating the difficulties that higher education continues to have in addressing the institutional real of its capitalist and white supremacist DNA.

Bring the Three Rs to Contemporary Higher Education

In response to the overwhelming power and impact of the institutional real in higher education, I argue we need a strong commitment to the three "R's": truth and Reconciliation, Reparations, and Radical consciousness raising.

1. *Truth and Reconciliation*—This idea is not new and for almost a decade now dozens of institutions have supported research, reports and even formal apologies for their role in promoting and benefitting from slavery (William and Mary 2016; Brown University 2011; Emory University 2011). All colleges and universities must follow suit, but not just about connections to slavery. Higher education must recognize its role in supporting and marketing economic and social stratification, often to the detriment of surrounding communities. Truth and reconciliation must extend to the ways in which universities have exploited local politics and development strategies for their own gain—not the general public's welfare.
2. *Reparations*—Again, this is not necessarily a new idea as many colleges and universities offer a modicum of scholarships to local youth and increasingly get involved in local public school districts. Yet, they continue to operate as elite economic development engines that benefit a few and harm many poor and working class neighborhoods. The same efforts now fueling research into past institutional relationships with slave economies and racist practices must also promote critical efforts to create new economic strategies that incorporate anti-discriminatory and democratically inspired forms of development. We should not be surprised that institutions are initially better at historical research on racial systems than they are on reflecting on and reconsidering economic structures that will democratize wealth, not just opportunity.
3. *Teach Radical consciousness*—In part, this effort involves teaching the institutional real. We should promote within our institutions a variety of methods for examining higher education itself and our own unique histories within the communities and regions we inhabit. Ideally, these would be akin to the freshman required courses that teach students how to be college students, improve study skills, be aware of college offices and services. They could easily be incorporated into freshman comp classes and other first year programs,

documenting the economic and social impact of institutional and local history, race relations, etc. Committed faculty may also have to develop other strategies to do this kind of work "outside" of traditional institutions for obvious reasons. Interdisciplinary faculty teams committed to putting such courses together will need to strategize based on courses offered and resources available. One key element would be to have committed faculty groups meet, plan, develop and evaluate curriculum and pedagogy.

The civic engagement movement could revitalize (or in Randy Stoecker's words "liberate" itself) by taking on these three R's and using them as guiding principles and fundamental goals. For example, much of the movement's partnership literature stresses collaboration and reciprocity but from a transactional approach. Instead, institutions and faculty must work with community partners also committed to radical practices and social justice—grass roots democracy, anti-racism, etc.—to create *transformational* partnerships. These relationships will challenge both the elite structures and practices of knowledge production as well as the elite goals of affirming and expanding elite power and wealth.

Meanwhile, all workers in higher education must organize and create forms of solidarity among and between staff and faculty units. Teaching assistants and adjunct faculty, kitchen workers and custodians, have maintained and even intensified unionization efforts in the past decade. But full-time faculty and professional units have been slow to support and often hinder such efforts. "An injury to one is an injury to all" rings true in all industries, including the knowledge factory. And we can't be vague about teaching such democratic principles to our students whose own futures are wrapped up in these struggles as well. It means training students with a more critical and engaged "political education." It also means moving from the very useful idea of "critical" service learning and civic engagement proposed by Mitchell (2008), to a "radical" or even "revolutionary" civic engagement that promotes radical citizenship, democratic and collaborative knowledge production, and constant strategizing about the political engagements that informs knowledge production and collective social action.

In conclusion, one cannot deny the power of the institutional real and the role that education, in general, and higher education, in particular, have played in buttressing capitalist exploitation and white supremacy. But all revolutionary movements must fight on multiple terrains to challenge the forces of domination and inequality. Mario Savio once told thousands of UC Berkeley student protesters demanding their free speech and civil rights that, if universities were corporations, then faculty were employees and students were the raw material. He suggested, however, that students would not be made into any product to be bought and sold by the university and clients—students were human beings. He concluded:

> There's a time when the operation of the machine becomes so odious, makes you so sick at heart, that you can't take part! You can't even passively take part! And you've got to put your bodies upon the gears and upon the wheels…upon the levers, upon all the apparatus, and you've got to make it stop! And you've got to indicate to the people who run it, to the people who own it, that unless you're free, the machine will be prevented from working at all!

We are rapidly reaching such a time where faculty and students and communities may no longer be able to even passively take part. Radical pedagogy and democratic engagement must be historically informed and politically courageous to not only stop the institutional real of capitalist exploitation and white supremacy, but to begin envisioning what a socially just university might look like.

References

American Association of University Professors (AAUP). (2016). Retrieved at https://www.aaup.org/our-programs/academic-freedom/censure-list. Accessed April 28, 2017.

Apple, M. (2004). *Ideology and curriculum* (3rd ed.). New York: Routledge.

Apple, M. (2015). Reframing the question of whether education can change society. *Educational Theory, 65*(3), 299–315.

Au, W. (2011). Teaching under the new Taylorism: High-stakes testing and the standardization of the 21st century curriculum. *Journal of Curriculum Studies, 43*(1), 25–45.

Baptist, E. (2014). *The half has never been told: Slavery and the making of American capitalism.* New York: Basic Books.

Barbush, B. Middle East stories: Images and words from a displaced community. https://bethbarbush.com/stories/middle-east-baltimore/. Accessed April 28, 2017.

Beins, M., Lapovsky Kennedy, A., & Lapovsky Kennedy E. (2005). *Women's studies for the future: Foundations, interrogations, politics*. New Brunswick: Rutgers University Press.

Billig, S., & Waterman, A. (2014). *Studying service-learning: Innovations in education research methodology*. New York: Routledge.

Bowles, S., & Gintis, H. (1976). *Schooling in capitalist America: Educational reform and the contradictions of economic life*. New York: Basic Books.

Boyles, D. (2000). *American education and corporations: The free market goes to school*. New York: Routledge.

Braverman, H. (1974). *Labor and monopoly capital: The degradation of work in the twentieth century*. New York: Monthly Review Press.

Brown University Steering Committee on Slavery and Justice. (2011). *Slavery and justice report*. Providence, RI: Brown University. https://www.brown.edu/Research/Slavery_Justice/documents/SlaveryAndJustice.pdf. Accessed April 28, 2017.

Bullock, H. A. (1967). *A history of negro education in the south: 1619-to the present*. Cambridge: Harvard University Press.

Butin, D. (2010). *Service-learning in theory and practice: The future of community engagement in higher education*. New York: Springer.

Camp, S. L. (2012). Reform to repatriation: Gendering an Americanization movement in early twentieth-century California. In S. M. Spencer-Wood (Ed.), *Historical and archaeological perspectives on gender transformations contributions to global historical archaeology*. New York: Springer.

Chomsky, N. (2014). How America's great university system is being destroyed. *Counter punch*. http://www.alternet.org/corporate-accountability-and-workplace/chomsky-how-americas-great-university-system-getting. Accessed February 28, 2017.

Chomsky, N., Nader, L., Lewontin, R., & Wallerstein, I. (1998). *The cold war and the university: Toward an intellectual history of the postwar years*. New York: New Press.

Churchill, W. (2004). *Kill the indian, save the man: The genocidal impact of American indian residential schools*. San Francisco: City Lights Books.

Conway, J. M. (2004). *Identity, place, knowledge: Social movements contesting globalization*. Halifax, Nova Scotia: Fernwood Publishing.

Daniels, R. (2002). *Coming to America: A history of immigration and ethnicity in American life*. New York: Harper Perennial.
Delucchi, M., & Smith, W. L. (1997). Satisfied customers versus pedagogic responsibility: Further thoughts on student consumerism. *Teaching Sociology, 25*(4), 336.
Doane, J. W. (2003). Contested terrain: Negotiating racial understanding in public discourse. *Humanity & Society, 27*(4), 554–575.
Dolgon, C. (1998). Rising from the ashes: The Michigan memorial Phoenix project and the corporatization of university-based scientific research. *Educational Studies, 24*(1), 5–32.
Dolgon, C., Mitchell, T., & Eatman, T. (2017). *Cambridge university handbook on service learning and civic engagement*. New York: Cambridge University Press.
Dolgon, C., & Roth, R. (2016). Twenty-first-century workers' education in North America: The defeat of the left or a revitalized class pedagogy? *Labor Studies Journal, 41*(1), 89–113.
Durkheim, E. (1956). *Education and sociology*. New York: Simon and Schuster.
Echols, A. (1989). *Daring to be bad: Radical feminism in America, 1967–1975*. Minneapolis: University of Minnesota Press.
Emory University. (2011). *Statement of regret*. History and Traditions. http://emoryhistory.emory.edu/issues/challenges/discrimination/slavery/index.html. Accessed April 28, 2017.
Evans, S. (1980). *Personal politics: The roots of women's liberation in the civil rights movement & the new left*. New York: Vintage Press.
Eyler, J., & Giles, D. E., Jr. (1999). *Where's the learning in service-learning?* San Francisco: Jossey-Bass Inc.
Faler, P. (1974). Cultural aspects of the industrial revolution: Lynn, Massachusetts, shoemakers and industrial morality, 1826–1860. *Labor History, 15*(3).
Fernandez-Kelly, P. (2016). *The hero's fight: African Americans in west Baltimore and the shadow of the state*. Princeton, NJ: Princeton University Press.
Fine, Michelle, Greene, C., & Sanchez, S. (2016). Neoliberal blues and prec(ar)ious knowledge. *Urban Review: Issues and Ideas in Public Education, 48*(4), 499–519.
Frost, J. (2001). *An interracial movement of the poor: Community organizing and the new left*. New York: New York University Press.
Frydl, J. K. (2009). *The G.I. Bill* (1st ed.). Cambridge: Cambridge University Press.
Geiger, R. (2004). *Research and relevant knowledge: American research universities since world war II*. New Brunswick, NJ: Transaction Publishers.
Geraghty, S. (2015). How the criminalization of poverty has become normalized in American culture and why you should care. *Michigan Journal Race & Law, 21*, 195.
Gerstle, G. (2002). *Working-class Americanism: The politics of labor in a textile city, 1914–1960*. Princeton: Princeton University Press.
Ginsburg, B. (2011). *The fall of the faculty: The rise of the all-administrative university and why it matters*. Oxford: Oxford University Press.
Gitlin, T. (1987). *Sixties: Years of hope: Days of rage*. New York: Bantam Books.
Gomez, M. (2012). *Race, class, power, and organizing in east Baltimore: Rebuilding abandoned communities in America*. New York: Lexington Books.
Gutman, H. (1977). *Work, culture and society in industrial America*. New York: Vintage Books.
Haney-López, I. (2006). *White by law: The legal construction of race*. New York: New York University Press.
Hatcher, J., Bringle, R., & Hahn, T. (2016). *Research on student civic outcomes in service learning: Conceptual frameworks and methods*. Sterling, VA: Stylus Publishing.
Higginbotham, L. (1978). *In the matter of color: Race and the American legal process: The colonial period*. New York: Oxford University Press.
Johns Hopkins University. (2016). Hopkins in the community. https://www.jhu.edu/about/community/. Accessed April 28, 2017.
Johns Hopkins University Schools of Nursing, Public Health and Medicine. (2016). SOURCE (Student Outreach Resource Center) The community engagement and service-learning center, annual report 2015–2016. http://SOURCE.jhu.edu. Accessed April 28, 2017.

Karabel, J., & Halsey, A. H. (1977). *Power and ideology in education*. New York: Oxford University Press.

Katz, M. (1989). *Reconstructing American education*. Cambridge: Harvard University Press.

Kerr, C. (2001). *The uses of the university* (5th ed.). Cambridge: Harvard University Press.

Kliewer, B. W. (2013). Why the civic engagement movement cannot achieve democratic and justice aims. *Michigan Journal of Community Service Learning, 19*(2), 72–80.

Koeber, C., Wright, D., & Dingler, E. (2012). Self-service in the labor process: Control and consent in the performance of "consumptive labor". *Humanity & Society, 36*(1), 6–29.

Lagemann, E. C. (1996). *Contested terrain: A history of education research in the United States, 1890–1990*. Washington, D.C.: Spenser Foundation.

Lehman Brothers Education Group. (1996). *Investment opportunity in the education industry*. New York: Lehman Brothers.

Leslie, S. (1993). *The cold war and American science: The military-industrial-academic complex at MIT and Stanford*. New York: Columbia University Press.

Lynd, R., & Lynd, H. (1928). *Middletown: A study in modern American culture*. New York: Harcourt, Brace and World.

McDew, C. (1966). Spiritual and moral aspects of the student nonviolent struggle in the South. In Mitchell Cohen & Dennis Hale (Eds.), *The new student left* (pp. 51–57). Boston, MA: Beacon Press.

McDougall, H. (1993). *Black Baltimore: A new theory of community*. Philadelphia, PA: Temple University Press.

Miller, J. (1987). *Democracy is in the streets: From Port Huron to the siege of Chicago*. New York: Simon & Schuster.

Mitchell, T. D. (2008). Traditional vs. critical service-learning: Engaging the literature to differentiate two models. *Michigan Journal of Community Service Learning, 14*(2).

Morton, M., Dolgon, C., Maher, T., & Pennell, J. (2012). Civic engagement and public sociology: Two 'movements' in search of a mission. *Journal of Applied Social Sciences., 6*(1), 5–30.

Naidoo, R. & Jamison, I. (2005). Empowering participants or corroding learning? Towards a research agenda on the impact of student consumerism in higher education. *Journal of Education Policy, 20* (3).

Nix, E. M., Hollowak, T. L., & Elfenbein, J. I. (2011). *Baltimore '68: Riots and rebirth in an American city*. Philadelphi, PA: Temple University.

Noble, D. (2003). *Digital diploma mills: The automation of higher education*. New York: Monthly Review Press.

Orser, W. E. (2015). *Blockbusting in Baltimore: The Edmondson Village story*. Lexington, KY: University Press of Kentucky.

Ozga, J. (2000). *Policy research in educational settings: Contested terrain*. Philadelphia: Open University Press.

Pai, Y., & Adler, S. (1997). *Cultural foundations of educations*. Saddle River, NJ: Prentice Hall.

Payne, M. C. (2008). *Teach freedom: Education for liberation in the African-American tradition*. New York: Teachers College Press.

Pearce, K. (2015). HUB https://hub.jhu.edu/2015/05/11/21cc-rapid-research-baltimore. Accessed April 28, 2017.

Peterson, P. (1985). *The politics of school reform, 1870–1940*. Chicago: University of Chicago Press.

Pietila, A. (2012). *Not in my neighborhood: How bigotry shaped a great American city*. New York: Rowman & Littlefield.

Power, G. (1983). Apartheid Baltimore style: The residential segregation ordinances of 1910–1913. *Maryland. Law Review, 42*, 289.

Puente, M. (2014, September 28). Undue force. *Baltimore Sun*. http://data.baltimoresun.com/news/police-settlements/. Accessed April 28, 2017.

Readings, B. (1994). *The university in ruins*. Cambridge: Harvard University Press.

Rhoads, R., Camacho, M. S., Toven-Lindsey, B., & Berdan Lozano, J. (2015). Massive open online course movement, xMOOCs, and faculty labor. *Review of Higher Education, 38*(3), 397–424.

Rice, M. J. (1913). *Scientific management in education.* New York: Hynes, Noble & Eldridge.

Ross, A. (2014). *Creditocracy: And the case for debt refusal.* New York: OR Books.

Saltmarsh, J., & Zlotkowski, E. (2015). *Higher education and democracy: Essays on service-learning and civic engagement.* Philadelphia: Temple University Press.

Sanchez, G. (1994). Go after the women: Americanization and the Mexican immigrant woman, 1915–1929. In V. Ruiz & E. C. Dubois (Eds.), *Unequal sisters: A multi-cultural reader in U.S. women's history.* New York: Routledge.

Saxton, A. (1990). *The rise and fall of the white republic: Class politics and mass culture in nineteenth century America.* London: Verso Press.

Schrecker, E. (2010). Academic freedom in the corporate university. *Radical Teacher, 93,* 38–45.

Scott, D. L. (2012). How the American university was killed in five easy steps. https://junctrebellion.wordpress.com/2012/08/12/how-the-american-university-was-killed-in-five-easy-steps/. Accessed April 28, 2017.

Simpson, J. (2014). *Longing for justice: Higher education and democracy's agenda.* Toronto: University of Toronto Press.

Stanton, T., Giles, D., & Cruz, N. (1999). *Service learning: A movement's pioneers reflect on its origins, practice and future.* San Francisco: Jossey-Bass.

Stoecker, R. (2016). *Liberating service learning and the rest of higher education civic engagement.* Philadelphia: Temple University Press.

Stoecker, R., Tryon, E. A., & Hilgendorf, A. (2009). *The unheard voices: Community organizations and service learning.* Philadelphia: Temple University Press.

Taylor, R. H. (1925). Humanizing the slave code of North Carolina. *The North Carolina Historical Review,* 2(3), 323–331.

Tirelli, V. (1997). Adjuncts and more adjuncts: Labor segmentation and the transformation of higher education. *Social Text, 51,* 75–91.

Trumpbour, J. (1999). *How Harvard rules: Reason in the service of empire.* Boston: Beacon Press.

Tuchman, G. (2011). *Wannabe u: Inside the corporate university.* Chicago: University of Chicago Press.

United States Department of Justice, Civil Rights Division. (2016). Investigation of the Baltimore police department. Washington, D.C. https://www.justice.gov/crt/file/883296/download. Accessed April 28, 2017.

Wallace, A. D. (1995). *Education for extinction: American Indians and the boarding school experience, 1875–1928.* Lawrence, KS: University Press of Kansas.

Washburn, J. (2006). *University, inc.: The corporate corruption of higher education.* New York: Basic Books.

White, G. (2000). *Campus inc. corporate power in the ivory tower.* Amherst, NY: Prometheus Books.

William and Mary. (2016). The lemon project: A journey of reconciliation. http://www.wm.edu/sites/lemonproject/index.php. Accessed April 28, 2017.

Williams, H. (2009). *Self-taught: African American education in slavery and freedom.* Chapel Hill: University of North Carolina Press.

Ziegler-McPherson, C. (2010). *Americanization in the states: Immigrant social welfare policy, citizenship, and national identity in the United States, 1908–1929.* Gainesville: University of Florida Press.

Conclusion
Final Words on Social Class and the Invisible Power Elite

By Leontina Hormel, University of Idaho, lhormel@uidaho.edu

It was 25 years ago that I first thought about social class stratification in US society, my place in that system, and how my educated middle class background had nothing on the power the elites of our society exercise and largely inherit. In the acknowledgements section, I mention my gratitude to the late Jeffers Chertok, to whom I credit with instilling in me the importance of workers' rights and protections and introducing me to intersectional analysis. Jeffers Chertok's 1960s graduate studies took place in the United States during a period of lively intellectual reflection, radicalism, and calls for change in higher education. He was part of a cohort of University of Oregon graduate students that included the late Joan Acker and Lawrence Carter, both of whom were influential in my graduate experiences and studies at University of Oregon in the 1990s. In fact, when I first met Larry Carter when considering studying at UO, he spent an hour reminiscing with me about being a young radical student hanging out with Jeffers and Joan, describing them both as fiery lefties who he held dearly in his heart. And, he couldn't help but share the story of a small bomb going off in the basement of Prince Lucien Campbell Hall, or PLC, where the editing work was done for the newly created journal *The Insurgent Sociologist* (now called *Critical Sociology*).

It was easy to imagine Jeffers palling about with Larry Carter and Joan Acker, as all three were the change that these times in academia represented and were promoting. Larry Carter was the first Black male faculty member hired in sociology at University of Oregon and Joan Acker was the first female faculty member hired in the same department—both made lasting intellectual contributions to sociology. With his passion for Marxist sociology, most especially his commitment to praxis, Jeffers taught passionately at Eastern Washington University, a commuter school out in Cheney, Washington (about a half hour drive west from the city of Spokane). His contributions were no less than his grad school buddies' as an EWU sociology instructor who inspired at least this one person to coauthor a book that captures the heart of what he wanted the thousands of students he eventually taught to comprehend and to use in making our world better.

What do I remember from Prof. Chertok's class that completely altered my way of thinking? First, after discussing Talcott Parson's insights about social class, he

K. Haltinner and L. Hormel (eds.), *Teaching Economic Inequality and Capitalism in Contemporary America*, https://doi.org/10.1007/978-3-319-71141-6

assigned an eye-opening essay that required we interview our paternal or maternal side of our family to figure out our social class location and to consider how Parsons helped us understand why we think we are in one social class versus another (see Family History and Social Class Location in Appendix A for a full description). I always thought of myself as lower class during my childhood. My dad was a lawyer, sure, but we faced lots of lean times as a family with five children. Moreover, dad defended a lot of people who couldn't afford him. He knew that and represented them, anyway. As a kid, I wore hand-me-down clothes dating from the early 1960s when I was an elementary student of the 1970s. To save money on meat, my parents went "halfsies" with one of our friends to purchase 100 retired laying hens, which both of our families slaughtered in our backyard one weekend, doing all of the cold-bath plucking and butchering in two days. (Add to this image, this all took place in the backyard of a house located in the middle of downtown Ephrata, Washington, on the town's main street.) Moreover, my parents did not pay for my college education—insisting that their kids would not learn to work hard if it were simply free for them. Of course, my siblings and I always understood this to be a way of saving face, since, besides instilling in us a proper work ethic, they probably couldn't cover the cost of higher education for all five of us.

This essay assignment, though, highlighted how much *privilege* I had in terms of education access on the paternal side of my family. I never thought about my last name—Hormel. Through Prof. Chertok's assignment, I learned that my grandfather was related to the wealthy family that founded Hormel meatpacking. Not only did he earn a college degree in the 1920s, but the aunt he loved so much also went to college in the late 19th century and had been marginalized by family because she was considered a "feminist," because of her "over education." My grandfather expected my dad to not only finish a four-year college degree, but to go on to study medicine. My father "let him down" by opting to become a lawyer, not a doctor. All of this I learned through the oral history essay assignment, including the fact my grandfather disowned the Hormel family after they tried to force him to break up with his one true love, Leontina Wilhelmina Weisenberger. Just one assignment, and I learned that much from it.

Second, Prof. Chertok assigned Harry Braverman's classic *Labor and Monopoly Capital*. As a student working her way through college as a retail associate and on-again, off-again food server in Spokane, Braverman's story of Taylorized, deskilled, and alienated labor helped me make sense of my work experiences. Not only that, but his conclusion that described how once-prestigious work, once it is deskilled enough, is feminized. It is not that women ought to be worth less in the paid workforce, but—thanks to the trusty gender pay gap—it becomes possible to replace men with the cheap, female workers who accept far less pay for a variety of institutional and interpersonal reasons. Braverman also noted that this deskilling and capital's constant pursuit of seeking cheaper and cheaper labor also meant that formerly "good jobs" would be filled with more women and people of color.

I was seeing this happen in my own experiences in retail. In 1988, when I was hired to work at the Northwest department store The Crescent, which was—soon after my hire—bought by the larger US department store chain Frederick & Nelson. I worked around women who had worked for the regionally-owned retailer for decades, who had likely replaced men from earlier eras (though many men still worked at the store in the men's department, furniture, and electronics). These women were covered by employer-provided health insurance and pensions that supported a timely retirement. At the time when I was taking this course, though, Frederick & Nelson was newly purchased by Federated Retailers, a corporation heavily promoting the passage of NAFTA with positive-messaging brochures conveniently left in the employee lunch room each week for us to read. At the same time, store management was offering severance pay to the older female sales associates to encourage early retirement and replace them with young, mostly female, associates who had to pay for health benefits themselves and had no pension plan. I was one of those young associates. After reading Braverman's book, I was bummed and a little bit indignant about the cruel practices under capitalism. It was clear to me that us Gen Xers were getting totally screwed in this new era. We were learning that we would be the first generation to experience multiple career changes and no upward mobility relative to our parents. In other words, my friends and I had a reason for our Gen X angst and this explains, undoubtedly, our love of watching free, live shows with the likes of Pearl Jam and the Posies in early 1990s Spokane. (Nirvana never played for free, just an FYI.)

Third, Prof. Chertok assigned William Domhoff's *Who Rules America?* If I wasn't already outraged after reading Braverman, well, a study of power elites and all of the ways they inherit and protect their social location in US society certainly tipped me over the edge. As someone raised in eastern Washington State, I had no inkling of this group's existence, to say the least of its level of power and privileged status. But, I did understand that I had a lot of friends and family members who were struggling under the weight of increasing debt from student loans and over-charged credit cards at the same time that housing prices and rents were rapidly growing. I started college with the 1987 Black Friday market crash and was about to end my studies with another economic recession in 1993. All of this was felt and in full view in Spokane, Washington, where I lived and worked while finishing my undergraduate degree. Learning that our abilities were practically nil to move up in the social ladder and be members of the elite class of people who dominate in decisions about American social policy, economic policy, and politics helped draw the curtain back for me enough to figuratively shout out, "The Emperor has no clothes!"

Though I could describe more about what I gained from Prof. Chertok's social stratification course, I am sure readers are wondering how I have determined this to be proper subject matter for concluding a book that multiple authors have helped Kristin and me to craft. This book's contributors are committed to teaching economic inequalities and capitalism in America and this commitment means they are generous enough to share their ideas with other instructors and professional learners. The learning experiences I share from my undergraduate education, though, help encapsulate the motivations and themes shared in this book's pages.

All of the authors seem to agree that students need to be able to personally connect to the subject of class inequality, no matter their particular social class membership. Without a student's personal connection, they may not comprehend the important role social class narratives and practices play in the United States to silence those positioned in the lowest tiers in the hierarchy. Silence will lead to ongoing sacrifices among an increasing number of people who are degraded through a variety of ways in the capitalist system. Part II, Making the Personal Political: The Stories of Capitalism is a direct reference to this understanding of student learning and praxis, though each book chapter is guided by the underlying assumption that students are most easily moved as engaged citizens if they can personally situate themselves in course literature, discussions, and exercises.

Just as the essay assignment and Braverman's book did for me, the emphasis in these chapters is the standpoint of low-income, working-class, and middle class members—the perspectives and life experiences we are most likely to encounter as instructors in the colleges and universities we represent. Several authors, for instance Retchitsky and Olsberg, Machum, and Backer, describe the role education plays in creating a class-unaware student population that has come to expect passive learning and to be blind to how their own behaviors in and outside of class reinforce classed social expectations and processes. Nowhere are the benefits of this type of education for the capitalist system more clear than in Rose Brewer's racial and class critique of capitalism and the neoliberal university and Corey Dolgon's historical critique of higher education's commitment to conservatism in US society. These observations are disturbing as we come to understand that students from working-class and poor families participate in their own subjugation, playing right in to the hegemonic relations Antonio Gramsci revealed nearly a century ago in his prison notes.

Kristin and I worked hard to be inclusive and to cast as broad a net as possible when seeking contributors so that the themes and angles of inquiry regarding economic inequalities and American capitalism would be represented. What we noticed, though, after all of the chapters were written and assembled was that the ever-so-important vantage point I learned in Prof. Chertok's stratification class—the position of C. Wright Mills' power elite, whose survival strategies were mapped out so effectively in William Domhoff's book—was missing. The different life chances between class-privileged Harold and working-class Bob during their different life stages that Gerbrandt and Strahm draw out in their interactive class exercise gives us a glimpse of how class privilege is protected through building exclusive environments. Barbara Chasin's chapter "Inequality and Violence" includes the way the United States as a world power uses military intervention as its means to secure its elite status in the global economy and geopolitics. In our book, though, we missed the opportunity to learn more about how people investigate the power elite and power structures in their courses.

We have important literature that updates and goes beyond C. Wright Mills' and William Domhoff's earlier, foundational works. These contemporary studies investigate how elites operate. A new book has been published this year (2017) *Elite White Men Ruling: Who, What, When, Where, and How* by Joe Feagin and

Kimberly Ducey that updates and exposes the major players in the early 21st century. Other books, such as Jane Mayer's *Dark Money* (2016), are exposing the level of strategic planning and collusion elite families in the United States have pursued in order to protect "business as usual," which has enabled the top one percent of the wealthiest individuals in 2013 to "hold nearly half of the national wealth invested in stocks and mutual funds" (Inequality.org). And, Leslie Sklair's *The Transnational Capitalist Class*, has helped us broaden the scope of these investigations to global social networks. In fact, this latter form of analysis helps us understand that the media buzz about possible connections between elite individuals like Donald Trump and Vladimir Putin are merely a reflection of social protocol among members of the TCC. Because power elite and power structure analyses are critical to students' comprehension of the full spectrum of class locations in society, I have contributed an assignment idea that may help students learn how to map power networks in their local communities (see Appendix A). We have even more access in the 21st century to the investigatory tools for mapping power elites' social, political, and organizational networks, which is yet another way to ensure that our students do not perpetuate the thinking and processes that serve this small group at the top.

Appendix A
Classroom Activities and Assignments

This Appendix consists of a variety of classroom activities and assignments to assist instructors in teaching about issues regarding economic inequality and capitalism. The activities were developed by the authors of chapters and pertain directly to the reflections contained in the book.

Active Learning Activities

Activity I: The Bob and Harold Presentation by Roxanne Gerbrandt and Ann Strahm
Activity II: The Income Quiz, by Charlotte Kunkel
Activity III: The Train Game by Charlotte Kunkel
Activity IV: Building Economic (In)Equality by Derek Robey and Jason Robey
Activity V: Mapping Local Social Networks by Leontina Hormel
Activity VI: Socialist Discussion Grades by David I. Backer
Activity VII: Discussing U.S. Military Interventions Since WWII by Barbara Chasin

Sample Assignments

Activity VIII: Envisioning Alternatives to Capitalism by Kristin Haltinner
Activity IX: Commodity Research Assignment by Eric Edwards

Activity I: The Bob and Harold Presentation by Roxanne Gerbrandt (Austin Peay State University) and Ann Strahm (California State University at Stanislaus)

Pedagogical Goal of Activity
Our exercise and presentation of a fictional "Bob and Harold" follows the lives of two people (from working class and upper-middle class backgrounds, respectively), their families, and especially their lived experience from the teenage years to mid-career. The goal of the exercise is to stimulate class discussion and reflection;

K. Haltinner and L. Hormel (eds.), *Teaching Economic Inequality and Capitalism in Contemporary America*, https://doi.org/10.1007/978-3-319-71141-6

enabling all students to see how ascribed class is structural in nature and often reproduced independent of individual effort, and challenging the hegemonic ideology of meritocracy.

Assignment Description and Instructions

The instructor will need to develop a method of presentation to allow for an interactive discussion with students, using a visual aid (we use a PowerPoint presentation, but this could also work with a whiteboard/chalkboard) to keep track of the various costs encountered by the two characters, a running tally of their indebtedness, and the intersection of their class position with each stage of their life course (described below). We typically take 80–90 min to go through the entire presentation. The typical class time will require the presentation be divided over two to three class periods. It is important to allow the time for the students to engage and interact with the story as it progresses. It's also important to not correct students. Rather, we find the nature of the class discussions allows them to reflect and analyze their way to the conclusion that social class is a structurally—not individually—created phenomenon.

As we move through the presentation, we also shift the focus; talking about social class from a micro-level first, then at the end looking at social class from a more meso-level focus. This shift then allows us to introduce the idea of macro-level social class structures, which can be very powerful while students are invested and connected with the two characters of Bob and Harold.

Bob and Harold are presented to the students as two white heterosexual and Christian young men, from different class backgrounds. We made the characters come from the dominant groups in an effort to allow students to have only one difference with which to grapple—class. This was purposeful so as to allow the students to compare/contrast Bob and Harold's experiences and life courses with their own. Students of color, religious, gender, and sexual minorities will be able to discuss the ways in which their own marginalized status(es) intersects with social class, when guided through such reflection by the instructor and each other. This open space allows the instructor to probe students' understanding of the intersectionalities of their own lives when it comes to social class, providing opportunity for students to engage the subject more deeply.

We take the students on the journey of Bob and Harold through their lives, highlighting various important life intervals, presenting keystone events in their lives. At each event, we ask the students to give us examples or comment on the choices made and outcomes of those choices for Bob and Harold (and what similar choices and outcomes might be for our students):

- Bob and Harold at 16—Getting a car
  - Bob must take out a loan for a car—$5000 @ 16% interest; $175/mo.
  - Harold gets a nice, used car from his family, worth $9000 with no interest; $0/mo.

Class prompts and comments: How does Bob get a car? He needs to get a job. How does he get a job? He takes the bus. Discussions can focus on public transportation; "Buy here-pay here" car lots, predatory lending, etc.

- Bob and Harold at 18/19—Decide to go to college
  - Bob gets students loans for undergraduate/graduate (MBA)—total $84,000 @ 7.35% interest; $990/mo.
  - Harold has his family pay for both undergraduate/graduate (MBA)—total $0; $0/mo.

Class prompts and comments: Discussions about the value of education and investment in your own future are appropriate here. However, the focus should then shift to how Bob and Harold pay for their college. This is a particularly good space to have students discuss their own journey to/through higher education—especially for first generation students. Approximately 30% of incoming freshmen and American colleges and universities are first generation students and most of these students have struggled to navigate the bureaucracy that is higher education. This is a good place to allow students who are first generation to tell their stories to students who aren't first generation, and it is a good place for the instructor to re/introduce Bourdieu's concepts of habitus and social/cultural/economic class, using higher education as the field where habitus impacts those different Bourdieusian classes, and in turn, how they intersect with social class.

- Bob and Harold at 26—Get jobs in Denver and decide it's time to buy a house (Housing costs are scaled in this presentation for this city; median price Junior Executive home @ $460K; median price home @ $270K as of this writing).
  - Bob buys a house for $240K some distance from work and other executives; 3% down, 6.75% interest, plus paying mortgage insurance for not having 20% down—$2020/mo.
  - Harold's buys a house for $380K closer to work and in the same neighborhood as other mid-level executives. His family provides him with a gift of the 20% down ($76K); 4.5% interest; no mortgage insurance needed—$1880/mo.

Class prompts and comments: This section requires some setup and exposition from the presenter. There are two main threads to follow as you lead the discussions. One centers on the mechanisms for home purchase (lending, mortgage rates, credit ratings, mortgage insurance, down payments, etc.) The other discussion should focus on the social capital related to each home purchase: what is social capital, how does it manifest; what is it's relation to social class. This is a great place to get into the details. Below is a couple of examples of ways to discuss this section.

Discuss the layout of junior executive homes versus working class homes:

- for entertaining
- floor plans

  - open versus traditional closed
  - powder rooms/half-bath versus traditional full

- outdoor spaces

  - entertaining
  - curb appeal

Discuss the neighborhoods

- what the neighborhood layout signify (lifestyle)

  - Bob's neighbors are more working class

    older homes and roads
    smaller lots
    family maintained lawns

  - Harold's neighbors are professionals and ascending executives

    - newer, larger homes
    - newer roads that are maintained/updated regularly (newer homes are often in what's called assessment districts)
    - larger lots with professional landscaping

These elements should lead to a discussion of the ways social class is reproduced using homes and neighborhoods as creator and reproducer of social capital.

- Bob and Harold—Grandma dies

  - Bob helps to pay for funeral expenses for his grandma; his family can't afford it all.
  - Harold's grandma has a $100,000 life insurance policy in his name—tax free! Harold uses the money to buy a nicer, newer house near his boss. His payments remain at $1880/mo.

Class prompts and comments: This is the introduction of a 'life event'; something that none of us can control. Again, the discussions can focus on two areas: This life event has different outcomes in part because of the differing social class between Bob and Harold (paying for the funeral vs. getting a life insurance policy). The other discussion can focus on the importance of Harold spending the money on a newer, nicer house near to his boss.

- Bob and Harold—Get married

  - Bob and Cathy get married; neither of their families can help, so Bob and Cathy pay $33,000 for their wedding (the average cost in Denver). They pay for the wedding using four different credit cards—now maxed out.
  - Harold and Tabitha get married; Tabitha's parents pay for the wedding, and Harold's family gives them a gift of Denver Country Club memberships.

Class prompts and comments: The discussions here can focus on the cost of the wedding, and the use of credit cards, but the presenter should shift the focus towards a deeper discussion of social capital, and social exclusion—the use of a wedding as a means for professional networking, for example. Also, and importantly, what does it mean to Harold and Tabitha if they have Country Club memberships?

- If students are unfamiliar with country clubs and other exclusionary forms of social capital accumulation, the instructor might wish to incorporate a section of the documentary, Born Rich, in which Christina Floyd (golf heiress) discusses how country clubs are exclusive.

- Summary of Bob and Harold's Financial positions

Bob's payments	Harold's payments
Car payment—$175/mo	Car payment—$0/mo
Student loan payment—$990/mo	Student loan payment—$0/mo
House payment—$2020/mo	House payment—$1880/mo
Credit card payments—$625/mo	Credit card payments—$0/mo
Bob total payments—$3810/mo	Harold total payments—$1880/mo

Class prompts and comments: The disparity in outflows is obvious, and can lead to discussions around choices for food, clothing, media, and other items in the family budget. We would suggest the presenter turn the discussion towards the Summary of Bob and Harold's Social Class.

- Summary of Bob and Harold's Social Class

Bob's social class	Harold's social class
Lives in small house in a low income neighborhood	Lives in a big house, near his boss
Drives to work in an older car	Drives a nice car
Wears suits from 3–4 years ago	Wears nice suits
Cannot entertain colleagues at home	Can entertain colleagues at home
Doesn't have a membership to Country Club	Sees his boss and the other executives at the Country Club on a regular basis

Class prompts and comments: At this point, some of the class have identified with either Bob or Harold. This "report card" view of their lives—from both financial and social capital perspectives—can be difficult for some students, as they realize the limitations of real meritocracy in society. As presenters, it is time to direct the discussion towards a more meso-level view of social class and social capital in the United States.

At the end of the presentation, we ask the following questions to the students:

- At the corporations where they work—who do you think is most likely to get promoted? Why?
- Did Bob just not work hard enough?

Class prompts and comments: Bob and Harold earn the same salary but, when it comes to purchasing homes, their social class plays an important role in intergenerational wealth creation (reproducing their social class). Harold and Tabitha will pay $134,400 in interest with a 30 year mortgage. They can also afford a 15 year mortgage. In that case, they would pay $74,800 in interest over the life of the loan. Bob and Cathy will pay $278,000 in interest on a $240,000 house with a 30 year mortgage, which means they will pay over $200,000 more in interest for a house worth half as much as Harold and Tabitha's. The bank will receive the money that could have been used to provide the important opportunities and material support for their children's social capital development.

Teaching Introduction to Sociology: When teaching race, an instructor could utilize the Bob and Harold exercise again and make Bob a racial minority. It is also an eye opening exercise to make Bob into Bobby for the sex and gender section. It illuminates many of our taken for granted assumptions about "workers".

Films: The Born Rich video is a useful tool to show the exclusionary nature of exclusive clubs, schools, etc. YouTube: https://youtu.be/8o46HH-TfNY; the PBS series, People Like Us: Social Class in America, provides a glimpse into the range of social classes in American Society.

Activity II: The Income Quiz, by Charlotte Kunkel, Luther College, kunkelch@luther.edu, 563-387-1624

For an extended narrative description regarding the employment of this activity, please see Chap. 10—Capitalism in the Classroom: Confronting the Invisibility of Class Privilege.

Pedagogical Goal of Activity

The income quiz seeks to help students understand the gap between social perceptions of "middle class" and their own socio-economic location. To do this, the activity simply asks two questions: what is your socioeconomic class identity/label and what is your parent's annual income. Students submit this anonymously on a piece of torn out notebook paper. They write two responses, class label and income. I create a chart with this data and present it to the class the next day, with data from the Statistical Abstracts of the United States about median family and quintile distributions of annual incomes.

Directions

To deploy this activity, first ask the students to get out a piece of scratch paper. Have them refrain from placing identifying information on the page—no names.

Then ask students:

(1) In your own words identify yourself by describing the family you grew up in. Give yourself a class label (if they grew up in two households, submit two papers, one for each). When I use this activity, I do not provide sample labels because I want students to identify their subjective notion of class identity.
(2) As best you can, estimate your family's annual income. Provide a dollar amount (pretax). Sample Distribution Table (as collected 2016)

Income	Class label
$300,000–$500,000	Upper middle
$450,000	Upper
$250,000	Middle
$200,000 but depends on markets	Middle
$200,000	Middle
$200,000	Middle/upper middle
$120,000	Upper middle
$115,000	Middle
>$100,000	Upper middle
$100,000	Middle
Dad and uncle: $90,000–$100,000	Middle
$75,000—$100,000	Middle class/wealthy white family
Mom: $80,000—$90,000	Middle
$75,000	Lower-middle
$75,000	Middle
$75,000	Middle
Between $45,000 and $50,000	Middle
$30,000	Well off
With child support and job $30,000	Lower-middle
$25,000	Poor
$8,000–$10,000	Middle class
$5000	Lower class/poverty

On the following day of class I present the students' responses back to them in an anonymous table with incomes ranging from high to low and their corresponding class labels adjacent to the income.

Quintiles for 2015 (Table A.1).

Students are forced to confront concepts of objective and subjective class, middle class bias, class consciousness (and false consciousness) invisibility, and relative deprivation, etc., while looking at their own class labeling and distribution. We debunk stereotypes of the poor and the rich, and introduce the concept of ideology. In discussion the students are further encouraged to problematize these labels and consider the effect of false consciousness and middle class bias on the economic conditions in the United States.

Table A.1 Income Limits for Each Fifth and Top 5 Percent of Families (All Races): 1947–2015

[Families as of March of the following year. Income in current and 2015 CPI-U-RS adjusted dollars (28)]

Year	Number (thous.)	Upper limit of each fifth (dollars)				Lower limit of top 5 percent (dollars)
		Lowest	Second	Third	Fourth	
2015	82,199	30,311	55,376	86,310	133,525	239,188
2014	81,730	29,100	52,697	82,032	129,006	230,030
2013 (39)	82,316	28,840	52,041	80,040	126,343	225,533
2013 (38)	81,217	28,894	50,520	78,000	121,059	217,032
2012	80,944	27,794	49,788	76,538	119,001	210,000
2011	80,529	27,218	48,502	75,000	115,866	205,200
2010 (37)	79,559	26,520	48,000	74,000	113,440	200,200
2009 (36)	78,867	26,934	47,914	73,338	112,540	200,000
2008	78,874	27,800	49,325	75,000	113,205	200,000
2007	77,908	27,864	49,510	75,000	112,638	197,216
2006	78,454	27,000	47,000	71,200	109,150	191,060
2005	77,418	25,616	45,021	68,304	103,100	184,500
2004 (35)	76,866	24,772	43,400	65,818	100,000 +	173,640

Source: U.S. Census Bureau, Current Population Survey, Annual Social and Economic Supplements. For information on confidentiality protection, sampling error, nonsampling error, and definitions, see //www2.census.gov/programs-surveys/cps/techdocs/cpsmar16.pdf

Activity III: The Train Game by Charlotte Kunkel, Luther College, kunkelch@luther.edu, 563-387-1624

Pedagogical Goal of Activity

This simulation game allows students to see the cultural assumptions of competitive individualism, capitalism, and its ideologies, and how we reproduce it in everyday practices such as childhood games, education, sports, and business transactions.

Directions

This simulation is modified from Harrod's articulation of a teaching game based on the prisoner's dilemma. I use it to demonstrate social cooperation versus competition. Students are asked to play a game wherein they decide what color cards to pass and earn various points. After playing we score points, expose assumptions and process why these were the choices they made.

Preparation

The instructor brings to class envelopes with two colors of cards inside. The classroom must have moveable chairs. Students are broken into groups which line up like a train in a circle—so one student is facing the next student's back—and are given the rules of scoring (I typically write these on the board) and told to pass cards—all without talking. Without explicit instruction they will most likely revert to cultural assumptions about competition and winning to play the game.

Procedure

A. The game has 4 stages:

1. Divide the class into groups of varying sizes, from 4 to 10. Have the students form a circle with their desks facing forward (like a wagon train). Conduct the first 10 trials.
2. Pause 5 minutes for students to assess their strategy and write messages to each other. Conduct 5 more trials.
3. Pause 5 minutes to allow discussion among group members and then conduct 5 more trials.
4. Classroom discussion.

B. The trials:

1. The trials move very quickly. Each student is provided with 2 colors of 3 × 5 cards (say, 10 white and 10 blue cards) and an envelope. When the instructor says, "go," each student puts a single card in the envelope and passes it to the student in front. The students are not to turn around or interact; they just pass the card (in the envelope) over the person's shoulder. After each pass, they score themselves as follows:

Give blue, get blue	0
Give blue, get white	+25
Give white, get blue	−15
Give white, get white	+10

2. This way of scoring sets up a payoff structure. As you can see, students maximize their self-interest by passing blue and hoping to get white. Since the person sitting behind has the same payoff structure, however, this pursuit of self-interest is likely to result in everyone getting zero scores.
3. The students are left to figure out this payoff structure (advantages and disadvantages of particular strategies) on their own and the first 10 trials are conducted quickly. Pause between each trial for the students to record their scores. It is essential that they all pass their envelopes at the same time.
4. After 10 trials, students are allowed to pass a message to the person in back of them. It can say anything they wish, but they are NOT allowed to discuss it. Conduct 5 more trials, again having the student score each trial.
5. After this second set of trials, have students turn their desks toward the center where they can discuss the activity with other members of their group. Someone will suggest that they could increase their average scores by passing white, white.
6. After a brief discussion, they play again for 5 more trials, recording their scores after each pass.
7. Announce that there will be ONE more round. (On this last round, many will figure out that it is in their interest not to give blue.)

C. Class Discussion:

1. After hashing out who did what and why, bring the discussion back to public issues. Ask students to deduce the conditions that induce cooperation: stable arrangements with the continuous interaction. (This is why many went back to a competitive strategy on the last play.)
2. Discuss socialism versus capitalism in terms of the game: also, discuss ideology, competitive individualism, cooperative play, and the problem of provision of public goods and the tragedy of the commons.

Supplemental Handout for Train Game:

Competition versus Cooperation

What social conditions encourage competition between group members? Which encourage cooperation? Which type of society do we live in? (Think about what types of board games did you play as a kid? Think about youth sports, high school sports; what are participants encouraged to do? Think about your grades; how do you achieve them? Think about a raise at work; Why is it awarded?).

How do individual actions reflect larger social structures?
Characteristics of two economic systems:

Capitalism versus Socialism

Capitalism	Socialism
Pursuit of personal profit Private ownership of property Free market competition	Pursuit of collective goals Collective ownership Government control of economy
Productivity high Inequality high	Productivity low Inequality low

Note Recognize that we know of neither system in a perfect form (ideal types)

Activity IV: Building Economic (In)Equality by Derek Robey and Jason Robey

Pedagogical Goal of Activity

The following activity is designed to cultivate students' ability to conceptualize inequality in various ways, understand how various forms of inequality are related, and develop a critical comparative lens on systems of economic inequality. Prior to this in-class activity, students should be familiar with the common terms and concepts addressed in this chapter.

Directions

In this activity, students will use the image of a building as a metaphor for thinking about various frameworks on inequality, identifying mechanisms for producing or reproducing inequality, and comparing socioeconomic inequality across contexts. Instructors should have students break up into small groups (between 3 and 8 students per group, depending on the total size of the class).

Begin the activity by prompting the students to reflect on the status of socioeconomic inequality in the United States. The instructor should visit small groups throughout in order to stimulate discussion and answer student questions. In their small groups, students should discuss and take notes on their perception of the following features of the United States economy:

- Distribution of wealth and income across social strata
- Access to educational opportunities
- Mechanisms for mobility or immobility
- Availability of support programs and services
- Relative size of various social strata (working class, middle class, upper class; can also conceptualize this as quintiles or percentiles)

Next, students will take their perception of the socioeconomic structure of the United States and translate it onto the image of a building. Each group should use one piece of blank printer paper to draw a building that represents the aforementioned features. Students can use various physical structures of a building to symbolically represent socioeconomic structures of the United States.

For example:

- The number of floors can represent the number of social strata in the United States (working class, middle class, upper class).
- Size of each floor can represent the total amount of resources each social strata controls (social, cultural, and economic capital).
- The number of people on a floor represents the relative population of that particular strata.
- Population density would refer to the ratio between the size of a floor and the number of people on that floor.
- Stairs and elevators can represent upward mobility opportunities (education). Some of these upward mobility mechanisms (stairs) require more labor than others (elevators). Trap doors might represent downward mobility mechanisms (incarceration).
- Certain services or resources may only be available to people in certain social strata. The quality of and competition for these resources may also vary from strata to strata.
- Other vectors of inequality (race, gender, nationality, religion, sexuality, and many others) may be represented, too.

The point of these depictions is not to capture objective reality about socioeconomic inequality. Rather, the focus is to identify hegemonic beliefs and perceptions students hold when they enter the classroom. Creativity and detailed depictions are encouraged. Instructors should circulate around the room to stimulate discussion and ensure students are drawing on course concepts (resource disparity, mobility or immobility, poverty, etc.).

After students have finished their visual representations of how the United States is currently structured, the instructor should prompt students to use another sheet of paper to portray their conception of what a "perfect" or "ideal" society looks like. This will require some deliberation about what makes a society fair, equitable, and desirable.

Finally, the instructor should call on several groups to present and discuss their portrayal of how the United States is currently structured. The remaining groups should then present and discuss their vision for an "ideal United States." This will naturally stimulate discussion and conversation, but additional discussion questions are provided below if needed.

- To what extent does the students' perception of the United States resemble their ideal society? Compare and contrast the U.S. model and the ideal model.
- Are there any students who have experience or knowledge of this structure in another society? Compared to the United States, is this other society closer or further from the ideal society?
- What are the most important structural aspects of an ideal society?
- Which is most important, equal distribution across the social strata, equal opportunity for mobility, or equal starting points?
- Should individuals beginning in the bottom strata be provided more opportunities for upward mobility? Should they be provided more protections against downward mobility?

Conclusion

This activity is designed to identify and understand the hegemonic and normative beliefs about the United States students hold when they enter the classroom. As a social scientist, the instructor is well-aware that many of these beliefs—and, therefore, many of the students' portrayals—will be inaccurate. Instructors should use the activity as an opportunity to challenge students to think more deeply about their perceptions and understanding of socioeconomic inequality. It is also an opportunity to provide students with high quality social science evidence about the nature of socioeconomic inequality in the United States. In addition to identifying students' perceptions, the activity cultivates students' abilities to think about inequality in a variety of ways and to understand how resource disparities, mobility or immobility, and poverty are related.

Activity V: Mapping Local Social Networks by Leontina Hormel, University of Idaho, lhormel@uidaho.edu

Pedagogical Goal of Activity

The value of this assignment is to teach students investigatory skills with tools available on and off campus and to increase their interest in local politics. Also, it is useful to tell students that if they wish to influence local politics, this information is exactly what you need to know to press for your ideas and proposals. You could have students work separately, or in groups, and they can perhaps identify key individuals, families, and organizations who shape different dimensions of community politics and economics.

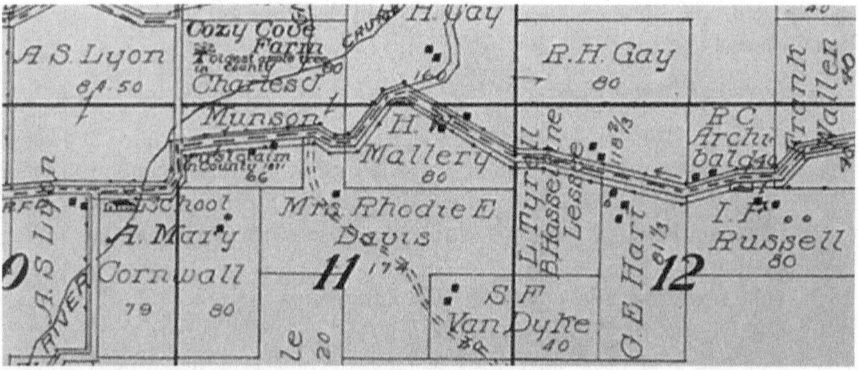

Fig. A.1 Plat Map of Land Owners on Eastern Edge of Moscow, Idaho. *Source* University of Idaho Library, Special Collections. Latah County Atlas, 1914

Context

Students seldom know much about the community where their college or university is located, thus they are unaware of how lessons about economic inequalities—notably the role of power structures—are going on right under their noses. This is an assignment I have developed for this textbook, without practicing it on students. Thus, you will need to adjust this to what resources you think are available for the networks you would like students to investigate and to the type of urban community within which you are situated. Since Moscow, Idaho, is a small city, some of the history of urban development summarized on Domhoff's website is not as relevant as it might be for your location.

Instruction Tip: One element I encourage you to either do with your class to launch this assignment after reading the "Who Rules America" website, or to have a group of students do as part of the assignment, is to use historical plat maps of your community. Plat maps lay out the names of families who own the land/properties, and looking at older maps (go back as far as you like: when your city/town was founded? When it was first settled, which may precede your city's founding?). Property ownership is a significant way individuals and families gain influential roles in communities, so looking at the names of early property owner may flesh out some influential families in the current political economic climate of your community. Figure A.1, below, is a snapshot of a 1914 plat map from the city outskirts of Moscow, Idaho.

Directions

This assignment will be ongoing for the next several weeks as we read about the power elite and power structures in the United States. The mission of this assignment is for each student to help the class reveal the power networks of Moscow, Idaho, and to piece together a map that traces connections between individuals, families, and organizations. You will find that powerful networks have significant influence in community politics, which affects the direction our community takes in development questions, anywhere from small business support to bike trail expansion and support of the arts.

I. **Background Preparation**

A. Go to the "Who Rules America?" website and find the page titled "Power at the Local Level: Growth Coalition Theory." Pay careful attention to these sections: The Political Economy of Urban Power Structures, The Creation of an Urban Policy-Planning Network, and Recent Challenges to the Growth Coalitions.

B. Take notes that give context for the information in Table A.2:

C. Entering the Field of Investigation
You and your peers have been assigned to look at different parts of your local "growth coalition": small and medium businesses (e.g., grocery stores, local shops and restaurants), major employers (e.g., hospitals, colleges/universities), city council, Chamber of Commerce, banks/credit unions, mortgage brokers, real estate firms, utility companies (gas, electric, telecommunications), and newspapers. Below, is a list to help organize your investigation:

Table A.2 Key background concepts for local network investigation

Key groups/organizations	Important dimensions
Growth coalition	Land ownership, local bank/credit union executives, telephone companies, gas and electric companies, major community employers like local hospitals and universities, major local merchants, newspaper executives
Place entrepreneurs	Individuals who do the research for development approaches
Local governments	City council and planning and zoning
Chamber of commerce	Network for local businesses
Key policy approaches	
Growth coalition approach	Key goal is to create optimal conditions for outside investment. To this end, policies focus on a "good business climate" including low business taxes, good infrastructure of municipal services, vigorous law enforcement, an eager and docile labor force, and a minimum of business regulations
Urban liberal regimes	Expand opportunities, employment, and services to minority populations without challenging growth coalition policies
Urban progressive regimes	Neighborhood empowerment approaches that directly challenge growth coalition and seek to slow growth or link growth pursuits to simultaneous investment toward areas like schools, parks, affordable housing
Urban conservative regimes	The reformulation of "growth coalitions" that more firmly grounds itself in private interests and deepening cuts to social service areas

1. Create an Excel spreadsheet that dedicates a column to the following: organization name, member name, member title (e.g., Director, Mayor, etc.), member's duties, member's credentials/background, ties to other organizations/people, policy positions or public image. Note: do not overlook memberships to churches or charity organizations.
2. Conduct an Internet search of organization/group/individual to fill in spreadsheet
3. Do an interview. If you are having difficulty filling out everything in the spreadsheet from an Internet search, you may need to conduct interviews with individuals associated with your study.

D. Research Analysis

Analysis should be going on during your data collection and will continue afterward. We will have class sessions dedicated to data analysis, for which you are expected to bring in your Excel spreadsheet that has record of your data and a written summary of your results.

You will need to visualize the connections you are recording in the spreadsheet. Go to this link to MovetoAmend for an example of how you might map these out.

In class sessions, as a full group, we will discuss students' findings and gradually combine them so we can build a comprehensive "network map" of local coalitions in Moscow. This will include a combination of individuals, groups, and organizations—the more times individuals are involved in different organizations in the community, the more central that person is to influence and power. The more times groups and organizations are tied to individuals and to political bodies, the more central they are to influence and power in the community.

E. Final Product

Once a class map has been created [Note: students may be charged with this, or the instructor], students can do one of two things: (1) Write out a traditional research essay that offers review of literature, description of their research process, analysis of data, and final conclusions, or (2) Prepare a class-written report of the community's power structure, what this means in terms of policy orientation in the community, and how this shapes how non-profits and individuals must work to pursue changes policy changes or actions.

Resources

Domhoff, G. W. Who Rules America? Website http://www2.ucsc.edu/whorulesamerica/ Accessed 23 April 2017.

Geo. A. Ogle & Co. (1914). *Standard atlas of Latah County, Idaho, including a plat book of the villages, cities and townships of the county. Map of the state, United States and world. Patrons directory, reference business directory and departments devoted to general information. Analysis of the system of U.S. land surveys, digest of the system of civil government, etc., etc.* Chicago.

MovetoAmend.org website. "Sample Power Map." https://movetoamend.org/sites/default/files/sample_power_map.pdf. Accessed 23 April 2017.

Activity VI: Socialist Discussion Grades by David I. Backer, West Chester University, dbacker@wcupa.edu

Pedagogical Goal of Activity

This activity serves two goals. First, socialist discussion grades seek to reduce the commodifying qualities of grading and work against the commodification of education. Secondly, through this activity students will learn about the hegemonic nature of capitalism and begin to see the ideology and its operation in the classroom more clearly.

Assignment Description and Instructions:

For this activity, discussed in detail in Chap. 7, sit with students in a circular formation, or around a table/series of tables. Make sure everyone can see each other. Then draw the class formation on a piece of paper, marking where everyone sits, including yourself.

During the discussion, as each participant takes a turn, mark it next to their name in some way. As students discuss, keep track of the number of times each individual has the floor. I draw arrows to signify who addresses whom as well.

After the discussion is over, count the number of turns taken by each individual. Array each individual number in the distribution. Find the arithmetic mean and median. Based on the students associated with these values (or most closely associated), as well as any particularities of the discussion itself, decide which number is the average number of turns for that discussion. For example, lets say a discussion had the following distribution of turns:

0 0 0 1 1 2 3 4 5 10 12 16

The median is 2.5 and mean 4.5, while the student who was most in rhythm with the group had three turns. I would therefore decide that three is average. Once you've decided what counts as average you can calculate grades either individually or collectively.

For individualistic grades: Determine the distance of each individual from the average as a positive number. Multiply that number by two and subtract from 100. In the class above, someone who said nothing would get 94/100, while the person that took 16 turns gets 68/100. The individual grades thus value listening and not dominating the conversational space.

For a collective grade: Align a scale of standard deviations with letter or number grades, where 0 is 100 e.g., then determine what the collective grade is for the particular class using the scale. In the class above, the standard deviation is 5.334. If we let 0 be 100 and go by tens, making 1 a 90, 2 and 80, etc., then this class would get a 50. Each student receives a 50/100. That would encourage all students to even out their participation, putting the emphasis on group behavior rather than individual behavior.

Activity VII: Discussing U.S. Military Interventions Since WWII by Barbara Chasin

Pedagogical Goal of Activity

Students, and the United States public generally, have little understanding or exposure to comprehensive works/data regarding US military interventions over time. This is a handout that I give students to help them begin thinking about how they can find well-researched information via different sources and also ways to be engaged. This is only a sample, as instructors may have further recommendations to share with students.

United States Interventions, Overt or Covert since World War II. (A partial list)

The date is the beginning of the intervention and/or support for a repressive regime, or counterrevolutionary movement. The involvement often went on for years. Not all of these involved U.S. troops but U.S. taxpayers paid for all.

Place	Years	Approximate non-U.S. deaths	U.S. military deaths	U.S. wounded[a]
Afghanistan	2001–?	13,000+	1894	15,460
Angola	1975	500,000	N/A[b]	N/A
Argentina	1970s	20,000	N/A	N/A
Chile	1973	30,000	N/A	N/A
Colombia	1990–2004	35,000	N/A	N/A
Congo/Zaire	1960s	N/A	N/A	N/A
Cuba	1959–2004	N/A	N/A	N/A
Dominican Republic	1963–1965	N/A	N/A	N/A
El Salvador	1981	60,000	N/A	N/A
Grenada	1983	45[c]	19	N/A
Guatemala	1954	200,000	N/A	N/A
Haiti	1959, 1987–1994	N/A	4 (1990s)	N/A
Indonesia	1965	500,000–1,000,000	N/A	N/A
Iran	1953	N/A[c]	N/A	N/A
Iraq	1990–1991 2003-?	280,000 30,000–600,000+	529 4247	467 69,807
Korea	1950–1953	2,800,000	36,562	103,284
Nicaragua	1981	9000	N/A	N/A

(continued)

(continued)

Place	Years	Approximate non-U.S. deaths	U.S. military deaths	U.S. wounded[a]
Panama	1989	1000–4000	N/A	N/A
Vietnam, Cambodia, Laos	1950s	2,300,000	57,900	153,303

Source William Blum (1995) Killing Hope: U.S. Military and CIA Interventions since World War II and Blum (2000) Rogue State: A Guide to the World's Only Superpower
[a]Wounded in all instances is only of physically wounded.
[b]*Notes* N/A = Not available.
[c]19 were killed when a mental hospital was bombed.

Military Operations (General)

United States Department of Defense (US DOD) website issues regular reports on casualties and other military news. This link takes you to the latest casualty count for different military interventions https://www.defense.gov/casualty.pdf. Accessed 16 2017.

This link https://www.defense.gov/ takes you to the homepage of US DOD where you may explore other subjects related to military defense and operations. Accessed 16 April 2017.

Gil, Leslie. (2004). The school of the Americas: Military Training and Political Violence in the Americas. Durham, NC: Duke University Press.

This book includes background to conflict in Colombia and Guatemala.

Grandin, Greg. (2014, 23 December). "How our 1989 invasion of Panama explains the current US policy mess." Mother Jones. http://www.motherjones.com/politics/2014/12/our-forgotten-invasion-panama-key-understanding-us-foreign-policy-today. Accessed 16 April 2017.

Hedges, Chris. (2003). War is a force that gives us meaning. New York: Anchor Books.

This book covers several places where US military intervention has been active, including Angola and Argentina.

Libcom.org website. "The US invasion of Grenada, 1983—Howard Zinn." http://libcom.org/history/articles/grenada-us-invasion-1983. Accessed 16 April 2017.

Parenti, Michael. (1988). The sword and the dollar: Imperialism, revolution, and the arms race. New York: St. Martin's Press.

Parenti's book includes important analysis regarding Chile, El Salvador, Indonesia, and Nicaragua.

Scahill, Jeremy. (2013). Dirty wars: The world is a battlefield. New York: Nation Books.

Scahill, Jeremy. (2008). Blackwater: The rise of the world's most powerful mercenary army. New York: Nation Books.

Jeremy Scahill is one of the founders (with Glenn Greenwald) of The Intercept (https://theintercept.com/) where you can find in-depth analysis of military interventions, conflict, and occupation. The Intercept is also good source for news investigating politics and economics in contemporary times.

Turse, Nick. (2013). Kill anything that moves: The real American war in Vietnam. New York: Metropolitan Books.

World Peace Foundation. "Mass atrocity endings—Korea: The Korean war." https://sites.tufts.edu/atrocityendings/2015/08/07/korea-the-korean-war/. Accessed 16 April 2017.

This site can lead you to other investigations in places throughout the world regarding conflict and casualties.

Military Intervention and Occupation in Afghanistan, Iraq, and Pakistan

"Costs of War" website from the Watson Institute of International and Public Affairs at Brown University in Providence, RI. Follow this site where you can find updated information regarding Human, Economic, Social & Political Costs of War in Afghanistan, Iraq, and Pakistan. http://watson.brown.edu/costsofwar/costs/human/civilians. Accessed 16 April 2017.

Icasualties.org: Iraq Coalition Casualty Count website conducts a running tally of war casualties by year (2001-present) in Afghanistan and Iraq. http://icasualties.org/. Accessed 16 April 2017.

Clark, Ramsey. (1992). The fire this time: U.S. war crimes in the gulf. New York: Thunders Mouth Press.

Activity VIII: Envisioning Alternatives to Capitalism by Kristin Haltinner, University of Idaho, khaltinner@uidaho.edu

Pedagogical Goal of Activity

The goal with this assignment is for students to envision an alternative economic system that would benefit all human beings, as well as the planet more broadly.

Assignment Description and Instructions:

It is required that students engage with sociology in the process of this activity. You must establish and present an awareness of the current economic systems (capitalism, socialism, communism) as well as their weaknesses and strengths, using course material. In the process of developing an alternative model the other social problems discussed in class (gender inequality, racial inequality, crime, health inequality, educational inequality, food and the environment, etc) must also be considered. It is expected that you will employ (and cite) course readings in this project.

The product can take many forms, not limited to the following suggestions: essay, charts, presentation, artwork, video, or a combination thereof. However, it must be of high quality and clearly employing your sociological imagination, analytical skills, and information from course materials.

It is my vision that there will be some "back and forth" between student and professor over the course of the semester. You are encouraged to present ideas to me as they arise and I will happily give you feedback throughout the semester.

To recap, the student must:

- Engage with course material about the current economic systems of:
  - Capitalism
  - Socialism
  - Communism
- Present the strengths and weaknesses of the current models, as explained in the class readings. This would include issues related to:
  - Gender Inequality
  - Racial Inequality
  - Crime and Punishment
  - Health Inequality
  - Educational Inequality
  - Food and the Environment
- Develop a well thought out alternative that would provide solutions to the aforementioned problems.

The final draft will be due on the final exam date, but students should present different elements of the project over the course of the semester.

Learning Outcomes:
The goal of this project is to help students understand hegemony and how it operates in society. In other words, the aim is to help students begin to see the invisible forces at play in our social world. Students are also expected to learn to think critically (and use their sociological imaginations) to interrogate current systems and develop (think and create) alternatives. Finally, students are tasked with communicating difficult concepts and ideas through writing and/or a creative project.

Activity IX: Commodity Research Assignment by Eric Edwards, University of Wisconsin—Superior

Pedagogical Goal of Activity
This activity seeks to help "remove the veil" of this commodity fetishism from students' collective eyes.

Guidelines for Instructors:
At the point in the semester when this assignment is used, one would have discussed in class that most commodities available for purchase go through a global production process. Often, this process is not a pretty one. Labor exploitation and environmental degradation are near-constant themes when commodities are produced by big corporations. Yet we, as individual consumers, do not see these harmful social and natural relations when we buy our products. Capitalists have no choice—they have to lower wages, pollute, and depress other social and environmental standards. If they did not, they would not be competitive, and would see their profits fall. This process of obscuring how and why commodities are produced in this exploitative fashion is what Marx called commodity fetishism.

Instructions for Students

You, of course, are aware that you will be giving a presentation to the class soon. Here is what I would like you to do:

You will choose a particular commodity either from a list I provide or one you think of yourself (which your instructor must approve). I want you to explore how this commodity is made. In other words, you will be tracing the production chain of a commodity. You will share this in two ways: an oral presentation delivered to the class late in the semester and a research paper due shortly after your presentation.

You will present a summary of your research of the particular commodity you chose. This presentation should be at least seven minutes long, and no longer than fifteen minutes. Ten people will present on each day (for a three hour course—the number would be three presentations per day for a standard fifty-minute class), beginning [day/date] and ending on [day/date]. Students will continue presenting until everyone has had a turn. I will determine the order of presentations by using a random sequence generator.

In order to receive full credit for the assignment, I require you to be an active and attentive audience member for everyone else's presentations. During each presentation, please write down either one main point that the presenter has talked about or one question that occurs to you about the presenter's topic. You will hand in these at the end of each class.

The most important parts of your presentation are discussing the labor process involved in producing your commodity, environmental harm caused by its production, connecting these to some of the relevant theories that we have encountered in class, and (perhaps) talking about how people are working to improve this process. The emphasis you place on labor vs. the environment will vary based upon the topic and/or availability of information. Coffee production, for example, would require an equal discussion of both factors. Both are important, and there is a lot of relevant material out there detailing how coffee is produced. If you cannot find much information on one or the other, emphasize the other factor. If you cannot find much information on both labor and environment, contact me immediately.

Themes

Here are some themes I would like you to try to find:

- Poor treatment of workers (long hours, poor pay, exposure to toxins, etc.—both in developed and in so-called developing countries associated with the commodity's production and consumption)
- Environmental harm caused by resource extraction, refining, transportation, use of the commodity, or other ways
- Association of your particular commodity's production process with the policies of the World Bank or International Monetary Fund, if applicable
- Attempts to improve the above problems, such as unionization or fair trade associations
- What you believe would be a better way of producing the commodity in order to minimize social and environmental problems (this might include not producing it at all).

The three parts of the assignment:

1. Annotated bibliography. Please turn in a bibliography by Monday, October 24. It should have at least four sources you plan to use. At least two of these sources should be from a book or peer-reviewed journal. Successful completion of this assignment will indicate to me that you've started working on this project and that you have a level of direction to your research.
2. Oral presentation. These are currently scheduled to take place during weeks twelve and thirteen of the semester. I will give you a separate assignment sheet for this part as we get a little closer to the presentation dates.
3. Presentation outline. This is due on the day of your presentation, which will be determined randomly within the block of time we have set aside for this endeavor.

Potential commodities for analysis:

Tea	Chicken
Tobacco	Pork/Bacon
Diamonds	Bananas
Gold	Electricity/coal
Biofuels (corn)	Electricity/nuclear
Biofuels (palm)	Coca cola and/or Pepsi
Vanilla	Cane sugar
Tomatoes	California-grown produce
Beef	Laptop computers
Smartphones	Roses
Cocaine	Automobiles
Heroin	Mangoes
Chocolate	Pineapple
Coffee	Marijuana
Bottled water	Timber/lumber
Nike shoes and apparel	Gasoline/oil extraction
Children's toys	Seeds (for planting crops)
Infant formula	Tech support/telemarketing (services are commodities!)

Here are some things to keep in mind when designing your presentation:

- You will create an outline that you will hand in on the same date you deliver your presentation. Please see the next page for more details.
- Your instructor and classmates are rooting for you to succeed, and will not judge you. Assigning a grade is not the same as judging. Relax and let us hear what you've discovered.
- Speaking of grades, I will evaluate your presentation primarily on content (see above for what you should include). Delivery of the content is a minor consideration. In other words, it does not matter to me if you are so nervous that it is

affecting your speech—I understand that this happens occasionally. As long as you make relevant statements about your commodity, you will do just fine.

- For your presentation to receive an A, you should make some connections between the material you've researched and a couple of the theories we have discussed in class and/or read about in the books. Some relevant theories/concepts are: monopoly-finance capital, structural adjustment, metabolic rift, and ecological modernization. (I assume you're talking about commodity fetishism, which is why it is not in the list.) You should talk about these connections—don't leave them to our imagination.
- You are welcome to use visual aids and/or Powerpoint slides, but certainly you are not required to do this.
- If you use a video clip (this seems to be popular), please limit it to only one clip. The video should be less than a minute long. I'd prefer it if you didn't use a video clip, though.
- There are some advantages to being one of the first people to present. The biggest one is that you get to sit back and listen to everyone else, knowing that your presentation is done. Some wise person called this feeling "the cool of the evening."
- If you need assistance with any part of this, please do not hesitate to talk to me. I am here to help.

Appendix B
Examples of Syllabi

This appendix provides syllabi, developed by chapter authors, to facilitate course development for instructors.

Syllabus I: Social Inequalities by Ann Strahm
Syllabus II: Sociology of Prosperity by Leontina Hormel
Syllabus III: Money and Society by Stephanie Bradley
Syllabus VI: Sociology of Conflict and Violence by Barbara Chasin
Syllabus V: Race, Class, and Gender by Kristin Haltinner

Syllabus I: Social Inequalities
Prof. Ann Strahm
California State University at Stanislaus

Course Description
This course will examine the nature and causes of social inequality in a national and international context. We will examine the economic, social, and political bases of inequality through a sociological perspective. Through reading, writing, lecture, presentations, and discussion we will analyze how race, class, gender, sexuality, and other statuses are mediated; as well as examine how privilege and inequality are reproduced ideologically and structurally.

This course is part of a broader theme that a wide range of disciplines participated in since the 2015/16 school year at CSU Stanislaus and at Modesto Junior College. Broadly speaking, the theme "Know Your Place" is a play on a negative phrase that many without privilege are often told both explicitly and implicitly by those who have power (you might recognize the implicitness of knowing your place as a student, for example). What we will do, however, is turn the phrase on its proverbial head and use it to understand ourselves and our society (this Great Central Valley). Through learning about ourselves, our families, our communities, as well as the broader socioeconomic organizations and structures that we are embedded in, we will better understand the social forces that impact us and will gain the tools necessary to disrupt and redirect that which squanders our full development.

K. Haltinner and L. Hormel (eds.), *Teaching Economic Inequality and Capitalism in Contemporary America*, https://doi.org/10.1007/978-3-319-71141-6

Required Texts

Poverty and Power, 2nd Edition by Edward Royce

Privilege: A Reader, 3rd Edition, by Michael S. Kimmel and Abby L. Ferber

The New Jim Crow, Michelle Alexander

ABCs of the Economic Crisis, Chap. 1, Magdoff and Yates [Dropbox]

"The Quiet Coup," Simon Johnson [Dropbox]

"Not a Citizen, Only a Suspect: Racialized Immigration Law Enforcement Practices" by Mary Romero [Dropbox]

"The Language of Terror: Panic, Peril, Racism" by Junaid Rana [Dropbox]

The Grapes of Wrath by John Steinbeck [Dropbox] (Also available in the CSUS Library) [**Note**: This book is not assigned for any particular class, it is to be read throughout the semester and utilized in your final paper]

Style Guide (Any style guide will do—I will post ASA and Harvard Style Guides to Dropbox—the Library has many to choose from (http://library.csustan.edu/citing-sources/how-cite-sources), and you can also find some online.

Digital Locations:

- Class Instagram feed is @SOCL3310
- Dropbox Link: https://www.dropbox.com/sh/4244bimobzgzw89/AAAylafUHsfe7JG3yYrXnmxSa?dl=0

Class Format

This class will include lectures, discussions, and video presentations. The lectures will include analysis of the most essential aspects of the readings, as well as additional information not available in the class texts. You will be given ample time and space to critically evaluate and question issues raised in this class. This course will challenge many of our self-evident truths so critical thinking is essential. Everyone should feel comfortable raising issues; even those deemed "taboo" by conventional wisdom and contemporary social norms. However, remember to be respectful to each other and to the professor. For those who feel uncomfortable bringing certain issues up in class, please come visit with me during my office hours and I will try to address the issue(s) in class. This course satisfies the upper-division writing proficiency requirement.

Course Requirements:

1. You should complete readings and assignments for each day/week before the start of class. Class should not be strictly lecture-style, but interactivity and discussion requires that students come prepared.
2. I expect that you will come to class each day, though I will not be taking attendance. Changes to the reading schedule, exams, assignments, or other changes to the syllabus will be announced in class. You are responsible for keeping up with these changes regardless of whether you have attended class.

Grading Criteria

Annotated bibliographies, in-class activities/assignments, classroom presentations*, and 275-word papers are worth 10 points each. *Note, the classroom presentation points include you being in class for all presentation days, not just your own. People not attending on days when they are not presenting will see their points reduced.

600-word papers are worth 25 points each.
1200-word papers are worth 50 points each.
3000-word papers are worth 100 points each.
Peer Evaluations and in-class writing assignments are worth 10 points each.
Instagram Pics & Posts (including chats) are worth 5 point each.
Grade percentages:

95–100% = A	73–76% = C
90–94% = A−	70–72% = C−
87–89% = B+	67–69% = D+
83–86% = B	63–66% = D
80–82% = B−	60–62% = D−
77–79% = C+	Below 59% = F

Classroom Policies:

Etiquette: Please arrive on time and plan on staying for the entirety of the class session. Please do not have conversations during class lectures/class discussions—direct your questions to the professor. Please do not do homework during the class lectures/activities. Attend class on presentation days regardless of your participation.

Studying sociology requires active and critical reading, listening, thinking and conversation. Since we all will have something to say, but may be saying vastly different, even contradictory things, the following guidelines will be adhered to while in this course:

- Acknowledge that prejudice and discrimination based on race, class, sex, sexual orientation, and physical differences exist.
- Acknowledge that all of us have learned misinformation about our own group and about members of other groups (whether we belong to a majority or minority group) from the mass media and other sources.
- Assume that people in this class are doing the best they can do.
- Never demean, devalue, or in any way "put down" people for their experiences, backgrounds, or statements. This does not mean that you can't disagree, only that you do so with respect. Personal attacks on the instructor and fellow students will not be allowed.
- Don't interrupt. Listen before speaking.

I encourage you to speak, as class discussion is an effective way of exploring concepts in this course, but please direct all your comments to the entire class. Engage each discussion using the sociological approach, stay on topic, speak in a respectful manner, disagree with ideas—do not attack individuals, share the "air time", listen carefully to what each speaker is saying. There is a difference between debate and disruptive, disrespectful behavior. Discussion and debate can be spirited, but do not consist of shouting-down others. Active disruption of class will not be tolerated and will lead to your removal from the class.

Reasonable Accommodations: Reasonable accommodations are available for students who have a disability. Please notify me during the first week of class of any accommodations needed for this course.

Academic Dishonesty: Plagiarism and cheating will not be tolerated. Plagiarism and cheating will be dealt with in accordance with the governing rules and regulations set forth by CSU-Stanislaus. *Anyone plagiarizing will automatically receive an F for the class and be reported to the Office of Student Judicial Affairs for tracking purposes.* For further information on these issues please consult with your student handbook and/or go to the following website for information on how to avoid plagiarism: http://www.library.csustan.edu/gorenstein/helpguides/plagiarism.htm and http://www.dartmouth.edu/~writing/docs/FINAL%20Sources%2011:12.pdf

Assignments: Please note that assignments are due at the assigned time and in the assigned format. Late assignments will not be accepted.

Extra Credit:

Syllabus and Class Changes/Adjustments: The professor reserves the right to make changes and adjustments to this syllabus. The professor will announce those changes in class. You will be responsible those changes regardless of your class attendance.

SCHEDULE

Date	Readings	Assignment due	Instructions
Jan 27	Class intro		Discuss syllabus and course requirements
Jan 30–Feb 3	Williams, "Why I Write," "The ABC's of the Economic Crisis," Johnson, "The Quiet Coup," Kimmel & Ferber, Chap. 7	Annotated bibliographies	Due Feb. 1—Annotated bibliographies
Feb 6–10	Royce, Chap. 1	Instagram chat	Due Feb. 6: Post on Instagram. Post a selfie and then write a paragraph-length (i.e. minimum five sentences) comment about what you learned in Royce, Chap. 1 Due Feb. 10: **THEN**, explore other Instagram followers in the class and respond to at least one other comment

(continued)

(continued)

Date	Readings	Assignment due	Instructions
Feb 13–17	Royce, Chap. 6	Annotated bibliography	Due Feb. 13—Annotated bibliography
Feb 20–24 2/24 out of class workday	Royce, Chaps. 3, 7	Instagram posts	Due Feb. 20: On your Instagram feed post: 1. A photo that represents Chap. 3 2. A paragraph discussion of the cultural theory of poverty 3. A photo that represents Chap. 7 4. Explain the cultural system and the impact it has on poverty MAKE SURE to link both photos/posts to @SOCL3310
Feb 27–Mar 3	Royce, Chaps. 4, 8		In-class writing assignment
Mar 6–10	Kimmel & Ferber, Intro	Instagram pics	Due March 6: On your Instagram feed post a picture that represents something from this chapter and add a paragraph comment about the chapter. Be prepared to present a 3-min analysis of your photo as it relates to the chapter. MAKE SURE to link your photo to @SOCL3310 **Presentations will be done on March 8 & 10**
Mar 13–17	Kimmel & Ferber, Chaps. 8–12 Special presentation—Bob & Harold go to college	600 word paper	Bob & Harold paper prompt will be provided on 3/13 as a special handout Paper due 3/17
Mar 20–24	Spring break		
Mar 27–31 No class 3/31	Kimmel & Ferber Chaps. 1–6 3/31 Cesar Chavez day		Select one of the readings to upload an Instagram post/discussion
Apr 3–7	Royce, Chap. 9	Instagram pics & presentations	Due Apr 3: Instagram a picture that represents something from this chapter and add a paragraph comment about the chapter. MAKE SURE to link your photo to @SOCL3310. Be prepared to present a

(continued)

(continued)

Date	Readings	Assignment due	Instructions
			3-minute analysis of your photo as it relates to the chapter. Students who make connections to previous course readings will have the best opportunities to achieve the highest points possible **Presentations will be done on 4/3 & 4/5**
Apr 10–14	Royce, Chap. 10 Kimmel & Ferber Chaps. 13–16, 19	1200 word paper	Due April 10: Discuss the issues faced by people as laid out in these chapters. Utilize your own experiences to discuss those obstacles. In what ways have you been privileged and/or oppressed by the structure of the system? Due on April 14: peer evaluations
Apr 17–21	Alexander, Intro—Chap. 4	600 word paper	Due on April 17: Discuss each chapter and relate each chapter to one or more of previous class readings Due Apr 21: peer evaluations
Apr 24–28	Alexander, Chaps. 5–6		In-class writing assignment: explain "The stigma of race was once the shame of the slave; then it was the shame of the second-class citizen; today the stigma of race is the shame of the criminal."
May 1–5	Romero, "Not A Citizen, Only A Suspect" and Rana, "The Language of Terror"	Annotated bibliographies	Due on May 1: annotated bibliographies
May 8–12	Know Your Place	Class presentations	Due: class presentations of "Know Your Place" final papers
May 15–17	Know Your Place	As above	Due: Class presentations of "Know Your Place" final papers. **Note**: If we need to we will finish them at the date/time of final **Final papers due at date/time of final**

Instagram Assignments

Instagram Pics and Chats: Please use your smart phones to post photographs/images and/or to write a response to a question/prompt. Those without a smartphone can post those images or responses via their computers.

Annotated Bibliographies

Annotated Bibliographies: provide you with the information necessary for doing research. This type of bibliography allows you to develop some general information about an article or book you have just read, allowing you to reference the material quickly and efficiently. Part of the training you receive via writing annotated bibliographies is the development of concise and clear writing. This allows you to capture what you sense is most important in a reading and keep track of it. When used for research projects annotated bibliographies allow you to working on your project without needing to hunt through readings to find a source applicable to what your are working on. Instead, you can simply scan your annotated bibliographies (which also serve to "jog" the memory) for the information and source you wish to reference in your work. In other words, developing this skill will serve you well in your college career and as you make your way towards either a career or graduate school path. An annotated bibliography is generally no more than one paragraph long.

Example of an Annotated Bibliography:

Cose, Ellis. "The Prison Paradox." *Newsweek*, Nov. 13, 2000. pp. 36–39.

The cover of this particular *Newsweek*, in bold letters, proclaims "Readell Johnson is one of 14 million Americans, mostly black or Latino, who will spend part of their lives behind bars. Inside the tangled world of America's prison generation." This headline leads one to assume there will be a cogent discussion of why 14 million have, or will have, spent some of their lives in jail. While there are a couple of small graphs that show the incarceration rate of Blacks and Latino's skyrocketing (while whites are increasing at a much slower rate), the bulk of the discussion is about how there are so many ethnic minorities in jail that people of color are becoming blasé about going to jail. In fact, the article says that in "some neighborhoods, prison has become such a part of the routine that going in can be an opportunity for reconnecting with friends" (43). When these people are not blasé about going to jail, the article quotes people of color who said that going to prison made them a better person—that they now have purpose in life. So, in a nutshell, I learned that people of color want to go to prison because it gives them opportunity to reconnect with friends and loved ones, as well as gives them purpose—a highly problematic analysis at the very least. While I can appreciate Cose's use of statistics to illustrate the phenomenal rise in Black and Brown incarceration, I found the overall discussion to be rather glib and individualistic in its analysis. Since it is clearly lacking in sociological analysis, I am unsure as to the overall usefulness of this article for anyone interested in a sociological examination of crime and punishment.

Paper Instructions
Many of you will be writing assessments, reports, proposals, plans, letters, etc. in your future careers. You may, for example, be called upon to turn a large binder of new policies, rules, and regulations into a concise two-page memo; or, you may be asked to develop a job description for a new hire. Many of you may also wish to attend graduate school, where you will be expected to write research papers, develop grant proposals, present at conferences, etc. Whatever the case may be the development of critical writing skills and collegial interpersonal communication skills are essential to your ability to be competitive on the job market, in the pursuit of a graduate degree, and for career advancement. *Successful completion of this course, along with willingness to work to improve your writing, ensures an advanced communication skill set, which will serve you as you navigate your college career.*

- On the top left of the first page for each assignment please include ONLY the following single spaced (you may allow one space between the title of the readings and the first line of your summary). Any additional information will result in point loss:

  Last four digits of your student ID
  Date Due

- Papers are to be written using either the MLA, APA, or ASA formats (this includes paper style, punctuation, grammar, quotations, and citations).
- Papers are to be double-spaced.
- Papers which do not or only marginally represent the content of the course will be given a failing grade.
- These are due at the beginning of class—in class. These are not accepted late, via email, under my door, nor in my mailbox. If you drop the paper off prior to or during the class session then leave class, your paper will not be accepted.

Peer Evaluating
Peer evaluating is intended to be an important part of your learning in this course. It serves as a review of the material and allows you to see how others are responding to the material. It is affirming to read that others agree with our views, and it is even more enlightening when we notice that someone else has a very different perspective than we do: we are challenged to rethink our own position. Learning to see the world through different sets of lenses is personally enriching. Peer evaluation also refines your writing, reading, and assessment skills because you are observing and processing other people's writing. By reading each other's papers, we realize that we are both teachers and students as we learn together.

Please give each other helpful, constructive, clear, and encouraging feedback on each paper you evaluate. Let your classmates know what you liked about their paper and how you think it could be improved. These are not accepted late, via email, under my door or in my mailbox.

Peer Evaluation Rubric

Level of performance expected in order to achieve each ranking and its related points

Criteria	Exemplary	Average	Marginal
Observance of guidelines	Your paper completely follows the relevant guidelines in terms of organization and format	Your paper doesn't completely follow the relevant guidelines in terms of organization and format	Your paper doesn't follow the relevant guidelines at all in terms of organization and format
Directness and accuracy of article interpretation	Your review suggests that you read and understood the articles completely before you wrote about them	Your review suggests that you probably read, but only partially understood, the articles before you wrote about them	Your review doesn't suggest that you read or understood the articles at all before you wrote about them
Writing style	Your review shows no problems with spelling, grammar, syntax or usage Your references are correctly and completely cited	Your review shows minor problems with spelling, grammar, syntax or usage Your references have missing or incomplete citations	Your review shows significant problems with spelling, grammar, syntax or usage You haven't referred explicitly to references at all OR your review appears to have borrowed heavily from other sources

Final writing assignment: "Know Your Place"

Write a 3000-word paper telling your story (a socioautobiography) in the context of *The Grapes of Wrath*, utilizing the sociological analysis you've learned through the other course materials.

- Where are you and family from? (Note: some of us may not have biological kin, so for purposes of this paper your family is whomever you choose to include in this story).
- How did your family come to where they are now and why?
- Why do you live in this area?
- What is your family's racial and ethnic heritage?
  - Does this matter to you? Does this matter to the people who are in your life? Why?
- Write about this region. What do you know about the geography, cultures, racial/ethnic groups, the environment, the industries, etc.? What do you know about this place?

Note: This paper is your opportunity to find out more about some of the people that have helped you to become the person that you are today, so you may want to interview members of your family to learn more about their experiences first hand.

In interviewing your family members, you are asking them to reflect upon themselves and their lives and to share that reflection with you so that you may learn from it. Those family members who agree to be interviewed will be sharing a precious gift with you; please treat that gift accordingly.

- **Compare/contrast you/your family's experiences with the materials we've utilized for this class.**
- Make sure you are using grammar appropriate to formal, academic, essay writing.
  - All quotes, all paraphrasing, and all references must be properly cited according to whatever style you choose to use (MLA, APA, ASA, Harvard, Chicago, etc.), and you must be consistent in the appropriate application of that style throughout your paper.
  - There are many style guides available in the CSUS library and online—please utilize these excellent resources.

In addition to the minimum word length, you must also provide a properly formatted bibliography or works cited page.

Deadlines:

Reflection and research papers must be handed in at the beginning of class for which the reading is assigned. See class schedule in the syllabus. Peer evaluation is due in class during the following class session. **ASSIGNMENTS ARE ONLY ACCEPTED IN CLASS THE DAY THEY ARE DUE.**

Syllabus II: Sociology of Prosperity

Prof. Leontina Hormel

University of Idaho

REQUIRED TEXTS

You are expected to read assignments by the beginning of each class session. For example, if we are to discuss Chapter One from Desmond on May 1, you are expected to have read Chapter One by the start of our class session on May 1.

Desmond, Matthew. 2016. Evicted: Poverty and Profit in the American City. New York: Crown Publishers.

Block, Fred, and Margaret R. Somers. 2014. The Power of Market Fundamentalism: Karl Polanyi's Critique. Harvard University Press.

Krippner, Greta. 2012. Capitalizing on Crisis: The Political Origins of the Rise of Finance. Harvard University Press.

*It is possible additional readings may be assigned. I will announce them in class and provide them in class and/or via our BbLearn site.

PURPOSE

Social philosophers have puzzled for centuries over how to make societies most prosperous, and differences emerge with regard to how to measure the success of their theories. The purpose of this course is to introduce students to the sociology of economics and how economic systems are integrally linked to social stratification. From the view of sociology, politics and economics are fundamentally interwoven, thus, this course will also take into consideration how democracy in the United States plays a major role in the way its economy is structured and changes.

GRADING

You will learn about key concepts and principles around which economic arguments are formulated. The assignments in this course are geared toward at least a couple of different forms of learning. One form of learning is traditional, in that students will be expected to memorize some concepts and general ideas attributed to specific theorists and historical periods. Knowledge acquired in this way (through careful note-taking when reading and during intensive lectures) will be tested with conventional instruments, like quizzes and exams. The second form of learning is cooperative and interactive, which I wish to encourage through using as much class time as possible working together in defining concepts and learning theoretical frameworks. Above all, I welcome you to explore the subjects in this course creatively. Please feel free to conceptualize how else we might shape the way things work at home and abroad and have confidence in your scholarly abilities to understand economics outside of the confines of the ivory tower.

3 exams (100 points each): exams will include a combination of multiple choice, true-false, and short answer questions. Questions will test student comprehension of economic, political, and social principles and how they operate together. As such, exams encompass reading, lecture, and discussion materials.

One take-home essay (100 points): Essay will be assigned to examine Matthew Desmond's book, Evicted. Students will apply concepts to experiences illustrated in the book. The essay will require students to demonstrate comprehension and will also require them to consider and substantiate solutions.

Class Contribution (100 points): reflects the level of preparedness you bring to class on a consistent basis. Students should demonstrate they have read text assignments before class and be engaged in class. Please note, I will consider regular mobile phone gazing (i.e., "electronic nose-picking") during class time a sign you are not engaged. Don't let others cost you your education and don't expect me to inform you that I have noticed you doing it.

Team Research Contribution (100 points each): See separate hand-out. This project is ongoing and will be built over the term. Each student will be tasked to complete different investigative errands and analyses to complete a team project we work on together as a research group.

COURSE SCHEDULE

By Monday, August 29, you are to complete CITI human subjects protection training. Instructions and explanation are available at this link on the UI IRB webpage.

Please look at this schedule as tentative, since I am going to be in the process all through the term of gaining access to experts and actors in our research project.

Students are advised to start reading Matthew Desmond's book Evicted before classes begin, as this will allow you time to enjoy it. As you read the book, try to map out different households and their members so you can follow the story. We will discuss these households in class, so any work you do on this will be helpful.

WHAT IT MEANS TO BE LOW-INCOME IN AN AMERICAN CITY

Week 1 (Aug 22) Introduction: What is Prosperity?

- Read over this week Prologue and Part One, RENT, of Evicted (pages 1–107).
  - When reading, document the two city regions compared and map out the households studied. This can be done in any way that helps you comprehend visually what Desmond is describing in these chapters.

Week 2 (Aug 29) Experiencing Precarious Housing and Eviction

- Assigned reading for this week is Part Two, OUT, of Evicted (pages 111–203). Also recommend Ruby Payne, *A Framework for Understanding Poverty & Bridges out of Poverty*;
  - Exercise today will ask students to pair up and identify characteristics of families in *Evicted* that seem to support Payne's description of poverty.
  - Wednesday, Aug. 31: Library research seminar—meet at UI Library reference desk.

Week 3 (Wed, Sept 7) Experiencing Precarious Housing and Eviction

- Assigned reading for this week is Part Three, AFTER, plus the Epilogue of Evicted (pages 207–313). Also recommend Paul C. Gorski (2008) "Peddling for Profit: Elements of Oppression in Ruby Payne's Framework."
  - Exercise today will ask students to pair up and discuss the main points Gorski makes. How does this sit with them? Does Matthew Desmond's conclusions avoid oppressive assumptions?

Week 4 (Sept 12) Experiencing Precarious Housing and Eviction: Wrap-Up

- Assigned reading for this week is About This Project of Evicted (pages 315–336).
  - Discussion (Sept 14) What have we learned so far about measuring prosperity?
  - Monday hand out essay assignment that will be due Monday, September 19.

- WEDNESDAY, September 14: Fieldtrip to Latah County Courthouse, Judge John Judge, Magistrate Court, will guide us. LT will reserve UI vehicle—*meeting place TBD*.

SOCIAL THEORIES ON PROSPERITY AND CLASS STRUCTURE
Week 5 (Sept 19) Classical Political Economy: How to Build Prosperity

- **DUE MONDAY:** Essay on Prosperity, Precarious Housing, and Culture of Poverty
- Read Adam Smith and Thomas Malthus this week (chapters from *Voices of the Industrial Revolution*, 1961).
  - Concepts: SMITH—Division of Labor, Use Value and Exchange Value, Human nature (self-interest regulated by moral sentiments), master and worker classes; MALTHUS—misery and vice as natural self-regulation of human populations
  - Stay Tuned: Field Trip Wednesday and/or Saturday? Monday September 19? Tom Lamar

Week 6 (Sept 26) Classical Political Economy: How to Build Prosperity

- Read David Ricardo this week (chapter from *Voices of the Industrial Revolution*, 1961).
  - Concepts: RICARDO—three different classes: landlords, merchants, and workers; comparative advantage
  - Stay Tuned: Field Trip Wednesday and/or Saturday?

Week 7 (Oct 3) Marx: Is this what prosperity really looks like?

- **ON MONDAY:** In-class Quiz 1 on Classical Political Economy
- Read "Karl Marx" in Heilbroner (1997) *Teachings from the Worldly Philosophy*
  - Concepts: commodity fetishism, formula for capitalist accumulation, the working day (class conflict/2-class system), primitive accumulation

Week 8 (Oct 10) Marx and Keynes

- Finish Karl Marx and read John Maynard Keynes this week.
  - Concepts: circular flow of money, 3 arguments against Say's Law, liquidity trap, multiplier effect
  - Read "John Maynard Keynes and the Turbulent Birth of Macroeconomics" in Sackrey et. al. (2016) *Introduction to Political Economy*

KARL POLANYI APPLIED: THE ROLE OF INSTITUTIONS AND IDEOLOGY
Week 9 (Oct 17) Karl Polanyi: Block & Somers' book The Power of Market Fundamentalism (TPMF)

- **MONDAY:** In-class Quiz 2 on Marx and Keynes
- Wednesday, October 19, Read Chap. 1, pages 1–43 of TPMF

Week 10 (Oct 24) Karl Polanyi

- Read Chaps. 6–8, pages 150–240 of TPMF
- Discussion with students to connect three devices in the armature to the historical events.

THE ROLE OF CORPORATIONS IN POLICY AND PRACTICE
Week 11 (Oct 31) Baran and Sweezy—Monopoly Capital

- **MONDAY:** In-class Quiz 3 on Polanyi
- No Reading for Baran and Sweezy this week—just lecture (relax and read Krippner's book)

Week 12 (Nov 7) History of Financialization

- Monday, Nov. 7, read Introduction (pp. 1–26), skim Chap. 2 (pp. 27–57), and Chs. 3 through Conclusion (pp. 58–150) of Krippner's book

Week 13 (Nov 14) Outcomes of Financialization and Monopoly Capital

- Privatizing Student Loans, Deregulation of Financial Transactions, and Banks Too Big to Fail

——THANKSGIVING RECESS NOVEMBER 21 TO NOVEMBER 25 ——
THEORIES OF THE ELITE: C. WRIGHT MILLS, WILLIAM DOMHOFF, AND LESLIE SKLAIR
Week 14 (Nov 28)

- No readings assigned, lecture only. Use this time to finish your part of the research project and to meet with classmates outside of class time this week.

Week 15 (Dec 5) TEAM PRESENTATION (LOCATION TBD—SYRINGA PARK OR COMMONS)

- Monday will be Team Presentation rehearsal—could continue to 6 pm, so plan accordingly
- Wednesday, December 7, TEAM PRESENTATION

FINALS WEEK—Tuesday, December 13, 3-5 pm:

- Final Quiz covering Monopoly Capital, Financialization, and Theories of the Elite.
- This will not be comprehensive or any longer than the quizzes assigned in the course.

NOTE from Leontina Hormel: I cancelled Krippner's readings, because we lost time as a result of conducting in-class discussions about Syringa. You will be forced to decide between more readings or more applied connections with the project.

Syllabus III: Money and Society

Prof. Stephanie Bradley
Florida State University

Course Description

Welcome to *Money and Society*! This course examines money in America from a sociological perspective. We will analyze the claim that money and society are inextricable concepts by exploring topics including the history, social construction, and social meaning of money; theories on money; the forms and uses of money; and the societal and institutional influences on, and effects of, money.

The first half of the course investigates sociological theories and the history of money, the causes and consequences of economic inequality, and how perspectives on money impact social relationships. The second half of the course devotes attention to the connection between institutions and money—paying specific attention to the government, tax policy, banking, corporate power, and the recent US financial crisis. We will end by exploring alternative forms of currency and consumption. Throughout the course we will examine the ways in which different groups experience money by asking who has it and who controls it.

Course Objectives: Specifically, the student should be able to…

1. Develop the language and knowledge required to critically analyze, think about, and discuss economic issues through a sociological lens.
2. Evaluate key theoretical frameworks concerning the sociological study of money.
3. Explain the consequences of market systems on economic inequality.
4. Analyze how "money" takes on different meanings and elicits different relational responses.
5. Recognize how economic thinking guides corporate and civic governance, and influences everyday beliefs and values.
6. Define the recent financial crisis as an economic, political, social, and cultural event.
7. Think critically about abstract concepts such as money, currency, capitalism, poverty, consumption, greed, inequality, and privilege.

Required Materials:

- *Money and Credit: A Sociological Approach* by Bruce G. Carruthers and Laura Ariovich. Publisher: Polity Press. Year Published: 2010. [ISBN: 9780745643922]
- *The Social Meaning of Money* by Viviana A. Zelizer. Publisher: Basic Books. Year Published: 1994. [ISBN: 9780465078929]
- One 3-ringed binder with lined paper (for your journal entries)

In addition to the two required books, **additional required readings and other pre-class assignments** will be available in the Course Library of our Blackboard website.

ASSIGNMENTS (aka "Celebrations of Learning") and GRADING

"Celebrations of Learning": I consider graded work "Celebrations of Learning." Assignments and exams are designed to provide evidence of your comprehension of course material… something I think is worth celebrating! When someone approaches assessments with doom and gloom, everything about it feels like drudgery. Instead, I encourage you to think about assessments as a way to "strut your stuff"—academically speaking—wherein you can provide evidence of your understanding and comprehension.

Item	Points possible	% of final grade
(A) Pre-class journal entries with glossary terms	50	10
(B) "Activities"	50	10
(C) Paper 1	75	15
(C) Paper 2	125	25
(D) Mid-term exam	100	20
(D) Final exam	100	20
Total	500	100

(A) **Pre-Class Journal Entries with Glossary Terms (50 total points; up to 5 points each):** In order to really digest a piece of text you have to not just read it, but write and think about it. Thus, in order to help you engage in the pre-class assignments and appropriately prepare for each class, you will keep a "pre-class journal" throughout the semester. I recommend you purchase a 3-ringed binder with lined paper specifically for this purpose. For each class with assigned pre-work, you will be expected to prepare by (1) writing a paragraph about each assigned reading or podcast prior to coming to class and (2) develop a glossary of assigned words. Twelve (12) random times throughout the course I will ask you to turn in your journal entry for that day. If your composition is two pages or more, please staple together all pages for each day's journal entry before class begins. I will collect the journal entries at the beginning of class. You must be present to receive any credit. Please make sure your handwriting is legible and that you are using complete sentences. At the end of the course, I will drop your two (2) lowest journal grades. If you have an excused absence, please see me immediately; make up work must be submitted within one week from the day the journal entry was collected, unless you are still excused from class.

Journal entry instructions: You are expected to come to each class having written one paragraph (5–7 sentences) about each assignment for that day. If there are multiple assignments for that day, you will write multiple paragraphs. Use this format to structure each paragraph:

- In the first sentence, explain the main argument that the author (or speaker, in the case of a podcast) is making. While most authors make several points in their writing, there is always an overarching argument that ties it all together. Ask yourself, "Broadly, what is this about?"
- In the next 2–3 sentences, explain some of the points the author makes to support their main argument.
- In the final 2–3 sentences, incorporate your own reaction, thoughts, or questions about what you just read/heard/watched. These sentences will provide evidence that you thought deeply about the assignment. An example of a bad reaction statement: "I was surprised by what the author said, I had not previously thought about the issue in that way before." A good reaction statement will convey deep thinking. For example, "The author argues X, but they should also think about Y because…", "If policymakers consider the author's perspective, our society would probably look different because…", or "I disagreed with what the author said about X because…"

In addition to the summary paragraphs, you are expected to define select terms related to each day's assignments. Each day's selected "Glossary Terms" are listed in the Course Library. Simply write each term and document its definition. The definition should be *in your own words*. While you will likely need to use a dictionary to develop your initial understanding, the definition should develop more fully as you complete the pre-work. Ultimately, it's important that you understand the terms, so it's best to use your own words. If you use outside resources in your definition, you must provide a citation (note: citation style isn't important here, but there must be enough information for me to find the source).

Each journal entry will be graded as follows:

- 5 = check plus: contains a thoughtful and thorough paragraph about each reading AND glossary terms with definitions
- 4 = check: satisfactory
- 3 = check minus: unclear, unfocused, underdeveloped, or otherwise incomplete
- 2 = present in class but did not complete journal entry (must submit a blank paper with name on it)
- 0 = absent from class when journal entries are collected

(B) **"Activities"—Pop Quizzes/In-class Activities/Take-home Assignments (50 total points; up to 5 points each):** Throughout the course, there will be twelve (12) <u>random</u> pop quizzes, in-class group activities, and take-home assignments, collectively called "activities." At the end of the course, I will drop your two (2) lowest activity grades. If you have an excused absence, please see me immediately; make up work must be submitted within one week from the day of the activity, unless you are still excused from class.

- Pop quizzes will cover material from the day's assigned readings, and will be in the form of multiple choice or short answer questions.
- In-class activities will provide you the opportunity to further explore course concepts, often with other students.
- Take-home assignments are intended to assess or supplement your understanding of course concepts and readings. These assignments will be given to you during the class period before the one in which they are due. *You must be present during both the class period in which the take-home assignment is distributed and the class period during which it is collected in order to receive credit.*

NOTE: You will receive full credit for an activity just by attending class on **Wednesday, January 28**. For full credit, you must arrive on time and stay for the full class period. You will receive no credit for arriving late or leaving early without advance approval.

(C) **Papers**: You are required to write two (2) papers. The first paper is worth 75 points and the second paper is worth 125 points. The first paper will require you to analyze song lyrics and connect the lyrics to sociological concepts and theories related to money and society. The second paper allows you to select two course objectives (from objectives #2–6) and document your mastery of the chosen objectives. I will discuss the details of these papers well before they are due and will post instructions on the Blackboard website for this course (under "Assignments"). Grading rubrics will be made available prior to the due dates.

Paper 1, February 20	75 points possible
Paper 2, April 17	125 points possible

Late Papers: Please contact me ASAP if you are unable to submit a paper on time. Papers that are submitted late for any reasons will be subject to the following penalties:

- Up to 12 hours late (8 a.m. the day after the due date) will be subject to a 10% penalty
- Between 12 and 24 hours late (8 p.m. the day after the due date) will be subject to a 20% penalty

Late papers should be emailed directly to me. After this late-day window, papers will not be accepted and will result in a zero, unless prior arrangements have been made with me.

(D) **Exams**: You will take two (2) exams, scheduled on March 2 and April 22. All pre-class assignments, lectures, and audio-visual presentations for that particular section should be expected on the exam. Although the exams are not cumulative, students may need to have an understanding of concepts covered earlier in the semester to answer some questions presented in the latter part of the course (e.g., Simmel's theoretical framework). Exams will take place in our classroom and may include a combination of multiple choice, true/false, matching, and short answer questions.

Do not schedule trips, flights, interviews, medical appointments, or any other events on exam dates. You will not be excused from the last exam if you have decided to leave town early. No alternate exam times will be offered simply for student convenience.

Mid-Term Exam, March 2	100 points possible
Final exam, April 29	100 points possible

Makeup Exams: Students will only be allowed to makeup exams if there is an excusable absence with supporting documentation (see "University Attendance Policy" below). Students are expected to review the course schedule early to determine any conflicts that may arise with exam dates. If you miss an exam, you are expected to notify me by the class period after the exam so that a makeup can be scheduled; notification concerning a missed final exam must be made immediately. Procrastinating makeups is unfair to other students. I reserve the right to administer makeup exams in a different format (e.g., essay instead of multiple choice) to insure that students making up exams do not have an unfair advantage over other students who took the exam earlier.

Evaluation/Grading Details:

A = 93–100%	B− = 80–82%	D+ = 67–69%
A− = 90–92%	C+ = 77–79%	D = 63–66%
B+ = 87–89%	C = 73–76%	D−= 60–62%
B = 83–86%	C− = 70–72%	F = 0–59%

Rounding: A final numeric grade that includes a decimal equal to or above .5 will be rounded up when it is on the cusp of the next letter grade. For example, if you earned a 92.46%, your final grade would be an "A−" while a 92.5% would be rounded to an "A." I reserve the right not to round a grade based on excessive unexcused absences or failure to meet course policies (listed below).

Blackboard Grade Center: Please review the My Grades feature on Blackboard to make sure all of your grades are accurate and up-to-date. Any inquiries about missing and/or inaccurate grades need to be made within a week following the Announcement that your grades have been posted (note: inquiries about grades posted the last week of class must be made immediately). Inquires that fall outside of this timeline will most likely not be considered. Do not wait until the last few days of the course to question your grades, as I may not be able to meet with you or adequately address your concerns with such little notice.

Extra Credit: I do not plan to offer any extra credit opportunities in this course. You should not need extra credit if you attend regularly, keep up with readings, seek out additional help during office hours (when needed), study for exams, and complete assignments on time.

Incomplete Grades: Missing work or not completing assignments are insufficient reasons for a grade of Incomplete. An Incomplete grade will not be given except under extenuating circumstances at my discretion. Note that College of Social Sciences and Public Policy guidelines require that students seeking an "I" must be passing the course.

Syllabus Change Policy: Except for changes that substantially affect implementation of the evaluation/grading policies, this syllabus is a guide for the course and is subject to change with advance notice. Class topics, assignments, required reading, and scheduling may be modified as circumstances dictate. I will announce in class meetings and/or via Announcements any changes in advance, so please stay tuned.

COURSE SCHEDULE
(Subject to change with advance notice)
*****Complete required assignments and journal entries <u>BEFORE</u> the class period*****

KEY:

Bullet points = pre-class assignments and important information

- Carruthers, Zelizer = required books
- Bb = Blackboard Course Library

<u>PART I: INTRODUCTION TO MONEY AND SOCIETY</u>

Wed./January 7: **OVERVIEW of the COURSE**

- Bb: Read the syllabus
- Obtain the required books

Mon./January 12: **FOUNDATIONS**

- Bb: Planet Money 2014 The Invention of 'The Economy'
- Bb: CNBC 2011 What is GDP?
- Bb: Swedberg 2007 defining 'The Market'
- Bb: Baker 1992 The Sociology of Money

Wed./January 14: **THEORIES of MONEY**

- Bb: Ingham, Chap. 3—"Money in Sociological Theory'
- Bb: Deflem 2003 The Sociology of the Sociology of Money

Mon./January 19: **Martin Luther King, Jr. Day. No Classes.**
Wed./January 21: **WHAT is MONEY?**

- Carruthers, Chap. 1—section titled "What is money?" on pp. 6–7
- Bb: Smithin (editor), Chap. 2—"'Babylonian madness': on the historical and sociological origins of money" by Ingham

Mon./January 26: **HISTORICAL DEVELOPMENT of MONEY**

- Carruthers, Chap. 2—"A Brief History of Money"
- Bb: "What exactly is money and why do we value it?" (poster)

PART II: MONEY AND INEQUALITY

Wed./January 28: **SOCIAL STRATIFICATION and STRUCTURAL INEQUALITY, PT I**

- No pre-work for today
- Full credit for one activity for each student who arrives on time and stays for the full class

Mon./February 2: **SOCIAL STRATIFICATION and STRUCTURAL INEQUALITY, PT II**

- Bb: Jackson 2007 defining 'Inequalities'
- Access the reading and related graphs here: http://scalar.usc.edu/works/growing-apart-a-political-history-of-american-inequality/index
- Bb: The Economist explains Thomas Piketty's "Capital" 2014

Wed./February 4: **INCOME GAP and the MINIMUM WAGE**

- Access the reading and related graphs here: http://scalar.usc.edu/works/growing-apart-a-political-history-of-american-inequality/the-minimum-wage?path=differences-that-matter
- Access the reading and related graphs here: http://scalar.usc.edu/works/growing-apart-a-political-history-of-american-inequality/fatter-cats-ceo-pay-and-corporate-governance?path=differences-that-matter
- Access the reading and related graphs here: http://www.npr.org/blogs/money/2014/10/02/349863761/40-years-of-income-inequality-in-america-in-graphs

Mon./February 9: **WEALTH GAP**

- Bb: Pew 2014 America's Wealth Gap
- Bb: Pew 2014 Racial, Ethnic Wealth Gap
- Bb: Conley et al 2014 Looking into the Racial Wealth Gap

Wed./February 11: **POVERTY**

- Bb: Block 2006 The Compassion Gap
- Bb: Rank 2011 Rethinking American Poverty
- Bb: The Washington Post 2014 Rental America
- Bb: Why Do Poor People 'Waste' Money on Luxury Goods

PART III: THE SOCIAL MEANING OF MONEY

Mon./February 16: **THE SOCIAL MEANING of MONEY: INTRODUCTION**

- Carruthers, Chap. 3—"The Social Meaning of Money"
- Zelizer, parts of Chap. 1—pp. 18–30

Wed./February 18: **MONEY in the HOME**

- Zelizer, Chap. 2—"The Domestic Production of Monies"
- Bb: Tichenor 2005 When She Earns More

Fri./February 20: **PAPER 1 DUE before 8 p.m.**
Mon./February 23: **POLICING POOR PEOPLE'S MONEY**

- Zelizer, Chap. 4—"Poor People's Money"
- Zelizer, Chap. 5—"With Strings Attached: The Earmarking of Charitable Cash"
- Zelizer, Chap. 6—"Contested Monies"

MID-TERM EXAM
Wed./February 25: **EXAM PREP**

- No additional pre-work
- Bring your notes and course materials to class

Mon./March 2: **MID-TERM EXAM**

- Bring a pencil and eraser

PART IV: MONEY AND INSTITUTIONS
Wed./March 4: **GOVERNMENT**

- Bb: Sorauf 1992 Politics and Money
- Bb: Lichtman 2014 Who rules America?
- Listen to and take notes on this full podcast: http://www.thisamericanlife.org/radio-archives/episode/461/take-the-money-and-run-for-office

March 9–13: SPRING BREAK—Enjoy! ☺
Mon./March 16: **TAXATION, PART I**

- Access the reading and related graphs here: http://scalar.usc.edu/works/growing-apart-a-political-history-of-american-inequality/who-pays-taxes-and-american-inequality?path=differences-that-matter
- Bb: Kenworthy 2009 Tax Myths
- Bb: Khan 2012 The Rich Haven't Always Hated Taxes
- Bb: America's Last Throwback to Plutocracy

Wed./March 18: **TAXATION, PART II**

- Bb: Brown 1996 The Marriage Bonus/Penalty in Black/White
- Bb: Time 2013 Windsor The Unlikely Activist

Mon./March 23: **BANKING and CREDIT, PART I**

- Carruthers, Chap. 1—section titled "Money and Credit" on pp. 8–11
- Carruthers, Chap. 4—"Credit and the Modern Consumer Society"
- Bb: Quinn 2010 The Credit Mines

Wed./March 25: **BANKING and CREDIT, PART II**

- Bb: Ritzer 1995 Chap. 1 in Expressing America

Mon./March 30: **CORPORATE GOVERNANCE, PART I**

- Carruthers, parts of Chap. 5—pp. 128–149

Wed./April 1: **CORPORATE GOVERNANCE, PART II**

- Bb: Davis 2003 American Cronyism

PART V: THE U.S. FINANCIAL CRISIS

Mon./April 6: **OVERVIEW of the CRISIS**

- Listen to and take notes on this full podcast: http://www.thisamericanlife.org/radio-archives/episode/355/the-giant-pool-of-money
- Listen to and take notes on the Prologue and Act Two of this podcast (Act One—5:13–36:15 is similar to the first podcast, so you can skip this part): http://www.thisamericanlife.org/radio-archives/episode/390/return-to-the-giant-pool-of-money
- Bb: Carruthers 2009 Sociology of Bubbles

Wed./April 8: **THE PLAYERS**

- Bb: Taibbi, Chap. 3—"Hot Potato: The Great American Mortgage Scam"

Mon./April 13: **THE IMPACT**

- Bb: Rugh and Massey 2010 Racial Segregation and Foreclosure Crisis

PART VI: MONEY'S POWER TO INSPIRE

Wed. / April 15: **ALTERNATIVE FORMS of CURRENCY**

- Bb: Dodd, parts of Chap. 8—pp. 342–383

Fri./ April 17: **PAPER 2 DUE before 8 pm**

Mon. / April 20: **THE SHARING ECONOMY**

- Bb: Forbes 2013 Airbnb and the Share Economy
- Bb: Ghoshal 2009 Surf's Up

FINAL EXAM

Wed. / April 22: **WRAP UP and EXAM PREP**

- No additional pre-work
- Bring your notes and course materials to class

FINAL EXAM: Wednesday / April 29, 2015 at 12:30–2:30 pm

- Bring a pencil and eraser

Syllabus IV: Sociology of Conflict and Violence

Prof. Barbara Chasin
Montclair State University

Classroom Policies:

- Students are expected to attend class regularly. More than three unexcused absences will result in a lowering of your grade. Material will be covered in class that is not in the readings and class discussions are an important part of this course.
- Students are expected to arrive on time and to remain in class for the entire class period. Frequent lateness will be counted as absences.
- If you leave before the end of a class session do not return, you will be counted as absent. Arriving late, walking in and out once class starts is distracting to fellow students and the instructor.
- Please do not bring food or drinks too the classroom and be sure phones and/or beepers are turned off.
- Students should exchange phone numbers or e-mail addresses with at least one other student in case you do miss a class. Do not call or e-mail the instructor for this purpose.
- Grades will not be given via-email or phone.

Evaluation:

- Three exams, each worth up to 28 points for a total of 84 points.
- One written assignment worth up to 10 points for a total of 10 points.
- Up to 6 points will be given for attendance and class participation.
- It is the student's responsibility to notify the instructor as soon as possible if an exam has been missed.
- You can earn up to an additional 5 points by handing in all the study questions that will be handed out.

Make-up exams are given only for documented reasons. There is no extra-credit work for low grades.

Final grades will be based on the following cumulative points

A	A−	B+	B	B−	C+
90 and above	88–89	85–87	80–84	78–79	75–77
C	C−	D+	D	D−	F
70–74	68–69	65–67	60–64	54–59	53–0

Course Outline and Reading Assignments

I. Introduction: What Is Conflict and Violence?

Chasin, Preface, Chap. 1

Cynthia Bogard, "Why Thousands May Die" and Richard A. Serrano and Nicole Gaouette, "Despite Warnings, Washington Failed to Fund Levee Projects" (Handouts)

II. Explanations of Violence

The Seville Statement (Handout)

Chasin, Chap. 2

III. Economic and Political Inequality

Chasin, Chaps. 3, 5

IV. Organizational Power and Violence

Chasin, Chap. 4

Chasin, Chaps. 6, 7

Gary Ruskin and Juliet Schor, "Junk Food Nation" (reserve)

Letter from the National Council of Churches (Handout)

Philip Zimbardo, "Power turns good soldiers into 'bad apples'" (Handout)

Esther Schrader, The Conflict in Iraq: These Unseen Wounds Cut Deep; Zucchino, "Iconic Marine Is at Home but Not at Ease" (Handouts)

Herbert C. Kelman and V. Lee Hamilton, "The My Lai Massacre: Crimes of Obedience and Sanctioned Massacres" (reserve); Megan Stack and Raheem Salman "A Town Awoke to Slaughter" (Handout)

V. Foreign Policy, Militarism, Terrorism

Martin Luther King, Jr., "Declaration of Independence from the War in Vietnam' in *Essays*

Chasin, Chaps. 13–15 (343–352, bottom of 357–367)

Clark R. McCauley, "The Psychology of Terrorism" (reserve); Scott L. Plous and Philip G. Zimbardo, "How Social Science Can reduce Terrorism" (Handout)

VI. Violence against Workers

Chasin Chap. 8

David Barstow, "U.S. Rarely Seeks Charges for Deaths in Workplace" (reserve)

Bob Herbert, "Where the Hogs Come First" (Handout)

Rebecca Clarren, "Fields of Poison" (reserve)

VII. Interpersonal Criminal Violence

Chasin, Chaps. 9, 10

David Beers, "Just Say Whoa" (reserve); John Tierney, "The Czar's Reefer Madness"; Paula Span, "Needles Without Strings" (Handouts)

Brent Staples, "How Denying the Vote to ex-Offenders Undermines Democracy" (Handout)

VIII. Interpersonal Violence and Ethnicity/Race

Chasin, Chap. 12; Frank Rich, "How Hispanics Became the New Gays" (Handout)

IX. Interpersonal Violence and Gender

Chasin, Chap. 11; 353–357

X. Strategies for Non-Violent Conflict Resolution

Martin Luther King, Jr. "Letter from a Birmingham Jail" in *Essays*

Chasin, Chap. 16

Syllabus V: Race, Class, and Gender (Truncated)

Prof. Kristin Haltinner

University of Idaho

COURSE OVERVIEW

This course investigates three major forms of inequality in the United States today: race, class, and gender (and its related topic: sexuality). In addition to mastering a conceptual understanding of these concepts, students will be able to recognize the ways in which they operate in social institutions and the lived experiences of people in the United States. Furthermore, students will leave class understanding how these inequalities operate autonomously, but also with and through one another (they are intersected).

COURSE EXPECTATIONS

Students must attend lectures, keep up with the reading, actively participate, and do the required work. The course is writing intensive (note the W after the number). Class periods will be primarily discussion based, with some lecturing, videos and in-class small group activities. There will be approximately 60–90 pages of reading per week drawn from course texts. Students are expected to critically reflect on their own experiences with race in light of the material covered in the course.

REQUIRED TEXTS

Shipler, David. 2005. The Working Poor, Invisible in America. New York, NY: Vintage. (ISBN: 978-0375708213)

Harris-Perry, Melissa. 2011. Sister Citizen: Shame, Stereotypes and Black Women in America. New Haven, CT: Yale University Press. (ISBN: 978-0300165418)

Feagin, Joe. 2006. Systemic Racism: A Theory of Oppression. New York, NY: Routledge. (ISBN: 978-0415952781)

Halberstam, Jack. 2012. Gaga Feminism: Sex, Gender and the End of Normal. Boston, MA: Beacon Press. (ISBN: 978-0807010983)

Smiley, Tavis and West, Cornell. 2012. The Rich and the Rest of Us. New York, NY: Smiley Books. (ISBN: 978-1401940638)

The final course grade is determined according to the following requirements:

Attendance and Classroom Etiquette (20%)

Reflections (40%)

Research Proposal (5%)

Rough Draft of Paper (10%)

Final Paper Draft (25%)

WRITING ASSIGNMENTS

Reflection Papers

Reflection papers are assigned for each book read. You are expected to complete three of the five throughout the semester (note the last one is due during finals week and others are due close together—choose wisely). Reflection papers are to be approximately four pages double-spaced and reflect on your personal experiences in light of the week's readings. 'A' papers will include terms or citations from the week's readings and connect them to your social world.

Final Term Paper

The final term paper is on a topic of your choice, approved by the professor. Topics will be selected early in the term and peer review sessions will be scheduled throughout the semester. Papers are expected to be 10–15 pages long, double-spaced, and include a formal reference section with at least five sources (two of which can be course materials). Examples of topics will be discussed in class.

There is no page requirement for this project. My guess is that most people will be able to write a satisfactory essay in 8–12 pages. You should use the relevant course texts and lectures, but also include five additional (scholarly) sources.

Your essay must use proper grammar. Please provide author's names and page numbers for quotations/cited material. You will need a formal bibliography. Be sure to include an introduction with a thesis and a conclusion.

Your paper can either be turned in on Moodle2 (by 12:30 pm on May 17th), in Kristin's mailbox in Social Sciences Tower, room 909 (by 12:30 pm on May 17th)

Service Learning Option (CSL)

Students who are interested in service learning must complete 30 h of service over the course of the semester. CSL students will have the option of writing their reflection papers about their experience in the field, in light of course reading and discussion. Additionally, CSL students will be expected to bring their experiences to bear on the discussion and write their final paper about their experience at their site. (If you chose to do community service learning your final paper will be a broader reflection on your selected organization based on readings and discussions from class. Outside research is not expected.)

In order to write this paper, it is important that you use notes from your experience at your service-learning site. Specifically, you may want to consider how your site deals with issues addressed in class and in the readings. How does your site make meaning of racial categories? How are stereotypes reinforced or challenged? Do you see labeling theory or the Pygmalion effect in action?

Questions to consider as you take notes include:

- How does my organization deal with X issue?
- In what ways could my organization better deal with X issue? In what ways do they deal with it well? What seems to be working? What doesn't? Why?
- What have I learned from class that would be useful to improve my organization? What do the readings say about this issue?

Your paper will be structured as follows:

(1) You need an introduction to the paper. Introduce your service-learning site and the topic on which you will be writing.
(2) Provide a summary of your organization. Include the goals and history of the group. Also describe what you did while completing your service learning tasks.

(3) Evaluate an element of your service-learning site in light of the class readings. For example, if your organization is fighting for racial equality, examine the ways they do that and evaluate them using Feagin's book or other course readings. Explain what efforts your site is making regarding the issue at hand. Highlight what seems to work well and what, in your opinion (based on the readings and class discussion), could be better.

(4) Write a conclusion summarizing your thoughts. You may also want to suggest changes/improvements the organization could/should make.

There is no page requirement for this project. My guess is that most people will be able to write a satisfactory essay in 6–10 pages. Your essay must use proper grammar. Please provide author's names and page numbers for quotations/cited material. You do not need a formal bibliography. Be sure to include an introduction and a conclusion.

Your paper can either be turned in on Moodle2 or in Kristin's mailbox in Social Sciences Tower, room 909 (by 12:30 on May 17th)

More information on Service Learning can be found on the CCSL website (http://www.cclc.umn.edu/) or by contacting Laurel Hirt, the class coordinator, at x3344 or hirtx002@umn.edu

Academic Integrity Also Applies To Community Work Done For Academic Credit. Any of the following actions constitute academic dishonesty within a community-based learning context and will be addressed in the same way as any other act of academic dishonesty:

1. Misrepresenting hours completed at a community site or spent working on a community project (students can count time spent off-site doing work that is required to complete a project for a community organization).
2. Writing reflections or completing other assignments about events or activities the student was supposed to attend and participate in, but did not actually attend or participate in.
3. Signing in at a site or training session and leaving before the hours or training was completed OR signing in for a friend or classmate at a site.
4. Writing reflections based on previous community work or documenting hours done at a community organization during a previous semester and misrepresenting it as your current service-learning experience.

Accommodations For Students Registered With Disability Services Doing Service-Learning

If you are registered with Disability Services, you are eligible to receive accommodations from the University when doing service-learning in the community. While not all buildings where community groups are located are 100% accessible to students with physical disabilities, service-learning staff can work with you to find a service-learning site that meets your needs. If you have an invisible disability, we encourage you to talk with your service-learning liaison and/or your DS specialist to discuss the type of work environment and structure you need to be successful during your community experience.

Confidentiality and Privacy Issues within the Service-Learning Context
Community organizations participating in service-learning expect students to work to the best of their abilities and act in a responsible manner. Furthermore, many service-learning students will be working with individuals who fall into protected categories, such as children, seniors, or individuals with disabilities. Be aware that through your service-learning, you may come to know information about individuals that is covered by rules and ethical guidelines about confidentiality. You should speak to your community supervisor about how confidentiality obligations apply to you. Examples of how these issues might arise in your service-learning include:

1. You should not take photographs of anyone at your service-learning site without following the policy the organization has in place. This often involves getting written permission from the individual and/or written permission or the parent/guardian of children under 18 years of age.
2. During class discussions, be careful about revealing any information that could be used to personally identify any individual you work with in your service-learning.
3. In written assignments and especially when using online learning tools (Moodle, class blogs, etc.), be particularly attentive about the information you disclose about your service-learning experience, in case the site you are using is publicly available online. Refrain from mentioning the name of your organization and change the names of any individuals you write about if you are utilizing these online tools for your class.

Please note that Criminal Background Checks are also required for many service-learning placements, especially those that involve working with "vulnerable populations" such as children, the elderly, and individuals with disabilities. If the agency asks about any convictions and you have a criminal record:

- Be honest. Failure to state convictions that are then uncovered in a background check will likely result in your immediate dismissal from your service organization.
- Ask the agency representative to explain what types of convictions are not acceptable (these often involve convictions such as those involving theft, violence, drug sales, and/or crimes against minors).
- If you believe that your record could disqualify you from the approved service-learning options, **please be proactive and talk to your service-learning liaison** to discuss alternative placement options.

WEEKLY ASSIGNMENTS

Date	Reading (to be done by class)	Assignments due
January 23rd		
January 28th/30th	Working poor, introduction—Chap. 3 *Library research orientation, 1/28* (**Meet in S30B of the library**) *CSL presentation 1/30*	
February 4th/6th	Working poor, Chaps. 4–6	**Research proposal due February 6th**
February 11th/13th	Working poor, Chaps. 7–9	
February 18th/20th	Working poor, Chaps. 10—epilogue; the rich and the rest of us, introduction—Chap. 1	
February 25th/27th	The rich and the rest of us, Chaps. 2–5	**Reflection 1 due February 27th**
March 4th/6th	The rich and the rest of us, Chaps. 6 and 7 Systemic racism, Chap. 1	
March 11th/13th	Systemic racism, Chaps. 2 and 3	**Reflection 2 due March 13th**
March 18th / 20th	No class—spring break	
March 25th/27th	Systemic racism, Chaps. 4 and 5	
April 1st/3rd	Systemic racism, Chaps. 6 and 7	
April 8th/10th	Systemic racism, Chaps. 8 and 9	**First draft of final paper due April 10th**
April 15th/17th	Gaga feminism, introduction—Chap. 3 **No class—1:1 Meetings**	**Reflection 3 due April 17th**
April 22nd/24th	Gaga feminism, Chaps. 4 and 5; sister citizen, introduction	
April 29th/May 1st	Sister citizen, Chaps. 1–4	**Reflection 4 due May 1st**
May 6th/8th	Sister citizen, Chaps. 5–7	

FINAL PAPER AND REFLECTION 5 DUE AT 12:30 PM ON MAY 17th ON MOODLE2 OR IN 909 SOCIAL SCIENCES

Printed by Printforce, the Netherlands